BUILDING THE RULE OF LAW IN CHINA

Elsevier

Asian Studies Series

Series Editor: Professor Chris Rowley,
Center for Research on Asian Management,
Cass Business School,
City University, UK; HEAD Foundation, Singapore
(email: c.rowley@city.ac.uk)

Elsevier is pleased to publish this major series of books entitled Asian Studies:

Contemporary Issues and Trends. The Series Editor is Professor Chris Rowley, Director, Center for Research on Asian Management, City University, UK and Director, Research and Publications, HEAD Foundation, Singapore.

Asia has clearly undergone some major transformations in recent years and books in the series examine this transformation from a number of perspectives: economic, management, social, political, and cultural. We seek authors from a broad range of areas and disciplinary interests covering, for example, business/management, political science, social science, history, sociology, gender studies, ethnography, economics, and international relations, etc.

Importantly, the series examines both current developments and possible future trends. The series is aimed at an international market of academics and professionals working in the area. The books have been specially commissioned from leading authors. The objective is to provide the reader with an authoritative view of current thinking.

New authors: we would be delighted to hear from you if you have an idea for a book. We are interested in both shorter, practically orientated publications (45,0001 words) and longer, theoretical monographs (75,000–100,000 words). Our books can be single, joint or multi-author volumes. If you have an idea for a book, please contact the publishers or Professor Chris Rowley, the Series Editor.

Dr Glyn Jones
Elsevier Publishing
Email: g.jones.2@elsevier.com

Professor Chris Rowley
University of Oxford, Oxford, United Kingdom
University of London, London, United Kingdom
Korea University, Seoul, Korea
Griffith University, Nathan, QLD, Australia
Nottingham University, Nottingham, United Kingdom
Email: c.rowley@city.ac.uk
www.cass.city.ac.uk/faculty/c.rowley

BUILDING THE RULE OF LAW IN CHINA

LIN LI

ELSEVIER

CP
CHANDOS
PUBLISHING

An imprint of Elsevier • elsevier.com

Chandos Publishing is an imprint of Elsevier
50 Hampshire Street, 5th Floor, Cambridge, MA 02139, United States
The Boulevard, Langford Lane, Kidlington, OX5 1GB, United Kingdom

ISBN 978-0-12-811930-3 (print)
ISBN 978-0-12-811930-3 (online)

British Library Cataloguing-in-Publication Data
A catalogue record for this book is available from the British Library

Library of Congress Cataloging-in-Publication Data
A catalog record for this book is available from the Library of Congress

For information on all Chandos Publishing publications
visit our website at https://www.elsevier.com/books-and-journals

Publisher: Glyn Jones
Acquisition Editor: George Knott
Editorial Project Manager: Naomi Robertson
Production Project Manager: Debasish Ghosh
Designer: Mark Rogers

Typeset by MPS Limited, Chennai, India

Published with financial support of the Innovation Program of the Chinese Academy of Social Sciences
Translated by Besteasy Translations

CONTENTS

PREFACE

The rule of law makes a country flourish; the rule of law makes a country strong.

The rule of law is an important achievement of mankind in political civilization and an essential criterion for evaluating the progress of human civilization. Advancing the building of the rule of law and realizing good law and proper governance are important goals for people all around the world in the long term.

China is an ancient country with more than 5000 years of history and civilization, and its legal system has also come a long way. As early as in the 21st century BC, there emerged the common law of slavery in China. In the Spring and Autumn Period and Warring States Period (770–221 BC), China began to enact statutory laws, and a systematic written code of laws appeared. In the Tang Dynasty (AD 618–907), China had a rather mature feudal code of laws that was passed on and developed in the following feudal dynasties. The Chinese legal system has developed a style of its own, and ancient China made important contributions to human legal civilization.

After the First Opium War in 1840, China was gradually reduced to a semicolonial and semifeudal country. Since then, the Chinese people have been fighting bravely for national independence, liberation, democracy, and freedom for generations and making unremitting efforts toward building China into a powerful, prosperous, and democratic republic.

The founding of the People's Republic of China in 1949 created unprecedented political, economic, social, and cultural conditions for the development of the people's democracy and the building of a socialist country based on a legal system in China.

In 1978, China initiated the reform and opening up policy and identified clear-cut goals for developing socialist democracy and improving the socialist legal system. The country's commitment to the establishment and strict and punitive enforcement of the law has opened up new vistas for building a democratic legal system.

At its 15th National Congress held in 1997, the Communist Party of China (CPC) decided to make the rule of law the country's fundamental governing strategy for managing its national, social, economic, and cultural affairs, and clearly made building a socialist country based on the rule of law the country's development goal. This marked China's transition from being a country ruled by law to one that is governed by law and her entering a new stage of socialist country based on the rule of law.

At its 16th National Congress held in 2002, the CPC made it loud and clear that developing a socialist democracy with Chinese characteristics requires sticking to an organic unity of the Party's leadership, the people's role as masters of the country, and the rule of law, which provided a correct path and direction for advancing the rule of law and building of a socialist country based on the rule of law.

After 2007, the CPC held its 17th and 19th National Congresses. At the two gatherings, the CPC pointed out that China needs to follow the development path of a socialist democracy with Chinese characteristics and unswervingly promote the implementation of the rule of law as a basic principle. As a result, China phased in the socialist legal system with Chinese characteristics as scheduled and took new steps in law-based government administration. China also achieved new results in judicial system reform and made remarkable achievements in building a socialist country based on the rule of law.

Promoting the people's democracy and building the rule of law in China represent the natural choice of history and the people. They are the inevitable requirements for building socialism with Chinese characteristics, deepening the reform comprehensively, and modernizing the national governance system and governance capacity. They are also necessary for promoting sustainable economic development, safeguarding social fairness and justice, and realizing the Chinese dream of national prosperity, people's happiness, and the great rejuvenation of the Chinese nation.

Based on the long-term practice of promoting democracy and the rule of law since the establishment of the People's Republic of China, especially after the 15th National Congress, the CPC as the ruling party has acted based on national conditions and reality to implement the rule of law as a fundamental principle across the board and to accelerate theoretical research, practical exploration, and institutional innovation in building a socialist country based on the rule of law. In doing so, the CPC has summarized national and local experience in actively building the legal system, drawn on best practices of other countries with developed and organized rule of law, and absorbed the essence of the Chinese nation's traditional legal culture. On top of that, the ruling party has constantly deepened its understanding of socialism and socialist democracy with Chinese characteristics, its understanding of the advancement of the rule of law, and its understanding of the building of a socialist country based on the rule of law. Gradually, the new concept of the rule of law has taken shape, and the new task of building the rule of law in China has been set.

In the report delivered to its 18th National Congress in November 2012, the CPC presented the new guidelines for the rule of law, which are to make laws in a scientific way, enforce them strictly, administer justice impartially, and ensure that everyone abides by the law.

The Third Plenary Session of the 18th Central Committee of the CPC held in November 2013 adopted *The Decision of the Central Committee of the Communist Party of China on Some Major Issues Concerning Comprehensively Deepening the Reform*. The *Decision* used the concept of building the rule of law in China formally for the first time and clearly raised the development goal and strategic task of promoting the rule of law in China.

The Fourth Plenary Session of the 18th Central Committee of the CPC held in October 2014 adopted *the Decision of the Central Committee of the Communist Party of China on Major Issues Concerning Comprehensively Advancing the Rule of Law*. According to *the Decision*, to comprehensively advance the rule of law, there is a need to stick to an organic unity of the Party's leadership, the people's role as masters of the country and the rule of law, and unswervingly follow the path of socialist rule of law with Chinese characteristics. There is also a need to resolutely safeguard the authority of the constitution and the laws, protect the people's rights and interests according to the laws, uphold social equity and justice, and maintain national security and stability. In so doing, there would be a strong legal guarantee for realizing the "two hundred-year strategic goals" and the Chinese dream of the great rejuvenation of the Chinese nation. *The Decision* also put forward the overall objective of "building the system of socialist rule of law with Chinese characteristics and a socialist country based on the rule of law." That is, to adhere to socialism with Chinese characteristics and implement socialist law-based theory with Chinese characteristics, i.e., phase in a perfect system of legal norms, an efficient system for implementation of the rule of law, a strict supervision system for the rule of law, a strong guarantee system for the rule of law, and a well-established inner-party system of laws and regulations. Moreover, this means sticking to common advancement of the rule of law, governance by law and administration by law, and integrated development of the country, government, and society based on the rule of law. In short, making laws in a scientific way, enforcing them strictly, administering justice impartially, and ensuring that everyone abides by the law. The aim is to promote the modernization of national governance system and governance capacity.

Building the rule of law in China is the Chinese people's lofty pursuit of freedom and equality, human rights and legal rights, fairness and justice, safety and order, dignity and happiness, among other values of the rule of law. Building the rule of law in China is aimed at improving and developing socialism with Chinese characteristics, boosting the modernization of national governance system and governance capacity, and realizing the rule of law in all undertakings with self-confidence in theory, path, and system. This means good law and proper governance for the people to realize state management, social governance, resource allocation, human rights protection, and power domestication in accordance with the constitution and the law.

Building the rule of law in China also requires combining general legal principles of the rule of law in human history with the socialist development path of the rule of law with Chinese characteristics, and organically unifying the Party's leadership, the people's role as masters of the country, and the rule of law. It also means making laws in a scientific way, enforcing them strictly, administering justice impartially, and ensuring that everyone abides by the law in a reinforced and all-around manner. Building the rule of law in China means promoting the rule of laws, governance by law and administration by law, and persisting in integrated development of the country, government, and society based on the rule of law. It also means practically safeguarding the authority of the constitution and the law, and effectively normalizing and restricting powers, i.e., sufficiently respecting and protecting human rights and promoting social fairness and justice according to the law. In short, we aim to build China into a strong, prosperous, democratic, civilized, and modernized country based on the rule of law where people live harmoniously and happily.

CHAPTER 1

Democracy and the Rule of Law in Contemporary China

Issues relating to democracy and the rule of law are the main concerns in the development of China's rule of law. When the reform and opening-up policy was implemented in 1978, Mr. Deng Xiaoping pointed out that there would be no socialism and socialist modernization without democracy. In this sense, there is a need to develop a socialist democracy, improve the socialist rule of law, institutionalize and legalize democracy, and bring all works of the state under the rule of law in order to build China into a modern socialist country. In the first two decades of the reform and opening up, China adhered to the idea that democracy is the premise of the rule of law while the rule of law is the guarantee of democracy. In this connection, democratic development was often prioritized. Thereafter, more and more developing countries suffered from setbacks, regressions, and failures in implementing the western mode of democracy. Today, China is all the more confident and determined in the development road of socialist democracy and rule of law with Chinese characteristics. China is putting more emphasis on refraining from indiscriminately copying the western mode of democratic constitutionalism. Instead, China must follow its own development path of democracy and the rule of law in line with its historical tradition, reality, and national conditions. When it comes to the relations between democracy and the rule of law, China continues to adhere to the basic concept that democracy and the rule of law are mutually complementary and interactive on the one hand. On the other hand, China believes that it should adhere to the principle of "stabilizing democratic development and speeding up the rule of law" at the current stage.[1]

[1]The so-called "stabilizing democratic development" principally refers to this developing socialist democracy, and boosting political restructuring at the present stage must be in line with China's national conditions and reality, adapt to the current economic and social development status, match the comprehensive quality and democratic ability of citizens, and proceed in a guided, progressive, active, steady, and step-by-step manner. China must not rush through things in this regard. As China continues to develop in its practice of democracy, more and more people have realized that democracy is a double-edged sword

Building the Rule of Law in China.
DOI: http://dx.doi.org/10.1016/B978-0-12-811930-3.00001-5

Beyond that, China must comprehensively implement the rule by law as a fundamental strategy and speed up the building of a socialist country under the rule of law.

---

in operation and practice. Democracy could either do good and become "a good thing" or do evil and become "a bad thing." "Stability" is key to seeking advantages and avoiding disadvantages, and fostering strengths and circumventing weaknesses. In terms of the development speed of democracy, what is of concern is not slowness but stagnation, especially regression. In this case, we must not sway back and forth, relax our efforts, or get sidetracked by developing democracy. Instead, we must proceed steadily and surely and consolidate progressively and step-by-step. In regards to the development mode of democracy, we must act on national conditions and avoid copying western models. We must drive people's democracy with inner-party democracy, propel high-level democracy with grassroots democracy, assist electoral democracy with deliberative democracy, promote direct democracy with network democracy, and implement economic and social democracy with political democracy. We must keep narrowing the difference of democracy, expand the scope of democracy, enrich the form of democracy, and raise the level of democracy with the development of the economy, society, and culture. The so-called "speeding up the rule of law" means that the development of the rule of law should be moderately faster than the expansion and increment of democracy in speed; the rule of law needs to be advanced with moderately greater efforts compared with innovation and reform of democracy; the rule of law should be prioritized to guide and guarantee a scientific development of democracy in practice; and the development of the rule of law should be used to promote and regulate the orderly realization of democratic rights. In specific practices of developing democracy and the rule of law, we should set rules before acting, decide procedures first before exercising rights, develop regulations before expanding democracy, and settle for legal reform (making, revision, and annulment of laws) before reformation. In particular, we must be careful to develop democracy by means of political restructuring and try to adopt law-based methods to proceed in a steady and orderly manner on the law-based track and under the guidance and regulation of the constitution and the laws. After China enters the peaceful development period, the functions of the rule of law, compared with that of democracy, are more conservative, stable, normative, and authoritative; more conducive to social relation adjustment, social benefit distribution, social behavior regulation, legal order building, equity and justice realization; more helpful for preventing social contradictions, resolving social disputes, mitigating internal conflicts, promoting social harmony, and maintaining national stability. Therefore it is relatively rational and practically necessary to implement the political development strategy of "speeding up the rule of law" in certain period and under certain conditions. Emphasizing the strategy of "speeding up the rule of law" is by no means "democratic stagnation" or "democratic regression." It means developing the rule of law one step ahead at this currently special stage so as to pave the way for and escort the development of democracy. The development of democracy could be advanced steadily only based on the rule of law. The development speed of democracy should be adjusted according to actual situations. The development of democracy should contribute to economic development, social harmony, political stability, ethnic unity, and national reunification, and help enable the people to become masters of the country.

1.1 INTERPRETATION OF THE CONCEPT OF "DEMOCRACY"

1.1.1 What is Democracy?

Democracy is a controversial concept, as different people have different interpretations of it. According to the original meaning of the term "democracy" from ancient Greece, "Democracy meant rule by the people or the many. But because the many were also poor, it was often taken to mean rule by the poor, or by the rabble."[2] Ancient Greek historian Herodotus was the first to describe the Athenian political system as democratic politics. Pericles, a famous Athenian politician, said that China's system was a democratic system because the state political power was in the hands of the many but not of the few.[3] Aristotle, a famous ancient Greek ideologist, used to divide the ancient Greek political system into three normal forms of government and three abnormal ones according to whether the state was ruled by one, by few, or by many. The former three forms refer to monarchy, aristocracy, and republic, while the latter ones refer to tyranny, oligarchy, and democracy. These are the earliest definitions of democracy in the history of human civilization. However, slaves were excluded from "the people" or "the many" in these definitions.[4] Women, foreigners, and the mixed-blood were also excluded from the main body of "democracy."

In the West, the Greek concept of democracy was not clearly defined until Rousseau and his *The Social Contract*, which was when democracy was revitalized. Democracy means that the people rule the government themselves. The people's sovereignty means that the people enact laws and elect their rulers that the rulers are servants of the people.[5] It was not until the European Renaissance Movement and the Enlightenment Movement that western political philosophers and legal thinkers held high the banner of democracy, freedom, equality, fraternity, human rights, and the rule of law to resist monarchy and theocracy, autocracy, and dictatorship, and hierarchical privilege, which set the foundation for bourgeois democracy in thought and theory. These western political philosophers and legal thinkers include Grotius, Hobbes, Bodin, Locke, Mill, Montesquieu, and Rousseau, among others.

[2]Anthony Arblaster: *Democracy*, translated by Sun Rongfei *et al.*, Jilin People's Publishing House, Changchun, Jilin Province, 2005 edition, p. 19.

[3]Thucydides: *History of the Peloponnesian War*, translated by Xie Defeng, The Commercial Press, Beijing, 1978 edition, p. 130.

[4]Li Tieying: *On Democracy*, People's Publishing House, Beijing, 2011 edition, p. 2.

[5]Anthony Arblaster: *Democracy*, translated by Sun Rongfei *et al.*, Jilin People's Publishing House, Beijing, 2005 edition, pp. 34, 40.

Beginning in the 19th century, and especially in the 20th century, the West witnessed many new developments and changes in democratic theories. Moreover, a number of theories and schools, such as Elite Theory of Democracy,[6] Theory of Pluralist Democracy,[7] Theory of Liberal Democracy,[8] Theory of Participatory

[6]The representatives of the Elite Theory of Democracy included German sociologist Max Weber and US economist Joseph Alois Schumpeter. The Elite Theory of Democracy takes democracy as a political method competing for political leadership. For example, Schumpeter believed that democracy does not require the sharing of powers among citizens and that power is exercised by a small number of leaders. The role of people is no more than to elect the government and social elites to govern the state. Democracy doesn't and is unlikely to refer to the case where people are indeed the rulers, as indicated clearly by the two terms "people" and "rule." In this case, Schumpeter put forward the definition of empirical democracy. "The democratic method is that institutional arrangement for arriving at political decisions in which individuals acquire the power to decide by means of a competitive struggle for the people's vote." See [US] Joseph Schumpeter: *Capitalism, Socialism and Democracy*, translated by Wu Liangjian, The Commercial Press, 1979 edition, pp. 355–356. The basic viewpoints of the Elite Theory of Democracy are that democracy doesn't mean rule by the people but rule by elites or politicians; democracy means the process of acquiring the power by pluralist elites by means of party competition; elites are open, and everybody has an equal opportunity to become an elite; and citizens elect political elites to become the rulers on a regular basis.

[7]American politicians represented by Robert Alan Dahl and Charles Edward Lindblom came up with the theory of Pluralist Democracy in a bid to make up for the shortage of the Elite Theory of Democracy through emphasizing the role of various interest groups in the democratic process. For their part, democracy is the process of ceaseless bargaining among many different interest groups. Election and political parties cannot alone guarantee the balance of a democratic state. Interest groups of all kinds must exist to maintain the democratic process. Dahl suggested using a "pluralistic form of government" to refer to the actual democratic system because the term "democracy" easily misled the people to an unrealistic ideal state. See [US] Robert Dahl: *Dilemmas of Pluralist Democracy*, translated by You Zhengming, Qiushi Press, 1989 edition.

[8]According to the Theory of Liberal Democracy, the establishment of a democratic system is the product of value ideas, and the core value of democracy is the freedom of individuals. Just as Lindblom stated that democracy was historically the pursuit of freedom, and the fight for democracy was the fight for political freedom in history. See [US] Lindblom: *Politics and Markets*, Shanghai Joint Publishing Press, 1996 edition. US economist Buchanan believed that modern democracy is the result of the market economy and the agreement gradually reached by the British in opposing autocratic monarchy and protecting their own properties. Refer to [US] James McGill Buchanan: *Liberty, Market and State*, translated by Ping Xinqiao and Mo Fumin, Shanghai Joint Publishing Press, 1989 edition. In the opinion of liberal democracy theorists, democratic principles revised by liberalism have changed from "all power belongs to the people" to "all power belongs to nobody." Democracy is no longer the rule of the people but the rule of rulers with voting and control powers. It has changed from direct to indirect democracy that is the representative

Democracy,[9] Theory of Deliberative Democracy,[10] Theory of Strong Democracy,[11] and Thought of Democratic Socialism also emerged during this time.[12]

American scholar Dahl said in his *On Democracy*, "Democracy has been discussed off and on for about 2500 years, enough time to provide

democracy. American politician Sartori observed that humanity is still trapped by the fact that the few are rulers while the many are ruled under present historical conditions. Contemporary democracy is only "the democracy being ruled." See [US] Sartori: *The Theory of Democracy Revisited*, translated by Feng Keli *et al.*, Orient Press, 1993 edition, pp. 89–133. According to the Theory of Liberal Democracy, democracy is not just the result of liberalism; it also takes the liberty of individuals as the basis for its existence and operation. Since the liberty of individuals can't be guaranteed, rulers can deprive citizens from participating in political affairs at any time. That being said, liberty doesn't mean democracy. The conflict between liberty and democracy is still present even if contemporary democracy contains liberty. Not limiting the government elected in democracy may also give rise to autocracy and infringe the liberty of individuals. Likewise, democracy doesn't mean equality. Otherwise, "more democracy" firstly and frequently means that democracy is not just a political form. Instead, it seeks more social security and economic welfare.

[9] British politicians Carole Pateman and James Ian Macpherson *et al.* put forward the Theory of Participatory Democracy. They argued that liberty and individual development can be realized only when citizens directly and continuously participate in social and state management. In modern western society, the participation of the people has been hindered by the unbalanced distribution of powers and resources and by the equality in class, gender, and race. The participation in election in the liberal democracy is only "limited" participation. They stand for expanding democracy to the system, which is closely related to the life of the many so that democracy could play its role in people's daily lives. That is to say, democratic rights need to be expanded to economic organizations and other important organizations in the society.

[10] The Central Compilation & Translation Press recently published a set of works about deliberative democracy, such as [US] *Deliberative Democracy: Essays on Reason and Politics* compiled by James Bohman and William Rehg, [South Africa] *Democracy as Public Deliberation: New Perspectives* written by Maurizio Passerin d'Entreves, [US] *Public Deliberation: Pluralism, Complexity, and Democracy* by James Bohman, and [Australia] *Deliberative Democracy and Beyond: Liberals, Critics, Contestations* by John S. Dryzek.

[11] Refer to [US] Benjamin Barber: *Strong Democracy*, translated by Peng Bin and Wu Runzhou, Jilin People's Publishing House, Changchun, Jilin Province, 2006 edition.

[12] In the opinion of democratic socialists, democracy must be incorporated in the political, economic, social, and cultural sectors, among all other sectors. A true democracy means that all people can equally and effectively participate in making decisions in their lives. A true democracy means that no official can have a reigning role in politics and that all forms of powers must be responsible for the people. They admitted that the prerequisite for political democracy is undoubtedly created by liberalism. (See [Germany] Willy Brandt, Bruno Kreisky, and Olof Palme: *Social Democracy and the Future*, Chongqing Publishing House, 1990 edition, p. 40.) The basic values of socialist ideology are liberty, justice, and unity. Democratic socialism is a movement for freedom.

a tidy set of ideas about democracy on which everyone, or nearly everyone, could agree. Ironically, the very fact that democracy has such a lengthy history has actually contributed to confusion and disagreement, for 'democracy' has meant different things to different people at different times and places."[13] British scholar Anthony pointed out in *Democracy* that democracy is an intrinsic, controversial, and changeable concept. Democracy is still being understood in a variety of different ways. These ways may have a common core or origin, but are not completely the same.[14] American politician Giovanni Sartori clearly stated in *The Theory of Democracy Revisited* that people are living in a time with a confusing concept of democracy because the concept of democracy is destined to result in mess and ambiguity.[15] Undoubtedly, the definition of "democracy" has been a controversial issue throughout history.[16] Different historical traditions, cultural origins, ethics and religions, economic and social backgrounds, political philosophies, political practices, and even national external environment and international factors, among others, may have a vital influence on people's understanding and interpretation of democracy, so no single definition of democracy has been widely accepted.[17] Different definitions of democracy have reflected the different appeals of different cultural traditions and even different political ideologies. Therefore, defining "democracy" has created a clash in ideology.[18]

[13] Robert A. Dahl: *On Democracy*, translated by Li Baiguang *et al.*, The Commercial Press, Beijing, 1999 edition, p. 3.

[14] Anthony Arblaster: *Democracy*, translated by Sun Rongfei *et al.*, Jilin People's Publishing House, Changchun, Jilin Province, 2005 edition, p. 8.

[15] Giovanni Sartori: *The Theory of Democracy Revisited*, translated by Feng Keli *et al.*, Orient Press, Beijing, 1998, 2nd edition, p. 3.

[16] Albert Breton *et al.*: *Understanding Democracy: Economic and Political Perspectives*, translated by Mao Dan *et al.*, Xuelin Press, Shanghai, 2000 edition, p. 89.

[17] Eric S. Einhorn, *Liberalism and Social Democracy in Western Europe*, published in [US] Chief Editor Howard J. Wiarda: *Comparative Democracy and Democratization*, translated by Rong Yuan, Peking University Press, Beijing, 2004 edition, p. 20. Eric argued that European democracy is established on three major pillars, namely constitutionalized political democracy, social democracy of welfare states, and economic democracy embodied by social market capitalism that relatively values equality. Therefore, modern European democracy has transcended the relatively narrow US-type liberal democracy at the social, economic, and even cultural level.

[18] Susan Marks: *The Riddle of All Constitutions: International Law, Democracy, and the Critique of Ideology*, translated by Fang Zhiyan, Shanghai Century Publishing Group, Shanghai, 2005 edition, p. 63.

The fight to define democracy is one of the inherent features of modern society.[19]

Today, to discuss democratic issues and define the concept of democracy, China needs to refer to the general meaning of democracy interpreted by western political cultures, but it cannot treat democracy with a focus on or from the viewpoint of western democracy and rule of law. Instead, China needs to take into consideration Chinese culture and Chinese political culture, political systems, economic and social development levels, and fundamental realities of China at the present stage. China should start from the basis of observing, studying, and solving issues in Chinese democratic political development. Based on this standpoint and perspective, China should understand the following basic points while discussing democratic political issues.

First, from the perspective of the main body, China should interpret the original meaning of "democracy" as "the rule of the many" or "the power of the many," just as Lenin said democracy is the rule of the majority[20] and the rule of the people. The rule of individuals or a small number of elites is not democracy in the real sense.

Second, from the perspective of state form and political system, China should understand that the "democracy" talked about by classical Marxist writers is a kind of state form and state power. Therefore "the first step taken in the revolution by the working class is to raise the proletariat to the position of the ruling class to win the battle of democracy,"[21] and to control the state power.

Third, from the perspective of the people's sovereignty principle, democracy as the embodiment of the people's fundamental rights and sovereign power means that other people are masters of the country and enjoy all rights to manage national, social, economic, and cultural affairs through direct or indirect democratic forms and by means of election, decision-making, participation, management, and supervision.

Fourth, from the perspective of the form of practice of today's democratic pluralism and diversity, especially from the practice of China's

[19]John Keane, *Democracy and Communication Media*, published in *Rethinking Democracy* edited by Social Science in China Press, Social Sciences Academic Press (China), 2000 edition, p. 291.

[20]Vladimir Lenin: *Constitutional Democratic Party and Land Issues*, *The Collected Works of Lenin*, volume 18, People's Publishing House, Beijing, 1959 edition, p. 273.

[21]Engels Marx: *The Communist Manifesto*, *Selections of Marx and Engels*, volume 1, People's Publishing House, Beijing, 1995 edition, p. 293.

democratic political development in the primary stage of socialism, fully realizing the people's democracy requires not only the support of economic, political, cultural, and social conditions of various kinds, but also the advancement of the institutionalization and standardization of the rule of law and the governance by law.

In the Chinese context, democracy can be interpreted from three main perspectives:

First, the democracy serves as the state power. It basically includes the public power of four layers: (1) the people's sovereignty, which is the supreme power of the state and belongs to the people, meaning the popular sovereignty; (2) the state power, which is the constitutional form of the people's sovereignty, the general term of public powers; (3) national legislative power, administrative power, judicial power, and the power of legal supervision, which are the major power fields and forms of state power; and (4) decision-making power, the power over personnel, financial power, management power, executive power, supervisory power, and other subordinate public powers, which are subject to superior powers like legislative power, administrative power, and judicial power, and have different representations and operation forms due to the differences in the superior powers. In the sense of democracy as the state power, democracy is a national public power and a power of the people in China.[22] See the chart in Fig. 1.1 for the structure of democracy as the state power:

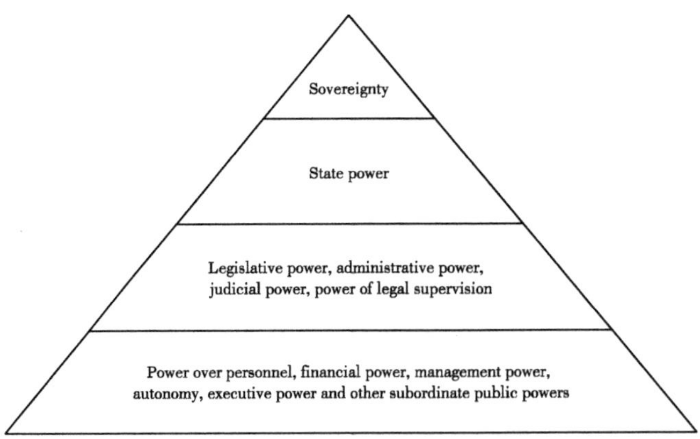

Figure 1.1 The structure of democracy as the state power.

[22] Douglas Lummis: *Radical Democracy*, translated by Liu Yuanqi, China Renmin University Press, Beijing, 2002 edition, p. 158.

Second, democracy serves as the state system (form), and generally includes four levels: nature of state, form of government, China's main political systems, and relevant democratic systems in political structure. "Nature of state" implies the status of all social classes in China, and it's the people's democratic dictatorship led by the working class (through the Communist Party of China (CPC)) in China. "Form of government" refers to the form of executing state power, and it's the system of people's congress that is the fundamental political system in China; "China's main political systems" mainly include the legislative system, administrative system, judicial system, and relevant systems of "the people's government, the people's court, and the people's procuratorate," namely the government administrative system, court trial system, and procuratorate legal supervision systems except for the legislative system, electoral system, personnel appointment and removal system, and the decision-making system for major issues under the people's congress system; "relevant democratic systems in political system," mainly includes the democratic electoral system, democratic decision-making system, democratic management system, democratic participation system, democratic supervision system, and democratic centralism. A system is a regulated behavioral model and thus all democratic systems belong to political systems. They have an acknowledged and direct link with political themes.[23] China can say that democracy is a state system and a state form. The structure of democracy as a state system is shown as below (Fig. 1.2):

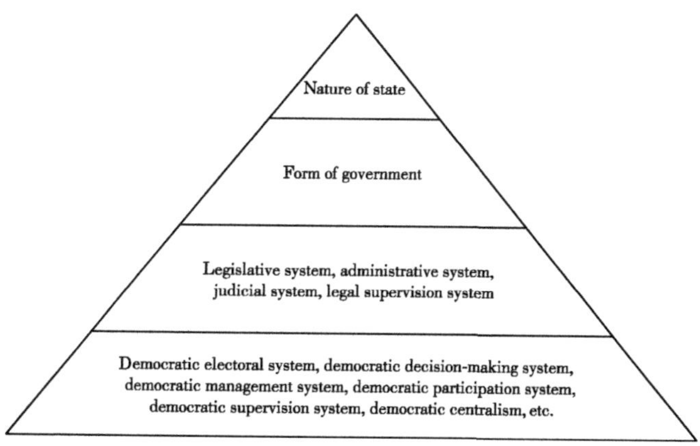

Figure 1.2 The structure of democracy as a state system.

[23] Keir O'Donnell: *On Delegative Democracy*, published in *Democracy and Democratization*, The Commercial Press, Beijing, 1999 edition, p. 49.

Third, democracy serves civil rights. There are three aspects to this idea: (1) civil rights and political rights (political democracy), including the right to life, right to personal dignity, rights to freedom of speech, right of assembly and association, right to parade, right of publication, right to vote and to be elected, right to know, participation right, right of expression, right of supervision, gender equality, and so on; (2) economic rights, social rights, and cultural rights (economic democracy and social democracy), including property right, labor right, right to a decent life, right to housing, right to food, right to education, right to social security, right to family life, and so on; and (3) the capacity for civil rights and acts, with the former referring to the capacity endowed by the law to enjoy democratic rights and undertake democratic obligations, which are the legal rights mandated or vested by law, while the capacity for acts means citizens can actually enjoy democratic rights and undertake democratic obligations independently, which are real behaviors decided by personal conditions. The capacity and qualification for democratic rights are vested by law and enjoyed by everyone according to the law. All people are equal before the law. The capacity for democratic acts is the result of acquired education, cultivation, and training, so it's subject to age, mentality, health, culture, and other subjective and objective conditions. The capacity for democratic acts has many personality characteristics. The capacity and qualification for democratic rights can't be directly incorporated into the inferior concept of "rights." That being said, we should pay attention to not only civil rights but also the principal factors determining the realization of civil rights if we want to make the following three points a reality. The first point is to turn constitutional and legal rights written on paper into real rights. The second point is to interpret clearly the differences and connections between idealistic rights and real rights. The third point is to determine why there are all kinds of differences among different people in realizing the rights under different cultural, economic, and social conditions. The principal factors determining the realization of civil rights are the capacity and qualification for democratic rights of citizens. At this point, rights are the main contents of democracy because if people choose democracy, they must choose to institutionalize a complete right and obligation system. These obligations are rooted in the fact that people must respect others' equal rights and guarantee that other people enjoy the shared structure of political activities.[24] In the sense that democracy is taken as civil

[24] David Held: *Models of Democracy*, translated by Yan Jirong *et al.*, Central Compilation & Translation Press, Beijing, 1998 edition, p. 398.

rights, and that the specific good point of democracy is reflected through important civil rights and political rights,[25] we can say that democracy is the rights of the citizens in China. Marxism argues that the development process of democracy is in essence an emancipation process during which the people get rid of external constraints, become free, realize their full potential, and finally experience political, economic, cultural, and social emancipation. This emancipation process in the field of democracy can be manifested as political democracy, economic democracy, social democracy, and cultural democracy. In the field of law, this emancipation process can be reflected as political rights, economic rights, social rights, and cultural rights. The contents of democracy as civil rights are shown in Fig. 1.3.

Moreover, democracy can also be interpreted as democratic value, democratic idea, democratic procedure, democratic method, democratic manner, democratic mechanism, and democratic principle, but this chapter mainly focuses on discussing democracy as state power, state system, and civil rights.

1.1.2 Essence and Forms of Realization

The basic difference between Marxist democracy and non-Marxist democracy or the view of democracy held by the exploiting class consists of their stance on whether class differentiation is essential to democracy. According to Marxism, to recognize class as fundamental to democracy is to be able to distinguish between democracy for the few privileged possessors of capital and democracy for all the people. In essence, the democracy of the exploiting class including the bourgeois democracy of the West is the democracy of the few, of hierarchical privilege, and of capital

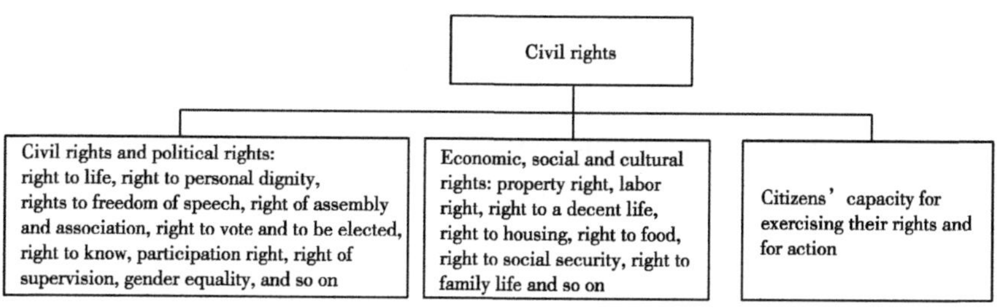

Figure 1.3 Democracy as civil rights.

[25] David Held: *Democracy and the Global Order. From the Modern State to Cosmopolitan Governance*, translated by Hu Wei *et al.*, Shanghai Century Publishing Group, Shanghai, 2003 edition, p. 204.

and money. The Marxist democracy emphasizes that socialist democracy is aimed at thoroughly eliminating the least democratic phenomenon of humanity under which a small number of exploiters rule a large majority of working people. The aim is also to enable the working class and other working masses making up a large majority of the population to have control over the state power and truly realize popular sovereignty, the people's role as masters of the country, and the rule of the many. Other objectives of socialist democracy are allowing the broad masses extensive democratic rights vested by the constitution and the law, managing national and social affairs through various means, and becoming masters of the nation, society, and themselves. It is in this sense of exposing the class essence of democracy that Lenin pointed out that "proletarian democracy is a million times more democratic than any bourgeois democracy, and the Soviet regime is a million times more democratic than the most democratic regime in a bourgeois republic."[26] Lenin not only exposed the nature of bourgeois democracy, but also attached importance to addressing the inner contradictions between the class nature and the realization form of bourgeois democracy, and in the separation of the state power from the people's rights. He also stressed the unity of the nature of state and the form of government, the unity of democracy and the legal system, and the unity of democratic form and democratic content in order to build a more ideal socialist democracy.

China's socialist democracy is a most extensive form of democracy that benefits people of all nationalities, and whose nature consists of people being the masters of the country.[27] People are masters of the country, and all powers in the People's Republic of China come from and belong to the people. The legal status and political role of all the people in national, political, economic, cultural, and social lives have determined and reflected the essence of China's democracy as truly the rule of the majority of the people under socialist conditions. However, the nature of China's socialist democracy can only determine but not replace the specific form, institution, and mechanism for realizing democracy. In China, the nature of state is the people's democratic dictatorship, and the form of government

[26] *The Collected Works of Lenin*, Volume 35, People's Publishing House, Beijing, 1985, 2nd edition, p. 249.

[27] Jiang Zemin: *Speech on the Occasion Marking the Twentieth Anniversary of the Third Plenary Session of the Eleventh Central Committee of the Communist Party of China*, published in *The Legal Daily* on December 19, 1998.

is the people's congress system, demonstrating that socialist democracy has Chinese characteristics and superiority in political nature and fundamental political system. However, historical experiences indicate that China needs to identify the realization form of socialist democracy while adhering to and improving the people's congress system if it wants to turn the superiority in political logic and political nature into a reality.

As early as the beginning of the 20th century, when analyzing the internal basic contradictions of the capitalist system at that time, Lenin pointed out that capitalism would be corrupted, dying, and destroyed when it developed into the stage of imperialism. However, after nearly a century of contest between socialist democracy and capitalist democracy, especially since the Second World War, capitalist countries have gradually completed their transformations under the prerequisite of keeping the nature of their state power and fundamental democratic political systems unchanged. They have transformed from a laissez-faire "free economy" to a "controlled economy" where the government has appropriately intervened. They have reformed, adjusted, and improved many realization forms and operation mechanisms of democracy and the rule of law accordingly. These efforts have to some extent facilitated the development of the productivity of capitalism, made up for the deficiencies of some capitalist political systems, and saved the moribund capitalism. At the same time, in the former Soviet Union[28] and Eastern European socialist countries, the socialist system had basically stagnated in essence and superiority, so the objective requirement of the economic base development for reforming and improving socialist democratic political system was neglected, and the institutional improvement and rule of law development for the realization of socialist democracy was overlooked. Beyond that, the rigid political system severely constrained the emancipation of productivity and the development of economy. Under the effect of these factors and some other complex factors, socialism finally ended in failure in these countries.

China should separate the nature of western capitalist democracy and political civilization from their realization forms and operation mechanisms. China should completely deny and abrogate their class nature while boldly

[28] Some western scholars believe that the collapse of the former Soviet Union exposed the fundamental deficiency of this kind of system and its doctrines. It failed as a kind of economic system; it lacked legitimacy as a kind of political system; and it seriously misunderstood humanity as a kind of ideology. [US] Steve D. Brad: *Whistling Little Shrimp: Russia-Democracy Getting in the Way*, published in [US] Chief Editor Howard J. Wiarda: *Comparative Democracy and Democratization*, Peking University Press, 2004 edition, p. 65.

absorbing, learning, and drawing upon their realization forms and operation mechanisms. Socialist democracy is a million times and even ten million times superior than capitalist democracy in nature. However, if the realization form of socialist democracy is less scientific, rational, and operable, is unable to adapt to the national condition and the essential requirement of socialist political civilization, and is unable to meet social, economic, political, and cultural development needs, then it would weaken the manifestation and exertion of the superiority of socialist democracy in nature. Additionally, these factors together with other factors would lead to loss of power of the ruling party and the collapse of the socialist system. Capitalist democracy is reactionary, hypocritical, decayed, and moribund in nature. However, if capitalist democracy could pay more attention to the improvement and innovation of the realization form and operation mechanism of democracy and even learn from the experiences of socialist democratic politics, then it would not only slow down the collapse of capitalism, but also enable capitalism and its democratic politics to be vigorous and vital under specific conditions through intelligent deployment of various specific institutions and mechanisms, such as democracy, the rule of law, party politics, and constitutional government.

History shows that the superiority of the democratic system of a society is decided by whether it can demonstrate the rule of the many (all the people) in nature and whether it can guarantee that all the people control and exercise the state power and act as masters of the country. Superiority is also decided by whether the realization form, operation mechanism, and operation process of democracy can adapt to the needs of the economic base, and whether it can continuously emancipate and develop the productive forces and guarantee national stability, social harmony, and people's happiness. The determining factor also includes whether it can guarantee concrete realization of democracy in technologies and procedures. Democracy is not only an abstract value and principle, but also specific rights and behaviors. The incomparable superiority of socialist democracy could only be demonstrated and brought into full play by acting upon national conditions and constantly adapting to the needs of the developing socialist market economy, democratic politics, advanced culture, and harmonious society. Beyond that, there is a need to combine the superior fundamental political system with realizing democratic value, enriching democratic form, improving democratic process, perfecting democratic mechanisms, safeguarding democratic rights, and promoting democracy level. On top of that, there is a need to combine the superiority of socialist democracy in nature with the scientific and rational nature of the realization form of democracy.

1.2 FUNCTIONS AND LIMITATIONS OF DEMOCRACY

In recent years, two noteworthy Chinese voices have been heard from concerning issues related to democracy (the rule of law). One opinion is that democracy has become "the most powerful religion in today's world" and "a democratic superstition."[29] What is suitable for the Chinese civilization is not democracy but the rule of law; China should follow the path of "a consultative rule of law" to develop its political civilization.[30] The other opinion believes that democracy is a good thing because it is relatively the best political system of mankind to this day and has the fewest drawbacks among all political systems invented and practiced until now. Democracy is also believed to be good because it is a political system guaranteeing popular sovereignty and the fundamental human rights; it provides equal opportunities to everyone and embodies the human fundamental value; the most substantive significance of democracy is the rule of people and the choice of people; and there can be no socialism and modernization without democracy.[31] As a matter of fact, there have always been arguments about the judgment of democracy in western countries. For example, John Keane, a British professor of political science, noted in the early 1990s that "most people of contemporary times say democracy is a good thing; ... but what's good about democracy exactly?" If democracy lacks confidence in philosophy, democracy can no longer be understood as a system of procedural rules with self-evidence and requiring no argumentations. The legitimacy of democracy is caught in a deep crisis.[32]

The opinions of the two voices are different and even opposite to each other in many aspects, but they also have some things in common. For instance, they both observe democratic problems from the perspective of China's background; they try to find better solutions to issues concerning China's democratic political construction and rule of law development; and they both admit that democracy or the rule of law have many

[29] Pan Wei: *The Rule of Law and "Democratic Superstition"—China's Modernization and the World Order in the Eye of A Believer of the Rule of Law*, Hong Kong Social Science Press, Hong Kong, 2003 edition, "Preface," p. 1.

[30] Pan Wei: *The Rule of Law and Democratic Superstition—China's Modernization and the World Order in the Eye of A Believer of the Rule of Law*, Hong Kong Social Science Press, Hong Kong, 2003 edition, p. 32, "Preface," pp. 2, 3.

[31] Refer to Yan Jianbian: *Democracy is a Good Thing: Dialogue with Professor Yu Keping*, Social Sciences Academic Press, 2006 edition.

[32] John Keane, *The Media and Democracy*, published in *Rethinking Democracy* edited by the Social Science in China Press, Social Sciences Academic Press, Beijing, 2000 edition, pp. 291, 292.

advantages but also limitations. The focus of their argument may involve a basic question: how do we look at the "democracy" learned from the West and understand the functions of democracy (the rule of law) in China from the standpoint and insight of the Chinese? From the perspective of its institution form and operation, democracy has always been a "double-edged sword," which means democracy can result in either good or evil. There is neither such democracy as absolutely good nor such democracy as absolutely bad. From the perspective of its political value, it is quite difficult to determine a universal subjective criterion for evaluating whether democracy is good or bad, and the objective criterion has also been questioned and criticized more often than not. In China, the criterion for testing whether the reform and development of democracy and the rule of law are good or not, successful or unsuccessful, is the practice of the Chinese people. The process and result of this practice should be conducive to strengthening the vigor and vitality of the Party and the state alike, and enhancing government service and management ability. The process and result should be beneficial for mobilizing the enthusiasm, initiative, and creativity of the masses, safeguarding the people's role as masters of the country, and realizing fairness and justice. The process and result should be helpful for maintaining national unity, ethnic unity, and social stability. The process and result should be good for safeguarding the unity of the rule of law and the constitution's authority and boosting the implementation of the strategy for ruling the country by law. The process and result should be good for realizing an organic unity of upholding the Party's leadership, ensuring that the people are masters of the country, and ruling the country by law ("an organic unity of the three"). The process and result should ensure the emancipation and development of productive forces and the promotion of economic development and social harmony and progress.

1.2.1 Functions of Democracy

By the functions of democracy, we mean the positive functions of democracy.[33] The negative functions of democracy will be included in the

[33] Professor Wang Huning divided the functions of democracy into three aspects: first, it is the overall function of the democratic political system; second, it is the institutional function of the democratic politics including citizen participation in politics, political stability, government efficiency, and government order; and third, it is the social function of democracy including promoting social members' capacity to make wiser decisions, propelling the realization of social justice, defusing political violence, advancing the development of citizen intelligence, and improving the personality of social members. See Wang Huning's *Democratic Politics* for details, Joint Publishing (Hong Kong) Company Limited, 1993 edition, pp. 97–114.

category of limitations of democracy for discussion, or we should say the limitations of democracy refer to the negative functions of democracy. In socialist China, democracy has the following main functions:

First, there would be no socialism without democracy. Before the October Revolution (1917), Lenin stated that socialism would not come true without the realization of democracy. This means two things: (1) the proletariat cannot realize the revolution if it is not ready for the socialist revolution in democratic struggles; and (2) the victorious socialism would not maintain its victory and would guide the people to the country's destruction without full democracy.[34] Deng Xiaoping also pointed out that there would be no socialism and socialist modernization without democracy. Here, democracy has three important functions. First, through democratic revolution, the working class seizes the state political power, becomes the ruling class, and establishes a new nature of state, new state, new regime, and new rule of law under the people's democratic dictatorship. Second, socialist countries should adopt the representative democracy to establish a new people's democratic form of government, consolidate the new regime, guarantee the people's role as masters of the country, and truly realize "the rule of the majority" required by the nature of democracy. Third, through continuous improvement and development of democratic superstructure, socialist countries and people should promote the emancipation and development of productive forces so as to provide an increasingly rich material basis on the one hand; and promote constant progress of their people's ideological and cultural level and continuous improvement of moral and rule of law, and cultivate a large number of high-quality citizens so as to provide hundreds of millions of qualified individual subjects for the realization of socialist modernization on the other hand.

Second, democracy guarantees "an organic unity of the three," namely upholding the Party's leadership, ensuring that the people are masters of the country, and ruling the country by law. "An organic unity of the three" is an essential feature of socialist political civilization and also an internal requirement of socialist democracy. Socialist democracy also provides solid and maximized public support for the leadership and governance of the Communist Party while safeguarding and implementing the people's role as masters of the country in politics and constitution. This function of socialist democracy can be seen by the following facts: that

[34]Vladimir Lenin: *A Caricature of Marxism and Imperialist Economism, The Collected Works of Lenin*, volume 23, People's Publishing House, Beijing, 1958 edition, p. 70.

the leadership and governance of the Party are the choice of the people; that the power of the ruling party is vested by the people; that the Party is the political party of the working class governing for the people; and that the leadership and governance of the Party are fully rational and legitimate. While safeguarding the people's democratic rights and respecting and guaranteeing human rights in constitution and laws, socialist democracy also offers institutionalized, normalized, and procedural guarantees for unifying the Party's propositions and the people's will, and can then turn these propositions and will into the will of the state. This function can be manifested as the legalization of the people's will and the Party's principles, policies, and guidelines, and as the basic strategy for the people's rule by law under the leadership of the Party.

Third, democracy adjusts important social relations and provides guarantees for building a harmonious society. Through the people's congress system, the constitution, and other institutional arrangements, socialist democracy normalizes and adjusts the relations between civil rights and the state power to guarantee that the two exist differently yet closely and harmoniously. Socialist democracy could also rationally allocate powers among state organs and regulate the setup, mutual relations, and limits of authority and responsibility of state organs. Socialist democracy could divide the respective limits of authority and responsibility, and form a rational power relationship and an appropriate interest structure between the central and local governments and between different local governments. Socialist democracy makes clear regulations between majorities and minorities and between different minorities in accordance with constitutional principles and basic political systems of regional autonomy of ethnic minorities, and can thus build an equal and harmonious ethnic relationship.

Socialist democracy can also help adjust various crucial national relations, balance various major social interests, and shape various norms governing basic national and social behaviors. Socialist democracy is an adjuster and safety valve in solving conflicts, balancing interest demands, maintaining social stability, national unity and a long-term stability of the state, and ensuring harmonious and orderly social relations. As such, it could guarantee an organic unity and close integration of the Party's political authority in governance and the authority of the constitution and the rule of law.

Fourth, democracy could prevent the worst and serious faults in decision-making. Democracy is the decision made by the majority and even all the people based on established procedures. The opinion of the majority is not always the best choice and is even unable to become the best choice due to the needs of mutual communication, compromise, and concession. But in most cases, rational opinions of the majority may prevent the worst decisions and thus avoid serious mistakes. If scientific and rational democratic procedures are available as the guarantee, decision-making could become increasingly scientific and optimized and less likely to result in mistakes. These democratic procedures may include investigations before decision-making, disclosure of matters and procedures in decision-making, citizen participation, listening to expert opinions and strengthening the supervision by public opinions in decision-making, and information feedback after decision-making. Democracy cannot guarantee that decision-making is always optimal, but it can effectively prevent the worst and serious faults in decision-making.

Fifth, democracy could normalize and constrain public powers and prevent abuse of power. Based on the principle of democratic centralism, socialist democracy builds the mechanism of using rights and powers to restrict powers through the Constitution and laws so as to regulate the state power and prevent the minority from using state power to endanger society and harm individual rights. When it comes to regulation and restriction of state power, socialist democracy firstly determines the people's sovereignty principle that the state power comes from the people and serves the people. Secondly, socialist democracy determines that the main body of national sovereign power is the people and uses systems and procedures to try to avoid "misplaced," "offside," and "inadequate" exercise of state power in operation. Thirdly, socialist democracy determines the contents, range, form, principle, and mode of the state power, and uses laws and systems to try to avoid abuse and excessive exercise of state power, guaranteeing operation of state power according to the law. Fourthly, socialist democracy determines the supervision of state power to prevent and avoid the possibility of corruption and sluggish state organs and staff.

1.2.2 Limitations of Democracy

Democracy is not omnipotent. It has intrinsic limitations and many external restrictions. Democracy does not necessarily produce "goodness," fairness, and justice. Under certain conditions, democracy may also produce "evilness" and destruct fairness, justice, and order under the rule of law. Democracy is a "double-edged sword," and thus it may become a great power with the ability to destroy the country and society if it gets out of control. No one can deny that democracy may also trigger economic crisis and social turbulence as well as aggravate social inequality.[35]

[35]Alain Touraine: *What is Democracy?*, published in *Rethinking Democracy* edited by Social Science in China Press, Social Sciences Academic Press (China), 2000 edition, p. 19.

First of all, democracy may generate the tyranny of the majority. The "tyranny of the majority" principally refers to the reckless and rash actions taken by the majority toward the minority as a result of lack of basic protection for the rights of the minority under the democratic system. The most typical example is that Athens "tried and executed Socrates on charges of impiety and corrupting the youth in 399 B.C." It has been said that that's evidence of the tyranny of the majority... evidence that ordinary people hate geniuses.[36] The anarchy, dictatorship, expansion, and final loss of independence caused by the tyranny of democracy happened not just in ancient Greece.[37] In 1932, Hitler won the presidential election in Germany by 19 million votes. Later, he disbanded other political parties, imprisoned and slaughtered a great number of Jews, and then started the Second World War. In China, the election of"chiefs" and the judicial decisions dominated by popular indignation and public opinions have been a common phenomenon that can be regarded as tyranny of the majority in some sense. In a pluralistic society, the rule of the majority leads to the dictatorship of the majority and civil war, but not to democracy.[38] Since democracy may give rise to tyranny of the majority, some countries adopt republicanism, aiming at preventing and avoiding the tyranny of the majority in institution.

Second, democracy may result in political and social disorder. Democracy is powerful, so it is likely to be abused and become a savage beast in the sense of state power or in civil rights. In fact, the representative parliament or the infinite or nearly infinite judicial power (direct democracy) of the simple majority of the people may endanger the security of property rights and the rule of law.[39] The abuse of public powers in democratic form will not only harm the rights of citizens, but also destroy

[36]Anthony Arblaster: *Democracy*, translated by Sun Rongfei *et al.*, Jilin People's Publishing House, 2005 edition, p. 25. Anthony made a further argument in the book *Democracy*, "The motion that Socrates was guilty was carried by 281 to 220, a close result which indicates that the decision was not the product of some universal mob hysteria.... This harsh judgment on Socrates was not in any way typical of Athenian democracy's attitudes toward its critics or even its enemies."

[37]Gustave Le Bon: *The Psychology of Revolution*, G. P. Putnam's & Sons (New York), 1913, p. 326; quoted from Tong Dezhi: *Between Democracy and the Rule of Law*, People's Publishing House, 2006 edition, p. 128.

[38]Albert Breton *et al.*: *Understanding Democracy: Economic and Political Perspectives*, translated by Mao Dan *et al.*, Xuelin Press, Shanghai, 2000 edition, p. 26.

[39]Albert Breton *et al.*: *Understanding Democracy: Economic and Political Perspectives*, translated by Mao Dan *et al.*, Xuelin Press, Shanghai, 2000 edition, p. 90.

the public power system itself. The abuse of civil rights in democratic form will infringe on other people's rights and freedom on the one hand and jeopardize the public power system and social order on the other. Pure democracy may either indulge state power or easily infringe on the rights of individuals, which is not only the conclusion of the development of ideological history, but also the manifestation of the democratic failures throughout history, such as the French Revolution.[40] If democratic powers or rights are abused, democracy may lead citizens to march on the street and abuse their freedom of assembly, parade, and demonstration, and thus may lead to political instability. Democracy may destroy the legal system, disrupt the social, political, and legal order, and even hinder social economic growth. Democracy may also undermine national peace and trigger domestic political division.[41] In extreme cases, democracy may also cause ethnic and national disintegration. Therefore we need to use rights to restrict powers and use powers to restrict powers and rights. The rule of law is an essential tool for restricting powers. In this sense, there would be no democracy without the rule of law. For either the state power or the civil rights, democracy is to do things permitted by the rule of law. Personal freedom is the right to do things not forbidden by law, but it's not democracy. Democracy is the rule of the majority but not the freedom of the majority.

Third, democracy is likely to be controlled and manipulated by money, violence, public opinion, and knowledge, and thus may be changed. As Winston Churchill said, democracy is not a perfect system.[42] Election is known as the starting point of vertical democracy. But the democracy of the West is usually influenced and manipulated by money, media, dark forces, and consortiums, and thus has become "a rich people's game" and "the democracy of wallets." Democracy is often controlled by the hands of the few. China is a country with 5000 years of feudal history. The old China has left us more tradition of feudal autocracy than tradition of democracy and legal systems. After liberation, China also failed to consciously and systematically put in place various systems to safeguard the people's democratic rights, and its legal system is neither complete nor

[40]Tong Dezhi: *Between Democracy and the Rule of Law*, People's Publishing House, Beijing, 2006 edition, p. 127.

[41]Yan Jianbian: *Democracy is a Good Thing: Dialogue with Professor Yu Keping*, Social Sciences Academic Press, Beijing, 2006 edition, p. 1–3.

[42]Chief Editor Howard J. Wiarda, *Comparative Democracy and Democratization*, Peking University Press, Beijing, 2004 edition, p. 104.

valued.[43] In this context, China needs to create conditions in all aspects for learning and advancing democracy. It will take a progressive and long-term process for China to realize democracy in a well-rounded way. While hundreds of millions of Chinese people studying and implementing democracy and making great achievements in this regard, "one packet of cigarettes, one meal, and a little money" may change the will of the voters in grass-roots elections in some places. In other places, democratic elections may be controlled and manipulated by family forces, religious forces, Mafia-like gangs, and even foreign forces. It's also not rare to see the phenomenon of news media, intellectual elites, experts, and scholars controlling and misleading democratic development due to information blocking and bias.

Fourth, democracy may also reduce efficiency and increase costs. Democratic states are not necessarily more efficient than other government organizational forms. Democratic states are also not necessarily more efficient in administrative management. Their decision-making may be even slower than the old systems.[44] Democracy is a kind of political "luxury" that requires not only a large amount of economic, cultural, and social resources, but also enough time. The amount of time and economic, cultural, and social resources has a positive correlation with the degree of democracy enjoyed and realized in operation to some extent. Democracy requires that the people can voice their opinions fully and listen to views from all sides, there are various procedures for repeated negotiations and discussions, People can be voted and also face unexpected results like being vetoed down or being pended. Therefore we say democracy and efficiency often form a pair of contradictions. In some cases, more democracy means less efficiency and more costs. Therefore the cost of democracy is sacrifice of efficiency and paying more.[45] The design and arrangement

[43] *Selected Works of Deng Xiaoping*, volume 2, People's Publishing House, Beijing, 1994 edition, p. 348.

[44] Philippe C. Schmitter and Terry Lynn Karl: *What Democracy Is...and Is Not*, published in *Democracy and Democratization*, The Commercial Press, Beijing, 1999 edition, p. 35.

[45] For example, the Swiss society overemphasizes democracy so that it has moved toward being conservative and sacrificed the efficiency that is essential to modern social development to a large extent. Swiss people believe that the importance of direct democracy is far better than the efficiency of legislation. Dictatorship is most efficient, but exercising full-fledged democracy should not choose dictatorship, so democracy has to be realized at the cost of efficiency. But the extreme democratic concept and system of Switzerland has slowed down national decision-making. It usually takes several or even dozens of years to enact a necessary legislation, from the consideration and motion to its final entry into force. This may easily result in a conservative trend of the entire society. This can be evidenced by the fact that Swiss women only began to enjoy gender equality in 1971. See *Legislative Theory and System* by Li Lin, China Legal Publishing House, 2005 edition, pp. 534–535.

of the democratic centralism, the chief executive responsibility system, the summary procedure, and the prescription system can integrate democracy and efficiency to a certain degree and realize a win-win scenario between democracy and efficiency.

1.3 RELATIONSHIP BETWEEN SOCIALIST DEMOCRACY AND THE RULE OF LAW

It is generally believed that the rule of law refers to the rule of the law.[46] That said, the rule of law can be understood in either a broad sense or a narrow sense. In the broad sense, the rule of law means all people should abide by the law and accept the rule of the law. In the narrow sense, the rule of law means a government should be ruled by law and should abide by the law.[47] The application and interpretation of socialist rule of law in this chapter have gone beyond "the rule of law in the broad sense" held by Raze. This chapter basically equates the socialist rule of law with governing the country by law as the fundamental strategy. Socialist rule of law hereby mainly includes six fundamental principles: the people's sovereignty, the supremacy of the constitution and the laws, human rights respect and protection, administration by law, impartial judicature, and supervision and restriction of public powers.[48]

What's the relationship between democracy and the rule of law? Is there a conflict, interactive, or master-slave relationship between them? Or is there no necessary connection between the two? Among western scholars, some believe that the rule of law (constitution) and democracy are mutually conflicting, while others have a different point of view. For example, American scholar Cass Sunstein insists that constitution and democracy do not necessarily conflict. He says that whether a constitution conflicts with democracy depends on the nature of the constitution available in China and

[46]The understanding of the rule of law in the West is mostly from the perspective of the political philosophy of liberalism. In the West, the ideal of the rule of law has the following implications at least: law has the supreme authority and thus can prevent the abuse of political powers; it guarantees personal priority through protecting individual rights; and it ensures that the principle of universality comes before particularity through implementing the principle of "all people are equal before the law." [US] Ellen S. Cohn and Susan O. White: *Legal Socialization Effects on Democratization*, published in *Rethinking Democracy* edited by Social Science in China Press, Social Sciences Academic Press (China), 2000 edition, p. 196.

[47]Joseph Raz: *The Authority of Law*, Clarendon Press, Oxford, 1983, pp. 211–213.

[48]See *The Rule of Law and Changes of Constitution* by Li Lin for details, China Social Sciences Press, Beijing, 2005 edition, pp. 223–234.

the democracy it pursues.[49] British scholar Susan Marks has incorporated the rule of law in democracy when discussing the theory of the minimum democracy. She observes that democracy is featured by regular elections, the multiparty system, the rule of law, and civil rights. She also believes that democracy equates to holding multiparty elections, protecting civil rights, and building the rule of law.[50] Josef Thesing also observes that the rule of law is one of the principles for supporting a democratic country and legal thought is one of the principles for designing the democratic political system. He believes that democracy requires social market economy, social justice, and the rule of law.[51] American scholar Dahl emphasizes in his *On Democracy* the decisive role of basic conditions in democracy. He also notes that if some countries enjoy favorable basic conditions, they could realize democratic stability no matter what kind of constitution they adopt. If what they enjoyed are extremely adverse basic conditions, then no constitution could save the democracy.[52] From the perspective of the people's sovereignty principle, people need democracy because people must participate in government decision-making under the rule of law.[53] People must be masters of their country. For democrats of dogmatism, the will of the majority determines not only what the law is, but also what a good law is. This "superstition" about democracy has resulted in the incorrect assumption that "so long as power is conferred through democratic procedure, it will not be arbitrary."[54] In fact, democracy must be subject to the rule of law. "However, for political life, like economic life, to be a matter of individual freedom and initiative, majority rule must be circumscribed by the rule of law. Only under these conditions can the majority principle function wisely and effectively."[55]

[49] Cass R. Sunstein: *Designing Democracy: What Constitutions Do*, translated by Jin Chaowu *et al.*, Law Press China, Beijing, 2006 edition, p. 9.

[50] Susan Marks: *The Riddle of All Constitutions: International Law, Democracy, and the Critique of Ideology*, translated by Fang Zhiyan, Shanghai Century Publishing Group, Shanghai, 2005 edition, pp. 91, 92.

[51] Josef Thesing and Winfried Jung: *The Rule of Law*, Law Press China, Beijing, 2005 edition, p. 6.

[52] Robert Dahl: *On Democracy*, translated by Li Boguang *et al.*, The Commercial Press, Beijing, 1999 edition, p. 137.

[53] Richard Williamson: *Why Democracy?* published in *Democracy and Democratization*, The Commercial Press, Beijing, 1999 edition, p. 41.

[54] Friedrich August von Hayek: *The Road to Serfdom*, translated by Wang Mingyi *et al.*, China Social Sciences Press, Beijing, 1997 edition, p. 72.

[55] David Held: *Models of Democracy*, translated by Yan Jirong *et al.*, Central Compilation & Translation Press, Beijing, 1998 edition, p. 329.

According to the Marxist democratic theory, bourgeois democracy is actually the dictatorship of the bourgeoisie as the few over the working class and the masses as the majority. Capitalist democracy and rule of law include some deep-seated inner contradictions: the contradiction between the publicity of representing social common interests in theory and the protection of capital special interests in practice; the contradiction between equality in political and legal forms and inequality in social and economic reality; and the contradiction between the separation of state power in form and the superiority of state power to the society.[56] In this connection, irreconcilable inner contradictions and conflicts exist between the bourgeoisie rule of law and democracy. Socialist democracy and rule of law have eradicated the root of these contradictions and conflicts between the nature of the state and the form of government, between state power and civil rights, and between the national system and the social system. No fundamental conflicts of interests exist between socialist democracy and the rule of law, although these need constant adjustments and adaptations.

1.3.1 Analysis of the Basic Relationship between Socialist Democracy and Rule of Law

It will further deepen our understanding of the relationship between socialist democracy and rule of law if we see them from different planes and perspectives while using the democratic forms of system, power, and rights as the principal line.[57] Looking from the perspective of socialist political civilization, socialist democracy and the rule of law are an inseparable entity that integrates democracy and the rule of law. In this entity, the rule of law is the procedural, normalized, and legalized form of

[56]Refer to *On Democracy* by Li Tieying, People's Publishing House, Beijing, 2001 edition, pp. 54–66.

[57]At the "theoretical workshop on the tenth anniversary of the implementation of the rule of law as the fundamental strategy" organized by the Institute of Law of Chinese Academy of Social Sciences on July 14, 2007, Xie Pengcheng, Qi Yanping, and other scholars observed that, in a general sense, democracy and the rule of law do not have necessary connections. Looking at the history of the rule of law in the West, freedom and human rights have a close relationship with the rule of law. However, democracy doesn't have necessary internal correlations with the rule of law. In socialist countries, democracy and the rule of law are closely connected, but democracy is not the foundation and precondition for the rule of law, and it is just the opposite. In my opinion, it is significant and necessary to rerecognize and rethink the relations between the two in line with China's actuality today, after 30 years of discussion of socialist democracy and socialist legal systems.

democracy while the democracy is the institutional, power, and right form of the rule of law. The combination of the two becomes the "state form" and the "form of socialist political civilization" and becomes an organic whole. In this sense, the concept of democracy has included the rule of law while the connotation of the rule of law has also contained democracy. When using concepts like "socialist democracy," "socialist rule of law," and "socialist democracy and rule of law," they are the same in essence in China, only with different emphasis.

From the perspective of the narrow concept of socialist political civilization, China can divide socialist democracy and rule of law into two concepts. In political science, democracy can be expressed as the concept of political philosophy comprised of state systems, state powers, and civil rights. In the science of law, the rule of law can be expressed as the concept of legal philosophy comprised of legal systems (norms), statutory powers, and legal rights. The difference between politics and law and the distinction between political science and the science of law have determined the difference between democracy and the rule of law as concepts and defined the relationship between the two: division of functions, interdependence, interaction, and close connection.

Looking from the perspective of hierarchical relations between the democratic political system and the legal system (the system of law), democracy and the rule of law have three primary relations. The first is determining relations top-down; the second is the interactive relations in parallel; and the third is the affiliated relations bottom-up.

First of all, the hierarchical relationship between the democratic political system and the legal system (the system of law) first constitutes a zigzag, determining relations top-down. In the relationship between democracy and the rule of law, the superior produces and determines the inferior, while the latter is produced by, and subordinate to the superior. For example, their relationship is like this: the nature of state and the form of government produce (determine) the constitution—the constitution produces (determines) the legislative (power) system, the administrative (power) system, the judicial (power) system, and the legal supervision (power) system, among other state political (power) systems—the legislative (power) system produces (determines) laws, the administrative (power) system produces (determines) regulations and government rules, and the judicial (power) system and the legal supervision (power) system produces (determines) judicial interpretations—laws, rules, government regulations, and judicial interpretations produce (determine) all kinds of specific rules.

Looking from the perspective of China's new democratic revolution, the people's democratic revolution is the foundation and premise for the rule of law. This is because the democratic movement overturned despotism, established the constitution and the electoral system, and adopted laws to restrict state powers and guarantee the people's power. Corresponding systems shall be put in place for the redistribution of property through reforming land ownership, changing inheritance law, levying taxes from the rich, and establishing a welfare system.[58] But after formulation of the constitution, it is inappropriate to say in a general and simple manner that socialist democracy is the foundation and premise for socialist rule of law and that socialist rule of law is the guarantee of socialist democracy. This is because the constitution has defined and produced a series of democratic political systems including the people's congress system and identified a host of constitutional principles. The constitution has become the cornerstone of socialist democracy and rule of law. The relationship between democracy and the rule of law has become a constitutional model in which the constitution determines democracy.

Second, democracy and the rule of law have an interactive relationship in parallel. Democracy and the rule of law are inseparable.[59] Under the conditions that China has taken the socialist constitutional path, applied the rule of law and governance by law, the zigzag relationship between democracy and the rule of law has changed. The relationship has changed to an interactive relationship in parallel with the democratic political system and the system of the rule of law with the constitution as the basis and the center. The rule of law is on a par with democracy, and they have become a parallel and interactive relationship with the same status. For instance, the constitution has regulated the country's nature of state, form of government, and fundamental political, economic, and social systems. The constitution has the supreme legal effect and status and represents the general principle for ensuring good administration of state affairs and national security. The constitution has defined the people's congress system, and thus the people's congress system has a direct basis for constitutionality. On the other hand, the National People's Congress is entitled to modify the constitution. The Standing Committee of the National People's Congress has the right to interpret the constitution and supervise

[58] Douglas Lummis: *Radical Democracy*, translated by Liu Yuanqi, China Renmin University Press, Beijing, 2002 edition, p. 159.

[59] Josef Thesing and Winfried Jung: *The Rule of Law*, Law Press China, Beijing, 2005 edition, p. 50.

its implementation. This has constituted the interactive relationship between the political democracy and the rule of law under the framework of a socialist constitutional system.

Third, democracy and the rule of law have formed a kind of reversed zigzag affiliated relationship between the inferior and the superior. In this relationship, the inferior is produced by and subject to the superior. Compared with the top-down zigzag determining relations, this is a reversed zigzag affiliated relationship. In this relationship, it is untenable to say that socialist democracy is the foundation and premise for the rule of law while the rule of law is the guarantee of socialist democracy. For example, in the specific affiliated relationship among the electoral law, the electoral system, and the electoral behaviors, the electoral system comes from the electoral law, and the electoral law is the premise and foundation for the electoral system. Electoral behaviors are based on the electoral system stipulated by the electoral law. The electoral law is the guarantee of the electoral system while the electoral law and the electoral system are the basis and guarantee of electoral behaviors.

Therefore it can be seen that socialist democracy and rule of law have a hierarchical relationship. In a specific up-and-down hierarchical relationship, socialist democracy can determine and guarantee the rule of law. But in another specific up-and-down hierarchical relationship, socialist rule of law may determine and guarantee democracy. In the parallel hierarchical relationship, democracy and the rule of law can determine, supplement, and act upon each other.

1.3.2 Revolutionary Party vs. Ruling Party: The CPC's Different Attitudes Toward Democracy and the Rule of Law

The CPC was a revolutionary party whose target was to overturn the Fascist rule of the Kuomintang and establish the people's democratic power. But after 28 years of bloody battles of the new-democratic revolution, the CPC became a ruling party defining its tasks as controlling the state power and making the people masters of the country. The *Report of the CPC to its Fourth Plenary Session of the 16th Central Committee* pointed out that it has experienced two fundamental changes in the 21st century. It has changed from a party that led the people in the struggle for seizing the state power to a long-term ruling party leading the people to control the state power; it has changed from a party that suffered external blockade and led the state building under a planned economic system to a party leading the state building under the conditions of opening up and developing a socialist market economy. As a whole, in the new-democratic revolution period, the CPC as the ruling party was denied and outlawed by the legal system, and laws of the Kuomintang reactionary regime and were to be wiped out politically, militarily, and even physically. Therefore the democracy, powers, and rights of the CPC existed in no way under the system of the fascist dictatorship of the Kuomintang. In order to lead the people of all nationalities to topple down imperialism, feudalism, and bureaucratic capitalism, establish a new China, and realize the revolutionary target of people's democracy, the CPC must use military, political, and other revolutionary forces to defeat the Kuomintang armed forces, smash state machines, and abolish its illegally constituted authority. In the opinion of Lenin, dictatorship means "unlimited power, based on force instead of on law." "The revolutionary dictatorship of the proletariat is the power obtained and maintained by violence of the proletariat against the bourgeoisie, without being restricted by any laws."[60] For the revolutionary CPC, the national legal system controlled by Kuomintang reactionaries and its so-called democracy actually looked to wipe out the CPC and the revolutionary forces under its leadership. Therefore the revolutionary CPC and the legal system and "democracy" of the Kuomintang reactionary regime could by no means coexist. The CPC must destroy the legal system and "democracy" of Kuomintang reactionaries so as to establish a legitimate foundation under its leadership and governance, to put in place a new rule of law of the people's democratic power, and to build a new country where the people are masters.

After founding the People's Republic of China, the CPC became the ruling party from a revolutionary party. The position and mission of the ruling party required and determined that, in the political field, the CPC must lead and support the people to establish the national political power, democratic system, and legal system under which the people are masters of

[60]Vladimir Lenin: *The Proletarian Revolution and the Renegade Kautsky*, published in *The Collected Works of Lenin*, volume 35, People's Publishing House, 1985 edition, p. 237. Lenin also mentioned this theory on many other occasions. For example, Lenin once pointed out that "dictatorship is the rule based directly upon force and unrestricted by any laws." Vladimir Lenin: *A Contribution to the History of the Question of the Dictatorship*, published in *The Collected Works of Lenin*, volume 39, People's Publishing House, 1986 edition, p. 374; "The scientific concept of dictatorship means nothing more nor less than authority untrammeled by any laws, absolutely unrestricted by any rules whatsoever, and based directly on force." Refer to *A Contribution to the History of the Question of the Dictatorship*, published in *The Collected Works of Lenin*, volume 39, People's Publishing House, 1986 edition, p. 380.

the country. The ruling party should also guarantee that the people manage national affairs according to the law and embody people's governance of the systems of the state and government. The ruling party should embody the unity of its advocates and the people's will in constitution and law, the unity of state powers and people's rights, and the unity of socialist rule of law and socialist democracy. In the economic field, the CPC should lead and support the people to control means of production, manage economic affairs in accordance with the law, and constantly release and develop productive forces. In so doing, it could create a rich material foundation and economic conditions for the people to enjoy a commonly prosperous and happy life, and fully exercise their democratic rights. In the social field, the CPC should lead and support the people to become masters of society, manage social affairs, enjoy social rights, undertake social obligations, and realize social autonomy of the people according to the law. The leadership of the CPC as the ruling party, the people's democracy, and the socialist rule of law are an organic unity. The CPC acts within the scope of the constitution and the law. It is committed to democratic and scientific governance by law. It takes a lead in enforcing and complying with the law and improving and developing the people's democracy through various channels and forms such as the rule of law. It leads, supports, and guarantees the people's role as masters of the country and obtains the power base and source and foundation of legitimacy continuously for its governance from its practices and development of the people's democracy.[61]

1.4 GUARANTEE OF DEMOCRACY BY SOCIALIST RULE OF LAW

The people's democracy is the life of socialism[62] and needs to be guaranteed by socialist rule of law. Socialist rule of law guarantees democracy mainly through three forms, namely its confirmation, guidance, and regulation of democracy.

[61] *The Decision* adopted at the Fourth Plenary Session of the 16th CPC Central Committee pointed out that the ruling status of the Party was not inherent and couldn't be realized once and for all. The Party should strengthen its governing capacity and entrench the democratic foundation and legitimacy for its governance so that it could always represent the interests of all the people and win the support of the people.

[62] Hu Jintao: *Hold High the Great Banner of Socialism with Chinese Characteristics and Strive for New Victories in Building a Moderately Prosperous Society in All—Report to the Seventeenth National Congress of the Communist Party of China*, CPC 17th national congress, CPC 17th national congress, October 24, 2007.

1.4.1 Socialist Rule of Law Affirms Democracy

The people's democracy means socialist democracy, with the rule of the many in a real sense and the democratic form most consistent with the original meaning of democracy. Democracy needs to be guaranteed by the rule of law. One of the major forms of guarantee is to ensure democracy in the constitution and the laws. Mao Zedong had profound insight on the function of the rule of law (constitution) in confirming democracy. He said that all constitutional governments in the world, no matter whether they were in the United Kingdom, France, the United States, or the former Soviet Union, would issue and accept a fundamental law after the success of a revolution and the availability of democracy, namely the constitution.[63] The existence of a constitution is widely regarded as an essential and prerequisite condition for democracy.[64] What has happened in many countries in modern times shows that the victorious ruling class in a revolution uses a constitution and laws to confirm the legitimacy of the power established by the revolution and to achieve the goal of consolidating power. American scholar Harold J. Berman illustrated the relationship between law and revolution in his book *Law and Revolution: The Formation of the Western Legal Tradition* with extensive supporting material and in-depth discussion. "Law is wholly subordinate to revolution. The overthrow of one set of political institutions and the replacement of another set of institutions lead to an entirely new law."[65] Berman further argues that "The legal tradition of the West was largely shaped by six great revolutions in its history, three of which are the Russian Revolution, the French Revolution and the American Revolution ... Each has sought legitimacy in a fundamental law ... Each has resulted in a new legal system.... The government and legal system of every western country are the result of this kind of revolution."[66] Each of the six revolutions of the West led to a new or greatly modified legal system within the context of the entire

[63] Mao Zedong: *Constitutional Government of the New Democracy*, included in Volume 2 of *Selected Works of Mao Zedong*, People's Publishing House, Beijing, 1991 edition, p. 735.

[64] B. Barry M. and Hager: *The Rule of Law: A Lexicon for Policy Makers*, translated by Mansfield Center for Pacific Affairs, China University of Political Science and Law Press, Beijing, 2005 edition, p. 35.

[65] Harold J. Berman: *Law and Revolution: The Formation of the Western Legal Tradition*, translated by He Weifang *et al.*, Encyclopedia of China Publishing House, Beijing, 1992 edition, p. 45.

[66] Harold J. Berman: *Law and Revolution: The Formation of the Western Legal Tradition*, translated by He Weifang *et al.*, Encyclopedia of China Publishing House, Beijing, 1992 edition, pp. 21–23.

changing society. The revolutionary goal specified in the new law reflects how successful the revolution was. "Each revolution successfully resulted in a new law, reflecting many primary targets sought by this kind of revolution."[67] The power established by the working class through revolution needs to be confirmed and consolidated by the rule of law. Among the first batch of decrees issued by the Bolshevik government in 1917, one was to announce the abolition of all laws issued before the revolution. The decrees applicable are only those of the new government.[68]

The precondition of the establishment of the people's democratic power of the People's Republic of China was the victory of the new democratic revolution. On the eve of the founding of the New China, Chiang Kai-shek published on January 1, 1949 the *New Year Proclamation*, proposing to have peace talks on five conditions and requesting the maintenance of the Puppet Legally Constituted Authority. Three days later, Mao Zedong published the *On the War Criminal's Suing for Peace* to refute the proposals of Chiang Kai-shek point by point and tit for tat.[69] Later, Mao Zedong published the *Statement on the Present Situation*,[70] showing the willingness to have peace talks with the Kuomintang reactionary government and any other Kuomintang local government and military bloc under the precondition of abrogating the bogus constitution and the Puppet Legally Constituted Authority. The Central Committee of the CPC issued the *Instructions Concerning Abolishing the Six Codes of the Kuomintang and Determining Judicial Principles for the Liberated Areas* in February 1949. It was stated clearly in the instructions that the law is the so-called state ideology enforced by the ruling class publicly with armed force. As with the state, the law is just an instrument for safeguarding certain interests of the ruling class. All laws of the Kuomintang were only instruments for protecting landlords and the reactionary rules of the bureaucrat-bourgeoisie and weapons for suppressing and restraining the broad masses. Under the people's democratic dictatorship with the worker–peasant alliance as the main body under the leadership of the

[67] Harold J. Berman: *Law and Revolution: The Formation of the Western Legal Tradition*, translated by He Weifang *et al.*, Encyclopedia of China Publishing House, Beijing, 1992 edition, p. 26.

[68] Harold J. Berman: *Law and Revolution: The Formation of the Western Legal Tradition*, translated by He Weifang *et al.*, Encyclopedia of China Publishing House, Beijing, 1992 edition, p. 24.

[69] Mao Zedong: *On the War Criminal's Suing for Peace*, published in *Selected Works of Mao Zedong*, volume 4, People's Publishing House, Beijing, 1991 edition, pp. 1381–1385.

[70] Mao Zedong: *Statement on the Present Situation*, published in *Selected Works of Mao Zedong*, volume 4, People's Publishing House, Beijing, 1991 edition, pp. 1386–1390.

proletariat, the "Six Codes" of the Kuomintang should be abolished. In September 1949, the Chinese People's Political Consultative Conference adopted the *Common Programme*. Article 17 of the *Common Programme* clearly stipulated that all laws, decrees, and judicial systems enacted by the reactionary Kuomintang shall be abolished. Instead, laws and decrees protecting the people shall be enacted, and the people's judicial system shall be established. The principle of the first constitution of the New China promulgated in 1954 was reflected by confirming the people's democracy and socialist principles with the constitution.[71]

After establishment of the nature of state and the form of government under which the people are masters of the country and during the socialist revolutionary period, especially in the period of socialist modernization, the socialist rule of law constantly confirms and safeguards the constitutional status and legitimacy of the leadership and governance of the CPC in the constitution and the laws. Also, the rule of law confirms and safeguards the authority and legitimacy of state organs of all kinds and at all levels to possess and exercise public powers. The rule of law confirms and expands the range of citizens' rights (and especially confirms and safeguards citizens' exercise of rights). The rule of law confirms the procedures and conditions for citizens to exercise their democratic rights and to realize full democracy.

After the Chinese people obtain democracy and establish the national regime, a major task faced by the CPC in its leadership and governance will be how to guarantee the people's democracy through state apparatuses. Deng Xiaoping pointed out that China must strengthen its legal system in order to guarantee the people's democracy. China must also institutionalize and legalize democracy so that this kind of system and laws will not change with the alteration of leaders or with the change of leaders' views and priorities.[72] The top priority for realizing democracy under the rule of law is to confirm all kinds of systems, powers, and rights of the people's democracy in constitutions and laws. However, the people's democracy cannot be confirmed by the rule of law once and for all, and the confirmation is not changeless. The rule of law needs to confirm the

[71] Mao Zedong: *On the Draft Constitution of the People's Republic of China*, published in *Selected Works of Mao Zedong*, volume 6, People's Publishing House, Beijing, 1999 edition, p. 328.

[72] Deng Xiaoping: *Emancipating the Mind, Seeking Truth from the Facts, and Looking Ahead in Unity*, published in *Selected Works of Deng Xiaoping*, volume 2, People's Publishing House, Beijing, 1994 edition, p. 146.

latest achievements in the development of democratic politics and political restructuring with the development of the economy, politics, culture, and society. In this way, it could broaden the content of the people's democratic rights, enrich the democratic participation form, expand the democratic participation channel, create new democratic participation mechanism, raise the democratic participation level, and improve the democratic participation system.

1.4.2 Socialist Rule of Law Guides Democracy

The rule of law is a code of conduct and way of life with the function of evaluating and guiding values. The socialist rule of law plays an obvious role in guiding the value choice, value judgment, and behavioral model of state organs, social organizations, and individual citizens.

First, socialist rule of law guides democracy in value. Democracy itself is not an objective, but a means by which the people effectively guarantee the highest political objectives. So, democratic movements must be limited. Democratic government should accept the limit within the scope of legal activities.[73] Democracy as a kind of systems, means, and forms will not necessarily lead to "goodness" that values fairness and justice. Democracy is not always right or doubtless.[74] Improper application of democracy may produce "evil" consequences such as unfairness, injustice, and disorder. Therefore it requires guidance from the rule of law by "restraining evilness and advocating goodness." An outstanding feature of socialist rule of law is its clear value orientation of denying the rule of man, pursuing fairness and justice, democracy, and human rights. The nature of socialist laws and rule of law is to demonstrate fairness and justice based on the people's interests and the people's will. The nature of socialist laws and rule of law is also to reflect the people-oriented political philosophy that respects and protects human rights. The nature of socialist laws and rule of law is also to embody the political value that the people are masters of the country and society and masters of their own.

Second, the socialist rule of law guides democracy in norms. Legal norms or statutory rules are basic paradigms for the rule of law to

[73] David Held: *Models of Democracy*, translated by Yan Jirong *et al.*, Central Compilation & Translation Press, Beijing, 1998 edition, p. 327.

[74] David Held: *Models of Democracy*, translated by Yan Jirong *et al.*, Central Compilation & Translation Press, Beijing, 1998 edition, p. 324.

function in social relations and behaviors. Modern countries implement the rule of law for not only promoting democratic activities but also guaranteeing human rights.[75] Legal norms are technical and operational in nature, but imply not only the requirements of some values, wills, and interests, but also the intentions of the people as legislators. The requirements and intentions of legislators in democracy are deeply embedded in legal norms through the processing of legal technologies like legal language, legislative technique, and behavioral models. Consequently, these requirements and intentions of legislators have become standard guidance for democratic powers, rights, and behaviors. The rule of law should not only guarantee the rule of the many but also protect the rights of the few. Respecting the many and protecting the few turns out to be a fundamental requirement of modern democracy for the rule of law. Democracy has a variable principle that stands for the supremacy of the people's will and the rule of the majority. Democracy also has a fixed principle that admits individual freedom and protects the rights of the few. These two principles supplement each other under the rule of law, so the democratic system can be perfect.[76] From the macro perspective, the constitution and laws shall determine and guide a country's nature of state, form of government, electoral system, structural form of state, form of ethnic relations, form of interparty relationship, and division and restriction of public powers. From the micro perspective, in most cases, norms of the rule of law determine various aspects such as which citizens could become the main body of citizens, what democratic rights citizens could enjoy, and how citizens could exercise democratic rights. The norms of the rule of law also regulate how citizens could supervise public powers and defend private rights as well as whether privileges are allowed to exist. For example, the right to vote is taken as the supreme right. It is the electoral rights that have made the people citizens. The right to vote is the basis for all other rights, including the right to life, right of freedom, and property rights.[77] It happens to be the constitution and the electoral law that have made institutional, procedural, and right arrangements of the right to vote and that have provided a basis for enjoying and exercising the right to vote. When it comes to the specification and guidance of democracy by the rule of law, there are

[75] Josef Thesing and Winfried Jung: *The Rule of Law*, Law Press China, Beijing, 2005 edition, p. 51.
[76] Josef Thesing and Winfried Jung: *The Rule of Law*, Law Press China, Beijing, 2005 edition, p. 56.
[77] Judith N. Shklar: *American Citizenship: The Quest for Inclusion*, translated by Liu Mangui, Shanghai Century Publishing Group, Shanghai, 2006 edition, p. 33.

prohibitive limits and incentive mechanisms as well as a wealth of requirements for "what should be done."

Third, the socialist rule of law guides democracy in behavior. From an operation perspective, the operation of specific democratic powers or the exercise of democratic rights are reflected in most cases as specific behaviors of particular democratic bodies. For specific state organs, social organizations, individual citizens, and other main bodies, the operation of democracy is further demonstrated as the interaction between specific behaviors (actions) of the main bodies of democracy for one part and statutory institutions and legal norms for another. The people is unable to guarantee that their opinions are beneficial or wise unless they are restricted by general rules in their actions.[78] The rule of law is responsible for guiding the main bodies of democracy in behavior from the following aspects: (1) enabling the main bodies of democracy to establish a socialist concept of the rule of law and promote a modern spirit of the rule of law through publicity and education of rule of law; (2) formulating all kinds of laws and regulations to institutionalize, normalize, and legalize the requirements of the ruling party and the people for enjoying democratic rights and exercising democratic powers and the requirements for the form, level, and limit of democratic behaviors by means of the state will so as to guarantee correct operation of democratic rights (powers) and prevent the abuse of democratic behaviors; (3) through correct law enforcement of administrative bodies and impartial judicature of judicial organs, the rule of law can better handle the relations between state powers and civil rights, between enjoying rights and undertaking obligations, between exercising powers and assuming responsibilities, between specific democratic behaviors and specific norms of the rule of law, and guide the main bodies of democracy to implement democratic behaviors on the track and within the range of the rule of law; and (4) through education, regulation, incentives, and punishments, among other forms and ways, the rule of law can guide citizens, especially the working staff, to actively fulfill their constitutional and legal obligations. In a democratic state under the rule of law, even those holding public offices are restrained by the constitution and the laws.[79] More importantly, the socialist rule of law needs

[78] David Held: *Models of Democracy*, translated by Yan Jirong *et al.*, Central Compilation & Translation Press, Beijing, 1998 edition, p. 324.

[79] Josef Thesing and Winfried Jung: *The Rule of Law*, Law Press China, Beijing, 2005 edition, p. 51.

to distribute, realize, and correct fairness through legislation, law enforcement, and judiciary, respectively. In this way, socialist rule of law can prevent fundamental conflict of interests, polarization between the rich and the poor, public power corruption, and alienation of democracy under democratic systems. If a country fails to develop and implement relevant laws after realizing democracy to address conflicts of interest, uneven distributed wealth, and corruption, the fragile new institution may be undermined by individual behaviors for accumulating wealth by unfair means,[80] and thus the socialist democratic power may be overthrown.

1.4.3 Socialist Rule of Law Regulates Democracy

Democracy as the state power, state institution, or a civil right has many positive and important values and functions. At the same time, democracy also has many inherent drawbacks and limitations. A democratic form of government does not mean a well-functioning government.[81] If a democracy chooses to destroy an institutional framework allowing the occurrence of consistency and conflict resolution by violence, that would mean suicide. Self-restraint is not only allowable but also obligatory. The majority of people must restrict their own powers to guarantee that they are followed by others.[82] Inappropriate application of democracy would lead to a catastrophe like the "cultural revolution" in the name of "great democracy" and tragedies such as German fascists led by Hitler who used democracy to seize the political power. Under certain conditions, democracy is nothing but another kind of unavoidable form of struggle, through which the people will decide who will obtain what things in what way at what time.[83] As can be seen, democracy does not necessarily result in

[80] Susan Rose-Ackerman: *Democracy and Grand Corruption*, published in *Rethinking Democracy* edited by Social Science in China Press, Social Sciences Academic Press (China), 2000 edition, p. 304.

[81] Mark E. Warren: *Democracy and Trust*, translated by Wu Hui, Huaxia Publishing House, Beijing, 2004 edition, p. 136.

[82] S. Holmes, "Precommitment and the Paradox of Democracy," in J. Elster and R. Slagstad (eds), *Constitutionalism and Democracy*, Cambridge: Cambridge University Press, 1988, pp. 239–249. Quoted from [Britain] David Held: *Democracy and the Global Order: From the Modern State to Cosmopolitan Governance*, translated by Hu Wei *et al.*, Shanghai Century Publishing Group, 2003 edition, p. 169.

[83] Friedrich von Hayek: *Law, Legislation and Liberty* (volumes 2, 3), translated by Deng Zhenglai *et al.*, Encyclopedia of China Publishing House, Beijing, 2000 edition, p. 268.

the realization of objectives such as goodness, justice, peace, trust,[84] stability, harmony, and order. Democratization does not necessarily bring about economic growth, social peace, management efficiency, political harmony, and a free market.[85] Democracy may sometimes produce results that are opposite to human ideals. Both a good democracy and a bad democracy are not unconditional. One of the conditions for democracy to become a good thing is to regulate democracy by (or through) the rule of law. A country under the rule of law, or a democratic country under the rule of law, is controlled and restricted by laws in all activities.[86] Democracy is a particular but limited ideal,[87] so regulating democracy is an approach to guarantee and restrict democracy by the rule of law, and the purpose is to maximally prevent or reduce possible drawbacks of democracy and give full play to the positive functions of democracy.

The first regulation of democracy by socialist rule of law is to regulate the main bodies of democracy:

1. In general, the constitution and laws stipulate who can become the main bodies of democracy. This involves two categories, namely politics and law. In politics, those who belong to the category of people can become the main body of people's democracy. In China, all laborers endorsing, supporting, and participating in socialist construction and all patriots endorsing socialism and supporting national reunification belong to the category of people. But they need to be confirmed by the constitution and the laws to become the main body of democracy in the sense of the nature of state and form of government.

[84]American Associate Professor in Politics Mark Warren pointed out that democracy can neither guarantee the trust nor ensure a dynamic society. Only in a society where the majority are willing to have a certain degree of trust in strangers, could generalized trust become an engine of the society. He added that historical evidence shows that democracy sometimes successfully leads to happiness and trust, but sometimes not. "To assume that democracy automatically makes people happy is to assume that the tail is wagging the dog." Political life is indeed in action, but it is generally a moderate effect. If the improvement of living standard and life quality come with democracy, then subjective happiness would be increased, which usually helps legalize democratic institutions. Refer to [US] Mark E. Warren: *Democracy and Trust*, translated by Wu Hui, Huaxia Publishing House, 2004 edition, pp. 135, 110.

[85]Philippe C. Schmitter and Terry Lynn Karl: *What Democracy Is... and Is Not*, published in *Democracy and Democratization*, The Commercial Press, Beijing, 1999 edition, p. 37.

[86]Josef Thesing and Winfried Jung: *The Rule of Law*, Law Press China, Beijing, 2005 edition, p. 6.

[87]Cass R. Sunstein: *Designing Democracy: What Constitutions Do*, translated by Jin Chaowu *et al.*, Law Press China, Beijing, 2006 edition, p. 278.

In law, all people with the citizenship of the People's Republic of China are Chinese citizens; all people meeting the conditions for being citizens of the People's Republic of China can become the main body of democracy of China. However, the qualification of citizens being the main body of a democracy would be greatly restricted, weakened, or canceled if their political rights were deprived.

2. In electoral democracy and consultative democracy, socialist rule of law regulates who can be elected as deputies to the National People's Congress (NPC) and local people's congresses and members of the Chinese People's Political Consultative Conference (CPPCC). Two important forms of realizing China's socialist democracy are: people exercise their rights through election and voting, people have full consultations before making major decisions and trying to agree on common issues. From the perspective of electoral democracy of the people's congress, the constitution and laws stipulate that all Chinese citizens aged 18 or above have the right to vote and the right to be elected irrespective of their nationality, race, gender, occupation, family background, religion, educational background, property status, and length of residence. From the perspective of consultative democracy, the constitution stipulates that the multiparty cooperation and political consultation system under the leadership of the CPC will exist and develop for a long time. The principal forms of consultative democracy are political consultation, political participation, democratic supervision, and collaboration.
3. Specifically, the socialist rule of law stipulates different democracies of some groups in line with special situations and specific national conditions. Typically, the NPC should have a proper number of female deputies and keep increasing their representative proportions; for ethnic minorities who are small in number and live in compact communities, each of which should have at least one deputy to the NPC, the election of deputies to both the NPC and the people's congresses above the county level shall apply special regulations; the NPC and local people's congresses in areas with more returned overseas Chinese should include an appropriate number of returned overseas Chinese deputies; if Chinese citizens living overseas happen to be in China during the election of deputies to people's congresses below the county level, then they can take part in the election in their domicile of origin or in where they lived before they went abroad; Chinese citizens of Hong Kong Special Administrative Region (SAR) and Macao SAR

participate in national affairs management in accordance with the law and elect their deputies to the NPC to take part in works of the highest organs of state power. The plan on Taiwan's participation in the consultation and election of deputies to the NPC was adopted. People who have been deprived of political rights have no right to vote or to be elected in accordance with the law. Those who are confirmed to be mentally incapable to exercise voting rights by legal procedures shall not take part in the election.

The second regulation of democracy by socialist rule of law is to regulate democratic institutions. Deng Xiaoping pointed out in *The Reform of Leading Institution of Party and State* in August 1980 that all kinds of mistakes made by China in the past had no doubt something to do with the thought and style of some leaders, but what are more important are the issues related to organizational systems and working systems. Good systems in these aspects can prevent bad people from running amok arbitrarily, while bad systems can prevent good people from doing good things and even make good people turn into their opposite. Even those people as great as comrade Mao Zedong may be also influenced by some unsound institutions, which cause misfortune to the Party, the country, and himself. Moreover, institutions are featured by fundamentality, stability, and overall importance.[88] The socialist rule of law guarantees that the republic and state powers (public powers) are always owned by the people and bring benefit to the people through the people's congress system, the system of regional national autonomy, the system of multiparty cooperation led by the CPC, and the political consultation and democratic systems at the grassroots level, among other democratic channels and forms.

The third regulation of democracy by the socialist rule of law is achieved by defining democratic rights and legal obligations. In a broad sense, all rights of citizens are democratic rights. Democracy is unconditional and its realization is subject to economic, political, cultural, and other external conditions and personality, mentality, age, and other internal conditions, so all rights of citizens will directly or indirectly affect and determine their understanding and application of democracy. All rights of citizens belong to democratic rights. Correspondingly, all legal obligations of citizens have something to do with democracy. In a narrow sense, political rights including the right to know, to vote and to be elected, and to make decisions,

[88] *Selected Works of Deng Xiaoping*, volume 2, People's Publishing House, Beijing, 1994 edition, p. 333.

and the rights of management, participation, and supervision, all belong to democratic rights. Correspondingly, the following civil obligations and civil rights have a much greater correlation with democratic rights. Citizens shall not damage national, social, and collective interests and other citizens' lawful freedom and rights when enjoying freedom and rights. Citizens have the obligation to safeguard national reunification and unity of all nationalities, citizens have the obligation to safeguard national security and the honor and interest of the motherland, etc.

The fourth regulation of democracy by socialist rule of law is to supervise and restrict public powers. For the sake of democracy, the rule of law needs all kinds of procedures and control methods to define government behavioral scope and pattern.[89] The regulation of public powers by the rule of law is first to use rights to restrict powers and use civil rights and social rights to supervise and restrict public powers, so as to prevent the abuse of public powers. Second, it is to use powers to restrict powers, i.e., to realize mutual supervision and restriction between powers through horizontal division of state powers and vertical division of central and local powers. Third, it is to use legal procedures to restrict powers, i.e., to formulate all kinds of procedural and legal norms through legislation and to define the precedence order and operating instructions for the exercise of public powers. Fourth, it is to use legal liabilities to restrict public powers, i.e., to preset legal liabilities of public powers at all levels and of all kinds based on the principle that there must be liability when there is power, and that more power leads to more liability. Once public powers are abused (including fulfilled, unfulfilled, and randomly fulfilled), the main body of public powers will be punished severely and immediately and be held accountable in accordance with the law.

1.5 SOCIALIST DEMOCRATIC RULE OF LAW AND HARMONIOUS SOCIETY

The so-called harmony is the cognition of the changes and the law of development of the nature and human society. Harmony is the values and methodology of the people for pursuing beautiful things and doing things. Harmony is a specific, dynamic, relative, and dialectical unity of opposite things under certain conditions. Harmony is the relations between different things, which supplement each other no matter whether they are

[89] Josef Thesing and Winfried Jung: *The Rule of Law*, Law Press China, Beijing, 2005 edition, p. 55.

the same, supplementary, or opposite, i.e., different things cooperate with and complement each other with mutual benefit and development. The essence of harmony lies in "seeking common ground while keeping differences" and "remaining harmonious in diversity."

A harmonious society is a good social state and a good social ideal of humanity. In this kind of society, all people work according to their ability, play their proper roles, and live in harmony. It is generally believed that a harmonious society means a powerful and prosperous nation, with ethnic unity, economic prosperity, social stability, honest and capable political administration, happiness of people, and peaceful coexistence guided by harmonious ideas. In ancient China, the "Great Harmony" pursued by the people was a harmonious society in a certain sense, which means "all people should show universal love, the elderly should be tended, the strong be employed, and the youth be nurtured, those who have no kin and cannot support themselves as well as the disabled and the sick be supported, doors are unbolted at night, lost articles are always returned."[90] Marx and Engels described the highest state of a harmonious society in *The Communist Manifesto*: "Bourgeois society will be replaced by an association, in which the free development of each is the condition for the free development of all."[91] That is a communist society.

Modern China is looking to build a harmonious socialist society that is characterized by "democracy and the rule of law, fairness and justice, integrity and friendship, vigor and vitality, peace and order, and harmony between man and nature." It is neither the unrealizable Plato's Utopia or the Confucian "Great Harmony," nor Utopian socialist "City of the Sun" and "Utopia" of Campanella and Mole. A harmonious socialist society is one where all people are in their proper place, and all people observe the public order and play their parts. It's a well-off society featuring the unity of democracy and the rule of law, the unity of fairness and efficiency, the unity of vitality and order, and the unity of man and nature.

To build a harmonious society, we should try to realize harmony between urban and rural areas, between different social classes, between and within different social areas, between different regions, between different ethnic groups, between central and local areas, between man and nature, and harmony of external environments.

[90] *Book of Rites·Rituals.*

[91] *Selected Works of Karl Marx and Friedrich Engel*, volume 1, People's Publishing House, Beijing, 1995 edition, p. 294.

To build a harmonious society, we should work to realize the strategic targets raised by the CPC at the Fourth Plenary Session of its 16th Central Committee. The targets and major tasks of building a harmonious socialist society by 2020 include the following. The legal system of a socialist democracy would be more perfect, ruling the country by law as a fundamental principle would be implemented across the board and the people's interests would be respected and guaranteed. The widening development gap between urban and rural areas and between different regions would be gradually reversed, a rational and orderly income-distribution structure would take shape, family property would be generally increased, and the people would live a more affluent life. There would be sufficient employment, and a social security system covering both urban and rural residents would be put in place. The fundamental public service system would be improved, and government management and service level would be enhanced significantly. The entire nation's ideological and ethical standards, scientific and cultural quality, and physical constitution would be enhanced remarkably, and moral integrity and harmonious interpersonal relationships would be further shaped. The creative vitality of the entire society would also be strengthened notably, and an innovative state would be established. The social management system would be modernized, and there would be good social order. Resources would also be used effectively and the eco-environment would see an obvious improvement. Last but not least, China would become a better society benefiting the entire Chinese population of more than a billion and all the people would do their part, have their places, and live in harmony.

To build a harmonious society, we need to make great efforts to meet the ambitious targets of realizing a well-rounded and well-off society by 2020. These ambitious targets were raised in the *Report to the 18th Central Committee of the CPC*. The first target is to realize a sustainable and healthy economic development. Significant progress should be made in the transformation of economic development mode. On the basis of apparent enhancement of balanced, coordinated, and sustainable development, the gross domestic product and urban and rural residents' per capita income would be doubled compared with that of 2010. The contribution rate of scientific and technological progress to economic growth would rise sharply, which would make China one of the most innovative countries. Industrialization would be basically accomplished, and the level of informatization would be improved substantially. Urbanization quality would be enhanced significantly, and remarkable achievement would be made in agricultural modernization and building new socialist countryside. The regional coordinated development mechanism would be formed, and China would open wider to the outside world and would witness enhanced international competitiveness. The second target is continuously to expand the people's democracy. The democratic system would be more perfect, democratic forms would be enriched, and people's enthusiasm, initiative, and creativity would be increased. The rule of law as a fundamental strategy would be implemented across the board, and a law-based government would be established. Judicial credibility would be improved continuously, and human rights would be respected and guaranteed. The third target is to enhance remarkably the cultural soft power. The socialist core value system would become popular among the people, and the civilization and quality of citizens would obviously increase. Cultural products would be enriched, the public cultural service system would be put in place, and the cultural industry would become the pillar industry of national economy. Chinese culture would go global with a larger step, and the foundation for building a powerful cultural socialist country would be more solid. The fourth target is to improve people's living standards. Therefore basic public services would be equalized, the level of education for all and the level of innovative training would be significantly increased, and China would become one of the stronger countries in talent and human resources. Education would be modernized, there would be more sufficient employment, and the income distribution gap would be narrowed. The middle-income group would keep expanding, the number of poor people needing support would decrease sharply, and the social safety net would cover the entire population, giving everyone access to basic medical care services. A housing guarantee system would be formed, and thus society would be harmonious and stable. The fifth target is to make great progress in resource-saving and environmental friendly social construction. The layout of main functional areas would be formed, and the resource recycling and utilization system would be preliminarily established. Energy consumption and carbon emission per unit of GDP would drop sharply, the total discharge of major pollutants would be cut significantly, and the forest coverage rate would be increased. The ecological system would be more stable, and the people's settlement environment would be improved substantially.

The report of the CPC to its 18th Central Committee notes that building a well-off society requires greater political courage and wisdom and taking every opportunity to deepen reform in critical areas. The report also put forward the requirements for resolutely discarding all old ideas and institutional drawbacks hampering scientific development and building a systematic, improved, scientific, regulated, and operationally effective institutional system. In so doing, systems in all aspects would be more mature and finalized. We also need to accelerate improvement of the socialist market economic system and optimize the basic economic system with public ownership as the main body while allowing diverse forms of ownership to develop at the same time. We need to perfect the distribution system with distribution according to work as the main body and allowing the coexistence of diversified modes of distribution. We need to give priority to the fundamental role of the market in resource allocation to a greater extent and in a broader range and improve the macro regulatory system. We need to improve the open economy system and encourage more effective, fair, and sustainable economic development. We need to speed up to make socialist democracy institutionalized, normalized, and programmed, to expand people's participation in politics on different levels and areas in an orderly way, to bring all works of the state under the rule of law. We need to expedite improvement of cultural management and cultural production and operation. We need basically to set up a modernized cultural market system, modernize the state-owned cultural heritage management system, and build a favorable cultural development environment for innovation and creation. We need to increase the formation of a scientific and effective social management system, improve the social security system, and perfect the grassroots public service and social management network. We also need to establish a system and mechanism guaranteeing a dynamic, harmonious, and orderly society. We need to speed up the establishment of an ecological civilization system and improve the system and mechanism for the development of national land space, resource saving, and ecological environmental protection. We need to propel the formation of a new pattern of modernization featuring harmonious development of man and nature.

From the perspective of political civilization, a harmonious socialist society is not only a democratic society where people are masters of the country, but also a society that is under the rule of law and upholds the supremacy of the constitution and the laws. Democracy and the rule of law represent the primary character and the most important element of a harmonious socialist society. Democracy and the rule of law realize the goal of harmony through their own special channels and functions. At the moment, China is still struggling with a lot of contradictions and issues affecting social harmony. These contradictions and issues mainly include unbalanced social and economic development between rural and urban areas and between different regions; growing pressure of the population on the environment and its resources; salient issues concerning the immediate interests of the masses in employment, social security, income distribution, education, medical care, housing, safe production, and public security; imperfect mechanisms and systems in the democratic legal system; and serious corruption in some areas.[92] Socialist democracy and rule of law are parts of the superstructure. They must adapt to and react to the economic foundation and production relations, address contradictions and issues in building a harmonious society, and play an indispensable and important role in the following aspects.

Society is a complex coalition composed of interconnected and interactioning factors, including the economic field, the political field, the cultural field, and other social fields as well as moral rules, legal norms, religious norms, and other social norms. In this complex coalition, the changes of any social factor may directly or indirectly exert a positive or negative effect on the balance and stability of the entire society now or later. This effect is independent of man's will. Just as Qu Tongzu put it in his *Chinese Law and Chinese Society*, the law is a product of the society and one of the social systems; it has a close relation with manners and customs, and it safeguards existing systems and values like morality and ethics. He added that the law reflects the social structure of a certain time and a certain society and has a very close relation with society. Therefore, he concluded, we cannot take the law as a kind of isolated existence and neglect its relations with society. According to him, the law of any society is enacted to maintain and consolidate its social systems and social order, and only a sufficient understanding of the social background of some laws could lead to understanding of the significance and functions of these laws.[93] That is to say, an effective law has a close relation with the society and its elements.

Building a harmonious society is a systematic project, requiring the synergy of material civilization with continuous economic development,

[92] *Decisions of the CPC Central Committee on Major Issues Regarding the Building of a Harmonious Socialist Society*, October 11, 2006.

[93] Qu Tongzu: *Chinese Law and Chinese Society*, Zhonghua Book Company, Beijing, 2003 edition, Introduction, p. 1.

political civilization with an increasingly improved system, and spiritual civilization with a constantly prosperous culture. Building a harmonious society also requires integrated promotion of economic, political, social, cultural, and ecological development and synthetic action of moral, religious, political, administrative, economic, and legal measures. A harmonious society is a democratic society under the rule of law. Without the rule of law, there would be neither true democracy nor social harmony. The rule of law, the rule of virtue, and politics are respectively the foundation, assistance, and guarantee of a harmonious society from the perspective of social interest, social behavior, social conflict, social order, and social justice.

The rule of law is the foundation of a harmonious society, which means that, under correct political leadership and decision-making, the rule of law plays a dominant, underlying, fundamental, and key role in various areas and aspects. These areas and aspects include the distribution of social interests, the regulation of social behaviors, the settlement of social conflicts, the building of social order and the realization of social justice; political, economic, and social life; the promotion of reform and development; the adjudication of conflict; and the maintenance of stability.

Relative to the rule of law, the rule of virtue plays an auxiliary role in the building of a harmonious society, which means that, the rule of virtue plays an auxiliary, subordinate, and nondominant role in the primary stage of socialism and in the process of building a harmonious society compared with legal norms and functions of the rule of law. We are not saying that morals, the rule of virtue and governing the country by virtue are not important or that we can underestimate or neglect the effect of the rule of virtue. As China is still in the primary stage of socialism with underdeveloped economics, culture, and society, there are still large gaps between people's moral consciousness and their behavior. We can only follow "law comes primarily with virtue as the supplement." So we say the rule of virtue assists a harmonious society.

Politics guarantee a harmonious society, and thus democratic politics provide a harmonious society with correct political leadership and decisions, correct lines, principles, and policies. Democratic politics also guarantee the building of a harmonious society toward people's happiness, ethnic unity, social stability, and national greatness and prosperity. Moreover, democratic politics guarantee smooth building of a harmonious society based on the people's will and through the guidance of the rule of law.

1.5.1 Rule of Law as the Basis for Maintaining Social Harmony and Stability

China's system of law is a judgment standard for social value and a legal standard for behaviors formed based on will of the people. The system of law is the accumulation of experiences of the New China in correctly dealing with various kinds of contradictions and relations in the last six decades plus. These contradictions and relations include contradictions among the people, ethnic relationships, central-local relations, relations between different local areas, relations between the state and society, relations between individuals and collectives, and all kinds of conflicts of interest. The system of law is the fundamental basis for judging lawful and unlawful social behaviors, rights and obligations, acts and responsibilities, rights and wrongs, and for the settlement of disputes in social relations. In a harmonious society, we must unswervingly keep to the principles of the rule of law and the fundamental strategy of governing the country by law. We must try to maintain the authority of the socialist system of law in building well-organized social behavior standards, social relation systems, social interest patterns, and social behavior orders. We must give full play to the system of law as a standard and criterion. Without evaluation and judgment standards, action principles and legal procedures of the system of law, and without various effective institutional rules established under the rule of law for solving social disputes, the authority of the rule of law would be undermined, and it would be difficult to address new issues occurring in social management. As a result, society would run into a ruleless and disordered state. Therefore we must refrain from doing unconventional or unorthodox things, or adopting other sets of standards.

In a harmonious society, we should have a correct "sense of maintaining stability" under the rule of law. On the one hand, a harmonious society is not a society without conflicts and disputes. Rather, it's a society with social conflicts and disputes that can be prevented, adjusted, controlled, and settled by the rule of law and other means. On the other hand, a harmonious society respects and protects human rights and realizes social stability through "safeguarding rights" under the rule of law. It should not only emphasize that "stability is a top priority," "maintaining stability is the primary task," and "making the maintenance of stability and the safeguarding of rights become opposite to each other." Consequently, it would fall into the vicious cycle where "more efforts in maintaining stability means a more unstable society." Maintaining stability of a harmonious society requires a new way of thinking of democracy and the rule of law. We should never make the people's interests antagonistic to social stability, make safeguarding people's rights in accordance with the law antagonistic to social harmony, and regard the people's proper interest expressions and right claims as factors of social instability. Trying to suppress and sacrifice the people's interest expressions and right claims by illegal means to realize so-called social stability would not result in social harmony and stability, but would produce more unstable and disharmonious factors.

1.5.2 Law as an Instrument for Adjusting Social Relations

What is the law? The law is enacted and approved by the state and implemented with the guarantee of the state. The law reflects the will of the people based on specific conditions of material life. The law is the system of behavioral norms consisting of rights and obligations. The law targets confirming, protecting, and developing the social relations and order anticipated by the people. The ethical principles of utilitarianism include the following: the nature of man is to avoid bitterness and seek happiness; people's behaviors are subject to utility; to pursue utility is to pursue happiness; each individual sets out to pursue his or her own greatest happiness; and the basic function of a society or government is to pursue the greatest happiness of most people that is the so-called "principle of the greatest happiness of most people." Based on these ethical principles, the utilitarian jurisprudence of the West (represented by Jeremy Bentham, James Mill, John Austin, and John Stuart Mill) believed that the choice of all behaviors of people lies in the weighing of utility, so legislators should follow the utilitarian principle of the greatest happiness of the most people when enacting laws. This is the purpose of legislation and the standard for judging whether a law is good or bad. Utility is also the basis for implementing a law. The purpose of a law and its corresponding punitive measures is to impose pains on people to force them not to do evil. The law is a means to meet the utilitarian goal (the principle of the greatest happiness of the most people). In a word, the utilitarian principle of the greatest happiness of the most people is not only the initial purpose of the law, but also the inevitable outcome of the law.

The law is an adjuster of social relations, an important social code of conduct, and the standard or principle that shall be followed by social members in social activities. The social code of conduct guides and regulates all social members about what can and cannot be done, as well as how.

It is part The social code of conduct is an essential form of social control. People's behaviors would be out of control without the guidance and restriction of the social code of conduct, and it definitely affects social functioning. American jurist Roscoe Pound said that the law is "a highly special form of social control that takes effect through authoritative commandments and is implemented in the normative system of judicial and administrative procedures." The law is the product of social development, and in return it also functions on social development. The law realizes its control and management of society through adjusting economic relations, political relations, marital and family relations, and property relations between different subjects of legal relations. The law as a basic norm for social behaviors is a fundamental standard for judging whether people's social behaviors are right or wrong, proper or improper, legal or illegal, lawless or criminal. The law is the fundamental criterion for evaluating social behaviors, resolving social conflicts, and settling social disputes.

For ancient Chinese people, the law likes "a measure, a carpenter's line marker, a rule, a scale, or a gauge."[94] This illustrates that the law is the code of social conduct and the fundamental basis for judging and resolving social conflicts and disputes. We must guarantee the availability of the law as a standard and basis, the availability of the procedures and system of the rule of law, and the availability of the final mechanism for settling judicial conflicts and disputes. We must not implement the rule of man in which a few or some individuals have the final say. We must refrain from "believing in authority and petitions rather than the law" and believing in or valuing the practices of settling conflicts and disputes case by case. Otherwise, social conflicts and disputes would not be settled fundamentally and for long, the authority of the law and the rule of law would be greatly undermined, and the national foundation for the rule of law and the social order would be endangered. Of course, emphasizing the role of the law in adjustment and regulation in a harmonious society does not reject and deny the function of other norms and means, such as moral rules, disciplinary rules, custom rules, rules and regulations, and ideological and political works. China advocates that, firstly we should unify and integrate all social norms, rules and other effective means into a system, which will form an organic whole to function on social management with clear division of work, mutual complementation, and interconnection. Second, given the current national

[94] *Guanzi: The Seven Standards (Qifa).*

reality and social conditions, and considering the mandatory, normative, and definite characteristics of legal norms and the characteristics of the state will, we can say that the law is a fundamental way to adjust social relations and regulate social behaviors. Therefore we need to highlight appropriately the distinctive role and function of the law in social management, to manage social affairs in accordance with the law, and to build a society based on the rule of law.

1.5.3 Legislation as an Instrument for Distributing Social Benefits

Legislation is the collection and expression of the will of the people. The main functions of legislation are to rationally distribute social interests and adjust social interest relations. According to the theory of justice put forward by Aristotle, the ancient Greek political philosopher, the legislative process is to distribute justice. Cicero, an ancient Roman political and legal thinker, believed that the formulation of a law is intended to ensure the welfare of citizens, national prosperity, and a peaceful and happy life for the people.[95] The nature of legislation is rationally to allocate social resources, distribute rights and obligations, and clearly define powers, responsibilities, and other practical interest arrangements through democratic means and legal procedures. The nature of legislation is also to regulate relevant procedures, set out rules for behavior, define behavioral limits and ways of acting, and thus to accomplish the goal of distributing justice. In order to realize a legislative distribution of justice, modern society needs to promote people's democracy fully through scientific and rational legislative procedures and allow various interest classes and groups to participate in the legislation. In this way, these interest groups could sufficiently and effectively express their interest demands and opinions while listening to those of others. Various social forces and interests often engage in games in legislative procedures, but finally make a compromise, reach a consensus, and write this consensus into legal provisions. This is the "good law and proper governance" or "the rule of good law." What does a good law mean? Shared values including justice, fairness, democracy, human right, order, security, happiness, and dignity promoted by the modern rule of law should be used to measure whether a law is "good" or not. They are also the values used to create good laws and the ethical

[95] Cicero: *The Republic and The Laws*, translated by Wang Huansheng, China University of Political Science and Law, Beijing, 1997 edition, p. 219.

principles for realizing good law and proper governance. "Proper governance" requires realizing effective social management and building good social order through the rule of law. Good law is the precondition while proper governance is the means, procedure, and target. Legislation should create good laws and provide the rule condition for proper governance of a harmonious society. However, there exit problems of departmental and special group's interest affecting, even predominating the legislative process in China. In particular, China is still faced with the phenomenon of "making national legislation by departments" and "making interests by department power and making department interest legalized." There are obvious influences from the departmental and group interest in some legislations, which has legalized the abnormal pattern and power relations. In some cases, the phenomenon of "expanding powers and removed liabilities in legislation" and "unjust and corrupted legislation"[96] have affected the quality of good laws, damaged the authority of the rule of law, restricted the implementation of the law, and affected social harmony and stability. In this sense, to realize a harmonious society with good law and proper governance, China should work to eliminate departmental legislation and legislative injustice, among other malpractices, from the legal system after the formation of the system of law. China should also work harder to promote democratic legislation and legislative games, eliminate hidden social conflicts in the designing stage of systems and regulations, and keep improving the system of law with distinctive Chinese characteristics.

1.5.4 Judiciary as a Defense for Rights

In the legal field, people's social interests are frequently reflected as all kinds of rights. When rights are violated or damaged, justice is needed for remedy. The essence and ultimate goal of judicature is to realize justice. Justice is a good and lofty pursuit of human society. In the western culture of law, justice is the highest value pursued by the law. The term "JUS" in Spanish is a polysemy that means justice, fairness, integrity, law, rights, and so on, and refers to just and rational viewpoints, behaviors, activities,

[96]Thomas Jefferson once said, "Of all the mischiefs … none is so afflicting, and fatal to every honest hope, as the corruption of the legislature." Quoted from [US] *End Legalized Bribery: An Ex-Congressman's Proposal to Clean Up Congress* by Cecil Heftel, translated by Huang Fuwu *et al.*, Foreign Languages Press, 2002 edition, p. 5. We say the corruption of the legislature is more detrimental because it is the corruption creating corruption through institutional arrangement.

thoughts, and systems. The minimum requirement of justice is that social interests and social responsibilities are not distributed and assumed randomly but follow certain norms, procedures, and standards. The general requirement of justice is to distribute equally social interests and obligations based on certain standards (such as equality in amount, contribution, or identity). Distributing social interests and obligations shall maintain the principle of neutrality. Justice can also be used to express good individual and social ethical states, like safety, order, harmony, tolerance, dignity, and happiness. In this sense, we can say that human society needs the law and a developed and organized rule of law because we want to pursue and guarantee the realization of the value goal of justice. Aristotle's theory of justice holds that judicature is to correct justice while the legislation is to distribute justice and the law enforcement is to realize justice. That is to say, when people's legal rights and interests are aggrieved and when other remedy channels and methods have proven ineffective, we need to use judicial channels to eliminate infringement, correct the wrong state of rights, and recover the normal state of rights, i.e., the rule of law and justice. China's courts and procuratorates are the main bodies of judicature. In what ways do they apply legislation justice? The court organic law stipulates that the people's courts through judicial activities punish all criminal offenders, settle civil disputes, and defend the system of the dictatorship of the proletariat. Also, through judicial activities, the people's courts safeguard the socialist legal system and social order, and protect the property possessed by all people of the social society, collective working people, and individual citizens. The people's courts also protect personal rights, democratic rights, and other rights of citizens, and guarantee a smooth socialist revolution and construction, among other undertakings. According to the Report on the Work of the Supreme People's Court, in 2013, the Supreme People's Court accepted and heard 11,016 cases and adjudicated 9716 cases, increasing 3.2% and 1.6%, respectively, from 2012. Local people's courts at different levels accepted and heard 14.217 million cases and adjudicated and verified 12.947 million cases, increasing 7.4% and 4.4%, respectively, on a year-to-year basis. In 2013, Chinese people's procuratorates at all levels approved the arrest of 879,817 criminal suspects of all kinds and instituted public prosecution against 1,324,404 people. Chinese people's procuratorates at all levels decided not to arrest 82,089 people who were suspected of being involved in criminal cases and not to prosecute 51,393 people whose crimes were minor and there was no need to punish them in accordance with penal stipulations, rising 2.8%

and 34.3% on a year-on-year basis. These figures indicate that Chinese judicial organs have played an important and indispensable role in punishing crimes, resolving social conflicts and disputes, protecting civil rights, and realizing social fairness and justice. Currently, China is still seeing frequent legal and judicial events. Among all protesting incidents in China, 35% are rights protection of peasants, 30% are rights protection of workers, 15% are rights protection of citizens, 10% are social disputes, and 5% are social riots and organized crimes. In the case of rights protection of peasants, 65% are related to land issues, and those related to villager autonomy and taxes and dues also constitute a significant proportion. At present, rural land disputes are mainly concentrated in more developed coastal areas, especially in Zhejiang, Shandong, Jiangsu, Hebei, and Guangdong. Disputes in these areas principally involve illegal or forced land acquisition, and the objects accused by peasants are mainly city and county governments. In central regions like Anhui, Henan, and Heilongjiang, the issues mainly concern the infringement of land contract rights, and the objects accused are mainly organizations at the township and village level. When it comes to the rights protection of workers, the main issues involved include state-owned enterprise reform, arrears of salary payment, social insurance, bankruptcy settlement, working hours, worker abuse, and so on. With the advancement of state-owned enterprise reform, workers in a traditional sense will gradually become employed workers, and workers' protection of rights will turn into conflicts between the hired laborers including peasant workers and employers.[97] An article in *Outlook Weekly* used the risk society theory of Beck, a German sociologist, to describe the social conflicts and social risks faced by China. According to the article, modern China is in a period of strategic opportunity and prominent contradiction with intertwined industrialization, urbanization, informatization, marketization, and internationalization. Modern China is undergoing a turning point of social transformation, and has accumulated energies in education, medical care, housing, employment, social security, income distribution, land requisition and demolishing, safety production, public security, ecological environment, and other hotspot areas. Mass disturbance and malignant extreme events are on the rise. The influence of negative corruption and serious crimes is grave. A host of natural and man-made disasters have shocked the inner mind of the general public. All these have

[97] Yu Jianrong, [US] Scott, *Bottom of Society and Social Stability*, January 24, 2008, *Southern Weekly*.

deepened the Chinese people's knowledge of "risk society."[98] "Risk society" requires the strengthening of government functions to prevent and manage the risks and the high attention required for effective judicial intervention and active disposal.

A harmonious society should put a new premium on and continue to give full play to the function of judicature in rights remedy. In particular, after the formation of the Chinese system of law, the focus of developing the rule of law should be shifted to promoting the implementation of the constitution and laws and to fully guaranteeing and leveraging the fundamental functions of judicature in implementing laws and regulations. The focus should be shifted to solving issues like failure to abide by the law, lax law enforcement, and unpunished lawbreakers. In sociology, performing judicial functions in a just, highly effective, authoritative, and honest way, and remedying rights in an active and effective manner in accordance with the law is a kind of essential social management form implemented through the judicial system.

1.5.5 The Rule of Law as a Stabilizer for Society

The rule of law is not only an important symbol of modern political civilization but also a stabilizer of social order. It is generally believed that socialist rule of law includes such links as governance by law, democratic legislation, administration by law, judicial justice, and legal supervision. The socialist rule of law also includes the establishment and strict and punitive enforcement of the law as well as scientific law making, strict law enforcement, impartial judiciary, and observance of the law by everyone. We can say that the socialist rule of law is a rigorous and scientific institutional system. Modern society is a large system, and building a harmonious society is a systematic project.

For the CPC to build a harmonious society, it needs to realize the transition from a revolutionary party to a ruling party. The ruling party needs to learn how to manage economic affairs, lead socialist market economic development, and emancipate and develop productive forces through restructuring the economic system. The ruling party also needs to learn to manage social affairs in an integrated manner, possess the ability to control and govern society, and guide socialist construction. The ruling party

[98]Yang Lin: *China Is Experiencing Social Transformation and Turning Point, Requiring Institutional Innovation of Social Management,* January 10, 2011, *Outlook Weekly.*

needs gradually to improve its governing ability and management level for one part, and adjust and reform productive relations and the superstructure for another. Therefore it could adapt to the productivity development level and the social development level of the current stage, and better meet the people's reasonable requirements for safety, order, and happiness. The ruling party should also try to limit actions frequently used in the revolutionary war periods when governing the country, dealing with politics, and managing the society. These modes include mass movement, revolutionary struggle, administrative order, policy means, and the emphasis on the will and final say of leaders. The ruling party should more frequently apply democratic and scientific methods to govern the country by law as well as other law-based thinking and ways that adapt to the ruling party's status and current social development situation. The ruling party should unite all aspects and links of socialist rule of law, go for a unified design, comprehensive arrangement, and coordinated operation, and use democratic legislation, administration by law, acting by law, judicial justice, and other law-based channels and ways to realize its guidance of the people and manage national, social, economic, and social affairs. Just as Deng Xiaoping put it, we still need to rely on the legal system, as it is more reliable.[99]

To build a harmonious society, we need to unswervingly uphold the rule of law as a fundamental strategy and keep to the principle of socialist rule of law and the principle of unification under the rule of law. There is also a need to comprehensively boost the development of the rule of law and to manage social affairs by legal means and through the rule of law. First, the socialist rule of law should be regarded as a systematic project. We need to comprehensively coordinate and integrate all kinds of works of the rule of law, including legislation, law enforcement, judicature, legal supervision, legal service, legal publicity, and education. In so doing, these links could be united organically and then formed into the synergic entirety of the rule of law. We need to comprehensively cope with and systematically address law-related issues in social management. Second, we need to weaken the model in which various departments dominate the development of the rule of law. We need to strengthen China's overall reform of the legal system under the leadership of the CPC and realize coordinated development of the rule of law. Third, we need to make the rule of law adapt to economic, political, cultural, social, and ecological

[99] *Selected Works of Deng Xiaoping*, volume 3, People's Publishing House, Beijing, 1993 edition, p. 379.

development, and make it a real facilitator and protector of modernization. Fourth, we need to practically guarantee that implementation of the constitution and laws is the focus of the development of the rule of law. We need to promote legislative improvement and facilitate governance and administration by law. We need to guarantee judicial impartiality and effective upholding of the constitution and guide citizens to believe in and abide by the law.

From the perspective of social rule of law, China has made considerable achievements in social legislation. Laws and regulations like *The Property Law*, *The Road Traffic Safety Law*, *The Employment Promotion Law*, *The Labor Contract Law*, *The Law of the People's Republic of China on Mediation and Arbitration of Labor Disputes*, *The People's Mediation Law of the People's Republic of China*, *The Social Insurance Law of the People's Republic of China*, and *Regulation on the Expropriation of Buildings on State-owned Land and Compensation* are highly relevant and significant to adjusting the relations of social interest groups, safeguarding the people's livelihoods, protecting social rights, and promoting social harmony and stability. However, these kinds of laws and regulations will not be implemented, or at least not effectively, without necessary property and material guarantees, without fair and timely execution and implementation, or without effective and impartial judicial guarantee. However, more formulation of laws and regulations and higher standard setting and better description of rights and interests would mean more conflicts and disputes. Also, the public would have more dissatisfaction with the government, which may further expand and even intensify social conflicts. For this reason, we need to unify legislation, law enforcement, judicature, and constitution upholding together as a systematic project for building a harmonious society and carrying out top-level designs. We should try to divide labors of different departments while keeping them integrated. We should guarantee coordinated and integrated operation of various links of the rule of law, and try to avoid their disjunction, contradiction, and inconsistency.

In particular, we need to persist in the effective practices generalized from the development of the rule of law and from governing the country by law since the reform and opening up. We need to keep improving and developing the practice model of local and industrial governance by law, urban construction based on the rule of law, and governance by law in local regions. We need to closely integrate the development of the regional rule of law with the development of economic, political, cultural, social, and ecological civilizations. We need to combine provincial governance under the rule of law with the promotion of safety, happiness, ecology, and civilization. Harmonious society is not a society without conflicts of interest. Rather, it is a society capable of settling and resolving conflicts of interest and thus realizing the balance of interest in general. To achieve this adjustment and balance, the law must be available. The history of the People's Republic of China proves that once the rule of law ends in failure, the rule of man will prevail, powers will be abused, and the society will fall into chaos. Historical experiences showcase that the greatest achievement of humanity over tens of millions of years is the taming of power. Only after the realization of the control of power and the rule of officials by law, could civil rights be guaranteed and fairness and justice be more brilliant than the sun.[100] James C. Scott, Professor of Politics at Yale University, pointed out that there is no absolutely stable and harmonious society, and the existence of disputes is a symbol of a society's success in realizing its targets. It is just like a good marriage, during which the couple may argue from time to time. He meant that a successful society should be good at managing conflict rather than completely eradicating it.[101] The world's practical experiences in social governance also prove that the rule of law is the positive result of human political civilization and a fundamental guarantee for realizing social harmony and people's happiness. Under the grand strategy and general trend of comprehensively advancing governance by law and accelerating the building of a socialist country based on the rule of law, we need to focus on two targets. First, we need to guard against and prevent the rule of law from going backward to the rule of policy, to the rule of administrative means, and to the rule of man. We need to refrain from irresolution, stagnation, and even regression of the rule of law as we seek to build a harmonious society. Second, we need to synergize various methods and means, including law-based thinking, law-based methods, ethical methods based on the rule of virtue, economic management approaches, public administration means, methods of public opinion guidance, methods of political and ideological education, methods of social autonomy, methods of industry self-regulation, and methods of psychological counseling. As such, they could supplement and connect to each other, and help guarantee and propel the building of a harmonious society.

[100] Huang Huo: *Eliminate Worries for "Class Solidification," Outlook Weekly*, Issue 2, 2011.

[101] Yu Jianrong, [US] Scott, *Bottom of Society and Social Stability*, January 24, 2008, *Southern Weekly*.

CHAPTER 2

Electoral Democracy and Deliberative Democracy Under the Chinese Constitution

Electoral democracy and deliberative democracy is a focus of politics and science of law research in China and a concern in various circles in the practice of democracy and rule of law in China. Democracy is the subject term that denotes both electoral democracy and deliberative democracy as well as the core idea of the democratic concept based on "the rule of the majority." It is an important way, means, and form for mankind directly or indirectly to manage the state, govern the society, and realize self-value. In modern countries, democracy is in essence a constitutional issue about the nature of state and form of government, power and rights, state and citizen, and legitimacy and illegitimacy. Electoral democracy is the prerequisite and essential condition of the legitimacy and validity of a modern democratic country and its constitution. It can be said that there would be no universally recognized democratic country and national constitution truly reflecting the will of the people without electoral democracy.

From the perspective of global constitutions, deliberative democracy is a new thing, a new mode generated from the operation of democracy, and an auxiliary means and supplementary method for the long-existing and widely adopted electoral democracy. The constitution of China clearly stipulates that the system of multiparty cooperation and political consultation under the leadership of the Communist Party of China (CPC) should exist for a long time with continuous development. However, this basic political system is not China's "deliberative democracy." In China's political life, deliberative democracy is not just an important democratic form for democratic parties and personages without party affiliation to participate in the political consultation and the administration and discussion in the state affairs, but also an important supplement to electoral democracy before and after decision-making of relevant political subjects. However, the constitution of China does not have any normative arrangement for this form of "deliberative democracy" at the operational level in the state

Building the Rule of Law in China.
DOI: http://dx.doi.org/10.1016/B978-0-12-811930-3.00002-7

system. If we explain it from the perspective of the constitution, electoral democracy is a state form, state power, and civil rights in essence while deliberative democracy is a democratic way, democratic form, and democratic means in essence. As far as the essence goes, electoral democracy and deliberative democracy are not at the same level. For democracy at the operational level, such as its operational form, way, method, and means, electoral democracy and deliberative democracy can supplement each other and bring out the best in each other.

In methodology, democratic issues of modern countries are essentially constitutional issues. This chapter will focus on the discussion of electoral democracy as state power, state system, and citizens' rights from the perspective of China's constitution, and the relationship between electoral democracy and deliberative democracy from the perspective of democratic form and method.

2.1 CHINA'S ELECTORAL DEMOCRACY AND ITS BASIS IN THE CONSTITUTION

As the starting point of the "state form" vertical democracy, electoral democracy refers to an important national system and operational mechanism under which the people enjoy and exercise sovereign power of the state and elect public representatives, leaders of state organs, and the ruling party, among other main bodies, through various modes of election such as referendum or direct and indirect election, in order to establish or maintain the state power and its institutions, uphold the nature of state and the form of government, and guarantee orderly operation of state apparatuses. The essence of electoral democracy is that people are masters of the country under the representative form of government, enjoy the most extensive and authentic civic rights and state power, and manage national, social, economic, and cultural affairs in accordance with the constitution and the laws. At the level of institutional design and practical operation, electoral democracy sometimes refers to citizens' right to vote and right to be elected, a specific way of operating democracy, a specific procedural system of democratic process, and so on. Thus there would be no democracy without electoral democracy. Electoral democracy is the foundation of democracy, the channel for political participation, and the regulator of social multi-interests.

Under the current constitutional framework and legal system, electoral democracy is a very important part of the democratic system in

China's constitution. There are many regulations on electoral democracy in China's constitution and laws. These institutional arrangements of constitution fully support the state power system of a republic where people are masters of the country. In China's existing constitution, concepts such as "election" and "the right to vote" appear 29 times. For example, article 3 of the constitution stipulates: the National People's Congress and local people's congresses at all levels are all constituted through democratic elections; article 34 provides that all citizens of the People's Republic of China aged 18 or above shall have the right to vote and the right to be elected; the 62nd article stipulates that the National People's Congress elects the President and Vice-President of the People's Republic of China, Chairman of the Central Military Commission, President of the Supreme People's Court, and Procurator-General of the Supreme People's Procuratorate; article 97 prescribes that the people's congresses of provinces, municipalities directly under the Central Government and cities divided into districts are elected by the people's congresses of the next lower level; the people's congresses of counties, cities without subdistricts, municipal districts, townships, ethnic townships, and towns are directly elected by voters; article 101 provides that local people's congresses at all levels elect and are entitled to remove the governor, vice-governor, mayor and deputy mayor, county chief and deputy county chief, district head and deputy district head, township head and deputy township head, and town chief and deputy town chief of their respective level of people's government.

In terms of China's constitutional laws, there are three laws that directly stipulate the national electoral system, namely the Electoral Law of the National People's Congress and Local People's Congresses at All Levels, Provisions of the Standing Committee of the National People's Congress for Direct Election of Deputies to People's Congresses at or below the County Level, and Provisions on the Election of Deputies to the National People's Congress, and People's Congresses above the County Level by the Chinese People's Liberation Army. Among the currently effective 35 constitutional laws, those have explicit provisions on the democratic electoral system including the law on deputies to the NPC and to local people's congresses at all levels, the organic law of local people's congresses and local people's governments, the organic law of the NPC, the organic law of the people's courts, the organic law of the people's procuratorates, the judges' law, the procurators' law, the organic law of urban residents' committees, and the organic law of villagers' committees. Moreover, legal guarantees for the rights of citizens to vote and to be elected are also provided to different extents in trade union law, in the law on the guarantee of rights and interests of women, in criminal procedural law, in civil procedural law, and in the law of PRC on penalties for administration of public security, among other laws of other legal departments.

Thus it can be seen that, from the aspect of China's constitution and laws, the electoral democracy is a state form, a state political system, the important part and democratic foundation of China's system of people's congress, and a basic right of Chinese citizens. This is because the NPC and local people's congresses at all levels are all constituted through democratic elections by the people in accordance with the provisions of the constitution and the electoral law. Deputies to the people's congresses at all levels have the right to attend the sessions of the people's congresses, deliberate all proposals and reports, and make proposals for addressing inquiries and proposals of recall. Deputies to the people's congresses at all levels have the right to submit proposals, make criticisms and suggestions, and attend meetings for election and vote. Deputies to the people's congresses at all levels also enjoy the privilege of immunity for speaking and voting. Deputies to the people's congresses are accountable to and supervised by the people, and try to serve the people. In this case, the system of people's congress designed through the constitution based on electoral democracy has closely combined the democratic rights of the people as masters of the country with the state sovereign power. The system of people's congress has also combined the dominant role of the people with state political power and the state political system. In addition, the principle of popular sovereignty has been specifically implemented in the state's fundamental and basic political systems. As the fundamental organizational form of state power, the system of people's congress has effectively realized the unity of people's democratic rights and the nature of state in the form of government, and has fully demonstrated the fundamental principle that all powers of the People's Republic of China belong to the people. On top of that, the system of people's congress has strongly guaranteed that Chinese people of all ethnic groups exercise the rights of democratic election, democratic decision-making, democratic administration, and democratic supervision according to the laws, and enjoy extensive democratic rights and civil rights stipulated by the constitution and the laws.

The importance of electoral democracy for the constitutionality of state power of the New China and the comprehensive establishment of the system of people's congress can be roughly seen in the background of the constitution of 1954. As is known, the foundation of the New China in 1949 was not realized through the establishment of one constitution. Rather, it was founded based on the *Common Programme of the Chinese People's Political Consultative Conference* (CPPCC) as the temporary constitution. Under the *Common Programme*, China had not yet established its organ of political power (the people's congress) through formal democratic election. Instead, the functions and powers of the people's congress were temporarily exercised by the CPPCC.

As early as July 1949, just before the founding of the PRC, Liu Shaoqi visited the former Soviet Union, during which Stalin suggested that the CPC prepare to establish a constitution. At the beginning of 1950, Stalin once again suggested that the CPC convene a NPC and establish a constitution as soon as possible when Mao Zedong first visited the former Soviet Union. According to Stalin, enemies could incite workers and peasants to oppose the CPC for two reasons: first, there was no election system and the government was not formed by election; and second, there was no constitution, and the CPPCC was not elected. He also said that these instigators could say that the CPC controlled the state by force and was self-elected. He added that the *Common Programme* was not adopted by representatives of the people but by the CPC, and approved by other parties, so the CPC should take this weapon from enemies and turn the *Common Programme* into China's fundamental law. Stalin also said that the contents of the constitution should be: first, general election participated in by all the people; and second, admission of the private property of enterprise owners and rich peasants.

Liu Shaoqi wrote a letter to Stalin in 1952 and explained why the New China was not in a rush to establish a constitution. He noted in the letter that China already had the *Common Programme*, which had prestige among the masses and classes, so it was acceptable to take the *Common Programme* as the fundamental law in the transition period. He also explained that if China formulated a constitution at that moment, then most contents, especially the relationship between bourgeoisie and petty bourgeoisie, would repeat the *Common Programme*, and there would be virtually no changes. The change would just be the form of article and the name of the *Common Programme*. Therefore the CPC was considering not formulating a constitution but using the *Common Programme* as the constitution in the transition period before China basically became a socialist country. Stalin agreed with the vision of the CPC for transforming China into a socialist country. But Stalin also pointed out that the CPC should make itself legitimate through election and constitution enactment and realize the transition to a single-party government through election. He said that the CPC should convene a NPC and formulate a constitution earlier. He also suggested that the CPC could go for election and adopt a constitution in 1954. At the end of 1952, the Central Committee of the CPC carefully considered the suggestions of Stalin in line with China's actualities at the time, and decided to convene the NPC and establish a constitution as soon as possible. The Central Committee of the CPC suggested to the CPPCC that the Central People's Government Commission hold the NPC regularly.[1]

It is easy to see from the above decision-making process that an important reason for the CPC Central Committee to convene the first NPC and enact the 1954 constitution was to establish the NPC through electoral democracy and then to enact a constitution to make the state government and the ruling of the CPC legitimate and constitutional.

There would be no representative democracy in a real sense without electoral democracy. When democracy is taken as a state form, electoral democracy is closely connected with the political concept of representative democracy (representative system) and the design of the form of government. Marx pointed out that it is the people of the state system in a monarchy and the state system of the people in democracy. A unique characteristic of democracy was that the state system was just a segment of people's existence in any cases.[2] It is not the state system that created the people, but the other way around. Marx further questioned whether people had the right to establish a new state system for themselves. He said that the answer was definitely yes, because the state system would become nominal if it could no longer represent the people's will.[3] Electoral democracy was the principal way to create the state

[1] Refer to *The 1954 Constitution and New China's Constitutionalism* by Han Dayuan, Chapter 3, the part about Stalin's suggestions on the establishment of constitution and the decision of the CPC Central Committee on the establishment of constitution, Hunan People's Publishing House, 2004 edition, pp. 53–57.

[2] Karl Marx: *Critique of Hegel's Philosophy of Right*, *Karl Marx and Frederick Engels*, Volume 1, People's Publishing House, Beijing, 1995 edition, p. 281.

[3] Karl Marx: *Critique of Hegel's Philosophy of Right*, *Karl Marx and Frederick Engels*, Volume 1, People's Publishing House, Beijing, 1995 edition, p. 316.

system after the people control the state power. In 1940, Mao Zedong said when explaining the design of the system of the people's congress in his *On New Democracy* that organs of state power that were inappropriate in form could not represent the state. He also said that China could at that moment adopt the system of people's congress at national, provincial, county, district, and even township levels, and the system of electing government by people's congresses at all levels. However, China must implement the electoral system under which all people are truly equal, regardless of their sex, belief, property, education background, and so on and so forth.[4]

As Lenin said just before the October Revolution of Russia, "Socialism is impossible without democracy because: (1) the proletariat cannot realize the socialist revolution unless it prepares for it by the struggle for democracy; (2) victorious socialism cannot consolidate its victory and bring humanity to the withering away of the state without implementing full democracy."[5] Deng Xiaoping also pointed out that there would be no socialism and socialist modernization without democracy. "Democracy" herein means that, first, the proletariat should take all means to realize democracy, become the ruling class and controlling the state power; second, it is to establish a representative organ of the people, enact the constitution and laws, and build and consolidate its own state power through electoral democracy; third, it's to guarantee that the masses are masters of the country through the electoral democracy featuring the people's universal, true, and extensive enjoyment of the right to vote and to be elected, and to maximally realize in state form the real intention that democracy is the rule of the majority. In the Marxist theory of democracy, the original meaning of electoral democracy is a political form and political system enabling the people to control the state power and realize the rule of the majority. Therefore it can be said in a certain sense that electoral democracy is the fundamental requirement of representative democracy, the foundation for building the country and establishing a constitution in China, and a fundamental and prerequisite system of China's system of people's congress.

[4] Mao Zedong: *On New Democracy, Selected Works of Mao Zedong*, Volume 2, People's Publishing House, Beijing, 1991 edition, p. 677.

[5] Vladimir Lenin: *A Caricature of Marxism and Imperialist Economism, Collected Works of Lenin*, Volume 23, People's Publishing House, Beijing, 1958 edition, p. 70.

2.2 CHINA'S DELIBERATIVE DEMOCRACY AND ITS POLITICAL NATURE

Deliberative democracy (also known as consultative democracy) started to attract the attention of the international academic community in the late 1990s. Deliberative democracy emphasizes reaching a consensus on public affairs including decision-making and legislation for public interests with universal participation of citizens under the background of a pluralistic society. Some Chinese scholars believe that the international theory of deliberative democracy has experienced three development stages since its emergence. Theorists of deliberative democracy at the first stage identified the normative nature of deliberative democracy. For example, Habermas and Rawls mainly discussed the legitimacy of democratic norms and observed that rational communication form may change the preference and help reach a consensus, but they did not take social complexity into consideration. Theorists of deliberative democracy at the second stage like Bohman, Gutmann, and Thompson believed that deliberation could produce deliberative democracy with practical significance only on the basis of acknowledging cultural diversity and social complexity. However, they did not provide enough details about how to guarantee deliberative democracy in a complex society. Theorists of deliberative democracy at the third stage put an emphasis on the "empirical turn" of deliberative democracy, such as Barber, Bartlett, O'Flynn, and Parkinson. They tried to seek the type of institutional practice of deliberative democracy through empirical evidence, which has facilitated the combination of normative theories and empirical studies of deliberative democracy.[6]

Of course, the Chinese academic circle generally believes that the socialist deliberative democracy with Chinese characteristics is essentially different from western deliberative democracy in economic foundation, social system, party system, cultural background, class basis, and political system, among other aspects. In this case, we cannot copy the theory of western deliberative democracy indiscriminately.

In the Chinese context, "deliberative democracy" has increasingly become a "hot word" of studies on theories of democratic politics, and there are also diverse academic statements and different theoretical

[6]Ma Ben: *Deliberative Democracy and Electoral Democracy: Origin, Relationship and Future Development, Journal of Literature, History and Philosophy*, 2014, Issue 3, pp. 146–152.

perspectives on the concept of deliberative democracy.[7] For instance, some research overviews conclude that deliberative democracy can be defined as follows. First, it is the theory of governance form. Some scholars think that deliberative democracy is the governance form in which different political parties, political organizations, and citizens give legislation and decision-making legitimacy through taking part in legislation and decision-making. Second, it is the theory of public decisions. Some scholars believe that deliberative democracy is where different political parties, political organizations, and citizens take part in public decision-making and political life by means of equal dialogues, discussions, deliberations, and so on. Third, it is the theory of democratic form. Some scholars observe that deliberative democracy is a democratic form of taking part in politics through dialogues, discussions, negotiations, communications, etc., in a certain political community. Fourth, it is the theory of compromise. Some scholars consider that deliberative democracy is not only a democratic form, a democratic decision-making process and mechanism, but also a form of state and social governance. These standpoints have different emphases, but all support that deliberative democracy should have important features such as negotiability, equality, and legality and multiple forms like dialogue, consultation, exchange, hearing, and communication.[8] From the perspectives of the emergence and development history of deliberative democracy in China and the stipulations of central files, this concept principally refers to a democratic form and a democratic method, which cannot be compared with electoral democracy in many aspects.

It is necessary to point out that the original meaning of the English word "deliberative" used in western theory of deliberative democracy was "consultative, discursive, and reviewed." The Chinese translation of "deliberative democracy" now is different from what it was in the 1980s and

[7] Zhang Feng: *Analysis of Eight Major Issues Concerning the Development of Deliberative Democracy, Studies on the Socialism with Chinese Characteristics*, 2015, Volume 1, Issue 2, pp. 49–55.

[8] Li Xiaoxi, Zheng Yazhuo: *Correctly Realizing and Understanding Socialist Deliberative Democracy – Research Overview of the Academic Circle on Deliberative Democracy*, March 25, 2015, quoted from "Academy of Marxism, Chinese Academy of Social Sciences," website: http://myy.cass.cn/news/662171.htm. For example, it is the generic term of rules and procedures of equal and extensive negotiations of all aspects of the Chinese people on major issues related to social and economic development and practical issues concerning the immediate interests of the masses through organs of state power, organizations of the CPPCC, and political parties and groups, among other channels. Liu Xuejun: *Several Issues Concerning the Improvement of Socialist Deliberative Democracy, CPPCC Daily*, December 12, 2012.

1990s.[9] The modern Chinese translation of "deliberative democracy" was adjusted and changed based on some of the realistic requirements of China's theoretical studies of deliberative democracy. The original meaning of the English word "consultative" used in "the Chinese People's Political Consultative Conference" is "negotiatory, advisory, and consulting." The two English words "deliberative" and "consultative" have obvious differences in meaning. We could say that "consultative democracy" is more appropriate for the understanding of current "deliberative democracy" in China. But the Chinese theory of deliberative democracy would be different from the concept of "deliberative democracy" commonly used worldwide in the theoretical origin. The effectiveness of the latter in providing proper theoretical and academic evidence to the former would be significantly decreased.

From a constitutional perspective, the convocation of the First Plenary Session of the CPPCC and the formulation of a series of constitutional legal documents like the *Common Programme* marked the great and historical victory of the Chinese people's movements for national independence and liberation over the previous 100 years, the complete formation of the patriotic united front and the great unity of the whole nation in organization, and the formal establishment of the system of multiparty cooperation and political consultation under the leadership of the CPC. It also opened a new chapter of the deliberative democracy and electoral democracy of the New China. The CPPCC contributed a great deal to the foundation of the New China.[10]

In the opening speech delivered at the First Plenary Session of the CPPCC held on September 22, 1949, Mao Zedong pointed out that the CPPCC would enact organic laws for itself and the Central People's Government of the PRC, the common program of the CPPCC, and

[9] Zhao Xuegang noted in the Chinese version of *The Constitution of Deliberative Democracy* that the initial Chinese translation of deliberative democracy was suggested by Mr. Zhai Xiaobo on the grounds that it is more consistent with the original meaning of the English word "deliberative," which means "carefully and prudently consider and consult (or discuss)," or "some people consider and review those reasons supporting and opposing some suggestion or action plan." In the Chinese political context, the almost defined "deliberative democracy" can also easily cause ambiguous understandings. [Argentina] Carlos Santiago Nino: *The Constitution of Deliberative Democracy*, translated by Zhao Xuegang, Law Press China, 2009 edition, p. 14.

[10] Xi Jinping: *Speech at the Meeting Celebrating the 65th Anniversary of the Chinese People's Political Consultative Conference*, September 21, 2014.

elect the national committee of the CPPCC and the Central People's Government Commission of the PRC.[11]

The Rules of Procedure of the First CPPCC Plenary Session adopted on September 23, 1949[12] clearly stipulated the procedures and contents of electoral democracy. For instance, article 3 of the *Rules* stipulated that the plenary session of the CPPCC should be convened only with the participation of more than half of the total members of the CPPCC, and resolutions must be voted or vetoed by more than half of the participating members. The Chairman will have the power to make a decision in cases where the votes and vetoes are the same in number. Article 4 stipulated that all participating members of the plenary session of the CPPCC have the right to vote. Alternative members have the right to speak but not the right to vote. Article 5 stipulated that, in terms of how voting for proposals and discussions should be done, first, general resolutions should be voted by raising a hand; secondly, if the resolutions concerning material issues or complex disputes, the Chairman proposed members to stand up to vote.

In the "Report on the Drafting Procedures and Basic Contents of the Organic Law of the Central People's Government"[13] on September 23, 1949, Dong Biwu explained the organizational principles of the new government: this principle is democratic centralism, which is represented by the government under the system of people's congress. That means the organs for the people to exercise state power are the people's congresses at all levels and the people's governments at all levels. The people's congresses at all levels are constituted through general election by the people. The people's congresses at all levels elect the people's government at all levels.

The Organic Law of the Chinese People's Political Consultative Conference[14] adopted on September 27, 1949 used "deliberative" as a verb in eight articles. Cases in point include: article 2 stipulated that all democratic parties and people's organizations endorsing the provisions of the first article may attend the CPPCC with the consent by negotiations of the National Committee of the CPPCC; article 3 stipulated that the participating units, numbers, and members of each plenary session of the CPPCC shall be determined by consultations of the last plenary session of the CPPCC, but that of the first session of the CPPCC shall be determined

[11] *People's Daily*, September 22, 1949, p. 1.
[12] *People's Daily*, September 23, 1949, p. 2.
[13] *People's Daily*, September 23, 1949, p. 1.
[14] *People's Daily*, September 30, 1949, p. 1.

by consultations of the first meeting of the CPPCC; article 13 stipulated that the functions and powers of the National Committee of the CPPCC include the negotiation and proposal of suggested plans to the Central People's Government of the PRC, the negotiation and proposal of a joint waiting list of ..., the negotiation and determination of the participating units, number, and members of the next plenary session of the CPPCC, the negotiation and handling of other matters related to internal cooperation of the CPPCC; article 18 stipulated that the local committees of the CPPCC are organs of local democratic parties and people's organizations negotiating and guaranteeing the implementation of resolutions. At the same time, *The Organic Law* had six articles clearly using the concept of "election." For example, article 7 stipulated that the plenary session of the CPPCC elects the Central People's Government Commission of the PRC and the National Committee of the CPPCC; article 9 stipulated that the plenary session of the CPPCC has a presidium elected by the plenary session; article 10 stipulated that the plenary session has one Secretary-General who will be elected by the plenary session; article 14 stipulated that members and alternate members of the National Committee of the CPPCC are elected by the plenary session of the CPPCC; and article 16 stipulated that the National Committee of the CPPCC has one Secretary-General who will be elected by the National Committee.

The CPPCC that served as the temporary constitution was drafted by the CPC after repeated studies and meticulous discussions of all democratic parties and representatives of all aspects under the leadership of the drafting group headed by Zhou Enlai. The *Common Programme* was adopted at the First Plenary Session of the CPPCC on September 29, 1949. The *Common Programme* as the constitutional and legal system of the New China was established through deliberative democracy, electoral democracy, and other ways based on people's democratic political basis and the democratic political system of the united front. Articles 4, 12, and 13 of the *Common Programme* include stipulations on "the right to vote and to be elected," "general election," "election," and so on, and directly stipulate democracy as part and parcel of national political life. The *Common Programme* had no direct stipulations on the systems, procedures, and methods of deliberative democracy. That being said, the foundation of the PRC and the establishment of the *Common Programme* are the greatest political achievements made by the CPC, democratic parties, mass organizations, democrats with no party affiliation, and other unit representatives through deliberative democracy. In a sense, it is the CPPCC that established the New China through democratic political forms including deliberative democracy. Just as the *Common Programme* declared, "the CPPCC represents the will of the whole nation, announces the founding of the PRC, and constitutes the Central Government of the people," this is "the founding of the nation through deliberation" by the CPPCC.

From a constitutional perspective, the reason why the CPPCC could "found the nation through deliberation" was not the adoption of deliberative democracy. Instead, it is because the CPPCC was convened on a completely new basis, and its essence was to represent the whole nation and thus was trusted and supported by the whole nation. Therefore the CPPCC declared to perform the functions and powers of the NPC.[15] In other words, it is constitutional and legitimate for the CPPCC to establish the New China and the power source was the "powers and functions of the NPC" rather than its inherent powers and legitimacy. Due to the specific historical conditions at that time, it was impossible to hold a general election and NPC immediately. Thus the CPPCC declared to act as the NPC to perform functions and had the right to develop the temporarily constitutional *Common Programme*, enact the *Organic Law of the Chinese People's Political Consultative Conference*, and the *Organic Law of the Central People's Government*, decide the name, capital, calendar era, national anthem, and national flag of the New China, and elect the Chairman of the Central People's Government. Just as Dong Biwu pointed out in the report on *The Drafting Procedures and Basic Contents of the Organic Law of the Central People's Government*, "Before the convocation of the national people's congress constituted through general election, the plenary session of the CPPCC, namely the conference, **perform** the functions as the national people's congress to elect the Central People's Government Commission of the PRC and empower it to exercise the state power."[16]

Of course, in the constitutional history of the New China, the 5 years between 1949 and 1954 were rather special for the first session of the CPPCC. During this period, the NPC was not yet held, and the CPPCC performed the functions of the NPC; at the same time, China was still in the transition period from a new democracy to socialism. Therefore the positioning, function, and role of the CPPCC cannot be simply compared with that of all subsequent sessions.[17]

[15] Mao Zedong: *The Chinese People Have Stood Up*, *People's Daily*, September 22, 1949, p. 1.
[16] *People's Daily*, September 23, 1949, p. 1.
[17] Zheng Wantong: *The Glorious Course and Important Enlightenment of the Chinese People's Political Consultative Conference in 60 Years*, *The People's Political Consultative Daily*, September 17, 2009.

After more than 60 years of practical development, deliberative democracy has now become a particular form and unique advantage of Chinese socialist democracy, an important demonstration of the Party's mass line in the political field, and an important part of deepening the political restructuring. Strengthening the development of deliberative democracy is conducive to expanding people's orderly participation in politics, better realizing the people's role as masters of the country, and promoting scientific and democratic decision-making. Strengthening the development of deliberative democracy can help boost the modernization of the state governance system and governance capacity, resolve contradictions and conflicts, and promote social harmony and stability. Strengthening the development of deliberative democracy can also help maintain the flesh and blood contact between the Party and the masses, consolidate and expand the Party's ruling foundation, give play to the political superiority of the Chinese political system, and enhance the confidence in the path, theory, and system of socialism with Chinese characteristics.

2.3 RELATIONS BETWEEN ELECTORAL DEMOCRACY AND DELIBERATIVE DEMOCRACY UNDER THE CONSTITUTION

It is easy to see from a simple recap of historical documents that deliberative democracy and electoral democracy coexisted and were used simultaneously in the process of founding the New China. However, from the perspective of founding the PRC, the CPPCC as the basic form of state political system performed the functions of the NPC through forms like deliberative democracy and played a crucial role in founding the New China. The electoral democracy at that time mainly played its role through democratic rights, democratic methods, democratic procedures, and democratic election as there were no conditions for general democratic election and the organizational form of political power as "the state form."

With the convocation of the first session of the NPC on the basis of the general election and the formulation of the 1954 constitution, electoral democracy was defined by the constitution as an important part of the people's sovereign power and the fundamental political system of the country and became the most fundamental democratic political rights of the people as masters of the country. After the convocation of the NPC in 1954, the CPPCC continued to play a pivotal role as a multiparty cooperation and political consultation mechanism and as an organization of unified front,[18] but its nature and functions had changed significantly.[19] At the end of 1954, Mao Zedong farsightedly answered the question about whether the CPPCC was a state organ or a people's organization in the article titled *Nature and Tasks of the CPPCC*. He said that the nature of the CPPCC was different from the organ of state power—the NPC—and not a state administrative organ. Some people said that the functions and powers of the National Committee of the CPPCC should equalize or generally equalize state organs to demonstrate its importance. If that were the case, would it have meant that the CPC was not important because it had no right to draw up a constitution, enact laws, and give orders, but only to provide suggestions? Obviously, we should not look at it in this ways. If the National Committee of the CPPCC was taken as a state organ, then there would be two of the same organizations in one country, which would not be workable. The functions of each should be distinguished.[20] Mao Zedong noted that the nature of the CPPCC was different from that of the state power. The people's congresses and the State Council were the organs of state power and state administrative agency. If the CPPCC had been taken as a state organ, then it would become a duality, which means a repeat and dispersion. Then, democratic centralism would not make sense. The CPPCC was not only a people's organization but also the deliberative organ of various parties and the organ of partisanship.[21] Although the CPPCC no longer exercised the functions of the CPPCC after 1954, deliberative democracy as an effective democratic method and a democratic procedure technique was still extensively applied. Since the reform and opening up, with the continuous development of socialism with Chinese characteristics, the continuous expansion of the main body, continuously enriched

[18] Xi Jinping: *Speech at the Meeting Celebrating the 65th Anniversary of the Chinese People's Political Consultative Conference*, September 21, 2014.

[19] The Preamble to the 1954 constitution stipulated that "China's united front of people's democracy will continue to play its role in mobilizing and uniting the whole nation to accomplish the general tasks and fight against internal and external enemies in the transition period of China."

[20] Mao Zedong: *Nature and Tasks of the CPPCC*. Speech of Mao Zedong at an informal discussion with invited representatives of democratic parties and democrats with no party affiliation on December 29, 1954.

[21] Zheng Wantong: *The Glorious Course and Important Enlightenment of the Chinese People's Political Consultative Conference in 60 Years*, *The People's Political Consultative Daily*, September 17, 2009.

contents, consistently improved form, increasingly extensive application, and continuous improvement of the effect, deliberative democracy has played an increasingly important and indispensable role in China's democratic political life.

Based on the above knowledge, we can comprehend the main differences between China's electoral democracy and deliberative democracy from the constitutional perspective as follows.

First, in the aspect of democratic theory, electoral democracy is the inevitable choice of the theory of representative democracy while deliberative democracy is the important form of elite democracy and participatory democracy. They have different foundations of democratic theory.

Second, in the aspect of the state political system, electoral democracy is an important part of the country's fundamental political system, while deliberative democracy is the major operation form of the country's basic political system. They have different positions in the country's political system.

Third, in the aspect of democratic operation, electoral democracy is the starting point of vertical democracy while deliberative democracy is an important form of horizontal democracy. They have different perspectives and ways in democratic operation.

Fourth, in the aspect of democratic function, electoral democracy is a common dominant democracy while deliberative democracy is a supplementary and auxiliary democracy. They have different functions and roles in democratic politics.

Fifth, in the aspect of democratic rights, electoral democracy is the most basic political rights of all citizens while deliberative democracy is the favor and attention to some citizens. They have different human rights foundations and rights values.

Sixth, in the aspect of national constitutional authority, electoral democracy is the main carrier and institutional content of state sovereignty and political power while deliberative democracy is the political arrangement without constitutional and legal force. They have different legal effects.

Seventh, in the aspect of democracy and efficiency, electoral democracy is the decision-making democracy giving consideration to both democracy and efficiency while deliberative democracy is the compromising democracy featuring surplus democracy but lacking efficiency. They have different democratic efficiency.

From China's constitutional perspective, the relations between electoral democracy and deliberative democracy can be further analyzed from the following aspects.

2.3.1 Electoral Democracy and Deliberative Democracy in the Level of State Power

According to Marxism, the first step of a workers' revolution is to elevate the proletariat to the ruling class, seek democracy,[22] and control the state power. The proletariat must establish a new country and a new political power where they are masters of their own affairs through electoral democracy after seizing the state apparatuses and controlling the state power through revolutions. In a socialist country, the political premise for electoral democracy is popular sovereignty; the people are masters of the country and society, and all powers of the state come from and belong to the people. The political essence of electoral democracy is that all people are masters of the country based on general election. Due to the large area, huge population, and inconvenient transportation of China, the proletarian authority was unable to guarantee that every citizen could exercise state powers and manage national, social, economic, and cultural affairs in organs of state power. Therefore the proletarian authority could only adopt the representative democracy of the people's congress system under which the people directly and indirectly elect their own representatives to exercise state powers in organs of state power. In *The Civil War in France*, Marx summarized the revolutionary experiences of the Paris Commune as that the commune was composed of city council members elected by each arrondissement of Paris through general election. He added that these members were held accountable to their voters and could be removed at any time, and most of them were naturally workers or recognized representatives of the working class.[23] Lenin pointed out when discussing the problems related to the building of the Soviet political authority that, under socialism, many parts of "original" democracy would

[22] Marx and Engels: *The Communist Manifesto, Karl Marx and Frederick Engels,* Volume 1, People's Publishing House, Beijing, 1995 edition, p. 293.

[23] Karl Marx: *The Civil War in France, Collected Works of Marx and Engels,* Volume 3, People's Publishing House, Beijing, 2009 edition, p. 154.

[24] Vladimir Lenin: *Immediate Tasks of the Soviet Government, Special Collected Works of Lenin – On Socialism,* People's Publishing House, 2009 edition, pp. 110–111.

inevitably be revived because the masses stood up for the first time in the social history of civilization. They would not only participate in voting and election independently, but also participate in daily management independently.[24]

It was stated in the preamble to the Chinese constitution that "After waging protracted and arduous struggles, armed and otherwise, along a zigzag course, the Chinese people of all nationalities led by the Communist Party of China with Chairman Mao Zedong as its leader ultimately, in 1949, overthrew the rule of imperialism, feudalism and bureaucrat-capitalism, won a great victory in the New-Democratic Revolution and founded the People's Republic of China. Since then the Chinese people have taken control of state power and become masters of the country."

Within the framework of a Chinese constitution and laws, deliberative democracy is neither a state power or a public power nor a civic right or a private right. Deliberative democracy is now mainly a democratic form, democratic method, democratic mechanism, democratic procedure, democratic means, and democratic responsibility.

2.3.2 Electoral Democracy and Deliberative Democracy in the Level of the Form of Government

The necessity and significance of electoral democracy for the form of government of a democratic state is self-evident. As Lenin said a long time ago, "Without parliamentarism and electoral system, the working class would not have been developing in this way."[25] Lenin also believed that the proletariat must get rid of the disadvantages of the bourgeois parliamentarism. The way to get rid of the disadvantages of the parliamentarism was certainly not by canceling the representative organization and the election system, but by turning the representative organization from an empty office into a "working" institution. A commune should not be parliamentary but a working institution and concurrently an administrative and legislative institution.[26] The Soviet is the direct organization of the exploited labors. The Soviet could help the masses to use all possible means to build and manage the country.[27] The Soviet democracy enabled

[25]Vladimir Lenin: *On State, Special Collected Works of Lenin – On Dialectical Materialism and Historical Materialism*, People's Publishing House, Beijing, 2009 edition, p. 295.

[26]Vladimir Lenin: *The State and Revolution, Special Collected Works of Lenin – On Marxism*, People's Publishing House, Beijing, 2009 edition, p. 218.

[27]Vladimir Lenin: *Proletarian Party and Renegade Kautsky*, selected from *Special Collected Works of Lenin – On Capitalism*, People's Publishing House, Beijing, 2009 edition, p. 243.

the workers' vanguard to lead the broad masses being exploited, attract them to take part in independent political life, and carry out political education based on their own experiences, and thus for the first time make all people learn and begin management.

The system of the people's congress is China's form of government, fundamental political system, and fundamental organizational form of state government. Article 2 of China's constitution clearly stipulates that all powers of the PRC belong to the people, and the organs for the people to exercise state powers are the NPC and local people's congresses at all levels. In the speech delivered at the Conference Celebrating the 60th Anniversary of the NPC, General Secretary Xi Jinping noted that the implementation of the system of the people's congress is the great creation of the Chinese people in the human history of political systems and the basic conclusion drawn from China's painful lesson on its political life after entering the modern era. He also said that the implementation of the system of the people's congress is the historical result of Chinese society after 100-plus years of sharp changes and surging development, and the ultimate choice of the Chinese people to stand up and to be masters of the country and control their own lives.

Under the system of the people's congress, electoral democracy has guaranteed that the people are masters of the country in three principal aspects. First, deputies to the people's congresses are elected and supervised by and responsible for the people, which realized the democratic authorization of the sovereign powers to deputies to the people's congresses by the people through electoral democracy. Second, deputies to the people's congresses elected directly and indirectly constitute the NPC and local people's congresses at all levels. The NPC and local people's congresses at all levels are the supreme organs of state power and local organs of state power, and exercise state powers on behalf of the people. As such, we have realized representative democracy, in which the whole nation exercises state powers through the NPC and local people's congresses at all levels. Third, state administrative organs, judicial apparatuses, and procuratorial organs are elected or determined and supervised by and responsible for the people's congress of the same level, which realized constitutional democracy, in which the people's governments, the people's courts, and the people's procuratorates are responsible for and supervised by the people. In a certain sense, in the early period after the founding of the PRC, without electoral democracy, the NPC and the first constitution of the PRC would not be established; the true establishment of state power on the basis of the nature of the state of the people's democratic dictatorship of the New China would be impossible; the legitimacy and legality of the state power of the New China would not be fully established. As we coordinately advance the strategic layout in "four comprehensive ways," without electoral democracy, there would be no people's democracy and a comprehensive rule by law as well as the modernization of socialism with Chinese characteristics and national governance.

The preamble to the constitution of China explicitly stipulates that the CPPCC is an organization of the united front with extensive representativeness. It has played an important role in history, and will continue to play its essential role in the struggle for socialist modernization and safeguarding the unity and solidarity of the nation. The preamble also stipulates that the multiparty cooperation and political consultation system led by the CPC will exist and develop for a long time. These stipulations indicate that China's constitution attaches great importance to and speaks highly of deliberative democracy and multiparty cooperation, and the political consultation system led by the CPC will exist and keep improving and developing for a long time as China's basic political system. However, within China's constitutional framework, deliberative democracy is neither the constitutional arrangement of state institutions nor the constitutional part of the form of government. On February 9, 2015, the CCCPC printed and issued the *Opinions on Strengthening the Building of Socialist Deliberative Democracy*, clearly requiring the enhancement of developing "the NPC consultation." *The Opinions* requires that the people's congresses at all levels shall perform their functions in accordance with the laws and hold full consultations before making major decisions as required. *The Opinions* also requires conducting in-depth consultations regarding legislative works, giving play to the role of deputies to the NPC in deliberative democracy, encouraging grassroots people's congresses to hold consultations according to the law in duty performance, and so on. These stipulations are an important innovation and development of the socialist democracy with Chinese characteristics and are of great importance to intensify the building of the form of government in the system of the people's congress.

2.3.3 Electoral Democracy and Deliberative Democracy in the Level of Civic Rights

The precondition of electoral democracy is to allow the people to enjoy political rights and basic freedoms as provided by the constitution and laws. In other words, the constitutional form of electoral democracy is, for citizens, typically reflected as the right to vote and to be elected and the relevant rights of equality and supervision and freedom of speech. The right to vote and to be elected directly comes from the political rights of popular sovereignty. In a democratic state, popular sovereignty can be exercised through either direct democracy or indirect democracy, but direct democracy does not need elections because the rights to vote and to be elected are the product of indirect democracy. In a socialist state, electoral democracy as a civic right has embodied more equality, universality, and authenticity. Lenin pointed out that Soviet institutions had profoundly and extensively developed bourgeois democracy, signifying great historical progress compared with medieval times. The great progress was the citizens' participation in the election of civil servants. In almost any democratic bourgeois state, the working masses have never exercised the right to vote as extensively, frequently, commonly, and simply as that in the Soviet regime.[28] Previously, universal suffrage had been misused as a tool for the parliament to approve the sacred state power, or as a plaything of the ruling class. Universal suffrage was only exercised once every few years to elect the tool for class rule under the parliamentary system. Now, universal suffrage is being used for its true purpose: the communes elect their civil servants for administration and legislation.[29] As a political right of citizens, electoral democracy is a statutory right clearly stipulated by the constitution and the electoral law, and the most fundamental political right of citizens. It is a basic right stipulated by Chinese laws and a basic human right, stipulated by international laws. It is sacred and cannot be deprived, limited, or transferred if it is not based on due process of law.

As a political right and basic human right of citizens, electoral democracy has the following features. First, the subject of right is definite, because the constitution and laws have clear-cut stipulations on which citizens have the right to vote and to be elected and which citizens do not have the right or who can be deprived of and barred from the right. Second, the ways of exercising the right of electoral democracy including time, location, procedures, and votes are statutory, and the right must be exercised in accordance with the laws. Third, the right of

[28]Vladimir Lenin: *Draft of the Programme of the Russian Communist Party (Bolshevik), The Collected Works of Lenin*, Volume 36, People's Publishing House, Beijing, 1985 edition, pp. 84–85.

[29]Karl Marx: *First Draft of the Civil War in France, Collected Works of Karl Marx and Frederick Engels*, Volume 3, People's Publishing House, Beijing, 2009 edition, p. 196.

electoral democracy is defined by equality. All Chinese citizens aged 18 years old and older have the right to vote and to be elected regardless of their nationality, race, gender, occupation, family background, religion, educational background, property status, and length of residence. Fourth, the right of electoral democracy is actionable. Judicial assistance and guarantee will be provided according to the law once it is infringed unlawfully. For example, article 181 of Chinese Civil Procedure Law stipulates that when a citizen refuses to accept the decision of the electoral commission on the appeal for electoral qualification, he or she may bring the case to the grassroots people's court of the electoral district at least 5 days before the election. Article 256 of Chinese Criminal Law stipulates that when electing deputies to the people's congresses at all levels and leaders of state organs, seriously sabotaging the election or interfering with the voters' and deputies' freedom of exercising the right to vote and to be elected through various means like violence, threat, cheat, bribery, forging election documents, and making a false report on electoral votes would result in a fixed-term imprisonment of no more than 3 years, put under detention, or deprived of political rights. Other laws like the Law of PRC on Penalties of Public Security Administration also have related provisions.

Deliberative democracy has not yet been included in China's constitution and laws as a basic political right of citizens, although it is very important. The dozens of international human rights and basic freedoms listed in the *United Nations International Covenant on Civil and Political Rights* do not include the right of deliberative democracy. According to the statistics of 142 constitutions in the world led by Dutch scholars, 67 of them addressed general elections, and 88 had stipulations on voting rights.[30] In most countries, the electoral system and the right of vote and to be elected, among other contents of deliberative democracy, are specifically stipulated in the form of a constitution. Furthermore, there are also specific laws like the electoral law providing institutional and procedural guarantees for citizens to realize electoral democracy.

Observing from the perspective of citizens' constitutional rights or basic human rights, deliberative democracy is neither a political right nor a political power of citizens. Deliberative democracy is at best a political arrangement, a policy measure, a democratic procedure and method.

[30] Henc Van Maarseveen, Ger van der Tang: *Written Constitutions: A Computerized Comparative Study*, translated by Chen Yunsheng, Huaxia Publishing House, Beijing, 1987 edition, pp. 131, 152.

There are no explicit constitutional and legal stipulations on whether the broad masses could truly become the subject of deliberative democracy and practically and effectively take part in policymaking and consultation processes. There are also no clear stipulations on whether the masses could express their appeals through various channels, forms, and levels of deliberative democracy. In addition, stipulations in this regard are also quite uncertain in the arrangement of various political agendas or regulations of policy documents. Such political or policy arrangements of deliberative democracy exist among some groups, but this kind of "deliberative democracy" is a giving (charity) but not a right (human right) for citizens enjoying such deliberative democracy. Electoral democracy is a basic right (human right) that should be generally enjoyed by all citizens, while deliberative democracy is a political treatment that only a few citizens may enjoy. Whether it is a basic right of citizens might be a major difference between electoral democracy and deliberative democracy.

2.3.4 Electoral Democracy and Deliberative Democracy in the Level of Method and Form

Relative to democratic idea, democratic value, and democratic intention, both electoral democracy and deliberative democracy are the technique, method, means, and procedure for the realization of democratic operation. In 2006, *The Opinions of the CPC Central Committee on Strengthening the Work of the CPC* put forward that the two major forms of China's socialist democracy are that the people exercise rights through election and voting, and that all circles of the people conduct full consultations before making major policies and try to reach an agreement on common issues. This statement indicates that both electoral democracy and deliberative democracy are important forms of democracy, but deliberative democracy usually happens before making major decisions. *The Decisions* of the Third Plenary Session of the 18th CPCCC proposed to carry out extensive consultations in the entire society and insist consultations before and in decision-making under the leadership of the CPC and focus on major issues related to social and economic development and practical issues bearing on the immediate interests of the masses. This statement on the Party's leadership over deliberative democracy has made clear the "main content" of consultations of deliberative democracy. *The Opinions of the CPC Central Committee on Strengthening the Building of Socialist Deliberative Democracy* has further defined the connotation of deliberative democracy as a democratic form: deliberative democracy is an important form of democracy, in which all circles of people under the leadership of the CPC carry out extensive consultations before decision-making and in decision implementation. They try to reach a consensus on major issues related to reform and development as well as stability and the practical issues regarding the immediate interests of the masses. This statement demonstrates that the leader of China's democratic consultation is the CPC, the subject of democratic consultation is the people, and the content of democratic democracy is the major issues related to the reform, development, and stability and practical issues regarding the intermediate interests of the masses. Democratic consultation is applied before decision-making and in decision implementation (it cannot replace decisions including those of electoral democracy). The purpose of democratic consultation is to try to reach a broad consensus.

In the aspect of democratic method and form, electoral democracy and deliberative democracy have no essential difference in status or importance. Both of them are the realization form and operation method of the socialist democracy with Chinese characteristics. *The Decisions* of the Third Plenary Session of the 18th CPC Central Committee proposed to expand the form of deliberative democracy and conduct in-depth legislative consultation, administrative consultation, democratic consultation, political participation consultation, and social consultation. *The Decisions* of the Fourth Plenary Session of the 18th CPC Central Committee stipulated to improve legislative organs and social public communication mechanisms, conduct legislative consultations, and give full play to the role of CPPCC members, democratic parties, federations of industry and commerce, personages with no party affiliation, people's groups, and social organizations in legislative deliberation. On February 9, 2015, the CPC Central Committee's *Opinions on Strengthening the Building of Socialist Deliberative Democracy* made a statement that the people's congresses at all levels shall perform their functions in accordance with the laws and conduct full consultations as required before making major decisions by pooling wisdoms of the people and hearing the will of the people to support and guarantee that the people exercise state powers through the people's congresses. We should carry out consultations on legislative works and give play to the role of deputies to the people's congresses in deliberative democracy. We should encourage grassroots people's congresses to carry out consultations, explore the form of consultation, and enrich the content of consultation in the process of fulfilling their duties. Obviously, socialist electoral democracy is the fundamental form of China's democracy while socialist deliberative democracy is the important form of China's democracy under the framework of China's existing constitutional and legal system. Electoral democracy and deliberative democracy supplement each other and bring out the best in each other.

At the same time, deliberative democracy and electoral democracy have many of the same or similar functions in method, way, and technological operation. Sometimes, deliberative democracy is superior to the competitive electoral democracy in the specific operational function for reaching a democratic consensus and agreement of various problems. That said, under the framework of China's constitutional system, deliberative democracy and electoral democracy are after all two different forms of democracy. Deliberative democracy can supplement, assist, enrich, and develop electoral democracy, but cannot surpass and replace electoral democracy in constitution. In other words, in the institutional system stipulated by the constitution and the laws of China, deliberative democracy is by no means meant to "surpass" and "replace" electoral democracy,[31] but is intended to supplement, enrich, and perfect electoral democracy.

Given the importance and innovation of deliberative democracy in the socialist democratic politics with Chinese characteristics, maybe we can consider including deliberative democracy in China's constitution in a future revision and improvement of the constitution, and thus gradually make deliberative democracy more constitutionalized and legalized.

[31]Yang Xuedong: *Misunderstanding and Modernity of Deliberative Democracy, Chinese Cadres Tribune*, 2015, Issue 5, pp. 70–72.

CHAPTER 3

The Culture of the Rule of Law in Contemporary China

Modern theoretical research on the rule of law indicates that three footstones must be available to build the rule of law in China: market economy, democratic politics, and culture of the rule of law (rational culture), and no one of these can be omitted. In modern China, it is relatively easy to build a legal system, but shaping a culture of the rule of law is beset with difficulties. It is relatively easy to create legal provisions on paper, but putting these provisions into practice is another story. An important reason for this phenomenon is the weakness and shortage of the culture of the rule of law in China. Therefore, focusing on and studying issues concerning the culture of the rule of law in modern China (as covered in this chapter) is theoretically valuable and practically significant to comprehensively advance the rule by law and build the rule of law in China.

3.1 DEFINITION OF CULTURE AND CULTURE OF THE RULE OF LAW

3.1.1 The Concept of Culture

According to scholarly research, "culture" is a concept with several meanings, and was first introduced in the West. The term "culture" is comprised of two characters in Chinese, namely "wen" and "hua" in Pinyin. In ancient Chinese, the two characters appeared very early but separately, such as in the *I Ching-Xi Ci II (Book of Changes)*, *The Liji-Yueji (The Book of Rites-Ritual Music)*, and *Huangdi Neijing-Suwen (The Inner Canon of Huangdi-Plain Questions)*. The *I Ching-Xi Ci II* recorded that the shape, stripe, and color of an object are interlaced, meaning "wen." *The Liji-Yueji* noted that "wen" is characterized by an integration of goodness, prosperity, and harmony. According to *Huangdi Neijing-Suwen*, "hua" refers to nature, so all natural things are irreplaceable. It was during the late Warring States Period that the ancient Chinese used the two characters in one paragraph. It was stated in the *I Ching-Ben Gua-Xiang Zhuan (Book of Changes-Divinatory Symbols of Bi-Overall Image)* that men and

Building the Rule of Law in China.
DOI: http://dx.doi.org/10.1016/B978-0-12-811930-3.00003-9

women together become mankind, meaning nature; mankind doing things in a civilized manner of life means humanity; observing the running path of the sun, moon, and stars to judge the seasonal changes; and observing music and literature, laws, and regulations to civilize the world. The two Chinese characters used together as the term "culture" can be traced back to the Western Han Dynasty (206 B.C.to 24 A.D.) in *Shuo Yuan-Zhi Wu* (*Garden of Anecdotes*). As recorded in the book, a saint should give priority to culture and morality first, followed by military force during his reign; all states reined by military force only without focus on the role of culture would be defeated in the end. The "culture" mentioned hereby is the education equivalent to "military force." The implication of the word is different from that used in current China. The basic concept of "culture" in ancient Chinese referred to "civil politics" and "education."

According to some scholars, the term "culture" (the same spelling in both English and French) used by Chinese people today was imported from the West through its Japanese translation in the late 19th century. The English word "culture" evolved from the Latin word "cultura," which originally meant "farming." Later, the word was used to represent manual activities, those with technique and the results of these activities. It was further expanded to include manners and customs as well as civilization systems.

In the West, the culture defined by British cultural anthropologist Edward Burnett Tylor in his *Primitive Culture* in 1871 was regarded as the classic definition. "Culture, or civilization, taken in its broad, ethnographic sense, is that complex whole which includes knowledge, belief, art, morals, law, custom, and any other capabilities and habits acquired by man as a member of society."[1] British cultural anthropologist Bronisław Kasper Malinowski (1884–1942) was the founder of the school of cultural function. He believed that culture should include spiritual culture, material culture, and language, and that social system was the real element of culture.[2] American cultural anthropologist Clyde Kay Maben Kluckhohn (1905–60) summarized 161 definitions of culture in *Culture: A Critical Review of Concepts and Definitions*. Kluckhohn thought these concepts were similar only different in the defining method, and stated that "Culture is a system which was formed by all historically created designs for living,

[1] Edward Burnett Tylor: *Primitive Culture*, Shanghai Literature and Art Publishing House, Shanghai, 1992 edition.

[2] Bronisław Kasper Malinowski: *A Scientific Theory of Culture*, translated by Fei Xiaotong, China Folk Literature and Art Publishing House, Beijing, published in 1987.

explicitly or implicitly it tends to be shared by all or specially designated members of a group in a certain period of time."[3]

In China, after the May Fourth Movement, scholars launched a hot debate over the implications of culture. The definition given by Liang Shuming in his *E astern and Western Cultures and Their Philosophies* in 1920, exerted the greatest influence of all. In his opinion, culture is "a kind of human life" that can be classified into three major categories, namely spiritual life, material life, and social life. Cai Yuanpei stated in his speech *What Is the Meaning of Culture?* in 1920 that culture represents the process of life. Liang Qichao elaborated on his understanding in *What Is Culture?* in 1922 and said that culture is all the valuable areas that can be interpreted by people's minds. Hu Shi pointed out in *Our Attitude toward Modern Western Civilization* in 1926 that culture is the way of life formed in a civilized society.

Pang Pu analyzed culture from three aspects: Material, institutional, and psychological. Material culture is the most superficial aspect. Esthetic tastes, values, moral rules, religious beliefs, and the ways of thinking are the deepest dimensions of culture, and what is in between are the institutions and theoretical systems.[4] Pang Pu asked Qian Zhongshu how to define culture in the early 1980s. Qian Zhongshu replied that "I kind of knew what culture was; but now I am confused when you ask me such a question."[5]

As stated in the *Modern Chinese Dictionary*, in the broad sense, so-called culture is an aggregation of material wealth and spiritual wealth created by humans during the course of social and historical development; in the narrow sense, culture refers to spiritual wealth, such as literature, art, education, and science.

Three kinds of cultural perspectives can be generalized in China based on the analysis of various concepts: the broad sense, the neutral sense, and the narrow sense.

In the broad sense, culture is everything created by humans, including spiritual culture, institutional culture, and material culture.

In the neutral sense, culture refers to social ideology and the corresponding system and institutional framework.

[3] Kluckhohn *et al. Culture and Individual*, translated by Gao Jia *et al.*, Zhejiang People's Publishing House, Hangzhou, Zhejiang Province, 1986 edition, p. 6.

[4] *Guangming Daily*, January 17, 1986.

[5] Zhejiang Young Academics Association of Social Science, *Collected Speeches on Eastern and Western Cultures and China's Modernization*, Zhejiang People's Publishing House, Hangzhou, Zhejiang Province, 1986 edition (temporarily published), No. 17, pp. 8–9.

In the narrow sense, culture only refers to social ideology, or social conceptual ideas, i.e. spiritual culture.

Professor Li Deshun from the China University of Political Science and Law noted that there are two essences in culture: first is to change the world by human ways, imprinting everything with the mark of humanities; second is to use these achievements from changing the world to cultivate, equip and improve the people, to make them grow in a more comprehensive and freer manner. The latter is a process, a result, a new height, and state of the former.[6]

Chinese influential theoretical works and political documents employed "culture" as follows:

In terms of time dimension and historical sense, creation of human beings means the birth of "culture," as culture is created by human beings and the symbol of human civilization. "Culture" was nonsense before ape men evolved into humans.

In a philosophical sense, materialism classifies the world into two categories: the material world and the spiritual world. Generally speaking, "culture" lies in the spiritual world and the dimension of human civilization. What was created by humans in the material world should also fall in the category of culture.

In the sense of human civilization, civilization was classified as material civilization and spiritual civilization in China in the first two decades of the reform and opening up. The socialist culture with Chinese characteristics was basically classified as a socialist spiritual civilization. For example, the report of the Communist Party of China (CPC) to its 15th National Congress pointed out that the contents of the socialist culture with Chinese characteristics were consistent with the socialist spiritual civilization, which has been advocated in China since the reform and opening up.

Entering the new century, civilization is classified into material, political, and spiritual civilization in China. Culture mainly falls into the category of spiritual civilization. For instance, the amendments to the constitution in 2004 stipulated that the basic task of the state is to promote coordinated development of material, political, and spiritual civilization, and build China into a strong, democratic, and civilized socialist country.

Based on the "principle of trichotomy," culture can be classified into economy, politics, and culture. For example, Mao Zedong noted in his *On*

[6]Li Deshun: *What Is Culture?* March 26, 2012, *Guangming Daily*.

New Democracy that a certain culture (culture as ideology) is the reflection of the politics and economy of a certain society and has a great influence and effect on the politics and economy of a certain society. He also noted that economy is the foundation while politics is the concentrated reflection of economy.[7] In regard to a new culture, it reflects a new politics and new economy in ideology and serves the new politics and the new economy.[8] The new democratic revolution led by the CPC not only sought to change the old China featured by political oppression and economic exploitation into a new country with political freedom and flourishing economy, but also aimed to turn the ignorant and backward China under the rule of the old culture into a civilized and advanced country under the rule of a new culture.[9]

Based on the "principle of quartering," culture is classified into economic development, political development, cultural development, and social development. For example, at the gathering celebrating the 60th anniversary of the victory of China's Anti-Japanese War, General-Secretary Hu Jintao pointed out in his speech that China needed to foster integrated development of its socialist economy, politics, culture, and society, continually meet the growing material and cultural needs of the people, and open a new vista for socialism with Chinese characteristics.

Based on "the quinquepartite principle," culture is positioned as economic construction, political development, cultural development, social construction, and the development of ecological civilization. For instance, General-Secretary Hu Jintao delivered a speech at the third collective learning of the 17th Political Bureau of the CPC Central Committee on January 29, 2008. He pointed out in his speech that China must comprehensively advance economic, political, cultural, social, and ecological civilization development, and promote coordination among various sections and aspects of modernization in order to implement the new requirements for the objective of building a well-off society in a holistic way. He also said that China must facilitate the coordination between productive relations and productive forces, between the superstructure and the economic foundation.

[7] Mao Zedong: *On New Democracy, Selected Works of Mao Zedong*, Volume 2, People's Publishing House, Beijing, 1991 edition, pp. 663–664.

[8] Mao Zedong: *On New Democracy, Selected Works of Mao Zedong*, Volume 2, People's Publishing House, Beijing, 1991 edition, p. 695.

[9] Mao Zedong: *On New Democracy, Selected Works of Mao Zedong*, Volume 2, People's Publishing House, Beijing, 1991 edition, p. 663.

There are many other classifications of culture. For example, the functions and powers of the State Council as stipulated in China's existing constitution are to play a leading and managing role in various aspects. The first is to lead and manage economic works and rural and urban construction. The second is to lead and manage the works related to education, science, *culture*, health, sports, and family planning. The third is to lead and manage the works related to civil administration, public security, judicial administration, and supervision. The fourth is to lead and manage national defense construction and ethnic affairs. The fifth is to manage foreign affairs.

The current setting of national institutions also reflects a kind of definition for the term culture in China. For instance, the organs of the State Council announced in 2008 include: the Ministry of Foreign Affairs, the Ministry of National Defense, the National Development and Reform Commission, the Ministry of Education, the Ministry of Science and Technology, the Ministry of Industry and Information, the State Ethnic Affairs Commission, the Ministry of Public Security, the Ministry of State Security, the Ministry of Supervision, the Ministry of Civil Affairs, the Ministry of Justice, the Ministry of Finance, the Ministry of Human Resources and Social Security, the Ministry of Land and Resources, the Ministry of Environmental Protection, the Ministry of Housing and Urban-Rural Development, the Ministry of Transport, the Ministry of Railways, the Ministry of Water Resources, the Ministry of Agriculture, the Ministry of Commerce, the Ministry of Culture,[10] the Ministry of Health, the National Health and Family Planning Commission, the People's Bank of China, and the National Audit Office.

In terms of connotation of culture, China has always interpreted cultural development as a crucial part of spiritual civilization over more than

[10] In terms of connotation, in China, the organizations related to the cultural works under the management of the State Council and local governments should include the Ministry of Culture, the Ministry of Education, the Ministry of Science and Technology, the State Administration of Radio, Film and Television, the General Administration of Press and Publication (National Copyright Administration), the General Administration of Sport, the State Intellectual Property Office, China's National Tourism Administration, the State Administration of Religious Affairs, the Research Office of the State Council, the State Council Information Office, the Archives Bureau, Xinhua News Agency, the Chinese Academy of Sciences, the Chinese Academy of Social Sciences, the Chinese Academy of Engineering, the Development Research Center of the State Council, the Chinese Academy of Governance, the State Administration of Foreign Experts Affairs, the State Post Bureau, the State Administration of Cultural Heritage, the State Language Commission, and the National Natural Science Foundation.

three decades since the reform and opening up. What calls for special attention is that, in the sense of two civilizations—material civilization and spiritual civilization—as the latter incorporates political restructuring and the building of democracy and the legal system, cultural development and spiritual civilization promotion seldom overlap with each other. However, in the sense of three civilizations—material, political, and spiritual civilization—as political civilization is independent from the other two, cultural development and spiritual civilization generally overlap. They are only different in the way of expression, in the issues to be solved, and in their focus of work.

The Report of the 17th National Congress of the CPC stressed that the main tasks for opening new vistas for the development of socialist culture with Chinese characteristics included the following aspects. First, make solid progress in building the socialist core value system and generate good results in Marxist theoretical studies and construction works. Second, extensively promote ideological and moral development to further improve the civilization of the entire society. Third, make significant progress in cultural system reform and accelerate development of cultural affairs and culture industry. Fourth, enrich the spiritual and cultural life of the people. Fifth, make new achievements in promoting fitness programs and competitive sports for all.

The Report of CPC to its 6th Plenary Session of the 17th National Congress clearly put forward the objectives of the reform and development of socialist culture with Chinese characteristics. These objectives include: further advance the construction of the socialist core value system, further promote fine ideological and moral integrity, and improve the quality of citizens. Meanwhile, produce more high-quality cultural products to meet people's demands, foster prosperity of cultural affairs, establish the public cultural service system for the whole society, and realize a basically equalized public culture service system. Moreover, make the culture industry the pillar of the national economy, significantly enhance the overall strength and international competitiveness, and form the cultural industrial structure where public ownership is the dominant form with diversified forms of ownership. The objectives also include the following: keep the cultural management system and the production and operation mechanism for cultural products vibrant and effective, attract foreign beneficial cultures with national culture as the subject, and encourage Chinese culture to go global. Last, but not least, strengthen the high-quality cultural talent team to guarantee cultural prosperity (Fig. 3.1).

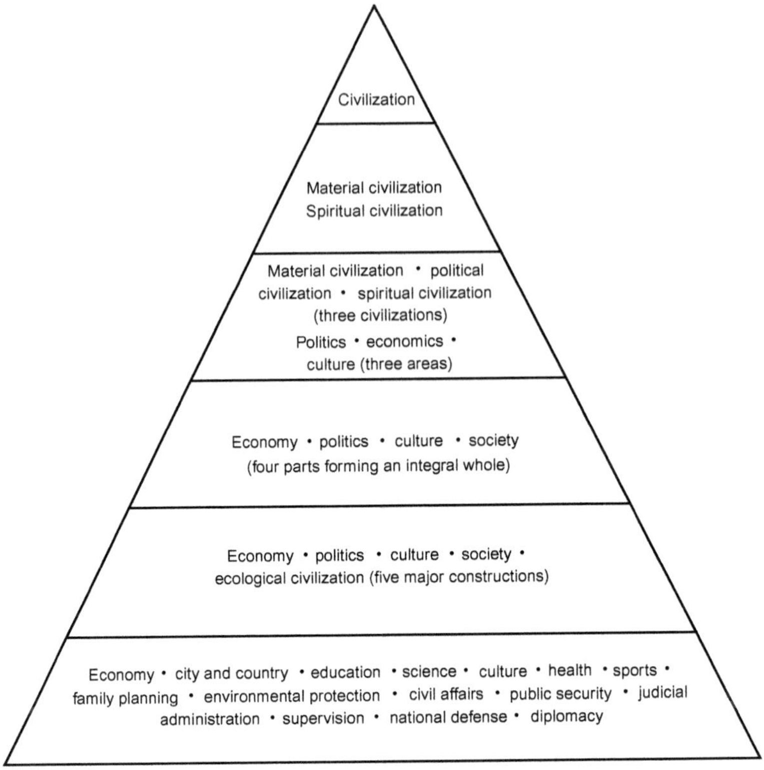

Figure 3.1 The Structure of the Definitions of Culture.

It can be seen that, in China's mainstream discourse system, the concept of culture has the following three features. First, it can be understood from many aspects with no fixed and single connotation and denotation. The concept of culture has different connotations at different levels, in different areas, with different references, and under different conditions. Second, it is a concept of relative meanings. Just as the pyramid structure shows, the broader meanings the concept has, the higher level it will become, and vice versa. Third, it is variable. The connotation, manifestation, and dominant ideology will keep developing and changing to a certain extent with the development of practices, the deepening of understandings, the ideological changing, practical needs, and other factors.

3.1.2 What is the Culture of the Rule of Law?

From a cultural perspective, the culture of the rule of law is a form of social culture where the state is governed "by rule of law." From the perspective of the rule of law, the culture of the rule of law is a form of rule of law in essence, with "culture" as the manifestation and the main content. The two perspectives are different on the surface but supplementary to each other in essence. The so-called rule of law refers to good law and proper governance with supreme authority and equal treatment. In the conceptual aspect, the rule of law mainly refers to a whole set of theories, thoughts, values, consciousness, and doctrines for controlling and governing the state. In the institutional aspect, the rule of law mainly refers to all kinds of institutional facilities that have been established or formed on a legal basis, covering legal principles, legal procedures, and legal norms. In the operation aspect, the rule of law typically refers to the legal order and the process and state of the implementation of law. In a deeper sense, the rule of law is a kind of culture, a kind of belief, and a kind of way of life. The rule of law is the continuum contained in universality and particularity, the combination of moral judgment and constraints of universal norms. The significance of the rule of law lies in the fact that it is an attribute of various kinds of systems, cultures, and the belief system of ordinary citizens. One special focus is that "the rule of law is a kind of culture." This is because the rule of law neither just means the establishment of a set of institutional system nor the formulation of a constitution or a set of laws. The most important part may be the law-based spirit embodied in a national culture. Therefore culture is of vital importance for understanding the significance of the rule of law in a country and plays a vital role in effectively exerting the operation value and normative functions of the rule of law.[11]

Based on the general understanding of culture and the rule of law, we can define the culture of the rule of law in a broad or narrow sense. In a broad sense, the culture of the rule of law is a cultural phenomenon and a state of the rule of law, which is comprised of spiritual civilization, institutional civilization, and the way of acts. Spiritual civilization includes law-based value, spirit, idea, thinking, theory, and ideology. Institutional civilization includes the legal system, legal norms, and law-based mechanisms. The way of acts includes enforcement, abidance, and application of law. In a narrow sense, the culture of the rule of law is the cultural

[11]James L. Gibson, [South Africa] Amanda Gouws: *Support for the Rule of Law in the Emerging South African Democracy*, published on the *International Social Science Journal* compiled and published under the organization of Social Sciences in China Press (Chinese version), May 1998, Issue 15-2, pp. 38–39.

phenomenon and the state of the rule of law concerning the unity of the achievements of spiritual civilization under the rule of law and the law-based way of acts.

The culture of the rule of law in a broad sense includes three aspects:

First, the culture of the rule of law as the achievement of spiritual civilization mainly includes the following:

1. Theories of law. It includes the following parts: what is law (such as law as the will of the state, the rule of nature, justice and rationality, the will of deity [or the ruling class], the system of standards and rules, specific actions and behaviors, political ruling tools and means), the essence of law, functions of law, relations of law, source of law, and the relations between law and state, law and morality, law and society, law and religion, law and political party, law and economy, law and politics, law and ideology, and law and culture.
2. Principles of the rule of law. For instance, the principles of the rule of law stated in the French *Declaration of the Rights of Man and Citizen* include: all men are equal before the law; there should be no conviction without a trial; laws are not retroactive; no one shall be deprived of the rights and freedom without due process of law; people shall reserve the rights that are not listed in the constitution; state organs shall not exercise powers without legal permission; judicial independence; constitution is the supreme law of the country, and no law or decree shall conflict with the constitution; separation of powers between state organs shall be strictly implemented. American legist Lon L. Fuller closely connected morality with law, and proposed eight principles of the rule of law: generality of law (laws shall be universal); laws shall be published to all; laws shall be clearly defined; laws shall be stable; laws shall not be retroactive; conflicts between laws shall be prevented; laws shall not have unrealistic requirements; and official behaviors shall be consistent with the published law.[12]
3. Values of the rule of law, including democracy, freedom, equality, human rights, fairness, justice, order, safety, harmony, and so on. There are "good laws" and "evil laws," likewise, the "law" upon which the rule of law is based is no exception. The first question the culture of the rule of law should answer is what laws shall be the basis for ruling. Not all laws can result in the rule of righteousness or help foster

[12] Quoted from Shen Zongling: *Modern Western Jurisprudence*, Law Press China, Beijing, July 1983 edition, pp. 204–209.

progress in social civilization. The German people were ruled under the legal system during the period of the Third Reich. However, the law was hated by many German people and people in other countries in many aspects.[13] Some legal clauses, such as conviction without trial, which have been applied for the racial segregation in South Africa in the past, were also implemented in the name of the rule of law.[14] Many atrocities made during the Cultural Revolution period in China were conducted based on the notorious *Regulations on Strengthening Public Security Work in the Great Proletarian Cultural Revolution*. History has repeatedly proved that the rule of law is a double-edged sword. It can be positive value-oriented and fully safeguard democracy, freedom, equality, human rights, justice and constitution, and guarantee people's welfare. On the other hand, it may be based on adverse values. The laws are then adopted as a tool for autocracy and the rule of man and safeguarding privilege and private systems. The law can even become the means for fascist dictatorship. Therefore, the rule of law must be based on rational value to build a country under the rule of law. What needs to be addressed for the rule of law in concept is the rational choice and positioning of the value of the rule of law.

4. Cognition of the rule of law, such as proper punishment for bad behaviors, life for a life, honoring commitment, getting debt paid, not committing murder or arson, not robbing or stealing, not swindling, not dominating the market, not giving short weight, and so on. These are the original perceptions and understandings of the law, legal value, the rule of law, law abidance, violation of law, crime, and punishment, among other legal norms and consequences based on social morality, religious discipline, and traditional customs of the social members. They are also the most extensive, most popular, and most original social moral basis of the culture of the rule of law of a country. They play a decisive and fundamental role in the development of law-based culture.

Second, the culture of the rule of law serves as the achievement of institutional civilization. The national political system, legal system, legal procedure, and law-based mechanism are the basic system carrier and important representations of the culture of the rule of law. They are also the institutional platform and important guarantee for the culture of the rule of law to play its role in national and social life as the achievement of spiritual

[13] *The Oxford Companion to Law*, Guangming Daily Press, Beijing, August 1988 edition, p. 791.
[14] J. W. Harris: *Legal Philosophy*. Butterworths & Co (Publishers) Ltd, London, 1980, p. 128.

civilization. The culture of the rule of law as the achievement of institutional civilization mainly includes the constitutional system, the legislative system, the law enforcement system, the judicial system, the legal supervision system, the law-abiding system, and the system of law, legal departments, legal norms, legal provisions, judicial precedents, and legal interpretations. For example, western countries usually implement the "tripartite" political system featuring the checks and balances of legislative power, executive power, and judicial power. China implements the people's congress system based on democratic centralism. China's system of law is divided into seven sections, namely the constitution and constitution-related law, civil and commercial law, administrative law, economic law, social law, criminal law, and litigation and nonlitigation procedural law. The Continental Law System in western countries is divided into public law, private law, social law, economic law, and other domains. In countries adopting the Anglo-American Law System, unwritten case law is a major form of law. In countries adopting the Continental Law System, written law is the principle form of law.

Third, the culture of the rule of law serves as the way of acts. If we say the life of the law depends on its implementation, then the realization of the rule of law will depend on belief. For a society, the rule of law is not only the mainstream value and theoretical concept but also the institutional norm and judicial machine. More importantly, it is a social belief, way of life, and behavioral habit. The culture of the rule of law as the way of act mainly refers to the attitude of social members toward the rule of law and the way of act they adopt in social activities. For general social members, why do they have to abide by the law? Are they voluntarily doing so, or are they forced to abide by the law? What cultural mechanism and reason make them observe the law voluntarily or forcefully? What are the reasons, conditions, and subjective and objective factors for them to violate the law? For civil servants, why do they have to follow the principles of governance by law, democratic legislation, and administration by law and judicial justice? Why do they have to act by law? Why could they not abuse public powers, abuse power for personal gain, commit corruption and accept bribes, commit illegalities for personal gain, commit judicial corruption, and sell offices and barter ranks? Why do they go for selective law enforcement and choose acts of omission or malpractice? For enterprises and businessmen, why do they have to operate by law, be honest and credible, compete equally, be fair in trading, and pay taxes according to the law? Why do they commit illegal and criminal activities, such as giving short weight, producing and selling fake items, evading taxes, committing contract fraud, and smuggling? All these social behaviors and social phenomena have something to do with the availability and unavailability, truth or fake, more or less, and strength and weakness of the culture of the rule of law. What especially needs to be considered is that, under what condition will the rule of law be truly believed by the people, internalized as their way of life, and developed in a society with several thousand years of feudal autocracy and cultural tradition. Just as Qian Mu said, "All problems come from culture and can be resolved by culture."[15]

The culture of the rule of law as the achievement of spiritual civilization is the idea, soul, and theoretical guidance of law-based cultural progress. The culture of the rule of law as the achievement of spiritual civilization determines the orientation of a country's rule of law, the nature and characteristics of the development progress, and affects the speed and quality. That so-called "further development of the culture of the rule of law means further development of the rule of law." But for a country without democracy tradition and the rule of law in history, there are many requirements for creation of the culture of the rule of law as the achievement of spiritual civilization: accumulation of democratic political culture, enlightenment of law-based thought, dissemination of legal knowledge and publicity and education on law, support of social and economic development, and democratic political construction. It will inevitably be a long-term, progressive, arduous, and tortuous historical process of going forward and backward at times.

The culture of the rule of law as the achievement of institutional civilization is the backbone, platform, and body of law-based cultural progress. It supports the development of the culture of the rule of law, builds the empire under the rule of law, and drives the advances of spiritual civilization and social behaviors based on the rule of law. Development of the culture of the rule of law as spiritual civilization and the way of act is progressive in essence. Relative to this, the development of the culture of the rule of law as an institutional civilization is a fast process that can be established under certain conditions, such as revolution, reform, or other ways of acts of man. Therefore for a developing country that is accelerating modernization, it is necessary to value and take the institutional improvement of the rule of law as the focus for development of the culture of the rule of law as an institutional civilization. It is also feasible and represents

[15] Qian Mu: *An Introduction to Culturology*, (Taipei) Taiwan Zhongzheng Publishing House, Taipei, Taiwan, 1981, p. 3.

an important channel for the development of the culture of the rule of law of radicalism.

The culture of the rule of law as the way of acts is the practical foundation and realization of law-based cultural progress. It requires every social member to follow the guidance of law-based thoughts and theories and the requirements of legal and institutional norms. It pursues the value and builds the order of the culture of the rule of law in all kinds of legal relations and turns laws into real practices. In so doing, we can move ahead with the developed and organized rule of law in a realistic and specific manner. However, for a country with a large population, deep influence of feudal culture, backward market economy, insufficient rational culture, and underdeveloped democratic politics, it is bound to be a long-term, difficult, and even painful process to put the advanced and civilized law-based cultural thoughts into practice and to make it a way of life and spiritual belief. It will not be accomplished overnight.

Apart from the above, we can also understand the rich connotation of the culture of the rule of law from the following dimensions: the subject, carrier, and history.

1. Subjects of the culture of the rule of law: (1) human—individuals, groups (such as cadres, workers, farmers, intellectuals, the aged, teenagers, consumers, the disabled, women, soldiers), ethnic groups, the people; (2) organization—organs of the ruling party, organs of participatory parties, legislative bodies, law enforcement agencies, judicial offices, legal supervision organs, organs of armed forces; (3) unit—factories, companies, and other enterprise units, schools, hospitals, and other public institutions. The ultimate subject of the culture of the rule of law is people. The culture of the rule of law is people-centered and is created, controlled, and enjoyed by people. The object of the culture of the rule of law is the culture in which people, the masters of the country, shall manage national, economic, social, and cultural affairs through the constitution and the law.
2. Carriers of the culture of the rule of law—direct carriers, such as legal text, court, tribunal, judge, procurator, layer, police, robe,[16] gavel, legal instrument, prison, prisoner; indirect carriers, such as broadcast, film,

[16]Wearing the robe produces a sense of professional dignity. Putting on the robe is to act as "the God" to judge what is right and wrong and what's criminal and innocent and then to take legal action against those who deserve it. Wearing the robe means the power to control other people's freedom and to decide the ownership of the disputed property. In this sense, the function of a judge is of great significance. Zhang Jianwei: *Court Dress in the Vision of Legal Culture*, February 3, 2012, *People's Court Daily*.

television, Chinese opera, Chinese folk art form, art works, journal, book, network, telephone, library, museum, cinema, publishing house, and book store. Carriers of the culture of the rule of law are the mode and form to reflect the rule of law. They are diversified and ever-changing. They turn the abstract contents of the rule of law (law-based spirit, soul, and idea) into concrete, overt, realistic existence, which is visible, touchable, and can be felt.

3. History of the culture of the rule of law—all historical relics, events, and stories related to the law may become the culture of the rule of law of a country or society. For instance, in China, historical relics include the totem, ancestral temple, memorial temple, county government, head of county government, indictment, private adviser, gavel, instrument of torture, punishment (such as ten unpardonable crimes, tearing a body limb from limb by five horses, putting to death by dismembering the body, immediate execution, and groundless charges), legal instrument (such as court verdict), cell, an indenture by which one sells oneself or a member of one's family, ancient legal codes and records (such as the *Land Law* of the Qin Dynasty, *Nine Chapter Law* of the Han Dynasty, *Law of the Wei Dynasty*, *Law of the Jin Dynasty*, *Law of the Northern QI Dynasty*, *Law of the Sui Dynasty*, *Law of the Tang Dynasty*, *Law of the Ming Dynasty* and *Law of the Qing Dynasty*). Historical events may include The Reform of Li Kui, Reforms of Shang Yang, The Political Reform of Wang Anshi, A Joint Petition of Imperial Examination Candidates to the Emperor Guangxu of the Qing Dynasty, The Hundred Days' Reform, and Law Reform in the Late Qing Dynasty. Historical stories may include The Chalk Circle, The Comedy of Mismatches, Snow in Midsummer, Susan Under Police Escort, The Adulteress, Justice Bao, Detective Dee Renjie, and Chen Shimei Betrayed His Wife.

3.1.3 Differences Between the Culture of the Rule of Law and Legal Culture

"Legal culture" is a general term used to describe the relatively stable and recognized systems, consciousness, and traditional theories related to the law and legal phenomena of a nation or country, which is formed in the long process of common life. The differences between the culture of the rule of law and legal culture are as follows.

Their conceptual hierarchies are different. Legal culture is a part of culture. Different nationalities have different legal cultures. The culture of the rule of law is a subcategory of legal culture, which emphasizes the element of modern rule of law in legal culture. Legal culture is a broader concept, including the culture of the rule of law, the culture of the legal system, legal civilization, legal tradition, and legal habit. The culture of the rule of law is subordinate to legal culture.

Their historical origins are different. Legal culture is historical accumulation. Where there is a human society and country, there will be laws and legal culture. The culture of the rule of law is the product of modern and contemporary bourgeois revolutions and social revolutions.

Their value orientations are different. Legal culture is neutral in value judgment, with no judgment of good or bad. Legal culture reflects its difference with other normative cultural phenomena like moral culture, custom culture, and religious culture.

The culture of the rule of law has an obvious value orientation. It stands for democracy while denying autocracy. It advocates that everybody is equal before the law while denying privilege. It proposes the rule of law while opposing the rule of man. It promotes human rights while denying imperial power and theocracy. It stands for the supremacy of law while denying dictatorial rule. It advocates values like restricting power by power, administration by law, judicial independence, fairness and justice, rationality, equality, freedom, and philanthropy.

3.1.4 Differences Between the Culture of Rule of Law and a System of Law Governing the Cultural Realm

As mentioned above, the culture of the rule of law is a kind of cultural phenomenon and state of the rule of law. It is comprised of the achievement of spiritual civilization, the achievement of institutional civilization, and the way of acts. There is also a system of law governing the cultural realm, including the cultural industry, cultural public enterprises, cultural system, cultural rights, cultural activity, and cultural education. In a society under the rule of law, a system of law governing the cultural realm is the manifestation and component of the culture of the rule of law. In an autocratic society, a system of law governing the cultural realm usually becomes an important part of the culture of rule of man, dictatorial culture and theocratic culture, such as the practices of "groundless charge," "unspoken criticism crime," "literary inquisition," and "burning books and burying alive Confucian scholars" in China's feudal system of law governing the cultural realm, and the "thought crime," "paganish crime," "presumption of guilt," and "cutthroat punishment" in western medieval systems of law governing the cultural realm.

Today, people in China often misuse "a system of law governing the cultural realm" to mean "the culture of the rule of law." They are confused about the differences between the two, which affects the progress of the culture of the rule of law. China believes that the culture of the rule of law cannot be equated to a system of law governing the cultural realm from the conceptual perspective, just as corporate culture differs from cultural corporation.[17] The culture of the rule of law and a system of law governing the cultural realm are different in the following aspects:

- First, "the rule of law" is different from "the rule by law," especially in value orientation, basic connotation, main principle, and practice requirement. Thus Chinese scholars uphold that development of the rule of law in China is a process "from the rule of man to the rule by law, and then from the rule by law to the rule of law." It took 20 years to change from "the rule by law" to "the rule of law."
- Second, research on the culture of the rule of law is different from that of a system of law governing the cultural realm. The culture of the rule of law emphasizes cultural significance, cultural attributes, and cultural characteristics to study and interpret the values, institutional norms, and ways of act of the rule of law. The "culture" under the concept of the culture of the rule of law is mainly a kind of perspective, method, and emphasis. It studies law-based phenomena in cultural science rather than in politics, economics, and sociology. "The rule of law" under the concept of the culture of the rule of law is mainly an object of observation and research from the perspective of cultural science (where there is the rule of law, there will be or should be the culture of the rule of law). If this object—the rule of law—remains unchanged, there might be different opinions and even brand-new understandings, due to differences in viewpoints and approaches to studying (e.g., politics focuses on the political rule and its legality, economics focuses on property relations and economic benefits, and sociology highlights class division and social conflicts).

[17] Corporate culture is the spiritual wealth and physical form of an enterprise, which are created in operation and management. It is imprinted with the characteristics of the enterprise. Corporate culture includes cultural concepts, values, enterprise spirit, moral rules, codes of conduct, historical traditions, enterprise systems, and cultural environments, among which, values stay at the core. All normal businesses have or should have their own corporate culture. Cultural corporations are different from chemical enterprises, iron and steel enterprises, construction enterprises, and food enterprises. This is because they are mainly enterprises engaged in producing, operating, and managing cultural products.

The focus of a system of law governing the cultural realm is the "system of law" that centers on and serves cultural development. This legal system emphasizes the differences and connections in the construction of a system of law governing the cultural realm and economic legal system, political legal system, social legal system, military legal system, administrative legal system, and environmental legal system. The system of law governing the cultural realm emphasizes issues related to policy, legislation, law enforcement, judiciary, law abidance, and legal guarantee from the perspective of the legal system. For example, in China, constructing the system of law governing the cultural realm means establishing the fundamental orientation, guiding ideology, and the core value of national cultural development in law. China's construction of a system of law governing the cultural realm has to determine the nature, status, and functions of all kinds of cultural subjects and draw up the principles, systems, and rules for various cultural activities. It has to determine the institutional mechanism for the creation, production, circulation, consumption, and service of various kinds of cultural products. It also has to determine the management, regulation, and guidance of the state in cultural activities and to adjust cultural rights and obligation relations. Finally, it has to move ahead with cultural reform and development on the legal track and ensure the establishment and strict and punitive enforcement of the law.[18]

- Third, the culture of the rule of law is different from a system of law governing the cultural realm in value orientation. The culture of the rule of law is the cultural paradigm that opposes the culture of the rule of man, dictatorial culture, theocratic culture, and culture not based on the rule of law. In value orientation, the culture of the rule of law puts emphasis on the rule of law while denying the rule of man, and stresses democracy while denying autocracy; it underlines human rights and freedom while denying theocracy, imperial power, and privilege. The culture of the rule of law emphasizes supervision and counterbalance while denying centralization of power and dictatorship and upholds conscious observation of laws while denying illegal and criminal activities. A system of law governing the cultural realm is a legal field that differs from economic, political, social, and administrative legal systems

[18]Shen Chunyao: *Strengthen the Development of Cultural Legal System*, November 10, 2011, *Guangming Daily*.

of the same value orientation. Compared with the value orientation of the culture of the rule of law, a system of law governing the cultural realm does not necessarily reject the rule of man, deny privileges, restrict powers, safeguard democracy, and protect human rights, and may not necessarily realize good law and proper governance in the cultural field.

- Fourth, the culture of the rule of law is different from a system of law governing the cultural realm in existing form. The existing form of the culture of the rule of law is principally the historical description and summary, real feeling and judgment, and future analysis and forecast of ideology and theoretical science. It is a kind of cultural style and theoretical description, featuring the connection between history and reality, between ideals and facts, between subject and object. The existing form of a system of law governing the cultural realm is the consideration of legal issues in cultural development, and also a kind of government behavior and governance mode focusing on the allocation of national legal resources, the improvement of the legal system, and the effectiveness of legal regulation and control.

3.2 SOCIALIST CULTURE OF THE RULE OF LAW

Socialist culture of the rule of law critically inherits and further develops the Chinese traditional culture of law. It takes reference and assimilation of all beneficial results of human development and organized rule of law. As an important part of modern China's advanced culture, it reflects the socialist basic values, such as fairness and justice, freedom and equality, human rights protection, democracy, and the rule of law. It also reflects the unity of the will of all the people, the proposition of the Party, and the unity of socialist ethics and socialist law-based spirit. Meanwhile, it reflects the unity of socialist law-based theory and socialist law-based practice, the unity of socialist law-based ideology, and the comprehensive implementation of the rule by law as the fundamental strategy. Moreover, it reflects the publicity and education of the legal system, and the cultivation of law-based behavior.

3.2.1 Meaning of Socialist Culture of the Rule of Law

Socialist culture of the rule of law is an advanced cultural phenomenon and state of progress of the rule of law. It is comprised of the achievements of spiritual civilization (law-based value, law-based spirit, law-based ideology, law-based idea, law-based thought, and law-based theory reflecting the intrinsic requirement of socialist advanced culture); the achievements of institutional civilization (legal system, legal norm, and law-based mechanism reflecting the nature of socialist democracy with Chinese features); and the way of acts (voluntarily acting by law and abidance by law).

1. The culture of the rule of law as the achievement of socialist spiritual civilization is a law-based value theoretical system, including socialist law-based spirit, socialist law-based ideology, socialist law-based concept, socialist law-based value, socialist law-based principle, socialist law-based thought, socialist law-based idea, socialist law-based theory, and socialist law-based doctrine.[19] It also includes the law-based attitude, law-based psychology, law-based preference, law-based standpoint, and law-based belief of citizens and civil servants.
2. The culture of the rule of law as the achievement of institutional civilization is a law-based institutional normative system that includes the socialist fundamental political system (the people's congress system) and basic political system (regional autonomy of ethnic minorities system, multiparty cooperation, and political consultation system led by the CPC, grassroots level democratic autonomy system, and special administrative region system[20]), economic system, social system, and cultural system as stated in the constitution. A law-based institutional normative system also includes the socialist constitutional system, the democratic

[19] Socialist law-based culture, socialist law-based spirit, socialist law-based ideology, socialist law-based notion, socialist law-based value, socialist law-based principle, socialist law-based thought, socialist law-based idea, socialist law-based theory, and socialist law-based doctrine all have been used by Chinese scholars in their writings; most of these concepts have also been used by the ruling party, the state, and state leaders in documents and speeches. However, what scientific connotations do these terms have and what relations do these concepts have in between? It seems that there have been no systematic research and in-depth analyses ever made, so most of these conceptual terms look similar. In particular, there is almost no difference among socialist law-based concepts, socialist law-based thought, socialist law-based ideas, and socialist law-based theory. It is also difficult to differentiate between them after translating them into foreign languages. The ruling party and the state should simplify and integrate these law-based concepts so as to make it easier for the people to learn, master, and implement these concepts.

[20] At present, the Chinese theoretical circle has not yet come to a conclusion about whether "the special administrative system" belongs to the national fundamental political system or not. Many scholars believe that it should not be defined as the basic political system, and the core viewpoint is that the basic political system needs to exist and be developed in the long run. But the capitalist way of life practiced in the Hong Kong Special Administrative Region and Macao Special Administrative Region will remain unchanged for 50 years.

election system, the human rights protection system, the democratic legislative system, the strict law enforcement system, the impartial judicial system, the legal supervision system and the conscious law-abiding system, the socialist system of law with Chinese characteristics, civil law, economic law, administrative law, legal department, various kinds of legal norms and legal provisions, legislation, and judicial interpretations.

3. The culture of the rule of law as the socialist way of act is a law-based behavioral system, including the governing act of the ruling party according to the law, the democratic and scientific legislative act and supervision act of legislative organs, and the administrative act of administrative organs. This law-based behavioral system also includes the impartial judicial acts of judicial organs and the conscious law-abiding and rational law using behaviors of the entire people. Furthermore, the law-based behavioral system also includes the law-based habit generated from law-based behaviors, law-based function, law-based actual effect, law-based authority, law-based order, law-based environment, and law-based situation.

Structure of socialist culture of the rule of law

	Three dimensions of the culture of the rule of law	Main contents
1.	**Socialist culture of the rule of law as the achievement of spiritual civilization**	1. Socialist law-based spirit, law-based ideology, law-based notion, law-based value, law-based principle, law-based thought, law-based idea, law-based theory, law-based doctrine 2. The law-based attitude, law-based psychology, law-based preference, law-based standpoint, and law-based belief of citizens and public servants
2.	**Socialist culture of the rule of law as the achievement of institutional civilization**	1. Socialist fundamental political system, basic political system, basic economic system, basic social system, basic cultural system 2. Socialist constitutional system, democratic electoral system, human right protection system, democratic legislative system, strict law enforcement system, impartial judicial system, legal supervision system, conscious law-abiding system 3. Socialist system of law with Chinese features, civil law, economic law, administrative law, among other legal departments, various kinds of legal norms and legal provisions, legislative and judicial interpretation

(*Continued*)

Structure of socialist culture of the rule of law (Continued)

	Three dimensions of the culture of the rule of law	Main contents
3.	**Socialist culture of the rule of law as the way of act**	1. Governing acts, legislative acts, administrative acts, judicial acts, supervision behavior, law-abiding conduct 2. Law-based habit, law-based function, law-based actual effect, law-based authority, law-based order, law-based environment, law-based condition

As the achievement of socialist spiritual civilization, the culture of the rule of law leads the development direction, determines the nature and characteristics, and affects the development speed and quality of a state's rule of law. However, for a country that lacks democracy history and rule of law, the true formation of the culture of the rule of law as the achievement of socialist spiritual civilization is bound to be a long and progressive process with arduous twists and turns. To strengthen the development of socialist culture of the rule of law as the achievement of spiritual civilization, we must stand firmly against the concepts and practices, including rule of man, autocracy, theocracy, rule of the few, and extrajudicial privileges. Moreover, we must abandon illusions and practices like illegal rights, believing in havoc, power and money not in the law, and the illusion that law cannot be enforced when everyone is an offender.

To strengthen the development of socialist culture of the rule of law as the achievement of institutional civilization, we must stick to the institutionalization and legalization of democracy and public powers and "the unity of the three." We must adhere to the political restructuring and innovative development in the top design of the socialist constitutional government and an organic unity of the law-based institutional norm system and the law-based spiritual theory system. We must prevent excessively abstract "emptiness" and "apotheosis" of socialist culture of the rule of law. For instance, the development of socialist culture of the rule of law is just to solve issues related to law-based spirit, law-based concept, law-based ideology, and legal theory. We also have to avoid the tendency of excessively specific "actualization" and "materialization" of socialist culture of the rule of law. For example, the main tasks of socialist law-based cultural development is interpreted as artistic performance, legal publicity activities, making of movies and television shows regarding the rule of law, and issuance of newspapers and periodicals as well as books relating to the rule of law.

Socialist culture of the rule of law as the way of acts is the practical basis and realization of the development of the culture of the rule of law. To strengthen the development of socialist culture of the rule of law as the way of acts, we must value the requirement for understanding the practicality, operability, and popularity of the culture of the rule of law and highlight the conceptual guidance, institutional norms, and national mandatory features of the culture of the rule of law; in practice, we must make a difference, move forward actively, and take a progressive and unconsciously influenced step. Moreover, we must avoid indulgent waiting or action with undue haste.

Socialist culture of the rule of law is the epitome of that mentioned above. The main idea is to realize a developed and organized rule of law under the guidance of socialist law-based spirit and concept. The socialist legal system is regarded as the backbone. Acting by law and conscious law abidance set the foundation. The goal is to build socialist order based on the rule of law.

The Sixth Five-Year Plan on law publicity and education clearly put forward the task of advancing the socialist law-based cultural development.[21] But compared with the requirement of the general connotation of socialist culture of the rule of law, the plan only described a narrow range of socialist culture of the rule of law. The plan was also limited to law-based cultural products, law-based cultural activities, and law-based cultural promotion. There has been no scientific definition of the key concept of socialist culture of the rule of law. In addition, the plan did not cover such contents as the value principles and institutional norms of the culture of the rule of law. These deficiencies make it hard for us to

[21]The functions of the publicity and education of the rule of law for the development of law-based culture are to: (1) promote socialist law-based spirit through the publicity and education of the rule of law to form the advocating atmosphere, encourage people to abide by the law, and safeguard the authority of the rule of law; (2) conduct different law-based cultural activities for publicity and education on the rule of law, to enrich the cultural life of the masses, carriers, and forms of law-based activities; (3) innovate and promote law-based cultural products, increase product quantity, improve quality, introduce competitive products, and create brands to constantly meet the growing demand of the masses for law-based cultural products; (4) encourage various kinds of cultural groups to engage in law-based cultural development, explore law-based cultural education, leverage the resource advantage of public cultural establishment in law-based cultural development; and (5) organize legal artistic performances and other law-based cultural activities favored by the masses.

understand the concept of socialist culture of the rule of law comprehensively and scientifically based on the plan, and advance the development of socialist culture of the rule of law.

3.2.2 Characteristics of Socialist Culture of the Rule of Law

Compared with the country's party culture, ethnic culture, social culture, corporate culture, unit culture, civic culture, religious culture, etiquette culture, folk culture, regional culture, and ethical culture,[22] socialist culture of the rule of law has the following characteristics.

3.2.2.1 The State Will

The culture of the rule of law is a cultural form where the law is regarded as the core element and precondition. Without the law, there would be no "rule of law" and rule by law. Socialist culture of the rule of law would be out of the question. In China, the law reflects the unity of the propositions of the ruling party, as the will of the state for one part and the will of the people for another. The law represents the social code of conduct implemented with the guarantee of the state by force. Socialist culture of the rule of law represents the symbol of national sovereignty, the majesty of state power, the way of state acts, the essence of state interest, and the guarantee for national strength. It is a part of China's mainstream culture.

3.2.2.2 Ideology

Marxism–Leninism and Deng Xiaoping Theory, the Important Thought of "Three Represents," the Scientific Outlook on Development, and the

[22]The concept of culture covers almost all aspects of human social life, and thus the classification of culture is diversified. Geographically, it can be divided into local cultural and foreign culture, urban culture and rural culture, oriental culture and western culture, and mainland Chinese culture and Chinese culture of Hong Kong, Macao, and Taiwan. In terms of time, it can be classified as primitive culture, slavery culture, feudal culture, capitalist culture, socialist culture, and so on. In terms of religious belief, it can be classified as Buddhist culture, Taoist culture, Christian culture, and Islamic culture. In terms of production mode, it can be divided into nomadic culture, agricultural culture, industrial culture and information culture. In terms of the instrument of production, it can be divided into Paleolithic culture, Neolithic culture, and bronze culture. In terms of human understanding of the world, it can be divided into scientific culture and humane culture. In terms of its nature, it can be divided as world culture, ethnic culture, elite culture, and pop culture. In terms of its structure and level, it can be divided as material culture, institutional culture, and spiritual culture. Refer to Wang Bingqin's *Cultural Translatology*, Nankai University Press, 1995 edition, pp. 3–4.

socialist core value system are the guiding ideology of Chinese legislation and the soul of the rule of law development. The leadership of the CPC in legislation represents the political principle of Chinese legislation. "The organic unity of the three" comes as the essential requirement of China's rule of law development. "The supremacy of the Party's cause, the supremacy of the people's interests and the supremacy of the Constitution and law ('the three supremacies')" is the guiding ideology for the works of the people's courts. All these indicate that socialist culture of the rule of law must be of distinctive class, political, party, and other ideological characteristics. Socialist culture of the rule of law is an important part of China's mainstream culture. Its value orientation, guiding ideology, theoretical basis, and spiritual ideas belong to the political ideology in nature, and are reflected as the state will.

3.2.2.3 People's Democracy

The people's democracy is the life of socialism. Without the people's democracy, there would be neither socialism nor socialist culture of the rule of law. The subject of socialist democracy and socialist culture of the rule of law is that all powers of the country belong to the people and people are masters of the country. The inevitable requirements of the people's democracy of socialist culture of the rule of law are that people exercise various democratic rights like democratic participation, democratic election, democratic decision-making, democratic management, and democratic supervision. The inevitable requirements of the people's democracy of socialist culture of the rule of law include that the people manage national, social, economic, and cultural affairs according to the constitution and the law. The inevitable requirements of the people's democracy of the socialist culture of the rule of law also include opposing the rule of man, guaranteeing restriction of powers, and governing officials in accordance with the law. The ruling party and organs of national public power insist on putting people first, people's democracy, building a party serving the interests of the people, governing for the people, and enforcement of justice for the people. These are reflections of the people's democracy of the socialist culture of the rule of law.

3.2.2.4 Institutional Construction

According to Marxism, democracy is a state form and a state system. The socialist rule of law is the institutionalization and legalization of socialist democracy and the institutional guarantee for people's democracy. In this sense, socialist culture of the rule of law is not only a culture of spiritual ideas but also a culture of institutional norms. This kind of institutional culture created and developed under the leadership of the CPC is legally continuous, stable, and authoritative. It represents the pillar platform for socialist culture of the rule of law.

From social and civilian perspectives, socialist culture of the rule of law also has social, folk, regional, and conscious characteristics. The state will, ideology, people's democracy, and institutional construction are not absolute. For instance, the public, experts, scholars, and news media all have different opinions from the government organs on several judicial cases including the cases of Wu Ying, Li Changkui, Yao Jiaxin, Li Zhuang, and Liu Yong. The culture of the rule of law has showcased diversified civil and social forms in various regional cultures, local regions, nationalities, and social groups and classes due to the different understandings and recognitions between national law and civil law, between hard law and soft law, between statutory law and common law, between legitimacy and rationality, and between custom and legal norms. To strengthen socialist culture of the rule of law, we must value its guiding role in national and institutional aspects and highlight its fundamental synergic function in social and civil aspects.

3.2.3 Basic Dimensions of the Socialist Culture of the Rule of Law

In the Chinese context, the concept of "socialist culture of the rule of law" actually refers to the socialist culture of the rule of law with Chinese characteristics. Under the comparative coordinate, the socialist culture of the rule of law with Chinese characteristics has the following four dimensions.

In the dimension of qualitative comparison, China's culture of the rule of law at the current stage belongs to the socialist culture of the rule of law. It must learn and draw upon all fine cultural achievements of human organized and developed civilizations, including the western capitalist culture of the rule of laws.[23] Moreover, the national constitution allows

[23] In February 2007, the then Premier Wen Jiabao pointed out in the article titled "Our Historical Tasks at the Primary Stage of Socialism and Several Issues Concerning China's Foreign Policy" that science, democracy, legal system, freedom, and human rights are not necessarily exclusive to capitalism. They are the common values and achievements of civilization created by mankind in a long historical process. In different countries at different historical stages, they may have different realization forms and channels and may not have a unified mode. This diversity of world civilization is an objective existence that is independent of man's subjective will. It is just the coexistence, connection, and integration of diversified cultures that have led to the progress of humanity. We need to acknowledge the cultural diversity of the world. Different cultures should not discriminate, reject, and be hostile to one another but respect each other, learn from each other's strong points to offset their weaknesses, and to form harmonious and colorful human cultures.

Hong Kong, Macao, and Taiwan to maintain the capitalist way of life for a long time under the "one country, two systems" policy. However, despite those mentioned above, in essence it is a kind of socialist culture of the rule of law where Marxism is the guiding ideology, socialism is the main body, and the proletarian party is the political leader. It is a kind of socialist culture of the rule of law where public ownership of the means of production is the economic basis, the people's democracy is the substantive characteristic, and the rule by law is the basic strategy for stage governance. It is a kind of socialist culture of the rule of law where fairness, justice, and common prosperity are the social values to realize people's freedom and all-round development.

In the dimension of orientation comparison, Chinese socialist culture of the rule of law is the culture of the rule of law with Chinese characteristics. China's national condition, Chinese culture, national tradition, political ecology, economic development, social development, cultural quality of citizens and the development path of democracy, and the rule of law have determined the formation and development of China's culture of the rule of law. It is forbidden to copy the development mode of western capitalist or from other developing countries. It is also impossible to copy from other socialist countries. Chinese socialist culture of the rule of law should reflect China's actuality and follow the development path of the socialist culture of the rule of law with Chinese characteristics. It is developed based on China's economic, political, cultural, and social conditions. This is the rule of law construction and developing path with three features: the unity of the Party's leadership, the people's role as masters of the country, and the rule by law.

In the dimension of phase comparison, China's socialist culture of the rule of law is still in its primary stage as China is still has a large population, with weak economic foundation, imbalanced regional development, and underdeveloped productivity. Furthermore, China is still facing an immature socialist market economy system, imperfect democratic legal system, wide influences of feudalism, decadent ideas of capitalism, and the force of the habits of small producers. China's socialist society is still in its initial stage.[24] In this context, while making remarkable achievements, China is bound to face unexpected challenges in many ways in its socialist law-based cultural development. These challenges include the habit of the rule of man, weak concept of the rule of law, weak capability in the rule of law, shortage of laws for observation, failure to abide by the law, lax law enforcement,

[24]Jiang Zemin: "Hold high the great banner of Deng Xiaoping Theory to completely advance the cause of building socialism with Chinese characteristics into the 21st century."

unpunished law breakers, unfair judicature, ineffective supervision, abuse of rights, and disregard of the rule of law to a certain degree. Some of these challenges are rather prominent. Thus we must pay more attention to the development of the socialist law-based culture with Chinese characteristics. We must also make constant reforms and improvement, keep learning, and move ahead. However, this is inevitably a long-term process of constant exploration, and it will develop gradually on a tortuous path.

In the dimension of international comparison, the socialist culture of the rule of law with Chinese characteristics is the culture of the rule of law rooted in the Chinese law system and cultural tradition. At the same time, it has absorbed and copied much of the content of the socialist law system represented by the Soviet Union including the definition, nature, feature, function and source of law, the legal system, the legislative system, the judicial system, the constitution, the electoral law, the organization law, the criminal law, the marriage law, and the economic law. It has also learned many theoretical principles and legal systems of the continental law system and the Anglo-American law system including the intellectual property system, the administrative legal system, the law of procedure system, the case law system, and the human rights system. In particular, Hong Kong, Macao, and Taiwan as inseparable parts of China have the law-based cultural tradition of the Anglo-American Law System and the Continental Law System, which has greatly enriched the connotation of China's culture of the rule of law and expanded the denotation and space of China's culture of the rule of law. In this way, China's culture of the rule of law has increasingly shown the characteristic of a "mixed law system" in the modern world law system.[25]

3.2.4 Socialist Law-based Ideas

In China, socialist law-based ideas are believed to be the core concepts of socialist culture of the rule of law. As a matter of fact, ideas of the rule of law, as an important part of the culture of the rule of law, are ideological and theoretical concepts about the nature, the basic connotation, the main task, and the fundamental requirement of the rule of law. Generally speaking, the culture of the rule of law is a kind of institutional culture and the concentrated expression of the rule of law in institution, system, social thought, and psychological basis. Therefore different systems have different

[25] In a broad sense, the mixed law system is comprised of two or more than two legal traditions or law systems; in a narrow sense, the mixed law system is comprised of the continental law system and the Anglo-American law system.

manifestations of the culture of the rule of law. To build the socialist culture of the rule of law with Chinese characteristics, we must stick to socialist law-based ideas.

Why did China propose the socialist law-based idea in the early 21st century? First, some phenomena occurred denying and weakening the Party's leadership and people's democracy during the advancing of the rule by law as the fundamental strategy; second, there was a trend of breaking away from China's national condition and excessively learning from western models of rule of law and the culture of the rule of law; third, some phenomenon occurred in judicial system reform, copying western judicial modes and breaking away from China's national condition; and fourth, there was a trend of "following western modes" in law education.[26]

How do we define the socialist law-based idea? We wonder whether the five phrases of the socialist law-based idea, namely "rule by law, law enforcement for the people, fairness and justice, serving the overall interests, and under the leadership of the Party" are scientifically and rationally applicable to the main body of China's legal relations, have sufficiently reflected the principles and requirements of socialist constitution, and have clearly conveyed the specific contents of the socialist rule of law for implementation? All these phrases need to be pondered and answered by more open, far-sighted, more scientific and rational visions that adapt to the law of the rule of law construction.

The applicable objects of the concept of socialist law-based idea include not only political and legal organs and their civil servants, but also the ruling party and participatory parties, armed forces, organs of state power, state administrative organs, social organizations, enterprises, public institutions, all civil servants, and all citizens. That means all main bodies of legal relations of the People's Republic of China should stick to and accept the socialist law-based idea. In addition, due to the Chinese law's principle provision of the legal effect of its main bodies, time and space,

[26]We cannot overlook the negative influence of various western law-based thoughts on China's law-based concept over the years. In the practice of law enforcement, some have simply applied some legal terminologies of the West, which has caused confusion for law enforcement; others have unilaterally advocated the legal thoughts and systems of the West, failing to act from China's national condition. Therefore we need to get to the root of issues in the ideological field of politics and law, use correct political and legal ideas to unify the thoughts of police officers in law enforcement, firmly understand the dominant right of Marxist ideology in politics and law, and unswervingly adhere to the socialist political direction of China's political and legal works. *Formal Proposal of the Socialist Law-based Idea.* http://www.fsa.gov.cn/web_db/sdzg2007/adv/BLDPX/bgcbg/gc026.htm.

ruling the country by law is to rule the country by the Constitution and that all people are equal before the law. Article 5 of the constitution of the People's Republic of China promulgates that state organs and armed forces, political parties and social organizations, enterprises and public institutions must abide by the constitution and the law. All acts violating the Constitution and the law must be prosecuted. No organization or individual shall have privilege over the law. Therefore all citizens of Hong Kong, Macao, and Taiwan, foreign and overseas organizations, enterprises and people must comply with the constitution and the law, accept national law enforcement regulation and judicial jurisdiction, and accordingly accept the socialist law-based idea to a certain degree.

In this connection, we need to have a broader and in-depth interpretation of the socialist law-based idea. This idea is a part of the socialist culture of the rule of law and the ideological and theoretical concept, reflecting the essential requirement and value orientation of the socialist rule of law. It is the policy and principle guiding socialist legislation, law enforcement, judicature, law abidance, legal supervision, and the implementation of the constitution and laws. It is the summary of historical experiences of the CPC as the ruling party in China's economic, social, and rule of law development in modern times, especially since the reform and opening up based on the reality and the larger picture of socialist modernization and the world experience in the rule of law development. It is not only a part of China's socialist construction planning, but also the ruling party's theoretical pursuit and improvement of China's experiences in the rule of law.

It is an organically united system of ideological theories and regulative principles that should include the following three levels and contents.

The first level is political philosophy, politics of law, and ideology. The socialist law-based idea at this level mainly includes five requirements: rule the country by law, enforce the law for the people, promote fairness and justice, serve the overall interests, and uphold the leadership of the Party. Among them, ruling the country by law is the core content of the socialist law-based idea;[27] enforcing the law for the people is an internal

[27] According to some Chinese writings, ruling the country by law is the core content of the socialist rule of law. This statement involves issues related to the basic relations between "ruling the country by law" and "the rule of law," and merits further studies and interpretations. Generally, the law community equates "ruling the country by law" to "the rule of law." Obviously, the presentation that "ruling the country by law is the core content of the socialist rule of law" takes "socialist rule of law" as a larger concept, and "ruling the country by law" is subordinate to it. Here, commentators need to make scientific a discourse and provide empirical proof for whether the relationship between "ruling the country by law" and "socialist rule of law" is equivalent, or inclusive, or which tolerates which. Otherwise, it is easy to cause confusion in both theory and thought.

requirement of the socialist law-based idea; promoting fairness and justice is the value pursuit of the socialist law-based idea; serving the overall interests is the political mission of the socialist law-based idea; and upholding the leadership of the Party is the fundamental characteristic of the socialist law-based idea. These five aspects supplement each other and have demonstrated as a whole "an organic unity of the three." They should be the core contents of the socialist law-based idea but not exactly the basic requirement of "socialist rule of law." This is because the socialist rule of law is required to "enforce the law for the people," "govern for the people," "make laws for the people," "practice justice for people," and "conduct legal supervisions for the people" based on the basic principles for the development of democracy and the rule of law since the Third Plenary Session of the CPC Central Committee. The socialist rule of law shall serve not only the overall interests but also "partial interests," not only the national "overall interests" but also local "partial interests," and not only economic and social construction but also political and cultural development. The socialist rule of law shall not only provide services but also make regulations, guarantees, restrictions, and even punishments. To develop the socialist rule of law, we must stick to the leadership of the Party and the people's role as masters of the country. On top of that, we must also stick to "an organic unity of the three." The socialist law-based idea cannot be equalized to the socialist rule of law. These five sentences should be the requirements of the socialist law-based idea.

Socialist law-based ideas are the ideological and theoretical concepts relating to the rule of law. In this sense, the socialist law-based idea at the first level should also include the socialist theoretical system with Chinese characteristics, the guiding ideology stipulated by the preface of the constitution and a series of thoughts, theories, policies, and guidelines of the Party, and the state for the development of socialist rule of law since the reform and opening up.

The first level of the socialist law-based idea plays a guiding role in the development of China's rule of law. Moreover, the socialist law-based idea is the political guarantee and theoretical premise for sticking to the socialist orientation and nature of China's rule of law. Moreover, the socialist law-based idea is a main feature differentiating the socialist culture of the rule of law with Chinese characteristics from the capitalist culture of the rule of law of the West.

The second level is socialist political civilization and the constitutional level. The socialist law-based idea at this level typically includes a host of constitutional principles. These constitutional principles include: the people's sovereignty under which the people are masters of the country;

the rule of law under which the constitution and the law are supreme; and human rights respecting and safeguarding people's rights. These constitutional principles also include the governing principle of democratic politics, scientific governance, and governing by law, and the legislative principle of democratic legislation, scientific legislation, and high-quality legislation. Other constitutional principles include: law-based government featuring the administration by law; the judicature featuring impartiality, high efficiency, and probity; and controlled and restricted power supervision.

The socialist law-based idea at the second level was put forward based on the constitution of the People's Republic of China and socialist constitutional principles. Compared with that at the first level and the third level, the socialist law-based idea at the second level serves as a link between the first and the third levels and comes as the requirement of implementing democratic and constitutional principles of the socialist law-based idea at the first level.

In a broad sense, the socialist law-based idea at the second level should also include the national fundamental political system, the basic political system, the legislation system, the administrative system, the judicial system, the legal supervision system, the special administrative region system, the human right protection system, and the citizens' law-abiding system built according to the constitution and the law. The socialist law-based idea at the second level should include in a broad sense the socialist system of law with Chinese characteristics and international laws and regulations applicable in China. The socialist law-based idea at the second level should also include libraries, museums, publications, films and television shows, various performances and expressions, and network news related to the socialist rule of law and to ruling the country by law.

The socialist law-based idea at the third level is the operation and implementation of the socialist rule of law. The socialist law-based idea at this level mainly includes the following specific law-based requirements: there must be laws for the people to follow; laws must be strictly observed and enforced; law breakers must be brought to justice; and all people are equal before the law. The socialist law-based idea at this level also includes the openness of law, the explicitness of law, the predictability of law, the authority of law, the unity of law, the justifiability of law, the nonretroactivity of law, independent exercise of judicial powers, and procuratorial powers in accordance with the law. Beyond that, it should also include the specific implementation process, implementation method, and implementation effect of legal norms; the capability and quality of leading cadres and civil servants in acting by law; the reason, method, degree, and effect of believing the rule of law and consciously abiding by the law by all citizens; and the restriction and reduction of illegal and criminal cases. The socialist law-based idea at the third level is the specific rule, method, and practical form of the rule of law in the operational aspect. It has reflected the specific requirements of the socialist law-based idea for the implementation of the constitution and laws.

From the contents of the socialist law-based idea at the three levels mentioned above, we can see the variable relationship brought by these different levels. A higher level of socialist law-based idea at the first level means a stronger level of thought, politics, ideology, and guidance and more obvious Chinese characters; vice versa, a lower level of socialist law-based idea at the third level means stronger universality, legality, normativity, and operability and weaker political and ideological nature.

3.2.5 Socialist Law-based Spirit

The report of the CPC's 17th National Congress proposed that China shall adhere to the "rule by law" as the fundamental strategy, build up the socialist law-based idea, socialist democracy and rule of law, freedom and equality, fairness and justice, and promote the law-based spirit. Law experts and scholars have debated this statement. First, what is the reason for putting forward these "two ideas" and what is the relationship between the two ideas? Second, since there is an attributive "socialist" before the "law-based idea" while there is no attributive before the "law-based spirit," does this mean the "law-based spirit" is universal while the "law-based idea" is socialist?

The 27th meeting for the collective study of the Political Bureau of the Seventeenth CPC Central Committee[28] convened in March 2011. The then General-Secretary Hu Jintao emphasized at the meeting that vigorously promoting the socialist law-based spirit in society has played a fundamental role in comprehensively implementing the rule by law as the fundamental strategy and building a socialist country under the rule of law. He also stressed that we must strengthen the implementation of

[28] On March 29, 2011, Professor Hu Jianmiao and Professor Zhuo Zeyuan gave their special lectures under the theme of *Administration by Law and Promoting Socialist Law-based Spirit* at the 27th meeting for the collective study of the Political Bureau of the 17th CPC Central Committee.

the constitution and laws to promote the socialist law-based spirit and keep advancing the process of scientific legislation, strict law enforcement, impartial judicature, and law observation by all the people. This clearly shows that law-based spirit can be either capitalist or socialist. In the process of comprehensively implementing the rule of law as the fundamental strategy, the law-based spirit promoted by China is socialist law-based spirit.

What is law-based spirit? The basic principle comes from "the spirit of law." The most classic theory was made in *The Spirit of Law* by Baron de Montesquieu, a French enlightenment political thinker. Montesquieu believed that "the spirit of law" meant that the law should conform to the necessity and regularity of human rationality, but he did not give a clear definition of what "the spirit of law" was. Instead, he expressed his understanding of "the spirit of law" through a lot of descriptions and interpretations. For example, Montesquieu advocated that laws should be associated with the state of the nature of the country; with cold, hot, and warm climate; with the quality, form, and area of land; and with the way of life of farmers, hunters, herdsman, and other people. Laws should be associated with the degree of freedom tolerated by the form of government and should adapt to the citizens' religion, leaning, wealth, population, trade, custom, and habit.[29] Laws enacted by a country shall be adapted to the people of the country. There were also relations between laws. Laws should also be associated with their sources, with the purposes of legislators, and basic things and procedures established as laws. All these relations constituted the so-called law-based spirit.[30] Montesquieu observed that there were different requirements of different climates that have shaped different manners of life, which resulted in different laws. While discussing ancient Chinese laws, Montesquieu said that Chinese legislators had two purposes: they wished that Chinese ordinary people could obey them and work harder. Due to climate and land factors, civilians were not living a stable life, so their lives were not guaranteed if they did not work hard.[31] The greed of the Chinese people was unimaginable due to the needs or the nature of climate, but there were no laws to restrict them. All things

[29] Baron de Montesquieu: *The Spirit of Law*, translated by Zhang Yanshen, Volume I, The Commercial Press, Beijing, November 1961, edition 1, p. 7.

[30] Baron de Montesquieu: *The Spirit of Law*, translated by Zhang Yanshen, Volume I, The Commercial Press, Beijing, November 1961, edition 1, pp. 6–7.

[31] Baron de Montesquieu: *The Spirit of Law*, translated by Zhang Yanshen, Volume I, The Commercial Press, Beijing, November 1961, edition 1, p. 314.

obtained through atrocity were banned while all things acquired by spell or cunning were permitted.[32]

There has been no scientific definition of "law-based spirit" or "socialist law-based spirit" in the Chinese law community. In the lectures given by Professor Hu Jianmiao and Professor Zhuo Zeyuan on *Administration by Law and Promoting Socialist Law-based Spirit*, we find the descriptive interpretation of law-based spirit: the so-called law-based spirit should mainly include respect for the constitution and the law, the supremacy of the constitution and the law, equality before the law, and fairness and justice.[33]

Law-based spirit is the achievement of developed and organized rule of law reflected in the unity of intrinsic and external adaptability of the rule of law. The intrinsic attribute of the rule of law refers to its attributive character differentiating it from other governing manners and theoretical concepts. On the one hand, it is to deny thoroughly the rule of man and autocracy, and to practice the rule of law by the majority on the basis of democracy. On the other hand, it pursues fairness and justice, freedom and equality, the supremacy of the constitution and the law, restriction of powers, and guarantee of rights, among other values and principles. It pursues governing the state by and building the society and country under the rule of law. The external adaptability of the rule of law is to combine the universal principles and value pursuit of the intrinsic attributes of the rule of law with the basic national, economic, social, and cultural conditions of a special nation or state, and adapt to the specific conditions of the nation or state such as the population, climate, soil, customs, and traditions. In this case, the rule of law could be established on the basis of a favorable climatic condition, geographical position, and the support of the people.

The intrinsic attribute of the rule of law is the ubiquity, commonality, and universality of the rule of law. Every society or country should meet the requirement for the intrinsic attribute of the rule of law and conform to the universal principle and value pursuit of the rule of law when practicing the rule of law, persisting in the spirit of the rule of law, and

[32] Baron de Montesquieu: *The Spirit of Law*, translated by Zhang Yanshen, Volume I, The Commercial Press, Beijing, November 1961, edition 1, p. 316.

[33] Hu Jianmiao and Zhuo Zeyuan: lectures under the theme of *Administration by Law and Promoting Socialist Spirit of the Rule of Law* given at the 27th meeting for the collective study of the Political Bureau of the Seventeenth CPC Central Committee on March 29, 2011.

building a socialist society and country under the rule of law. Of course, with the theoretical class analytical method of Marxism, there should have further and in-depth revelation of the essential attributes of the rule, i.e., to reveal the unity of the class nature and the social nature of modern national laws and rule of law, and then to make a qualitative judgment on whether it is the rule of law of socialism, capitalism, or of others (such as Russia, India, Brazil, Mexico, and Egypt).

The external adaptability of the rule of law is to apply the universal and common principles and values of the rule of law to a specific society and country. It is influenced and determined by the national cultural tradition, economic development level, social and natural conditions, political institutional choice, major historical events, and other factors of the specific society and country. Therefore the diversity, particularity, and specificity manifested by its realization form and development mode of the rule of law have determined the difference between the country (such as the United Kingdom) and other countries (such as Germany, France, and the United States[34]).

The socialist law-based spirit is an important achievement of constantly deepened the understanding of socialist rule of law. It is the achievement of the developed and organized rule of law formed and reflected in the construction practice of the socialist rule of law with Chinese characteristics. It features the unity of the intrinsic attribute and external adaptability. The socialist law-based spirit is an important part of the socialist culture of the rule of law with Chinese characteristics.

The essential requirements of socialist law-based spirit stress "an organic unity of the three" and oppose the multiparty system and the separation of three powers (legislative, administrative, and judicial power) of the West in politics. In thought, the emphasis is on guidance of Marxism with Chinese features while opposing the liberalism and diversified guiding ideology of the West. In ideology, the emphasis is on the class, political, and socialist nature of the rule of law while opposing capitalist rule of law, democracy, human rights, and absolute "judicial independence" of the West. In practice, the emphasis is on the development of the socialist rule

[34]German and France have chosen the Continental Law System while the United Kingdom and the United States have chosen the Common Law System. They are quite different in terms of legal tradition alone. They are also somewhat different in constitutional system, constitutional review system, judicial system, the system of law, and in the understanding of "the rule of law," "constitutionalism" and "the rule by law."

of law with Chinese characteristics while opposing indiscriminate imitation of the western model of the capitalist rule of law.

Based on its essential requirements, the socialist law-based spirit formed and reflected in China's rule of law and its practices does not stand for abstract or western fairness and justice, freedom and equality, restriction of powers and guarantee of rights. Rather, it is the law-based value determined, guaranteed, and realized in line with China's national conditions of socialist development within the framework of the constitution and the law. It does not stand for abstract or western law-based ideas. Rather, it seeks to build up the socialist law-based idea with the rule by law, ruling for the people, fairness and justice, serving the overall interests, and the Party's leadership as the main contents. It does not stand for abstract or western supremacy of constitution and law. Rather, it upholds the supremacy of the Party's cause, the supremacy of the people's interests, and the supremacy of the constitution and the law. It does not advocate abstract or western rule of law. Rather, it establishes the rule by law as the fundamental strategy under which the CPC leads the people to govern the state and act as masters of the country. It does not stand for building an abstract or western country under the rule of law. Rather, it looks to build a socialist country under the rule of law with Chinese characteristics.

To strengthen the development of the socialist culture of the rule of law, there is a need to define the connotation and extended connotation of "socialist culture of the rule of law" in a scientific way, i.e., not to "generalize" and excessively "virtualize" the socialist culture of the rule of law, which will make the term ubiquitous and difficult to understand or implement and thus overlook its normative and practical characteristics. Thus there is a need to avoid the undertaking of "narrowing" and "oversubstantiating" the socialist culture of the rule of law such as cultural undertakings, cultural industry, cultural activities, and cultural barriers, therefore avoiding overlooking the due value, spirit, and idea of the rule of law.

3.3 RULE BY LAW AND RULE BY MORALITY

According to the report of the CPC to its Sixth Plenary Session of the 17th National Congress, since the reform and opening up, especially after the convocation of the 16th National Congress, the CPC has always set cultural development as a strategic priority of its workings and the state's overall workings, focusing on both material civilization and spiritual civilization; the CPC has combined the rule by law with the rule by morality, facilitated a common development of the cultural undertakings and the cultural industry, and promoted continuously new achievements in cultural development. The CPC has identified a road toward building socialism with Chinese characters. *The Decisions* of the Fourth Plenary Session of the 18th Central Committee of the ruling party emphasized that comprehensively advancing the rule of law must stick to the combination of the rule of law and the rule of virtue. National and social governance required the law and morality to play their roles jointly. There was a need to focus on the rule of law on the one hand and the rule of virtue on the other, energetically promote socialist core values, and carry forward Chinese traditional virtues. There was a need to cultivate social morality, professional ethics, family virtues, personal morality, and highlight the regulatory role of laws and the educational role of virtues. There was a need to reflect moral ideas with the rule of law, strengthen the role of laws in promoting moral construction, and nourish law-based spirit with virtues. There is also a need to enhance the supporting role of virtues in the culture of the rule of law, and make laws and virtues supplement each other and bring out the best in each other. Practices prove that law and morality are inseparable in any modern country. So the rule of law and the rule of morality must be integrated. In China, the rule by law as the fundamental strategy should be unified with the Party's leadership, people's democracy, and rule by morality. But in the primary stage of socialism and under the historical condition of China's deep economic reform and rapid social transformation, the combination of the rule by law and the rule by morality should be supported by the principle of "making the law play a leading role while making the morality play an auxiliary role." There is also a need to give play unswervingly to the guiding role of the rule of law and the rule by law in state administration, social governance, relation adjustment, power allocation, behavior regulation, human rights protection, and the maintenance of stability. In the above areas, the rule by morality should be the supplement to the rule by law.

3.3.1 Practicing the Rule of Law Reflects the Basic Requirements of Rule by Morality

In China, the relationship between the rule by law and the rule by morality is actually the relationship between law and morality and between the rule of law and the rule of morality. Reviewed from the perspective of jurisprudence and ethical philosophy, there are three basic relations between law and morality[35]:

- First, it is the legalization of morality, i.e., to add most of the general requirements of most political morality, economic morality, social morality, and family morality of the country into the legal system. They will become part of the state will and the binding social behavioral norms, which are implemented with the guarantee of the coercive force of the state. Generally speaking, morality is the basis of the legitimacy and rationality of the law. Many behaviors required or prohibited by morality are more often than not the important basis for implementing relevant provisions of the law. Thus most legislations for adjusting social relations and regulating social behaviors are the results of the legalization of morality. For example, national legislative rules prohibit murder, burning, robbing, and stealing stipulate life for life, paying debt in full, supporting parents, raising children, no pay no goods, and returning things picked up. In general, all these rules and stipulations have demonstrated the basic requirements of morality. In China, socialist morality is the source of laws, the guiding thought, and internal requirement for enacting laws and the important standard for judging whether a law is good or not. Since the reform and opening up, the Party and the state have attached great importance to legislative works and kept strengthening democratic and scientific legislation. By August 2014 after 30 years of effort, China had enacted 242 current constitutions and effective laws, 737 administrative laws and

[35]The difference between law and virtue is also reflected in their consistent or inconsistent attitudes toward the same object. It basically includes the following. (1) There is no obvious difference between the two in attitude. Instead, they are consistent in attitude toward some behaviors. For example, both deny murder, injury, and burglary. (2) What is approved by virtue may not be approved by the law. For instance, the possession of others' property for a certain period of time would mean obtaining of ownership; rights that are not exercised for a certain period of time would be abrogated; prosecution of criminal offenders would be time-barred. (3) What permits by virtue may not be permitted by law, such as some behaviors violating procedures, laws, and rules. (4) What is permitted by virtue may be acquiesced and or may not be banned by the law. For instance, it is immoral but not illegal to be unpunctual for meetings or to be inefficient. (5) Virtue and law have no direct relations in some situations. For example, love relations and friendships are adjusted by virtue while the division of powers of state organs must be stipulated by the law. Refer to the *Rule of Law and Construction of Socialist Spiritual Civilization* by Liu Hainian, Li Lin *et al.*, China Legal Publishing House, 1997 edition.

regulations, and more than 8700 local laws and regulations. They have formed the socialist system of law with Chinese characteristics. In this system of law, the contents of many legal provisions have embodied the internal requirement of socialist morality and come as positive results of the legalization of social morality. For example, under Chinese law, people shall not commit murder, arson, robbery, and burglary and shall pay life for intentional murder, pay debt in full, support parents, and raise kids. The Chinese law also provides for respect and protect of human rights, ethnic unity and social stability and promote material civilization, political civilization, and spiritual civilization. All these have demonstrated the value orientation and basic requirements of socialist morality in general. Therefore, speaking from the significance of the already legalized moralities of a country or a society, adhering to the implementation of the rule by law means implementing the rule of morality through law-based means. But the following situations should be excluded: The law lacks proper support of social morality, such as the stipulation of human trafficking, racial discrimination, and genocide as legalized; the law violates ethical and moral rules, such as allowing random deprivation of others' lives, restricting others' freedom, allowing incest between family members, maltreatment and swindling, allowing embezzlement and bribe-taking of public servants, deceiving both superiors and subordinates, and abusing powers for personal gain. Obviously, the rule by law would not reflect or demonstrate the basic requirements of the rule of virtue if the law itself (or some of the laws) of a country or a society is "evil" or "bad." Because of this, the rule by law in China is the fundamental ruling strategy under which the Party leads the people to govern the state. Its basic requirement for the combination of law and morality is "good law and proper governance" rather than "evil law and autocracy" or "bad law and the rule of man."

- Second, it is the delegalization of morality. Morality and law are, after all, two different kinds of social behavioral norms. A country or a society must admit that the minority or some moralities cannot be legalized while the majority of social moralities have been or can be legalized. For example, the following are generally difficult to be included in legal adjustments and mandatory rules and become legalized, including: love relationships between men and women, amicable relationships between colleagues, caring relationships between superiors and subordinates, ethical requirements for honoring parents, the ethical pursuits of selflessness, helping those in distress, and aiding those in peril. Under the circumstance that some moralities cannot be or are inappropriate to be legalized, related moral issues shall not be made into legal issues randomly in order to avoid "tyranny and terror of the law."

- Third, some moral requirements can be either legalized or delegalized. For instance, China has implemented criminal punishment for being a "mistress," written voluntary actions against injustice into the law, abolished the crime of counter-revolution, reduced and abolished death penalties, and stipulated the principle of no-fault liability and the privilege of silence. All these stipulations depend on the changes of time, concept and situation, and legislators. At the moment, it frequently happens when people are "daring not to and unwilling to help others for just cause" and "showing indifference to others' deaths." It seems impossible to eradicate poisonous and harmful food and products, such as poisonous steamed bread, toxic capsules, substandard milk powder, clenbuterol pork, illegal cooking oil, and shoddy cottons. In some fields and local regions, the boundaries between right and wrong, good and evil, beauty and ugliness are ambiguous. Money worship, hedonism, and ultraindividualism have developed to some extent. Moreover, events of forgetting friendship for profit and benefiting oneself at the expense of public interests happen occasionally. On top of that, incredibility and fraud have become social hazards. Abusing power for personal gain and becoming corrupt and degenerate are serious. All these phenomena have reflected the lack of certain moral rules and the anomie of moral functions as well as insufficient punishment for evil conduct and immortal behavior. These phenomena have also shown a lack of Chinese laws promoting and guaranteeing development of socialist morality. Here legislation should realize the legalization of some moralities through legislative means, determine and strengthen the value pursuits, and regulate implementation of socialist moralities through the law. Laws and morality should ban and punish all evil conduct and immortal behavior. When there are good virtues that need to be awarded and supported by laws, legislation should be made accordingly. It is of utmost urgency to strengthen legislation further in socialist moral development and to roll out laws and regulations for behaviors such as helping others for a just cause. It is also urgent to improve existing laws and regulations, fix legislative loopholes, and reinforce the punishment of evil conduct and immortal behavior. Certainly, when it comes to behaviors deviating from socialist moralities, including forgetting friendship for profit, loving indolence and hating work and being extravagant and dissipated, the questions of whether laws can intervene, what laws can intervene, and when and how the laws can intervene require in-depth study and scientific conclusion. All moral requirements that can be regulated by laws, or guaranteed or punished by the rule of law, should be included in the range of legal adjustments in a scientific and rational manner. Thus they can be normalized and legalized through legislative procedures. Legislation shall avoid stepping into all areas of ideological categories (such as ideological problems, conceptual problems, and belief problems) and moral relations (love relationships, friendships) that are inappropriate to adjust by legal norms.

A civilized country or a state of etiquette should stick to "the separation of law and morality." The "empire" of law should be moderate to some extent, and the existence of morality should be rational. At the current stage, we need not only keep vigilant to "the omnipotence of laws" but guard against "the supremacy of morality." The availability of more laws does not mean a better society. Instead, it should follow the old saying that "the gods' mill grinds slow but sure." More moralities also do not equate to a better society. Rather, "good moralities mean good moralities." If the law generalized and peculated or replaced all moralities, the result would be "autocracy and terror of the law." The generalization and denial or replacement of all laws by moralities will result in utopian dreams and social disorder. The law and morality shall have the best proportional relations with the characteristic that the law plays a leading role while morality plays an auxiliary role, and the two shall supplement each other and bring out the best.

3.3.2 The Rule of Law Should Play a Leading Role as a Social Code of Conduct

Both law and morality are social behavior norms and codes of conduct. But on the whole, law and morality are different standards or measures. Socialist morality pursues values like truth, goodness, and beauty, which are lofty states and higher standards of conduct. The rule of law pursues values like fairness, justice, and interests, which is an ordinary and lower standard of conduct that most people can meet. Socialist morality is realized mainly through education and self-discipline, reformatory education, and pressure from public opinions. Socialist morality represents an intrinsic "soft" restriction. It is true that realization of the rule of law depends on education and cultivation, but what is more important is the extrinsic heteronomy, which is reflected as "rigid" restriction on violators supported by the coercive force of the state. The punishment of criminals and even the deprivation of life is "rigid." What is stipulated by state laws is the people's social behaviors of a lower standard, including prohibitive behaviors like killing people, committing arson, poisoning, robbery, burglary, rape, embezzlement, and taking bribes. Also, it includes obligatory behaviors, such as paying taxes, serving in the army, supporting parents, raising children, fulfilling obligations, and performing contractual obligations. What is stipulated by social morality has a higher standard of people's social behaviors, such as helping others for a just cause, returning money found, and placing righteousness above family loyalty. The social behaviors of a higher standard include forgetting selfishness in the interest of the public, self-sacrifice for the sake of others, and helping those in distress and aiding those in peril. Other social behaviors of a higher standard include disregarding fame and fortune, healing the wounded and rescuing the dying, taking pleasure in helping people, working in unity, and helping one another.

In today's China, many lower standards and requirements provided in state laws are unrealizable (unattainable). Various kinds of social conflicts occur frequently. The number of various cases keeps increasing. Thus the implementation of laws is worrisome. For example, the number of cases accepted by people's courts for first instance, second instance, and retrial rose from 613,000 in 1978 to 7.462 million in 2009, up 11.2 times; of which, the number of criminal cases increased from 295,000 to 872,00, up 1.9 times; the number of civil cases grew from 318,000 to 6.436 million, up 19.2 times; and the number of administrative cases rose from more than 6000 in 1987 to 154,000 in 2009, up 23.7 times.[36] During the 5 years from 2008 to 2012, the Supreme People's Court accepted 50,773 cases and completed the investigation of 49,863 cases, up by 174% and 191%, respectively, compared with the previous 5 years. Local courts accepted 56,104,964 cases and completed the investigation and implementation of 55,258,651 cases, up by 29.30% and 29.76%, respectively, compared with the previous 5 years. The amount of settled cases were Chinese Yuan (RMB) 8.174783 trillion, up by 47.10% compared with the previous 5 years. Among these settled cases, 4661,527 were criminal cases, accounting for 8.44% of the total; 34,108,826 were civil and commercial cases, making up 61.73% of the total; 797,276 were administrative cases, representing 1.44% of the total; 558,956 were appeal cases and retrial cases, comprising 1.01% of the total; 8684 were cases of state compensation, accounting for 0.02% of the total; 12,039,065 cases were executed, representing 21.79% of the total; and 2870,623 were commutation and conditional release cases, making up 5.19% of the total. From 2008 to 2012, the number of cases accepted by courts nationwide increased

[36] Zhu Jingwen: *Analysis of the Number of Lawsuits in China over the Past 30 Years—<Report on China Law Development> (Excerpt)*, published on *Legal Daily* on January 18, 2012.

by 6% annually on an average basis to 13,242,945 in 2012 and increased by 26.38% compared with that of 2008, hitting a record high.[37]

According to the statistics, from 1981 to 2009, the number of criminal cases registered in public security organs rose from 890,000 to 5.58 million, up 5.26 times. The rate of exposed criminal cases increased from 89.6 to 419.1 per 100,000 people, up 3.68 times. Among these cases, the number of violent crimes including murder, injury, despoliation, and rape rose from 84,000 to 504,000, up 4.99 times, and the number of stealing and fraud cases rose from 763,000 to 3.77 million, up 3.94 times. At the moment, violent crimes account for 9% while burglary and fraudulent crimes account for 67.6%. The crimes, according to the proportion, can be categorized as burglary, rape, robbery, injury, fraud, and murder in 1981, and burglary, fraud, robbery, injury, rape, and murder in 2009. These changes show that the structure of crimes in China has changed significantly. The crimes related to economic interests have become the main category. Since the reform and opening up, the crimes with the fastest growth are robbery, fraud, burglary, injury, murder, and rape.[36]

Statistics of Registered Criminal Cases of Public Security Organs between 2011 and 2012

Type/year	**Place on file (case)**		**Composition (%)**	
	Year 2011	**Year 2012**	**Year 2011**	**Year 2012**
Total	6004,951	6551,440	100.00	100.00
Murder	12,015	11,286	0.20	0.17
Injury	165,097	163,620	2.75	2.50
Robbery	202,613	180,159	3.37	2.75
Rape	33,336	33,835	0.56	0.52
Abduction of women and children	13,964	18,532	0.23	0.28
Pilferage	4259,484	4284,670	70.93	65.40
Fraud	484,813	555,823	8.07	8.48
Smuggling	1350	1577	0.02	0.02
Forgery and alteration of currency	688	2194	0.01	0.03
Sell, purchase, transport, hold and use counterfeit bank note others	831,581	1299,746	13.86	19.85

[37] Hu Yunteng: *Enumeration of Cases*, *People's Court Daily*, March 10, 2013.

Under these circumstances, it is impractical to require people to have higher ideological and moral standards, ethical conducts of high quality, and higher standards of behaviors promoted by socialist morality on a voluntary and general basis. The general public should be encouraged to pursue moral ideals and try to use the standard of moral behaviors to be strict with themselves. But in practice, they should start from the lower standard of social behaviors that have demonstrated many moral requirements as provided by law. They should start from the code of conduct of legalized moralities and gradually build up their belief in the rule of law after continuous guidance, education, regulation, and repeated practices. In so doing, people could develop the habit of acting by law and strengthening their awareness in law observation, and China could gradually realize its transition from a country ruled by law to a society ruled by morality.

Morality lies in obedience. After the legalization of most social moralities, the various social subjects are required to seriously implement the constitution and the law, so as to realize the legalized moral requirements of social life. For instance, *The Marriage Law of the People's Republic of China* stipulates that people's courts can enforce the judgment and ruling for payment of alimony, cost of maintenance, and support. *The Law of Succession* stipulates that successors will lose their right of inheritance in case of abandoning or maltreating decedents. Reviewing the implementation of laws, execution of legalized moral rules by law enforcement agencies and judicial offices could effectively guarantee in the rule of law full realization of social moralities, professional ethics, and family virtues. On the contrary, a socialist moral system and moral development would be damaged inevitably and severely if national constitution and laws cannot be effectively implemented, or laws are not observed and enforced strictly, or law breakers are not published, or people could commit illegalities for personal gain. On the one hand, in the process of enforcing a law, concerned personnel and judicial officials should take facts as the basis, take laws as the criterion, and act strictly by law. Also, they should adhere to the principles of equality before the law, impartial law enforcement, and judicial justice. Beyond that, they should not bend the law for personal gain; they should adhere to the principle of being upright and outspoken, and implement the legalized socialist moral requirements in practice. On the other hand, law enforcement personnel and judicial officials should balance the relations among the law, ethics, and human feelings, and focus on the moral and ethical factors behind general legal rules and complex facts. In this way, they could attempt to implement laws (such as court judgment) consistent with the required evaluation of socialist morality and at least not conflict with socialist moral values. If a court decision may lead to people's reluctance to help others for a just cause, daring not to heal the wounded and rescue the dying, reluctance to help the aged and the young, and return money found, then the judge needs to be particularly cautious. Otherwise, this kind of judicial judgment may fall into the dilemma of "winning the law while losing morality." Law enforcement personnel and judicial officials should also take the lead in setting a social moral example, resolutely preventing law enforcement corruption and judicial corruption, and guaranteeing pure and sacred legal weapons. British political philosopher Francis Bacon once said that an unjust judgment is more than ten times the evil crime, because a serious crime contaminates the river while an unjust judgment contaminates the source of water. Socialist morality is one of the "headwaters" of China's rule of law. Unjust administrative law enforcement and judicial judgment and despised corruption in law enforcement and judicature have not only directly damaged the authority and credibility of the socialist rule of law, but have also severely damaged the value basis of socialist virtue.

3.3.3 The Rule of Law Should Play a Leading Role as Analyzed From the Difference Between the Rule of Law and the Rule of Morality

A large amount of research has shown that there are obvious differences between the rule of law and the rule of morality when both are taken as a method to govern the state: from the perspective of the governing subject, the rule of law is the democratic governance of the majority while the rule of morality is the governance of a few elites; from the perspective of the governing process, the rule of law is the rule of process while the rule of morality is the rule of human feelings; from the governing perspective, the rule of law is the rule of external control while the rule of morality is the rule of internal restraint; from the perspective of the governing standard, the rule of law is the rule of a lower behavioral standard while the rule of morality is the rule of a higher behavioral standard; from the perspective of governing method, the rule of law is the state compulsory rule while the rule of morality is the social educational rule; and from the perspective of governing emphasis, the rule of law is to govern officials while the rule of morality is to govern the people.

Because there are both differences and similarities between law and morality, between the rule of law and the rule of morality, the rule of law and morality are mutually complementary, mutually affected, and organically united. The rule of law is the bottom line and backup force of socialist morality. Usually what is prohibited by the rule of law is also opposed by socialist morality. Likewise, all those encouraged by the rule of law are generally supported by socialist morality. Socialist morality is the altitude and foundation of the rule of law and the internal basis for the rationality, legitimacy, and legality of the rule of law. The value, spirit, principle, and theory of the rule of law are mostly built on the basis of socialist morality. Quite a number of systems and norms of the rule of law are the institutionalization and legalization of socialist morality. For instance, in terms of social behaviors, "endangering the motherland" is a behavior denied by socialist morality and prohibited by China's Constitution and criminal law. "Harming others for personal gain" and "forgetting friendship for profits" not only go against ethics and moral rules, but also violate socialist law-based ideas and legal norms under certain conditions. Behaviors violating the law and discipline and committing fraudulence will be sanctioned by socialist morality and discipline and condemned by socialist law-based ideas. Illegal criminal activities will be punished by national laws. In terms of the legal system, the socialist rule of law sticks to "good law and proper governance" in legislation. The socialist rule of law stresses "justice for the people" in law enforcement. It advocates fairness and justice in judicature, and requires equality, honesty, and credibility in law abidance. All these features and requirements have demonstrated the requirements for socialist morality to varying degrees and have become legalized socialist morality.

In the constitutional aspect, the current constitution stipulates the practice of ruling the country by law and the building of a socialist country under the rule of law. As the fundamental strategy for the ruling party to rule the state and make politics, the rule by law puts forward a number of requirements. The people under the leadership of the CPC should manage national, social, economic, and cultural affairs in accordance with the constitution and law. The ruling party must act within the framework of the constitution and law and stick to democratic, scientific, and law-based governance. Legislative organs should persist in democratic and scientific legislation and keep improving the socialist system of law with Chinese characteristics. Administrative organs should adhere to administration by law and try to build the government under the rule of law. Judicial organs should keep to judicial justice and try to be just, highly effective, authoritative, and clean. All citizens should learn, respect, observe, and apply the law and consciously maintain the unity and authority of the rule of law.

In reality, China's socialist market economy is the economy under the rule of law rather than the economy under the rule of morality. China's socialist democratic politics is the politics under the rule of law rather than the politics under the rule of morality. China's socialist harmonious society is a democratic society under the rule of law rather than a society bound by relationship.

Given the differences mentioned above, the rule of law and the rule of morality should be closely connected and mutually supplemented. The rule of law shall not regulate and adjust people's thoughts. It is usually powerless in issues of the category of thought. Ideological and moral constraints are often of no use for anomic and conscienceless behaviors. It is just the so-called "an inch may prove long while a foot may prove short." Therefore China needs to oppose the practice of using the rule of law to replace the rule of morality and the tendency of valuing the rule of morality while neglecting the rule of law. For all this, the rule of law should play a leading role in the process of state governance at the primary stage of socialism.

3.4 BUILDING A STRONGER SOCIALIST CULTURE OF THE RULE OF LAW

The following aspects should be carefully studied and emphasized in order to strengthen the development of socialist culture of the rule of law.

3.4.1 Understanding the Rules and Features of Law-based Cultural Development

The following rules and features should be understood to build the socialist culture of the rule of law with Chinese characteristics at the current stage.

3.4.1.1 Political Guidance

Socialist rule of law has distinctive class, political, and party characteristics. In this connection, to build a socialist culture of the rule of law, we must organically unify politics and the rule of law. We should not just emphasize the rule of law but also paying no attention to political awareness; we should emphasize political awareness but paying no attention on the rule of law. Rather, we should persist in "an organic of the three" as they are supplementary to each other and no one can be omitted. We should focus on the central tasks, serve the overall interests, and insist on realizing an organic unity of political effect, social effect, and legal effect through the rule of law. We should put people first, protect human rights, and persevere in applying socialist rule of law to realize "an organic unity of the three" in law enforcement, judicature, and legal supervision. We should adhere to the socialist orientation and realize an organic unity of five aspects in promoting a socialist culture of the rule of law. These five aspects include establishing a socialist law-based idea, promoting socialist law-based spirit, upholding socialist law-based values, enhancing socialist law-based concepts, and strengthening socialist law-based awareness.

3.4.1.2 Legal (Law-based) Character

The socialist rule of law is the behavioral norm for adjusting social relations in the form of the state will and through institutions and rules. Legal character is an important feature of the rule of law for differentiating from behavioral norms like moralities, disciplines, religious taboos, village rules, and Party rules. To build the socialist culture of the rule of law, we must fully embody its legal (law-based) nature, and establish and improve the system of law with the constitution as the essence. We must also build and operate various systems (including the legislative system, law enforcement system, judicial system, legal supervision system, law popularizing system, the system of acting by law, law-abiding system, and lawsuit system) with laws as the foundation. We must follow and create various kinds of legal principles and legal theories with the science of law as the scientific support. To build a socialist culture of the rule of law, there is a need to prevent law-based nihilism and the culture of rule of man, and guard against omnipotent and ideological forms of the rule of law.

3.4.1.3 Cultural Background

On the one hand, in the formation and development process, the socialist culture of the rule of law with Chinese characteristics has been influenced by traditional Chinese political and legal culture, the socialist legal culture of the Soviet Union and Eastern Europe, the culture of the rule of law of western continental law system, and the Anglo-American law system. It has also absorbed moral, religious, social, political, behavioral, and management cultures, among other cultural elements. It has become a mix of human advanced cultures. On the other hand, it is in itself "cultural development," so it is bound to be featured by soft powers of "culture." These soft powers are applied to national cohesion, international influence, social stability, ethical influence, centripetal unity, historical inheritance, guidance of public opinions, religious substitution, literary creativity, space and time positioning, information control, trendy assimilation, fashion advocacy, knowledge protection, spread of civilization, ecological balance, and cultural sovereignty.[38] To build a socialist culture of the rule of law, we should combine the general features of cultural soft powers with the professional features of the culture of the rule of law and combine the general requirements of cultural development with the special requirements of law-based cultural development, so as to truly reflect the cultural essence of socialist law-based culture and the intrinsic features of cultural soft powers.

3.4.1.4 Long-term Process

The development of a socialist rule of law and law-based culture with Chinese characteristics includes interdependent but closely connected practical processes as well as the following factors. First, the old China had left the New China more autocratic traditions and less democratic and legal traditions.[39] These historical characteristics and conditions determined that it would be a long and arduous historical task to promote the socialist law-based culture, deny and eradicate the culture ruled by man, and eliminate and reform the culture not ruled by law. Second, western societies and cultures were formed under the rule of law over a long history of more than a thousand years that included ancient civilization, ancient Greek culture, the Roman Empire, and the rule of theocracy, and hundreds years of development in modern times. Rome was not built in a day. Likewise, the socialist culture of the rule of law would not realize development right away. Third, China is still and will be for a long time in its primary stage of socialism. Therefore it will take a long-term practical process to keep improving the socialist system, fully embody the superiority of socialism, realize highly developed productivity, comprehensively develop scientific and technological culture, and improve social civilization and moral accomplishment in an all-round way. Fourth, it is bound to be a long-term process for the general public to truly acknowledge the rule

[38] Zhu Xiangyuan: *Capital Cultural Development and Soft Power*, see *Advancing the Construction of Cultural Centers Nationwide* compiled by the Research Group of the Standing Committee of Beijing Municipal People's Congress, Red Flag Press, Beijing, 2012 edition, pp. 194–196.

[39] Deng Xiaoping: *The Reform of Party and State's Leadership System*, *Selected Works of Deng Xiaoping*, Volume II, People's Publishing House, Beijing, 1983 edition, p. 332.

of law, believe in it, and develop good behavioral habits based on this rule of law.

3.4.1.5 Practicability

Culture is always human culture, life is always human life, and history is always human history.[40] The development of a socialist culture of the rule of law cannot be realized without the influence and education of the people, the communication means, and the teaching process. From individual and social perspectives, why should we implement the rule of law, accept the restriction of the rule of law, and believe in law-based culture? Western societies under the rule of law and their culture of the rule of law were gradually established and formed after the success of the bourgeois revolution, which was based on the political and legal theories propagated by the Renaissance and the Enlightenment. In China, the ruling party and state elites applied the trial and error approach and picked the democratic and political path of "developing socialism and improving the socialist system" in the process of introspecting the lesson of the Cultural Revolution and denying the rule of man. It is impracticable to mainly rely on external forces to change the path of the rule of law chosen by the ruling party and states elites into the choice and way of life of the general public and to make the general public consciously abide by the rule of law. Implementing the rule of law and the rule by law-based on the actual requirements and reality has determined the need to internalize the requirements of national rule of law into the value identification, belief, and habit of the general public. The internal driving force is bound to be primarily "practical," which is the usefulness and effectiveness of the rule of law. Western countries mainly rely on popularized religion, cultural education, and moralization with the support of interest induction and state coercive force to address issues regarding the internal demand of the general public for the rule of law. In China's culture of the rule of law, the lack of support of religious culture has led to the adoption of law dissemination, compulsory execution, and adoption of interest induction by drawing on advantages and avoiding disadvantages. On this basis, the culture of the rule of law could be gradually switched to the internal demand from an interest-driven basis and then become a way of life.

[40] Zhou Ximing: *Urgent Problems in China's Cultural Construction, Advancing the Construction of Cultural Centers Nationwide* compiled by the Research Group of the Standing Committee of Beijing Municipal People's Congress, Red Flag Press, Beijing, 2012 edition, p. 209.

3.4.2 Enhance Citizen Education

The socialist culture of the rule of law is the culture that citizens consciously respect, study, abide by, and use the laws. In a certain sense, the main purpose of strengthening the development of socialist culture of the rule of law and carrying out publicity and education on law for all entire citizens is to educate citizens and increase their awareness (i.e., citizenship education). Enhancing citizenship education lays the foundation for development of socialist culture of the rule of law. Citizenship education gives citizens a correct understanding of their subject identity through appropriate means of education. Consequently, citizens could shape their political attitude and legal awareness, accurately understand their relations with the state, and adjust their attitudes and behaviors. Citizenship education cultivates the citizens' value, knowledge, and skills to manage social public affairs.

From the perspective of politics, citizenship education cultivates citizens into qualified social citizens, meaning "social men" and "political men." In the perspective of law, citizenship education cultivates citizens' democratic and law-based ideas and their sense of freedom, equality, fairness, and justice, so they can enjoy their rights, fulfill their obligations, assume their responsibilities, and have the capacity to act.

The goal of citizenship education is to educate citizens about right consciousness. Every citizen should know that he or she as a citizen has the basic rights and freedoms guaranteed by the constitution and the law, such as the right to life, the right to property, and the right to freedom of speech and thought. While enjoying the basic rights and freedom prescribed in the constitution and laws, citizens shall assume the obligations stipulated by the constitution and laws. Citizen is a concept relative to the state. It cannot be talked about without the state. The task of citizenship education is to: cultivate citizens' sense of belonging and their cognition of the state; improve the citizens' recognition of the state and the constitution; entrench their loyalty and belief and confidence in the state; make all citizens understand that protecting the country and safeguarding national interests are their fundamental obligations; and foster qualified citizens to meet the requirements of the state and society, namely, citizens with a positive attitude toward life, enthusiasm for political participation, attainment in democracy and rule of law, and who could cooperate with other citizens and social organizations.

Many countries and regions attach great importance to citizenship education (and human rights education), despite the lack of publicity and education on law. For example, the Republic of Korea has set up a special moral curriculum and national ethic course and carried out "national spiritual education." In Singapore, the comprehensive training program for citizens was issued as early as 1960 and the textbook *Good Citizen* has been adopted since 1992. *American Civics* is used in the United States and the contents involve relations between citizens and the government, between citizens and society, between citizens and the world, and the economic obligations of citizens. In Germany, citizenship education mainly includes education on citizens' rights and obligations, collective spirit, sense of authority, sense of nationality, and laboring. In Japan, the purpose of citizenship education is to give citizens the self-consciousness of becoming citizens conforming to democratic principles, with the attitude to become builders of society and the country in the future. The purpose is also to cultivate citizens with a culture for caring about politics, economy, society, and international relations, with good abilities to take active action in the form rights and obligations. Internationally, the "Global Citizenship Education" has been proposed. Furthermore, the Research Committee on International Political Socialization and Education made "political consciousness and citizenship education in institutional transformation" the theme of the round-table conference held in 1992.

The Education Commission of Hong Kong introduced *The Guidelines on Civic Education in Schools*, stipulating that citizenship education shall start from kindergarten. The *Guidelines* have detailed requirements for the content, form, channel, and model of citizenship education. In Taiwan, senior high schools should take the course of "citizenship and morality" with civic virtue and civic knowledge, covering education, society, law, politics, economy, culture, and other aspects.

Improving citizenship education is both main work and foundation work to advance implementation of the rule by law as the fundamental strategy and strengthen development of the culture of the rule of law. Improving citizenship education is also an important measure to implement the rule by law in an all-round way.

To improve citizenship education and develop a socialist culture of the rule of law, we must resolutely eliminate and reform the citizen culture not developed based on the rule of law. At present, the citizen culture exists among Chinese citizens to varying degrees, and the manifestations have four aspects: first, some citizens do not believe in law but in power, petition, making trouble (minor issues can be solved through small-scale disturbance; big issues can be solved through large-scale disturbance; issues will not be solved without disturbance), relationships, money, leaders, and rumors. Second, some citizens are proud of evading the law, exploiting loopholes of laws, and breaking the law for profit and wealth. Instead, they feel stupid if they respect and abide by the law. For instance, they laugh at poverty but not prostitution, believe that it is difficult to become rich without breaking the law, and that the honest man always suffers losses. Third, the so-called "illegal experiences" are quite popular. They spread like wildfires among some groups, such as tax evasion, swindling, making and selling fakes, cheating on workmanship and materials, violent resistance against the law, bribing, and cultivating contacts. Fourth, the ideas and proverbs against the rule of law are repeatedly copied and propagated through films, television programs, literary works, street gossip, and other channels. For example, a crime committed by more people would not be punished; stealing books does not equal stealing; money makes the mare go; free things would be taken definitely; those who do not pick up money on the ground are thought to be foolish; no warning, no-fault; winning a relation means winning a lawsuit; beheading is nothing but a bold big scar, and another brave man would be born 20 years later; someone telling the truth would be put in prison; and one stubbornly refusing to acknowledge a crime would be set free.

In citizenship education, some content is similar to that of the publicity and education of the rule of law, but some is new. Improving citizenship education can better solidify the foundation for developing the ideology and culture, morality and ethics, and political ideas of the rule of law, and help solidly advance the implementation of the rule by law as the fundamental strategy.

3.4.3 Strengthen the Education of Leading Cadres on the Rule of Law

Leading cadres are important organizers, facilitators, and practitioners for the development of the rule of law. *The Decisions* of the Fourth Plenary Session of the 18th CPC Central Committee pointed out that laws are treasures for state governance while good laws are the precondition of proper governance. To comprehensively advance the rule of law, there need to be scientific legislation, strict law enforcement, impartial judicature, and law observation by all the people. The realization of these major tasks would be impossible without leading cadres at all levels. Adhering to the leadership of the Party is the fundamental guarantee for ruling the country by law. The Party leads legislation, guarantees law enforcement, supports judicature, and takes the lead in law observation, so the legal consciousness and legal quality of leading cadres have a direct effect on the advancement of the rule of law. In the process of comprehensively advancing the rule of law, leading cadres at all levels should shoulder responsibilities and missions, take the lead, and serve as good examples. General-Secretary Xi Jinping emphasized that "leading cadres at all levels shoulder great responsibilities in advancing the rule of law. They shall be the paramount part as 'the key minority' of the rule of law. Leading cadres should set an good example in respecting, studying, abiding by and using laws and mobilize the entire party and the whole nation to work together to conspicuously achieve new results in building the system of socialist rule of law with Chinese characteristics and building a socialist country under the rule of law. Xi Jinping required that Leading cadres should set an good example in respecting the law and holding the law in awe, and take the lead in honoring the rule of law; Leading cadres should serve as examples in studying the law and take the lead in realizing and understanding the law; Leading cadres should play a vanguard role in law abidance and take the lead in observing the law and guarding the rule of law; Leading cadres should serve as models in using the laws and take the lead in strictly enforcing the law and acting by law."[41]

The socialist culture of the rule of law is the culture that leading cadres at all levels take the lead and set examples. The key to promoting socialist culture of the rule of law is to strengthen the education of leading cadres on the rule of law. The attention of leading cadres at all levels is related to the development of the socialist culture of the rule of law. This is because, first, China's rule of law development is a historical development process from the rule of man to the rule by law and then from the rule by law to the rule of law. Its success depends on the attention, support, and participation of leading cadres. Second, Chinese leaders are models of society and the public, so their words and deeds, actions by law, and law abidance have a highly positive and demonstrative effect on society. Third, Chinese political culture in history has always followed the practice where subordinates follow the behaviors of superiors, and the masses follow the behaviors of cadres. In this case, when superiors behave wrongly, subordinates will do the same. Illegal criminal activities and corruption of Chinese leaders will have a negative effect on the socialist culture of the rule of law.

[41] Xi Jinping: *Speech at the Opening Ceremony of the Special Seminar on Implementing the Spirit of the Fourth Plenary Session of the Eighteenth Central Committee of the CPPCC for Leading Cadres at Provincial and Ministerial Levels, it's published in a newspaper People's Daily*, February 3, 2015.

For leaders at all levels, improving the development of the socialist culture of the rule of law requires firmly developing the law-based concept and improving its qualities. It is also to enhance their ability to act by law, resolutely oppose and eliminate various kinds of cultures ruled by man. At the moment, some leading cadres value the rule of man while neglecting the rule of law, which can be manifested mainly from the following aspects: (1) value law over power, meaning individual wills outmatch the constitution and the law; an individual or the few have the final say; what is said by leading cadres are laws; and the law will change with the changes of the opinions and attention of leading cadres; (2) make frequent changes, meaning laws are stable, normative, constant, and authoritative, and replacing legal norms with policies, documents, orders, and instructions makes laws and systems exist in name only; (3) give instructions to judicial cases and randomly intervene in courts' independent exercise of judicial powers and in procuratorates' independent exercise of procuratorial powers; (4) take the law and the rule of law as the means and tools to deal with and punish others, and use the law to rule the citizens, the masses, and the people rather than using the law to control powers, govern officials, and themselves; (5) prevailing corruption culture, meaning being proud of abusing powers for personal gain, feeling stupid when acting by law, believing that the identity of official means the earning of gold, sacrificing oneself for the whole family, being an official is to make money, powers are not being supervised but abused, playing favoritism, and committing irregularities and corruption; (6) advocate administrative means and the means of the will and order of officials, despise and even give up law-based principles, legal means, the legal system, and the democratic rule of law; and (7) official standard, praising privilege, despising human rights protection, and violating the principle that all people are equal before the law, among others.

The awareness of leading cadres at all levels should be strengthened in four aspects through education of the socialist culture of the rule of law. First, strengthen their consciousness as public servants, make them bear in mind that they are always servants while the people are masters, and their powers come from the people and belong to the people. Second, enhance their consciousness in the rule of law and try to improve their capacity and level in making decisions, governing, administering, and acting by law. Third, heighten their service awareness, and make them bear in mind that the idea of public servant means to take people's interests above all; the behavioral norms of public servants are serving the people wholeheartedly; and keep to the people-oriented principle and the principle of governing for the people. Fourth, improve their consciousness of responsibility, make them remember that the powers bestowed by the people are not privileges but obligations and responsibilities. They must be responsible for the state, the people, and the law. They shall bear legal responsibilities if they abuse their powers.

Leading cadres are required to develop five concepts through education of the socialist culture of the rule of law. First, the concept of building a party serving the interests of the people, governing for the people, and governing by law. Second, the people-oriented concept that puts people first, uses power in the interests of the people, bears feelings for the people, and seeks interests for the people. Third, the concept of respecting and guaranteeing human rights and the concept that everyone is equal before the law. Fourth, the law-based concept of democratic legislation, admonition by law, judicial justice, and supervising by law. Fifth, the democratic concept that people are masters of the country, and the concept of democratic election, democratic decision-making, democratic management, and democratic supervision.

3.4.4 Strengthen Cultural Legislation

The socialist culture of the rule of law is culture on the basis of law. The legal basis is not only an important premise for the implementation of the rule of law but also an instrumental basis for strengthening the development of the socialist culture of the rule of law. The socialist system of law with Chinese characteristics has taken shape and the law is generally available. However, the socialist system of law and the availability of legal basis still cannot fully meet the needs of economic, political, social, cultural, and ecological civilization progress. China's legislative works need to be further strengthened. The system of law needs to be improved continuously.

When it comes to improvement of the system of law, there needs to be more theoretic research on "the socialist system of law with Chinese characteristics" and "the system of law with Chinese characteristics." There is also a need to intensify legislative works in weak links of the system of law, especially cultural legislation at this point. Among the seven legal departments of China's system of law, cultural legislations are few in number and have not yet formed into an independent legal department. Cultural legislation is scattered in the constitution and other department laws. Quite a number of cultural acts of legislation are administrative laws and regulations and few in number.

Major issues and demands exist in building of the legal environment for Chinese culture. First, cultural legislation is weak in general. It is even nonexistent in some vital areas. For instance, there are no laws available on public cultural service, cultural creative industry, artwork management, professional literature and art development, cultural exchange with foreign countries, and performance art, among other aspects. Second, there is a lack of criterion and promotion for new types of businesses in the cultural field. For example, the number of websites and the amount of information available on them are far more than that provided by traditional media, as a result of the rapid development of the Internet. But how to regulate this scenario through legislation is still not well established. There is also a shortage of legal constraints and norms on microblogs, Tencent QQ, network audio and video on demand, outdoor video advertisements, unwanted messages to mobile phones, broadcasting stations, and TV station channel allocation. Third, the contents of some laws and regulations can no longer meet the needs of reality, so they need to be revised and improved. Some legislation principles need to be refined, such as *Regulations on the Administration of Ground Receiving Facilities for Satellite Television Broadcasting*, *Regulations on the Administration of Internet Access Service Business Establishments*, *Regulations Concerning the Management and Protection of Underwater Cultural Relics*, and *Regulations on the Administration of Commercial Performances*.[42]

Therefore, China should strengthen cultural legislation in the following aspects:

- First, create laws for promotion of the film industry, and strive to address issues like unsound development of the film market and film ticket prices that are unaffordable to ordinary people. Furthermore, more issues need to be addressed, such as the relatively fewer number of cinemas that are accessible for many people; too many restraining factors in the film-making process that are not good for operating and producing films and thus result in lower film quality; fewer quality films; a higher risk of the film investment industry; and a lack of stable funding and talent resources.
- Second, enact a library law to energetically address issues related to establishment and facility construction of libraries, assurance of

[42] Liu Jigang, Zhang Yin *et al.*: *Research Report on Cultural and Legal Environment Construction*, published on *Advancing the Construction of Cultural Centers Nationwide* compiled by the research group of the Standing Committee of Beijing Municipal People's Congress, Red Flag Press, Beijing, 2012 edition, pp. 70–78.

investment for libraries, cobuilding and sharing of documents and information resources, modernization of libraries, the building of library teams, and the guarantee of citizens' rights to access to library services.

- Third, formulate a law to guarantee radio and television transmission and vigorously solve issues concerning the licensing system for radio and television transmission businesses, operation systems for radio and television transmission, systems for guaranteeing the interests of the general public in radio and television transmission, systems for protecting radio and television transmission facilities, emergency systems for radio and television transmission security, and two-way access systems for facilitating integration of broadcast networks, telecommunication networks, and the Internet.
- Fourth, improve laws and regulations on culture management, such as enacting regulations on museums and revising the *Regulations on the Administration of Ground Receiving Facilities for Satellite Television Broadcasting*, *Regulations on the Administration of Internet Access Service Business Establishments,* and *Regulations Concerning the Management and Protection of Underwater Cultural Relics.* There is also a need to establish and improve the news legal system, understand the right direction of news and public opinion, and give full play to the important role of news and public opinion.
- Fifth, perfect laws and regulations to promote healthy development of network culture, intensify the effort to build a network legal system, formulate a telecommunication law, improve the legal system for network information, strengthen network information service and management, and protect individual information and network information security.
- Sixth, improve laws and regulations closely related to cultural activities, enact a tourism law, a natural heritage protection law, a voluntary service law, and a philanthropy law, and establish and perfect the legal system for giving national medals and honorary titles.

CHAPTER 4

Rule by Law and Governance by Law

4.1 THE RULING PARTY, THE NATURE OF STATE, AND THE RULE OF LAW

China is a socialist state under the people's democratic dictatorship led by the working class (through the Communist Party of China (CPC)) and based on the alliance of workers and peasants, indicating the fundamental nature of the Chinese state, i.e., China's nature of state. What then is the form of government? China's form of government is the people's congress system based on democratic centralism.[1] In terms of politics and science of law or constitutional democratic theory, as the ruling party of the People's Republic of China (PRC), the CPC should hold state power in both the nature of state and the form of government. The CPC should directly or indirectly exercise national legislative power, administrative power, judicial power, procuratorial power, and supervisory power in the capacity of national public powers.

4.1.1 The Ruling Party and the Nature of State

4.1.1.1 Constitutional Relationship Between the Ruling Party and the Nature of State

Most political scientists believe that political party is closely related to democracy and democratic politics. Without political parties, there would be no democracy and democratic politics in a modern sense. "Political parties created democracy; it is beyond imagination how modern democracy can be judged from any other point of view except in terms of political parties."[2] In China's political life, the ruling party plays dual political roles.

[1] *Jiang Zemin's Thought on Socialism with Chinese Characteristics* (special excerpts), Central Party Literature Press, 2002 edition, pp. 306–307.

[2] E. E. Schattschneider, *Party Government*, New York, Rinehart, 1942 edition, p. 1, quoted from Lipset: *Indispensable Political Parties*, published on *Comparative Studies of Political Parties* edited by Rong Jingben and Gao Xinjun, Central Compilation and Translation Bureau Press, 2002 edition, p. 274.

Building the Rule of Law in China.
DOI: http://dx.doi.org/10.1016/B978-0-12-811930-3.00004-0

According to Marxism, the nature of state is the status of social classes in a state and the nature of the ruling party determines the nature of a state. From the perspective of nature of state, the CPC as the ruling party is not only the core of leadership for the cause of socialism but also the leading political force of the entire state. From the perspective of the form of government, the CPC represents the controller of state political power, the center of state political power, and the ruling party. South Korean scholar Dr. Ham Tae Young believed that the dual nature of a ruling party has determined that it must face the challenge of having to handle the relations between its leadership role and its ruling methods.[3] There are mainly two choices in this regard. First, the party's leadership is realized through the party's ruling. Second, the party's ruling is represented by the party's leadership. In past practices, the CPC took the lead not as the ruling party but as the leading force whose existence did not rely on state institutions. The tradition of nonseparation between party and government and of a high degree of centralization of political power in the hands of the party was formed thereby. The constitutional meaning that the Party's leadership is realized through the party's ruling is: the Party operates the state system and leads national life as the leading force within the state system rather than outside the state system. That means the Party operates the state system and leads national life as the ruling party. Establishing this kind of relation between the Party and the government within this constitutional framework will help guarantee the Party's ruling status, strengthen the Party's ruling capacity, and regulate the Party's ruling behaviors as the value orientation.

The constitutional relations between the ruling party and the nature of state is in effect how the ruling party, as the bridge between the masses and the state (the government), represents the political, economic, and other interest appeals of the majority to exercise public powers. This has reflected the ruling party's relations with the masses, with the state, with public powers, and with the society. The CPC represents the will and interests of the overwhelming majority of the people in its ruling, which is reflected in the relations between the ruling party and the people. The CPC does not have any special interests and powers of its own except for building the party for the interests of the people, ruling for the people, and serving the people wholeheartedly.

China is a socialist state under the people's democratic dictatorship led by the working class (through the Communist Party) and aimed at

[3] Ham Tae Young: *Party Government and Market of China*, Economic Daily Press, 2002 edition, pp. 203–204.

making the people masters of the country. This can be manifested in the relations between the ruling party and the nature of state. First, the CPC is the core and soul of the people's democratic dictatorship and determines the attribute, value orientation, functions, and principles of the nature of state. Second, the CPC as the ruling party must stick to its political leadership of the state power, always play a leading and central role in national state power system, and try to maintain a stable ruling status. Third, the CPC as the ruling party is not only the vanguard of the Chinese working class but also the vanguard of the Chinese people and the Chinese nation. Therefore the CPC must always represent the most extensive interests conforming to its advancement, i.e., to represent the interests of not only the Chinese working class but also the Chinese people and the Chinese nation. Fourth, the CPC as the ruling party must exist in the nature of state under the people's democratic dictatorship and leverage all national facilities and resources to lead and support the people to be masters of the country in politics and improve the people's well-being.

4.1.1.2 Constitutional Relationship Between the Ruling Party and the Form of Government

The form of government is the organizational form of state power. The nature of state and the form of government are inseparable with unified nature and form. The CPC as the ruling party should be a part of the state and its government system. The CPC must always represent the fundamental requirements for the development of China's advanced productive forces, the trend of the development of China's advanced culture, and the fundamental interests of the overwhelming majority of the people in China.[4] The nature of state is intrinsic and abstract, while the government

[4] Mao Zedong pointed out in his *The Tasks of the Communist Party of China in the Anti-Japanese War Period* that the leadership of the proletarian party over all revolutionary classes of the country is the political leadership. Realizing the political leadership, first of all, is to raise the fundamental political slogan based on the historical development process and put forward the mobilization slogan for every development stage and every major incident to realize the former slogan. Second, based on the nationwide movement for this specific target, the proletariat, especially its vanguard, the Communist Party, should show its infinite initiative and loyalty and become the example for realizing these specific objectives. Third, it is to establish an appropriate relations with allies and develop and consolidate this alliance in the principle of maintaining the identified political objectives. Fourth is the development of the team of the Communist Party, the unity of thoughts and the stringency of discipline. The leadership of the Communist Party over the whole nation is realized through implementing the above-said conditions. *Selected Works of Mao Zedong*, Volume 1, People's Publishing House, 1991 edition, pp. 262–263.

system is extrinsic and concrete. The CPC is the ruling party of the state, the source of government authority in China.

Lenin once made the correct interpretation on the relationship between the ruling party and the national structure of government. He pointed out, "CPC is the ruling party."[5] The authority and power of the CPC (and its central committee) and the Soviet regime must be clearly defined in terms of the relationship between the CPC and the national government, between CPC and the state organs. The Party's task is to exert overall leadership over operation of all the state organs, rather than interfere over-frequently or frequently, or tinker with the details.[6] The Communist Party, serving as the ruling party, should lead over the state political power on one hand and execute political power on the other. How to coordinate and unify these two functions appropriately should be seriously addressed by the ruling Communist Party. As Lenin stated in his *Report on the Party Program*, "Although the Soviet is a government administrated via the working masses in terms of the guiding principles, in fact, it is administrated via the vanguard of the proletariat for the working class instead of the working class itself."[7] Lenin stated more specifically, "The ruling party is the vanguard of the proletariat, the leader."[8] But how to rule the political system directly? The answer is, "As is known by the Chinese, as China's ruling party, the CPC cannot but confuse the upper class of Soviet and that of the Communist Party as a whole. We should do so now and in the future."[9]

Given the constitutional definition of the ruling party, the leadership of the CPC is the ruling of power, which should operate within rather than beyond the state government. The party should operate within rather than beyond the scope of the constitution and law. As Deng Xiaoping pointed out in *The Party and the Anti-Japanese Democratic Government* on April 15, 1941, "The Party should shoulder its leadership responsibility on defining the political principles rather than keep everything in hand, or interfere in all issues, or put the party right over everything." The Party should carefully study, through the party members in the administrative organ and the public opinion organ, to correctly make the policies, decrees, and administrative guidelines for the government. The Party holds the power to give

[5] *The Collected Works Of Lenin*, Volume 38, People's Publishing House, 1986 edition, p. 311.
[6] *The Collected Works Of Lenin*, Volume 43, People's Publishing House, 1987 edition, p. 64.
[7] *Lenin Selected Works*, Volume 3, People's Publishing House, 1972 edition, p. 789.
[8] *Lenin Selected Works*, Volume 4, People's Publishing House, 1995 edition, p. 423.
[9] *The Collected Works Of Lenin*, Volume 41, People's Publishing House, 1986 edition, p. 11.

orders to the party members or the political parties in the government and to put forward proposals to the government in the name of the Party whenever necessary. By no means can the Party have the power to command the government.[10]

According to *The Regulations of the Central Committee of CPC on Unifying the Party's Leadership and Adjusting Relations between Organizations in Anti-Japanese Base Area* adopted by the Political Bureau of the Central Committee of CPC on September 1, 1942, the relationship between party committees and the government system must be clearly defined. The Party should lead the government system in principles, policies, and fundamental guidelines, rather than interfere in all issues and keep everything in hand. The Party should lead the Consultative Council and the government only through party members and groups. Party committees and Party organs have no rights to give direct orders to the Consultative Council and government agencies.

Zhou Enlai also emphasized in 1950 that a state government had been established in China nationwide. The CPC played the leading role in the government. Therefore all decrees should be issued by government institutions. In the past China had been fighting for a long period. Under such context, orders were often given in the name of the Party. Entering the time of peace, China established its national government, so this practice should be changed. To organize and implement the Party's policies and guidelines, the government should play a critical role and the Party organization shall play the role to guarantee the implementation process. The Party should not give orders to the masses.[11]

How could the ruling party and the government merge into one organic whole in China's political reality? Mr. Dong Biwu proposed in October 1951 that party committees at all levels should lead government organs at all levels through party members working in government organs.[12] Deng Xiaoping pointed out in *The Report on the Revision of the Party Constitution* of the Party to its Eighth National Congress that the CPC faced new challenges due to its status as the ruling party. He added that since the CPC had become the ruling party of the entire country, it

[10] *Selected Works of Deng Xiaoping*, Volume 1, People's Publishing House, 1994 edition, pp. 12–13.

[11] *Selected Works of Zhou Enlai about United Front*, People's Publishing House, 1984 edition, pp. 174–175.

[12] *Selected Works of Dong Biwu*, People's Publishing House, 1985 edition, p. 314.

is more risky to isolate the party from the masses, which would result in greater disadvantages for the Party. How to guarantee that, the ruling party maintains a close contact with the masses, and always represents the fundamental interests of the people, in terms of politics? The most important institutional arrangement is to guarantee that the ruling party exercises its power and leadership through the government system—the system of people's congress within the framework of the constitution and the law.

However, for quite some time, the national legislative bodies, state administrative organs, state judicial organs, and national military authorities are not established in accordance with the ruling behaviors of the ruling party. The state system has lost its function to regulate the subject of state powers. Consequently, the Party's leadership has gradually broken away from the state system.[13] The leadership and ruling of the CPC are not abstract but concrete and require institutional and legal guarantee. The ruling party should operate within but not beyond the state system, and firmly control all public powers as many of the Party members enter into different government bodies and departments.

In western countries, what modern political parties desire most is to quickly control the masses, enter the political system, become an important part of the political and institutional structure, and ultimately the ruling party. The main characteristics of western ruling parties include: (1) they are elected into the administrative system, and have to be tested again once every few years to determine their status; (2) after entering the system, they must act based on the rules and regulations of the administrative system; and (3) they can only turn their party policies into laws of the country through legislative procedures within the parliament.[14] As for the functions, political parties should firstly and mainly belong to the representative system. They are the tools or agencies of the people. They represent the people and express their requirements. With their development, political parties have become the tool for passing the people's will to the power.[15] But just as the British famous politician Professor David Held had summarized, citing the opinions quoted from Weber, the modern

[13] Nie Gaomin *et al.*: *Theoretical Discussion on Separation of the Functions of the Party from Those of the Government*, Chunqiu Publishing House, 1988 edition, p. 122.

[14] Cao Peilin: *Parliamentary Politics*, Joint Publishing (Hong Kong) Company Limited, 1993 edition, pp. 61–62.

[15] Giovanni Sartori, *Part of the Political Party*, published on *Comparative Studies of Political Parties* edited by Rong Jingben and Gao Xinjun, Central Compilation and Translation Bureau Press, 2002 edition, p. 217.

development of the parliamentary rules controlled by party government in the West has irreversibly changed the nature of parliamentary politics and triggered the bankruptcy of the western party system and the parliamentary system. The features of this kind of "bankruptcy" include: (1) political parties have become bureaucratic organizations; (2) party machines have established the mechanism to control the supporters including senators, and the representatives have become the people saying "yes;" (3) bankruptcy of the idea that the parliament serves as the center of deliberation and argumentation; and (4) political parties control the parliament while the leading figures control political parties: "autocracy of election."[16]

According to socialist constitutional principles, exercising political powers beyond the national government could not be regarded as the controlling behavior of the state power. It is not ruling. Political parties acting beyond the national government are usually opposition parties. They cannot be called the ruling party. In the state system of government, the organizations and members of the ruling party have a dual identity. First, they are members of the ruling party. *The Constitution of CPC* and other intraparty laws and regulations are the basis of their identity and the standard for their behaviors. Second, they are the subject of public powers. *The Constitution of the People's Republic of China* and other laws are the basis for the legitimacy of their identity and the standard for their public powers. As ruling the government is a legal act to exercise public powers, only when acting within the state system of government can the members of the ruling party become the subject of public powers, obtain the legal qualification for exercising public powers in the government, and then exercise various public powers for controlling the state power as authorized by the constitution and the law. After all, the ruling party should enter the national government through legal and institutionalized channels conforming to the requirements of democracy and then lead the state and society in strict accordance with national laws.[17]

4.1.2 The Ruling Party and the Rule of Law

In a certain sense, modern party politics refer to the politics under the rule of law. Political party is derived from Western democracy. Western scholars

[16] David Held, *Models of Democracy*, translated by Yan Jirong, Central Compilation and Translation Bureau Press, 1998 edition, pp. 249, 215, 216.

[17] Zhang Zhiming: *Governing for the People and the Party's Leadership*; refer to the questions and answers between Zhang Zhiming from the Party School of the CPC Central Committee and the netizens.

have different definitions of political party. Some believe that a political party is a group aiming at the realization of some doctrine; some take it for an election tool; some regard it as a kind of institutional framework for political powers; and some others argue that a political party is an instrument for people to seek public employment.[18]

Marxism combines political party with class interests with the view of historical materialism, which has unveiled the nature of a political party. Just as Mao Zedong said, a political party is a kind of society and a kind of political society. The first class of a political society is a party faction. A party is a class organization.[19] From the Marxist point of view, a political party can be defined as the leading political force of a specific class. It is the political organization formed by the backbone elements of a class with specific political objectives. "Ruling party" usually refers to the party controlling the government of a state. Sometimes, political scientists also use "dominant party" to refer to an overwhelmingly influential party in a specific political party system, but it cannot be equalized to the party in power for long.[20]

The substantive legitimacy of the CPC as the ruling party comes from "three represents," its wholehearted service to the people, and its performance in governing the state and dealing with governmental affairs recognized by most of the people. The legitimacy of the CPC in form comes from democratic election and constitutional procedures. The substantive legitimacy of CPC as the ruling party is the focus of analysis here.

Under the democratic constitutional system, any political power (authority) may face the issue of legitimacy. What is legitimacy? French scholar Jean-Marc Coicaud defined it as the evaluation of the relations between the ruled and the ruler, the process in which the political authority and its followers prove their legitimacy. It means recognition of the ruling power. Approval by the ruled is the first requirement for legitimacy. Getting the approval of social values and the society is the second requirement. Recognition of the ruling power and values by the law is the third requirement. Jean-Marc Coicaud made three points when discussing why legitimacy is also applicable to China. First and foremost,

[18] Chief Editor Wang Puqu: *Basis of Political Science*, Peking University Press, 1995 edition, pp. 263–264.

[19] *Selected Works of Mao Zedong*, Volume 5, People's Publishing House, 1977 edition, p. 335.

[20] *The Blackwell Encyclopaedia of Political Thought*, China University of Political Science and Law Press, 1992 edition, p. 208.

political legitimacy was a political issue concerned by the Chinese people. How did the people evaluate government behaviors? For the Chinese people, what were or what should be government responsibilities? All these questions shall not and cannot be overlooked by the Chinese government. Second, China was undergoing profound changes. In particular, the profound changes that China had witnessed since it was forced to open the door to the West in the nineteenth century have given special significance to legitimacy. Third, the economic reform led by Dong Xiaoping enabled China to enter into a transitional stage. All aspects of society were impacted. One aspect was the legitimacy of the government form. Without doubt, economic growth and its far-reaching influence on the Chinese society came as the source of the legitimacy of the Chinese government.[21]

People have recognized the importance of legitimacy for the ruling party. In the opinion of some western scholars studying the causes for the collapse of the Soviet Union and the dramatic changes of Eastern Europe, the recession of legitimacy and the decrease of trust in official ideology turned out to be damaging to the foundation of communist morality. This led to the loss of confidence of elites, the "emergence and maturity" of civil society, and ultimately the collapse of the system.[22] This explanation may be one-sided or limited to a certain extent, but at least it helps China realize that legitimacy should not be neglected.

Concerning the importance of legitimacy to political rule, Habermas profoundly warned that if China equated legitimate political power to political rule, then China must understand that any kind of political system without legitimacy would not permanently gain loyalty from the masses (to what it possesses). That is to say, it could not always guarantee that its members would closely follow its step.[23] In western countries, the ruler (political party) claims through election that its power is legitimate in the public opinion. China needs to consider why the political party of the bourgeois could win the votes of a large number of voters from the middle and lower class of society and keep consolidating its political ruling in the capitalist society where the working class and the bourgeoisie

[21]Written by Jean-Marc Coicaud, translated by Tong Xinping and Wang Yuanfei: *Legitimacy and Politics*, Central Compilation and Translation Press, 2002 edition, Chinese version, pp. 1–7.

[22]Edited chiefly by Rong Jingben and Gao Xinjun: *Comparative Studies of Political Parties*, Central Compilation and Translation Bureau Press, 2002 edition, p. 292.

[23]Written by Jurgen Habermas, translated by Guo Guanyi: *The Reconstruction of Historical Materialism*, Social Sciences Academic Press, 2000 edition, p. 264.

engage in sharp conflicts and mutual struggles. Democratic election, can defuse conflicts and prove power's legitimacy. The mechanism and functions are not specific to the bourgeoisie. China can learn from this.

Generally speaking, legitimacy is classified into substantive legitimacy and formal legitimacy. Substantive legitimacy refers to conforming to rationality, justice, and natural law, based on the thoughts of natural science of law; and the principle "conforming to the greatest happiness of the most majority of people" based on the theory of utilitarianism. Formal legitimacy refers to conforming to the procedures, rules, and means stipulated by the constitution, laws, and other regulated documents. However, formal legitimacy does not evaluate the value of "good law" or "bad law" of these regulated documents in general.

In contemporary China, there is little discussion about what the substantive legitimacy of political power and power is. According to the principle of judgment commonly used in practice and the ideological line of seeking truth from facts, the standards for judging substantive legitimacy can be "the three benefits" (benefiting the development of the productivity of socialist society, the comprehensive national strength of socialist country, and people's living standardards), "the Important Thought of Three Represents," and scientific outlook on development. The legitimacy of the power of the CPC as the ruling party of the PRC has a profound historical origin and realistic basis. This legitimacy has its historical necessity as the CPC led the people to overthrow the imperialism, feudalism, and bureaucrat capitalism. People chose to support the leadership of the CPC in the new democratic revolution period.[24] The legitimacy of the power of the CPC also comes from the advancement of the Communist Party, the internal rationality of the program, nature, purpose, and mission contained, and revolutionary actions adopted based on this rationality. The advancement of the CPC has adapted to the people's requirements, reflected their wishes, and represented their fundamental interests. Beyond that, the legitimacy of the power of the CPC comes from the extensive democracy and the public opinion demonstrated by electing deputies to

[24] In 1949, the convocation of the Chinese People's Political Consultative Conference and the formulation of the *Common Programme* as well as the establishment of the Central Government established the political leading core of the Communist Party of China. The ruling status of the Communist Party had been recognized by democratic parties and supported by the entire Chinese people, which was the foundation for the Party's political legitimacy. *Social Ecological Analysis of Chinese Political System*, by Wang Bangzuo *et al.*, Shanghai People's Publishing House, 2000 edition, p. 117.

the People's Congress by the people in the socialist construction period. On top of that, the legitimacy comes from the constitutionality defined by socialist constitution and laws.[25]

The legitimacy of the ruling of the CPC in the past and the present is not an issue. But the legitimate foundation for its ruling should be highly valued and continuously entrenched if the CPC wants to maintain long term ruling in the entire primary stage of socialism and realize the lofty goal of communism through controlling the state power.[26] In particular, against the background of globalization and with the deepening reform and widening openness, China has increasingly integrated itself into the international community. This is evidenced by China's entry into the World Trade Organization (WTO), approval of *International Covenant on Economic, Social and Cultural Rights* and other international covenants of human rights, and treaties signed with other countries.[27] China has also participated in the United Nations and regional peacekeeping operations. China has close connections with the international community in environmental protection, energy utilization, economic cooperation, human rights protection, humanitarian aid, fighting against terrorism, and international crime prevention. In the process, China may encounter issues

[25]After several revisions, the preface of *The Constitution of the People's Republic of China* formulated in 1982 made it clear: the Chinese people of all nationalities will maintain and develop the multi-party cooperation and political consultative system led by the Communist Party and build China into a prosperous, democratic and civilized socialist country. Article 3 of the *Legislation Law of the People's Republic of China* adopted by the National Congress of the CPC in 1999 stipulated that legislation should follow the basic principles of the constitution and stick to the leadership of the CPC.

[26]In the masterpiece titled *The Issue of Legitimacy and Its Chinese Context*, Mr. Liu Bin from the Management Department of Zhongnan University of Economics and Law analyzed in an exploratory way that, after 1978, the government worked harder to rebuild legitimacy. The passivity can be reflected in: building a new and negative legitimacy through denying and clearing the far-left route; and rebuilding a negative legitimacy of historical materialism through stressing the continuity of the socialist system and ideology and the socialist system and ideology before the Cultural Revolution. When it comes to the initiative to rebuild legitimacy, it is to rebuild "the legitimacy of performance" through the reform and opening up and build its legitimate foundation through strengthening the democratic legal system.

[27]By 2013, the Chinese Government had signed 27 international conventions including the *International Covenant on Economic, Social and Cultural Rights*. As of early 1999, China had signed about 14,040 treaties with other countries, of which 13,820 were bilateral treaties and more than 220 were multilateral treaties. *Relations between International Treaties and Domestic Law*, edited by Zhu Xiaoqing and Huang Lie, World Affairs Press, 2000 edition, p. 238.

related to the legitimate foundation of the ruling subject, so it needs to keep strengthening and consolidating the legitimate foundation.

Substantive legitimacy is the intrinsic ruling basis for the ruling party. Informally speaking, it is the support or opposition of the people, the so-called "getting the support of the people means getting control of the world, while losing the support of the people means losing control of the world," and "water can float a boat but can also overturn it." Fundamentally speaking, if a political party could hold the power, then it could win the support of the majority and lead the country to grow stronger with continuous progress across the times. Therefore, the biggest concern of the ruling party and the biggest challenge it faces is losing the support and trust of the masses, eventually losing the state power due to falling behind. Ultimately it will fall from power.[28] In the new democratic revolution period, the CPC led the people to fight bloody battles to seek liberation and happiness and won the support of the people. Finally, the CPC under the support of the people won the state power and established the PRC, changing from a revolutionary party to a ruling party. History has chosen the CPC to rule the country.[29] The CPC was elected as the ruling party by the people not by votes in the parliament, but by gaining the support of the people for its performance on the battlefield. In the socialist construction period, the CPC led the people to vigorously develop productivity and keep improving people's living standards. It resulted in an increasingly stronger state and united nationalities, a stable society, and better lives for people. All these visible and remarkable achievements made by the CPC have helped win the support of the great majority of people.[30] All these have repeatedly proved the substantive legitimacy of the Communist Part as the ruling party.

[28] Li Junru: *Interview Record "Three Represents" and Party Building – Records of Interview of Li Junru*, published on *Hundred Year Tide*, 2000, Issue 9.

[29] However, what to choose in the future and "who will win or lose" in the future of China will depend not on any preach and surmise but on whether the ruling party will always guarantee the implementation of "The Three Represents" in institution, whether the ruling party will serve the people wholeheartedly and whether the ruling party will maintain a flesh-blood relationship with the people.

[30] As Deng Xiaoping pointed out, in a socialist society, a true Marxist political party, after taking the state power, must commit itself to developing the productivity and improving people's living standards. *Selected Works of Deng Xiaoping*, Volume 3, People's Publishing House, 1994 edition, p. 39.

When it comes to theories, Mao Zedong proposed the thought of serving the people wholeheartedly; Deng Xiaoping emphasized the standard of "three benefits" (benefit the development of the productivity of socialist society, benefit the comprehensive national strength of a socialist country, and benefit people's living standards) and the statement that "development is of overriding importance;"[31] Jiang Zemin put forward the Important Thought of "Three Represents;" Hu Jintao proposed to stick to the scientific outlook on development; and Xi Jinping has come up with the strategic thought of "four comprehensives" (comprehensively build a moderately prosperous society, comprehensively deepen the reform, comprehensively rule the country by law, and comprehensively govern the Party in a stricter manner). All these thoughts have scientifically generalized the substantive legitimacy of the CPC in governance in different stages and added more requirements for the governance of the ruling party.

4.2 THE COMMUNIST PARTY OF CHINA MUST ADHERE TO THE RULE BY LAW AND GOVERNANCE BY LAW

4.2.1 Legalization of the Policies of the Ruling Party

Policy is the principle for activities as well as the standard of behaviors established by a certain social group to realize certain interests and accomplish certain tasks. The policies of the ruling party are different from state policies, the policies of nonruling parties, and the policies of other social groups. Policies of the ruling party represent important measures taken by the party to control the state power and manage national political,

[31] Mr. Kang Xiaoguang pointed out in the article *Economic Growth, Social Justice, Democracy, Rule of Law and Legitimate Foundation – Changes since 1978 and Choices of the Future*: after 1978, the new government has focused on building a new legitimate foundation while highlighting the consolidation of the legitimate foundation vested by historical materialism. First, it has chosen the so-called "performance legitimacy." Second, it has strengthened the construction of the democratic legal system and built its own democratic legitimate foundation. However, in the entire 1980s, the new government paid more attention to development of "performance legitimate foundation." It developed its legitimacy on the basis of economic development and worked to win the support of the people by improving people's living standards. Entering the 1990s, the dramatic economic slowdown triggered by the Soviet radical reform provided the new government of China another new legitimate foundation, which is the so-called negative legitimacy benefited from the failure of democratic power. This has proved conversely that China's strategy of "progressive reform" is correct. Not all issues can be resolved by democratized reform of politics.

economic, social, and cultural affairs. They are the main means to conduct political activities. Policies of the ruling party are different from laws mainly in the following points.

First, they are created by different parties in different ways. Policies of the ruling party are developed and issued by ruling party organizations. Laws include statutory laws of legislative organs, customary laws acknowledged by the state, and case laws formed by judicial judgments.

Second, they are applicable to different targets. There are some common adjustment objects and ranges. But they also have their respective applicable areas. For instance, both have prescriptive requirements to regulate party members and national public servants. Policies do not adjust legal issues like judicial procedures and legislative techniques, while laws generally do not regulate and adjust interparty relationships.

Third, they are different in adjustment method. Policies are implemented or realized through ideal and faith, persuasion and education. Laws are implemented and realized through coercive force of the state.

Fourth, they are different in manifestation. Policies are diversified in different forms. They can be manifested by declarations, programmes, resolutions, decisions, statements, slogans, speeches, documents, notices, announcements, notifications, and approvals. Policies are arbitrary and uncertain to some extent. Laws are generally manifested as statutory laws, case laws, customary laws, and treaties. Most laws are normal, certain, and stable.

Of course, laws and the political party's policies have some similarities. The most outstanding similarities are that both have reflected the ruler's interests and wishes, represent the order or requirement of the ruling party representing the people to control the state power, and are the application and manifestation of the people's democratic power. As the common social superstructure, both are finally determined by certain conditions of common material life.

The policies of the ruling party are not legal norms reflected as the will of the state. They play an essential role in democratic countries under the rule of law. Policies of the ruling party are decisions made by highly organized people of the society. They are used to guide, require, or regulate the entire social members. The political ruling to govern the state with nonstate regulative forms, regulate and constrain the entire social members with decisions made by a small percentage of people, must be realized by means of legalization. This is the most reliable choice conforming to democratic constitutional requirements. Compared with laws, policies generally lack strict and normative democratic procedures, normative contents, and poor operability. The implementation of policies lacks governing and ruling strength and authority. Therefore in order to realize the leading principles and policies, the ruling party should turn its principles and policies into the will of the state, into laws, and realize its ruling purpose through laws.

In political aspect, legalization of policies of the ruling party is necessary for political civilization. Democratic politics is a type of politics with the involvement of most people. Democratic politics is featured by the concept, belief, and institutional design of popular sovereignty, supremacy of the constitution and the law, division and restriction of powers, administration by law, judicial justice, and independence. Democratic politics require all individual citizens and social groups to act within the government system and the law.

In a society with perfect rule of law, these activities are conducted by law. That means all kinds of social subjects, no matter what position they hold in society, must act in accordance with legal provisions and proceedings when they are engaged in social behaviors and individual behaviors. At the same time, these activities are conducted based on the law. That means if social subjects have the powers allowed and endowed by law, they shall follow the legitimate authorities to further improve their legal behaviors and elaborate the behaviors into normative documents with legal effects. They shall exercise their powers and fulfill their obligations by legal means. Policy legalization of the ruling party is the specific requirement of political civilization for the ruling party to govern by law. On the one hand, the ruling party should obtain its legitimate status within the constitutional and legal framework, behave in accordance with the law, and implement activities according to the principle that "all what not permitted by the law are prohibited." On the other hand, the ruling party should also translate its policies into laws through its political and legal status and authority. The laws should reflect the will of the overwhelming majority of the people, and be taken as the will of the state through democratic proceedings and means. The ruling party should also use the law to control and manage the society and implement and promote its routes, principles, and policies. Political civilization does not allow the existence of extrajudicial privilege. Any organization, group, or individual is not superior to the constitution and the law. The constitution and the law represents the people's will and the people's sovereignty. So anyone breaking the constitution and the law or placing themselves superior to the law means violation of the people's will and power, setting themselves above the people.

From a legal perspective, legalization of policies of the ruling party is an internal demand of law-based order. Every society needs order. The order established in a society ruled by law is the democratic order ruled by law. Since all people are equal before the law, the democratic order ruled by law should be the order of equality. The democratic order ruled by law has provided all lawful subjects with the mechanism and opportunity for participating in political decisions on an equal basis. Exercising the rights to participate in decision-making based on this mechanism is an internal demand of law-based order. The ruling party as the representative of the fundamental interests of the overwhelming majority of people is integrated and equal with the people. Policies rolled out by the ruling party shall also be recognized and accepted by the people in the law-based mechanisms. The best way for the people to recognize and accept policies is to legalize the policies through legal procedures by using the will of the people—the law. The process of making laws by the people is usually the legalized and concretized process of policies of the ruling party. If this process is successfully completed, then it is considered that the policies of the ruling party are recognized by the people. Otherwise, the policies are denied, revised, or improved by the people in procedure or content. Speaking in the language of political civilization, the legalized process of the ruling party's policies is the process during which the ruling party has to accept the test of the people. The policies of the ruling party truly representing the will of the people would not be denied in the process of legalization.

From a technical perspective, legalization of the ruling party's policies is a necessary means and process for transformation of norms. As previously mentioned, policies in technology have some limitations, such as uncertainty, nonnormative nature, internality, and certain arbitrariness. Policies of the ruling party must be transformed into legal and open norms so that the entire society will follow these policies. Transformation of these policies into laws is not simply and automatically to copy the contents and form. Rather, transformation means integrating the policies to comply with legal requirements in form and content, based on constitutional and legal provisions and normative requirements of legal procedures and legal techniques. Through thorough changes of structure, manifestation form, and corresponding legal procedures, these policies would be transformed into legal norms.

Legalization of the ruling party's policies will produce the following results:

- First, the ruling party's policies will be recognized by both the people and the state. As a result, it will gain a legitimate foundation in the people's will in legal system in a real sense. The principle of making the people masters of the country is not just a political system. More importantly, it is a kind of system design. Making laws by the people is a critical link of democratic system design. The ruling party's policies are accepted by the people through legislative processes. It is thus based on the most extensive public opinions in system. Legislation is also an act of the state, so recognition of the ruling party's policies by the state turns the legislation into political will. Externally, legalized policies are a part of state sovereignty. Any foreign or international force shall not destroy or violate the law of other sovereign states. Internally, legalized policies are symbols of the state and the state power. Any citizen and organization of the country must respect and accept the rule of law.

- Second, once legalized, the ruling party's policies would have legal effect guaranteed by coercive force of the state. The legalization fundamentally guarantees the ruling party's policies will be implemented with fairness and justice, backed up by state coercive force, and observed by all social subjects.
- Third, laws are characterized by relative stability, effect continuity, explicit normativity, great authority, and judicial justifiability. After being transformed into laws, the ruling party's policies are bound to have these characteristics, the legal effect supported by these characteristics, and unmatchable by any other social behavioral norm.

4.2.2 The Ruling Party Acts within the Framework of the Constitution and the Law

The constitution of the PRC clearly stipulates that no organization or individual shall have the privilege to stand above the constitution and the law. All state organs and armed forces, all political parties and social organizations, and all enterprises and public institutions must abide by the constitution and the law. All acts in violation of the constitution and the law must be investigated. The Party constitution also provides that the Party must act within the framework of the constitution and the law. The precondition is that the constitution and the law are the supreme authority. But in practice, there is a view that states that upholding the supremacy of the constitution and the law and requiring the ruling party to act within the framework of the constitution and the law is to deny the leadership of the ruling party. This point of view is seemingly to uphold the leadership of the ruling party, but in essence, it turns the constitutional and legal authority against the ruling party's authority, turns the legalized policies of the ruling party against the entire leadership of the ruling party, turns the leadership of the ruling party against ruling the country by law, and against building a socialist country under the rule of law. Finally it turns the people against the ruling party. It is bound to end up with loss of people's interest, loss of the ruling party's leadership, and failure to build a socialist country under the rule of law.

Upholding the supremacy of the constitution and the law is consistent with adhering to the leadership of the ruling party and upholding the authority of the ruling party. As the preface of the constitution of the PRC clearly stipulates: implement the reform and opening up program; uphold four fundamental principles (the socialist road, Marxism-Leninism and Mao Zedong Thought, the people's democratic dictatorship, and the leadership of the Communist Party); and Chinese constitution and laws are crystallized, normalized, and legalized policies of the ruling party. Therefore upholding and safeguarding the supreme authority and status of the constitution and the law are actually to confirm the ruling party's leading authority and ruling status and the supremacy of its policies. It also means the party is using law to safeguard the authority of the leadership of the ruling party, and to implement policies of the ruling party. In this way, the leading and ruling mode of the ruling party could be brought under law. Implementation of the principle that "the party should act within the framework of the constitution and the law" could be guaranteed in the system and in the rule of law.

Ruling the country by law is to strengthen and improve the leadership and ruling of the ruling party, continuously meet the growing material and cultural needs of the people, make the people exercise their divine powers as masters of the country, and safeguard the fundamental interests of the people. Some of the reasons for establishing the strategy of ruling the country by law are to make the political system and legal system meet the needs posed by the establishment and development of the socialist market economy and to guarantee and realize a major transformation of the ruling party's style of leadership and management of the political, economic, and social life. Under the context that the CPC holds the power, the Party's leadership and ruling are the fundamental guarantee to ensure people are masters of the country. Without the Communist Party, there would not be a people's country and people's democracy. In order to practically and effectively guarantee people's democracy and fully realize the role of people as masters of the country, the leadership of the ruling party should be institutionalized and legalized, i.e., to confirm the leading status of the ruling party through the constitution, and turn the ruling party's routes, principles, policies, and other major decision-making representing the people's will and interests into the will of the state and legal norms through legal procedures. In this way, the leadership of the CPC would have the authority and coercive force for the entire society to follow.

After establishing the rule by law as the fundamental strategy for ruling the country, how we further bring the Party's ruling under the rule of law is of great significance to upholding and developing the ruling party's leadership and guaranteeing the ruling party's governance by law. Various levels of organizations of the ruling party are required to follow the principles of the Party constitution—"the Party must act within the framework of the constitution and the law"—and the provisions of the constitution—"no organization or individual shall have the privilege of being placed above the constitution and the law." The ruling party shall go for unified leadership over the works of organs of state power, economic and cultural organizations, mass groups, and all other aspects. The ruling party should play the leading role in all relevant legislative, administrative, judicial, and economic issues and other major decision-making. But the ruling party is not an organ of state power, nor an administrative organ, nor a judicial organ. It should not directly exercise the functions of government agencies. The ruling party should support and guarantee that these organs and agencies could exercise their powers and perform their duties. In practice, Party organizations at all levels should guarantee that state legislative, judicial, and administrative organs, economic and cultural organizations, and mass organizations could proactively, independently, responsibly, and coordinately carry out works based on the requirements of the Party constitution.

Ruling the Party by law is derived from ruling the country by law. It means to implement the basic spirit of ruling the country by law in the ruling party's leading activities and self-building. The ruling party's activities within the structure of the rule by law should also be included. Ruling the Party by law has two meanings. First, the Party must act within the framework of the constitution and the law. The Party exists as a part of the state but is not independent from the state. The Party acts within the limitations as stipulated by the constitution and the law and does not override the constitution and the law. The Party shall not be placed above the constitution and the law. Second, the ruling party must intensify its institutional building and development of laws and regulations. The Party should use improved institutions and standards to vitalize its party under the rule of law and democracy.[32]

[32] Hou Shaowen: *The Rule by Law and the Party's Leadership*, Zhejiang People's Publishing House, 1998 edition, pp. 258–259.

The ruling party has led the people to enact the constitution and the law. It also needs to lead the people to abide by the constitution and the law. The constitution and the law demonstrate the unity of the propositions of the ruling party, the will of the people, and the will of the state. Party members' abidance by the constitution and the law means to follow the people's will, safeguard national interests, and obey the leadership of the ruling party. Liu Shaoqi pointed out that the CPC is the core of China's national leadership. This status of the Party shall by no means enable the Party to enjoy any special rights in national life. This status of the Party shall only endow Party members with greater responsibilities. Members of the CPC must play an exemplary role in abiding by the constitution and all other laws.[33] The words and deeds of all party organizations, party members, and especially party cadres shall not go against the constitution and the law. All ruling behaviors violating the constitution and the law may cause damage to the ruling party, the state, and the people's undertakings. It goes against the advancement of the Party. All ruling behaviors violating the constitution and the law shall be prevented and avoided. Once they occur, the parties involved shall be investigated for legal and political responsibilities.

4.3 UNDERSTANDING GOVERNANCE BY LAW: DEFINITION AND BASIC REQUIREMENTS

In modern China, governance by law means that the CPC sticks to the rule of law, acts within the framework of the constitution and the laws, and leads legislation, guarantees law enforcement, supports judicature, and takes the lead in law observation. Some Chinese scholars have studied and discussed the idea of governing by law. Some have proposed that the following basic ideas should be entrenched and followed unswervingly for governing by law: (1) establish the idea of the people's sovereignty for governance, when considering the source of ruling power; (2) adhere to the idea of restriction of power for allocation of power; (3) follow the idea of the supremacy of the law when considering the fundamental basis of ruling; (4) establish the governing idea to protect human rights when considering the ruling purpose; (5) follow the governing idea of due process in a specific ruling process; and (6) maintain honesty and credibility as the ruling morals.[34] Some others observe that governing by law is the core idea

[33] *Selected Works of Liu Shaoqi* (Volume II), People's Publishing House, 1985 edition, p. 168.
[34]Yang Ping: Basic Idea of Governing by Law, *Marxism and Reality*, 2005, Issue 5.

of modern political civilization and the basis for judging the legitimate foundation and proper activities of the ruling party. In the process of governing by law, the ruling party shall follow the following basic principles: power priority, integration of power and responsibility, honesty and credibility, pluralism and tolerance, and sustainable development.[35]

4.3.1 Enter the State Government System or Government Organizations According to the Law to Directly Control the State Power

Under the people's congress system, the ruling party should handle its constitutional relationship with the people's congresses properly in order to realize its governance by law within the state government system. The ruling party should enter into the political governmental system and become the leading party of government organs through certain means.

The relationship between the ruling party and state organs is actually the relationship between the ruling party and the people, between the ruling party and the people's sovereignty. In this constitutional relationship, all state powers come from the people and belong to the people. The governance of the ruling party is to support and guarantee that people are masters of the country, that the sovereign power is always in the hands of the people. Under the system in which only delegacy can be adopted and direct democracy cannot be implemented directly, the National People's Congress (NPC) and local people's congresses enjoy and exercise national public powers for the people as their representative.

In *A Critique of the Draft Social-Democratic Program of 1891*, Engels said "What, however, in my opinion should and could be included in the program is the demand for the concentration of all political power in the hands of the people's representatives."[36]

In 1919, the Russian Communist Party (Bolsheviks) pointed out in its Eighth Congress that it should obtain absolute political dominance in the Soviet and implement its decisions within the framework of the Soviet constitution through Soviet organs.[37]

[35] Jiao Bo: On Basic Principles of the Political Party's Governance by Law, *Social Sciences in Nanjing*, 2005, Issue 3.

[36] *Karl Marx and Frederick Engels*, Volume 22, People's Publishing House,1965 edition, p. 274.

[37] *Resolutions and Decisions of the Communist Party of the Soviet Union*, Volume 1, People's Publishing House, 1964 edition, p. 571.

In terms of the supervision system, Lenin used to propose the model of "identification of party and government": merge the Party's supervisory committee with the procuratorate of workers and peasants and change the parallel Party and government supervising organ into a unified and strong people's supervision system.[38]

In the period of socialist modernization construction, Jiang Zemin put forward in line with China's actuality that the CPC was the ruling party, and the ruling party's ruling status was realized through the party's leadership over state organs. Its ruling status would be out of the question if the leadership were given up. State organs at all levels, including people's congresses, governments, courts, procuratorates, and the army must accept the leadership of the Party. Of course, the Party is different from state organs in nature, function, organizational form, and working procedure. The Party cannot replace people's congresses to exercise state powers.[39]

The institutionalization of the ruling party's functions is reflected in the constitutional relationship between the ruling party and the people's congresses. This constitutional relationship means that members of the ruling party are elected deputies to people's congresses at all levels and backbone members of the ruling party become main leaders of the standing committees of people's congresses at all levels through democratic elections. As Lenin pointed out, "The people need a republic in order to educate the masses to act in the methods of democracy. Democratic organs are required to set to represent the people. Meanwhile, a mechanism should also be set up for the masses to engage in state administration from the bottom up, actively participate in all aspects of life, and play the active role in the administration." "We need to educate the mass of proletarians and semi-proletarians to learn the art of state administration and administer the whole state power."[40] The thought of managing all state powers is the requirement and reflection of the principle of people's sovereignty.

The CPC had accumulated certain experiences in the period of revolutionary base. The Chinese Soviet Republic founded under the leadership of the CPC issued the *Detail Rules on Election of Chinese Soviet Republic* in 1931. In 1933, the Central Executive Committee of the Chinese Soviet Republic promulgated the *Soviet Provisional Election Law.*

[38] *Basic Problems of Marxism-Leninism*, People's Publishing House, 2002 edition, p. 312.

[39] *Thought of Mao Zedong, Deng Xiaoping and Jiang Zemin on Party Building*, Central Party Literature Press, Press of the Party School of the Central Committee of the Communist Party of China, 1998 edition, p. 555.

[40] *The Collected Works of Lenin*, Volume 29, People's Publishing House, 1985 edition, p. 287.

During the Anti-Japanese War period, various anti-Japanese bases led by the CPC rolled out a number of regulations including *Regulations on Election of the Shanxi-Chahar-Hebei Border Area*, *Regulations on the Senate Election of Shanxi-Hebei-Shandong-Henan Border Area*, *Regulations on the Senate Election of Shanxi-Suiyuan Border Area*, and *Regulations on the Election of Senate of All Levels of Shaanxi-Gansu-Ningxia Border Area*. For the first time in Chinese constitutional history, these regulations adopted the universal, direct, equal, and secret ballot system. In February 1953, the CPC formulated *The Electoral Law of the National People's Congress and Local People's Congresses of the People's Republic of China*. The Second Plenary Session of the 5th National People's Congress held in 1979 adopted the new electoral law. The new electoral law became more perfect after revisions in 1982, 1986, 1995, and 2010. The CPC should enter into state organs through the procedures and means regulated by these laws.

In accordance with the provisions of the constitution and organization laws of the PRC, party organizations can recommend to the NPC candidates for the state chairman and vice chairmen, candidates for the chairman of the Central Military Commission, candidates for the president of the Supreme People's Court; candidates for the chief procurator of the Supreme People's Procuratorate; candidates for the prime minister of the State Council to the NPC through the elected state chairman; candidates for provincial governors and vice governors, mayors and vice mayors, county chiefs and deputy county chiefs, district chiefs and deputy district chiefs, township heads and deputy township heads, town chiefs and deputy town chiefs; and candidates for the presidents of local people's courts and for the chief procurators of local people's procuratorates. These laws have guaranteed that the ruling party could recommend important cadres to state organs based on the rule of law, and that the recommended cadres could hold major leading posts of state organs in accordance with the principles of the rule of law through party organizations and members inside state organs. Party organizations must also guarantee that party members take up the majority in state organs, and the Party plays a leading and core role in national government so as to realize governance by law.

4.3.2 Give Legislative Suggestions through Legal Procedures and Guarantee Institutionally to Turn the Party's Guidelines and Policies into Laws With a General Binding Force

The ruling party turns its guidelines and policies into national policies and laws through its organizations and members in the people's congresses in accordance with legal proceedings, and then realizes its leadership and governance through the rule by law and other channels and means. These are important constitutional and institutional arrangements and contents of the ruling party for its governance. In the people's congress system of China, the ruling party concentrates the unitary wills of the overwhelming majority of people it represents, expresses the fundamental interests of the broadest masses it represents, and then turns these wills and interests into the wills of the state and enacts laws and regulations. The ruling party realizes its governing functions through the rule by law, governing by law, and other channels and means. This process is the process in which the ruling party connects with the masses, concentrates and expresses the people's will, implements its democratic decision-making, and realizes its leadership and governance.

For quite a long period after gaining power, the CPC was not good at turning its guidelines, policies, and propositions into the laws reflecting the people's will through statutory and legislative procedures, or implementing its propositions by enforcing and applying laws. The CPC was not good at governing by law. Instead, the CPC was good at releasing intraparty documents. Party and government organs at all levels were required to directly convey and implement the Party's meeting resolutions, decisions, and instructions to all citizens. The Party's documents certainly have a general disciplinary and binding force for the all party members but not for people other than party members. However, it does not make any sense to require social members who have not joined a political party to follow the decisions and instructions of the political party. If they are required to do so, then there would be no difference between party members and nonparty members. This political party likely considers all social members as members of the party in subconscious.[41]

However, the CPC as a political party, especially as the ruling party, must implement its major economic, political, cultural, military, diplomatic, and social administrative policies, propositions, and decisions that are formed through certain procedures. It requires the ruling party to learn to submit its propositions and decisions to national legislative bodies, so as to turn them into laws. Since the reform and opening up of China started in 1978, the CPC has also started to explore and reform its ruling style while developing socialist modernization, democracy, and

[41] Shi Taifeng, Zhang Hengshan: *On the CPC's Governance by Law*, published on *Social Sciences in China*, 2003, Issue 1.

the legal system. For instance, the CPC made it clear at its 14th National Congress that the objective of China's economic system reform was to build a socialist market economic system, a major policy decision made by the CPC in leading the people to reform the economic system. To guarantee implementation of this policy decision in the entire society, the Central Committee of the CPC put forward the suggestion to revise some of the content of the constitution to the Standing Committee of the 7th National People's Congress on February 14, 1993. It suggested establishing a socialist market economic system in the constitution, which was under discussion at the 30th Session of the Standing Committee of the 7th National People's Congress. The amendments to the constitution was adopted and submitted to the First Session of the 8th National People's Congress for approval. On March 29, 1993, the First Session of the 8th National People's Congress adopted the amendments to the constitution, making the socialist market economic system a common will of the people, which is a law recognized by the constitution. The CPC convened its 15th National Congress in September 1997. The political report adopted at the congress put forward the ruling strategy to rule the country by law and build a socialist country under the rule of law. In order to make the principles of the rule of law by this ruling strategy the principles to guide the activities of the state organs, the CPC suggested revising some of the content of the constitution to the 9th National People's Congress on January 22, 1999. This suggestion was accepted at the 7th Session of the Standing Committee of the 9th National People's Congress. The Standing Committee of the 9th National People's Congress proposed the draft amendment to the constitution to its 2nd Session. This amendment was adopted with an absolute majority of votes, making the rule by law a general principle that must be followed nationwide.

In particular, the CPC adopted *The Decision of the Central Committee of the Communist Party of China on Major Issues Concerning Comprehensively Advancing the Rule of Law* in October 2014, creating a comprehensive strategic plan on building the rule of law in China in the new era. When talking about the background of *The Decision*, General-Secretary Xi Jinping said that the CPC Central Committee had begun to study and consider the topics for the 4th Plenary Session of the 18th Central Committee of the CPC after the convocation of the 3rd Plenary Session in 2013. The 18th National Congress of the CPC proposed the objective of building an all-around well-off society. The 3rd Plenary Session of the CPC Central Committee came up with a top design to comprehensively deepen the reform. Realizing the struggle of implementing the objective the top design mentioned above required a reliable guarantee from the rule of law. Since the convocation of its 18th National Congress, the CPC Central Committee has put a high premium on the rule of law and emphasized that there is a need to boost scientific legislation, strict law enforcement, impartial judicature, and law abidance by all the people in order to implement the rule of law as a fundamental strategy and speed up the building of a socialist country under the rule of law. The CPC has also put emphasis on adhering to the Party's leadership and paid more attention to improving the Party's way of leadership and governance. Ruling the country by law is firstly to rule the country by the constitution. The key to governance by law is to govern the state by the constitution. Under the new situation, to perform its major duties of governing and rejuvenating the country, our Party must govern the Party members strictly according to the Party constitution and govern the state and deal with governmental affairs according to the constitution. The Party leads the people to enact and implement the constitution and laws, and the Party must act within the framework of the constitution and the laws and truly realize the Party's leadership in legislation and law observation and guarantee of law enforcement. Comprehensively advancing the rule of law has a bearing on our Party's major strategies, such as the governance and rejuvenation of the country, the people's happiness and health, and the lasting political stability of the Party and the state. Comprehensively advancing the rule of law is an essential aspect of improving and developing the socialist system with Chinese characteristics and boosting the modernization of the state governance system and governance capacity. We must make an overall plan, adopt practical measures, and take firm steps in comprehensively advancing the rule of law if we want to realize the series of strategic plans of the 18th CPC National Congress and the 3rd Plenary Session of the 18th CPC Central Committee, build an all-around well-off society, realize the Chinese dream of the great rejuvenation of the Chinese nation, comprehensively deepen the reform, and improve and develop the socialist system with Chinese characteristics.

4.3.3 Reform of the Leadership System of the Ruling Party to Ensure State Administrative Organs Act by Law and the Independence of the Exercise of Judicial and Procuratorial Power by Judicial Organs

The ruling party takes the leading role through national government, which means the Party has indirect relations with state administrative organizations and judicial organs except for its direct relationship with state organs.[42] The ruling party can neither replace the government to exercise state administrative powers nor replace courts or procuratorates to exercise state judicial powers and procuratorial powers.

Therefore the ruling party has an indirect ruling relationship with administrative organs and judicial agencies in the constitutional system. This means the ruling party generally does not exercise administrative powers and judicial powers directly, either in the division of functions or in institutional arrangement. Principally, the ruling party requires party organizations and members in these organs and departments to act by law, practically administer by law, and exercise judicial independence and impartiality.[43] Socialist laws reflect the unity of the will of the people, the will of the ruling party and the will of the state, the unity of people's role as masters of the country, and the Communist Party's governing guidelines and policies. The constitution and law are materialization, normalization, and legalization of policies of the ruling party. They are major policy decisions as the will of the state made by the ruling party through state organs. Therefore correct and legitimate governance means sticking to the ruling party's leadership and representing the fundamental interest of the overwhelming majority of the people. State administrative organs, judicial

[42]Jiang Qiuming: *The Leadership of the Communist Party of China and the Rule by Law*, published on *Academia Bimestris*, 2000, Issue 5.

[43]According to the *Minimum Standards of Judicial Independence* adopted by the International Bar Association at its 19th meeting in 1982, *The Universal Declaration on the Independence of Justice* adopted at the First World Conference on the Independence of Justice in 1983 and the *Basic Principles on the Independence of the Judiciary* adopted at the 7th United Nations Congress on the Prevention of Crime and the Treatment of Offenders in 1985, judicial independence refers to the independence of judicial powers and the independence of judges. Judicial independence as a principle mainly includes three rules. First, it is the specific rules for judicial powers. The judicial powers of a country could only be exercised by the country's judicial apparatus. No other organs are allowed to exercise these powers. Second, it is the independent and autonomous principle for exercising judicial powers. Judges and trial organizations comprised of judges or other nonprofessional judges independently exercise judicial powers without the interference, influence, and control of any organ, group, and individual. Third, it is the legitimate principle for exercising judicial powers. Judicial apparatus must and could only abide by the constitution and the law in exercising national judicial powers. This is not only the right but also the obligation of judicial apparatus. According to the provisions of China's constitution and relevant laws, judicial independence means that people's courts and people's procuratorates at all levels independently exercise their judicial powers in accordance with legal provisions without the interference of administrative organs, social groups, and individuals.

apparatus, procuratorial organs, and armed forces should all act by law. All national staff, the broad party members, and especially the cadres of the ruling party in state organs shall take the lead in abiding by the law, enforcing the law strictly, prosecuting law breakers, and acting by law.

Administrative power is established to enforce law. The principal function is to quickly and accurately enforce the will of the people and the will of the ruling party reflected as laws. Most of the laws enacted by the people under the leadership of the ruling party are enforced by administrative organs and their staff. Whether the ruling party could play its due leading and governing role depends neither on the number of CPC members holding administrative posts nor on the number of party organizations in administrative organs. Rather, it is determined by how to administrative organs and their staff administer by law with respect to institution and mechanism.[44] Chinese administrative authorities are responsible for management works and affairs in economy, education, science, culture, health, sports, urban and rural construction, social and welfare service, finance, civil administration, public security, safety, ethnic affairs, judicial administration, supervision, and family planning. The administrative management involves political life, economic life, cultural society, and social life, and in effect uses

[44]Mr. Liu Zhifeng accurately analyzed the sticking point of the relations between the Communist Party of China and the government. In his opinion, the relationship between the Party and the government from the perspective of government administration is reflected as the unique structure of "dual administration" or "dual-track administration" of the Party and the government. That means party organizations have not only the rigorous bureaucratic system corresponding to government agencies but also systematic functions from decision-making to execution. Some scholars argued that government agencies are nothing more than the Party's auxiliary governance system (Hu Wei: *The Process of Government*, Zhejiang People's Publishing House, 1998 edition, p. 292). This "dual-track administrative" pattern lacking strict and normative restrictions on the relationship between the Party and the government in institution and law has brought about quite a lot of negative effects to government agencies. First, institutions are overlapped, and there are too many staff members. The Party's institutional setup corresponds to government agencies. This kind of parallel dual-track structure is bound to cause institutional expansion. Second, the functions are overlapped that has lowered the administrative efficiency. Overlapped institutional setup will inevitably result in the overlap of functions. The Party and the government deal with the same thing without a clear division of institutional responsibilities and powers. At the same time, there is also the phenomenon of separated responsibilities and powers between the Party and the government, so it is easy to trigger their contest for powers and profits, or buck passing, and finally result in low efficiency of administration and bureaucratism. Beyond that, the overlap may also cause decentralized administrative powers that have added management and

the legal norms to adjust various kinds of social relations, such as relations between the state and the society, between government and people, between citizens, between different citizens and legal persons, and between different nationalities. The NPC as the legislative body represents the fundamental interests of the overwhelming majority of the people to make legislative decisions from the perspective of value judgment and interest choice, which have taken full consideration of and reflected the ruling party's governing decisions and requirements to adjust social relations. Under this precondition, the fact that the administrative bodies and their civil servants administer in strict accordance with the law and build the government based on the rule of law has actually demonstrated the leadership and governance of the ruling party in administrative organs. Thus administration by law and building the government under the rule of law is consistent with the governance of the ruling party and the persistence in improving the ruling party's leadership. It is unified with the people's role as masters of the country. On the contrary, if administrative bodies fail to abide by the law or strictly enforce the law, act willfully, seek private gains through power abuse, replace the law by personal views of administrative leaders, annul laws by powers of administrative leaders, or advocate for departmental protectionism and local protectionism by administrative organs, it will cause direct damage to the legal

disposal links, virtually increased the opportunity for rent seeking and rent setting, and encouraged the occurrence of corruption. Third, government administrative ability and authority are reduced, which is an inevitable result of replacing the governance by the Party. Also, the practice of the dual-track administration and the unity of the government's rights and the party's rights have restricted government agencies to exercise their functions and prevented full realization of institutional rationalization. This is reflected in the rough division of labor of administrative organs, in insufficient administrative powers, and lower administrative ability. Therefore it is difficult to provide good public products to the society. Fourth, it is not good for the legalization of government organizations. The realization of the legalization of government organizations should include the supervision and restriction on the functions, formation, and personnel of government agencies from outside administrative powers. Theoretically speaking, this kind of restriction should come from people's congresses as power organs. But actually, the power and status of people's congresses are unworthy of their name and are less and lower than the government. Also, the powers of people's congresses are controlled by the Party's system, and have formed the Party→government→people's congresses relations. In the realistic condition of China, there is no foundation for separating the functions of the Party from those of the government. We could only institutionally and legally regulate the relations between the Party and the government over time in line with China's actuality. *Major Issues on the Existence of Chinese Government Agencies* by Liu Zhifeng, published on *Strategy and Management*, 1999, Issue 5.

relationship between the people's government and the masses. What is more, serious damages would be caused to the flesh–blood relationship between the ruling party and the people, to the authority of the ruling party in the people's heart, and to the ruling party's foundation for Party building, the cornerstone for its governance and the source of its strength.

In socialist countries, neutrality and impartiality are the main characteristics of justice. Impartiality is the core of justice and the value pursuit of justice for realizing its functions as a social regulator and stabilizer. For parties involved, judicial impartiality means that they get the deserved results. For the society, judicial impartiality means social stability and legal order. For the state and the ruling party, judicial impartiality means the popular support maintained by fairness and justice. In order to guarantee judicial impartiality, the state needs to endow a relatively independent status to judicial organs to prevent all illegal interference and intervention. Marx used to express his views on the independence of judges—the core of judicial independence. He said that judges did not have other superiors except for the law. The responsibility of a judge is to interpret the law based on his sincere understanding of the law when applying the law to individual occasions.[45]

Liu Shaoqi once said that independent adjudication of courts was right, and it is the regulation of the constitution. Neither the Party nor the government shall interfere with the judgment of courts. Procuratorates should fight against all phenomena, all organs, and all those violating the law and disciplines. Judicial organs should not absolutely obey the leadership of party committees at all levels. As long as they violate the law, they would not be followed. If the decisions of local party committees are inconsistent with the law and the decisions made by the Central Committee, then which one should we follow? In this case, we should follow the law and the decisions made by the Central Committee.[46] Judicial organs are subject to the law, which means obedience to the leadership of the Party Central Committee, to the decisions of the supreme organ of state power, and the people of the country.[47] People's courts and people's procuratorates should be independent and just in exercising judicial powers. However, judicial independence must be conducive to maintaining

[45] *Karl Marx and Frederick Engels*, Volume 1, People's Publishing House, 1956 edition, p. 76.

[46] *Selected Works of Liu Shaoqi* (Volume II), People's Publishing House, 1985 edition, p. 452.

[47] Peng Zhen: *On Political and Legal Works in the New Era*, Central Party Literature Press, 1992 edition, p. 178.

and realizing judicial impartiality. This is the bottom line for realizing judicial independence in the primary stage of socialism. If the individual, the legal environment, the material condition, and other factors cause far too independent justice and damage judicial impartiality, or if judicial impartiality is destroyed due to the lack of due judicial independence and guarantee, then it should be reexamined and readjusted in the institution system. In socialist countries ruled by the Communist Party, judicial independence and judicial impartiality supplement each other. They are indispensable.

Judicial independence is by no means against the Party's leadership and governance. Instead, it is used precisely to maintain and adhere to the Party's leadership and to implement the Party's ruling actions by adapting to the professional characteristics of justice. Judicial impartiality and independence are the systems designed to help maintain and adhere to the Party's leadership and governance. This is because China's constitution and laws are enacted by the people led by the ruling party. It is also because China's judicial organs act upon the setup of the constitution and the law, backed by the leadership of the ruling party and the democratic supervision of People's congresses.[48] Therefore the higher degree of judicial impartiality and independence, the bigger role of judicial organs in maintaining the ruling party's leading authority and the people's interests. On the contrary, judicial organs and personnel could not make independent and impartial judgment according to the law, if they are interrupted by

[48] In the article *A Revelation of American Presidential Election: Party Politics, Judicial Independence*, Li Yahong accurately analyzed the influence and control of China's ruling party on justice. The analysis indicates that the close relationship between the ruling party and the judicial system is stable and unchangeable in the context of judicial independence. It is thus totally unnecessary to worry that judicial independence would weaken the authority of the ruling party. Li Yahong pointed out the influence of China's political party on the judicial system. First, its leading status in constitution has made it easy for the Communist Party of China to promote its political ideas and other ideas and policies. Second, the Communist Party of China has established strict organizations in the judicial system from top to down, which is extremely helpful for promoting its ideas and policies. Third, most judges who are also members of the Party may be restricted and influenced somewhat by their identify as Party members when handling cases. People often try to convince themselves and other people like this: China's justice is led by the Party, so the Party's idea represents the idea of justice. For instance, many laws were enacted under the leadership of the Party. In addition, as the Communist Party of China is the permanent ruling party and its ideas and policies have long-term and consistent influence on the judicial system, no other ideas can replace them except for revision by the Party itself.

random instructions, approvals, and interferences from various parties. This would certainly damage the authority of the ruling party and impair the Party's status. That is to say, in China, the Party leads the formulation of national laws and the establishment of judicial organs, so disrespect of laws and judicial powers by anyone would damage the Party's leadership and authority.[49] The Party mainly leads judicial works in policies and guidelines. Party committees at all levels should stay firm to change their past customs and practices to substitute the Party for the government and substitute the words for the law. In the past, the ruling party did not act by law and neglected both judicial and administrative matters.

4.4 POLITICAL SYSTEM REFORM: SEPARATION OF PARTY AND THE GOVERNMENT?

In the past, emphasis was put on the relationship between the Party and the government when discussing the mode and path of China's political restructuring. Separation of party and government has been the core mainstream viewpoint as well as the breakthrough and key to China's political restructuring. In 1987, the report of the ruling party to its 13th National Congress made it clear that "separating the functions of the Party from those of the government" was the target and emphasis of China's political restructuring. However, this political restructuring idea proved to be a failure to a certain extent with the occurrence of the political disturbance at Tian'anmen Square. China has acquired a great deal of experience and learned many lessons in the past 30 years plus of reform and opening up, especially in terms of political system reform. Today, China needs to consider soberly and rationally a question under the constitutional concept: Should it adopt the mode of "separation of party and government" or find a new path for "identification of party and government?"

4.4.1 Definition of "Party" and "Government"

In the first place, China needs to define clearly the meaning of "party" and "government" in order to address this question.

[49] September 9, 1979, *The Instructions of the Central Committee of the Communist Party of China on Guaranteeing Practical Implementation of Criminal Law and Criminal Procedural Law*, published in the *Compilation of Documents of the National People's Congress of the People's Republic of China 1949–1990* compiled by the research office of the General Office of the Standing Committee of the National People's Congress, China Democracy and Law Press, 1991 edition, p. 384.

In a general sense, the term "party" seems to contain the following aspects:

- First, it is the CPC as the leading party and the ruling party. It should not be interpreted as one (some) individual(s) party member(s), leader(s), or organization(s) of the ruling party.
- Second, the CPC exercises powers in party affairs, formulates policies, implements management, and other activities. For example, the CPC practices intraparty democracy, holds Party's congress, revises the Party constitution, introduces party members, safeguards the rights of Party members, and punishes party members and cadres.
- Third, the ruling party takes the lead and carries out ruling actions in state power and related affairs, such as suggesting revision of the constitution and formulation of important laws, turning the ruling party's guidelines, policies, and other important decisions into national policies and laws, determining and suggesting principal appointments, and removal or decapitation of central and local authorities, administrative organs, procuratorates, and judicial apparatus.

The term "government" contains the following aspects:

- First, as the nature of state, it means the people's democratic dictatorship and the political power of the PRC.
- Second, as the form of government, it refers to the people's congress system, and the unitary form of the state, the system of regional ethnic autonomy, the "one country, two system" policy implemented in Hong Kong and Macao, and the NPC, the State Council, the Supreme People's Court, the Supreme People's Procuratorate, the Central Military Commission, and other systems of state institutions.
- Third, as the government, it means the legislative organs, administrative bodies, procuratorial organs, and judicial offices of the central and local governments.
- Fourth, as state organs and legislative actions, it means the NPC and local people's congresses and their standing committees and their behaviors for exercising legislative powers.
- Fifth, as administrative bodies and administrative behaviors, it means central and local administrative organs and their behaviors for exercising administrative powers as provided in the constitution and law.

Obviously, in terms of "party," the "first" and the "third" meanings refer to the CPC as the ruling party and its administrative behaviors. In this regard, "party" and "government" are closely related and inseparable. Otherwise, there would be no guarantee for the existence and realization of the leading status and governing functions of the Communist Party. All political parties aim to take and control the state power. The CPC after taking control of the state power as the ruling party has formed a solid and completely harmonious relationship with the state power, politics, and political power.

As for "government," the "first" and the "second" meanings actually refer to the nature of the state and the form of government of the PRC. In this regard, all Chinese citizens, enterprises, public institutions, political parties, and armed forces exist and act in the nature of state and the form of government. Here, "party" and "government" are mutually tolerant or integrated. The "ruling party" should never be separated from the nature of state and the form of government.

In the "third" meaning, "the people's government" mainly refers to the functions, powers, and statutory behaviors of the central and local people's congress, administrative organs, procuratorial organs, and judicial apparatus. In the "fourth" meaning, the subject of "government" refers to people's congress as legislative bodies and their standing committees. The behaviors of "government" refer to legislative behaviors (including legislation, interpretation, decision, appointment, removal, supervision, and so on) in the broad sense of legislative bodies. The "fifth" meaning refers to the functions, powers, and other statutory behaviors of administrative organs (government in a narrow sense).

The relationship between the Party and government discussed in China typically refers to two aspects: (1) how to understand the relationship between the governing functions and behaviors of the ruling party, and the statutory powers and behaviors of state organs; and (2) how to realize an organic unity of the ruling party's ruling style and ruling the country by law under the precondition to stick to the leadership of the Communist Party.

4.4.2 Why is it Inappropriate to Implement the Principle of "Separation of Party and Government?"

In 1978, China took political restructuring into full consideration when designing the reform and opening up and modernization programs. Deng Xiaoping pointed out that China had already included political restructuring in the reform program. Now we feel it is necessary to reform the political system during the advancement of the economic restructuring.[50]

[50] *Selected Works of Deng Xiaoping*, Volume 3, People's Publishing House, 1994 edition, p. 176.

The political restructuring process is the process of developing political civilization. Just as Deng Xiaoping put it, the leading system and other systems of the Party and the state need to be reformed in many aspects in order to adapt to the needs of socialist modernization construction, meet the needs of democratic political life of the Party and the state, and promote what is beneficial and abolish what is harmful.[51] We need to better handle the relationship between the rule of law and the rule of man and between the Party and the government through reforms.[52] Political restructuring includes democracy and the legal system.[53] Only political restructuring could address the issue of separation of party and government, the devolution of administrative powers to lower levels, and streamlining of government organs. Strengthening the development of political civilization and the legal system in reform could better realize the people's role as masters of the country. Lastly and most importantly, political restructuring must be led by the Party. The unity of the Chinese people, the stability of the society, the development of democracy and the reunification of the country all rely on the leadership of the Party.[54] Only an organized, planned, systematic, active, and steady political restructuring led by the Party could guarantee better handling of the relationship among reform, stability, and development and realize an increasingly improved people's democracy. The CPC clearly proposed in the report to its 16th National Congress advancing the political restructuring in an active and steady manner. At the same time, China has also noticed that formal documents of the Party and the state mentioning political restructuring have stopped using "separation of party and government" since the convocation of the 4th Plenary Session of the 13th Central Committee of the CPC. Moreover, separation of party and government is not the key to political system reform. It has not even been listed in the political system reform. China needs to think more when considering the relationship between the ruling party and the state power.

[51] *Selected Works of Deng Xiaoping*, Volume 2, People's Publishing House, 1994 edition, p. 322.
[52] *Selected Works of Deng Xiaoping*, Volume 3, People's Publishing House, 1994 edition, p. 177.
[53] *Selected Works of Deng Xiaoping*, Volume 3, People's Publishing House, 1994 edition, p. 244.
[54] *Selected Works of Deng Xiaoping*, Volume 2, People's Publishing House, 1994 version, p. 342.

If separation of party and government[55] means that "the Party manages party affairs," or "the party manages its own affairs while the government manages government affairs"—the second meaning of "party," or "exercising official powers by law" of "government" as mentioned above—then there is clear differentiation of the functions, powers, and behaviors between the ruling party and state organs. The functions are clearly defined in the constitution of the CPC, other party rules and party laws, the constitution of the PRC, relevant organization laws, and other laws and regulations. It would not be necessary to put forward the question of "separation of party and government." Clear differentiation has been made between party affairs and state affairs in institutions and regulations. There are no direct connections between the activities of the ruling party to manage party affairs and the behaviors of state organs to exercise statutory powers. State organs are not supposed to interfere in and get involved in party affairs.

If separation of party and government refers to separating the governing powers and behaviors of the CPC, jurisdictions of state organs, their behaviors of exercising powers based on the law, then it is not scientific which can only be called "division of labor between the Party and the government." It is necessary to divide the labor between the Party and the government. Except for the requirement for dividing the labor between the Party and the government, the division of labor and cooperation can be found everywhere in modern society with even more detailed and specialized process. For instance, the division of labor and cooperation exist between the ruling party and enterprises, between the ruling

[55]"Separating the functions of the Party from those of the government" is quite different from "the division of labor between Party and government." The latter means that the Party allocates some powers to the government while the former means the government has its own range of action and represents an independent unit. The political report of the Party to its 13th National Congress clearly stated the principles for separating the functions of the Party from those of the government, but in 1988, some local areas encountered difficulties in drawing a clear line of demarcation between party and government while implementing the pilot project of separating the functions of the Party from those of the government under the precondition of sticking to the leadership of party committees. Failure is inevitable in separating the functions of the Party from those of the government. [ROK] Ham Tae Young: *Party Government and Market of China*, Economic Daily Press, 2002 edition, p. 169. The paradox faced by this theory is that it would be impossible to realize the separation of the functions of the Party from those of the government without the interference of the ruling party. However, separating the functions of the Party from those of the government under the interference of the ruling party in itself goes against the principle of separating the functions of the Party from those of the government.

party and the society, between the ruling party and participatory parties, between the ruling party and mass organizations and social organizations, between the central government and local governments, and between central administrative organs and between local administrative organs. The method of labor division includes not only the division of functions and responsibilities, but also the division of powers, rights, and jurisdictions. Labor division is a means and method to cut costs, increase efficiency and quality, and realize a higher level of cooperation and harmony.

The CPC would not be the ruling party if it is separated from the state, the state power, and its institutions. It means giving away the state power obtained through bloody battles by leading the people. In this aspect, a painful lesson was learned from the collapse of the Soviet Union and the drastic changes in Eastern Europe.[56] Even in western countries of the multiparty system, the ruling party would not easily give up the already obtained powers. Leadership of the CPC means holding of power. The CPC must firmly control the state power and must not relax and give up the power for a moment. When it comes to the importance of the state power, just as Mao Zedong said, everything of revolution would be non-existent without the power of revolution.

When handling the relationship between the Party and government under the principle of separation of Party and government, it is implied that in general, state organs are unlikely to interfere and meddle in Party affairs, if no such extreme events like the coup of state organs occur. According to the principles of rule by law, state organs and civil servants are banned from everything not allowed by the law. The functions and powers of state organs come from the constitution and the law. They are subject to the constitution and the law. So long as state organs step into Party affairs without permission of legal provisions, they would violate the constitution and the law. However, the CPC needs to make contact in its ruling with legislative organs, administrative organs, procuratorial organs, and judicial organs, and realize its leadership over state power through its ruling. However, there are no clear provisions in the constitution and laws on how and to what extent shall the ruling party enter into the government and lead state administrative organs. Because the national

[56]When the Soviet Union under the leadership of Gorbachev implemented the political restructuring, it advocated the separation of the functions of the Party from those of the government, upheld that the state was not subject to any party, and the Soviet Communist Party needed to exit from the state management system. Today, it seems that the grave consequences of this proposal in practice are obvious to all.

constitution and laws have no general principles on the range of activities of the ruling party and state organs, and their mutual relationship, their boundary is anomic and their relationship has become vague since the very beginning.[57] It can easily lead to the situation that the ruling party could lead and govern (at least in theory) any affairs of state organs while state organs could not interfere in Party affairs. This relationship featuring power exchange and power placement is asymmetric. When talking about separation of Party and government, the most possible semantic meaning is to target the ruling party for "separation," breaking the ruling party away from state organs weakening the leading status, ruling functions, and powers of the ruling party in state organs. Past practices in political restructuring based on the idea of "separation of party and government" have proved the possibility to a certain extent. Looking from another perspective, during the process of implementing the strategy of ruling the country by law under the principle of "Party acts within the limit of the constitution and the law," should China consider the constitutional arrangements for ruling of the CPC as well as a series of issues confirmed by legal norms?

As early as in the period of revolutionary struggle in Jinggangshan, Mao Zedong proposed that the Party should assume the task of leading the government. He also said that, except for publicity purposes the Party's propositions must be implemented through government organizations. The Party should also avoid giving direct orders to the government, just as the Kuomintang did.[58] These statements are taken as a classic exposition on straightening out the relationship between Party and government put forward earlier by the Communist Party. Later, during war time, especially during the peaceful construction period, the CPC and its leaders proposed separating the functions of the Party from those of the government. More opinions were also uttered about no separation of party and government and practicing centralized leadership of the Party. These opinions on and practices of identification of party and government have produced many disadvantages. It even brought undeserved losses to China's revolution and construction cause. But should China give serious thought to the question of why the CPC faced issues concerning the relationship between party and government in the very beginning of the political power building? The question has not yet been resolved effectively. The core issue is that the

[57] Edited by Wu Zhenkun: *Lessons Learned by the Communist Party in Its Ruling in the 20th Century*, Central Party School Press, 2002 edition, pp. 389–390.

[58] *Selected Works of Mao Zedong*, Volume 1, People's Publishing House, 1991 edition, p. 73.

Party and the government are not separated.[59] Does it mean that Chinese communists lack experience and political wisdom? Or that "separation of party and government" is itself a pseudo-issue? The latter is probably the main aspect of the issue. Seen from the conceptual logic of party politics and constitutional democracy, the practices of western political party systems, the lessons learned from the collapse of the Soviet Union, and the drastic changes of Eastern Europe, the experiences of China in sticking to the leadership of the Communist Party, it can be seen that separation of party and government is impracticable to a large extent. "Party" and "government" are inseparable. Once they are separated, the political party would lose the meaning of existence.[60] Since they are inseparable, the opposite path might be identification of the Party and the government.

We can see from some analyses that the ruling party's ruling status, ruling functions, ruling powers, and ruling behaviors can easily be virtualized under the principle of separation of party and government. The ruling party will find it difficult to lead the people to effectively control the state power and exercise the functions of the state.[61] It is naive or ignorant to

[59] Lin Shangli: *Study on Contemporary China's Political Form*, Tianjin People's Publishing House, 2000 edition, p. 424.

[60] Zhu Guanglei: *The Governmental Process of Contemporary China*, Tianjin People's Publishing House, 1997 edition, p. 76.

[61] Before the collapse of the Soviet Union, the Soviet Communist Party believed that the separation of the functions of the Party from those of the government was to return all powers and functions that do not belong to it to state organs. That is to shift the center of powers from party organs to Soviet state organs. At its 19th National Congress convened in June 1988, the Soviet Communist Party took a major step to reform state organs in order to strengthen government decision making and executive capability. At the same time, the Soviet Communist Party limited the responsibilities and powers of its party organizations at all levels and required them not to make any decisions that include direct instructions to state organs, economic organs and social organizations. The Soviet Communist Party abolished various production functioning departments established inside the party and set up the committees related to the party's works. These committees only took charge of rolling out relevant principles and policies and did not undertake specific management functions. A large number of office workers of party organs were laid off. By March 1989, the number of central-level organs were cut by half, and 40% of their employees were dismissed. The party organs of the governing area of the republic were reduced by 44%, and their employees were decreased by 30%. This reform brought about quite many problems. In theory, it resulted in the conflicts between sticking to the party's leadership and separating the functions of the Party from those of the government completely. In practice, the reform measures of the Soviet Communist Party fundamentally shook the traditional party functional way and method. At the same time, it failed to enable the broad party members and party organizations to master new ways and methods for action, which caused grave intraparty chaos. It exerted crucial influence on the collapse of the Soviet Communist Party.

propose that the ruling party's ruling process can be realized without the legislative power, administrative power, procuratorial power, judicial power, supervision power, and other domains. Could the ruling party realize its ruling beyond or without the state power? Without its ruling in these areas of state apparatus, could it be called the ruling party? The answer is self-evident. To rule the country, the CPC needs to handle its relations better with national legislative organs, administrative organs, procuratorial organs, judicial organs, and military organs. But it should not replace the government and substitute it to exercise statutory state powers. The ruling party should not interfere in organs' affairs. But this is only the question about how to divide their works, which should not be taken as the reason for their separation. The opposite train of thought should be how to realize "the integration of the Party and the government" and how to realize the division of labors and cooperation between the ruling party and state organs based on "the integration of the Party and the government."

4.4.3 The Basic Concept of "Identification of Party and Government"

Based on the spirit of democratic constitution and the rule by law, the basic meaning of "identification of party and government" is that the ruling party leads and supports the people to control the state power within the framework of the constitution and the law and the state power system. It means to organically unite the Party's leadership, the people's role as masters of the country, and the rule by law through the people's congress system; and to realize the people's will, the state's will, and the ruling party's will, which are reflected as laws through the legal activities of administrative organs and judicial organs. The ruling party's leadership and ruling are completely consistent with the rule by law. The ruling party leads the people to formulate the constitution and various laws through state organs and turns its propositions into the will of the state. The ruling party acts within the framework of the constitution and the law. Governments at all levels administer by law. In this way, the ruling party could unify its leadership and ruling with the rule by law in major aspects.[62]

The principle of the people's sovereignty has determined that all powers of the socialist China belong to and come from the people. This is not only the political and philosophical idea on which the PRC relied

[62] Jiang Zemin's *Thought on Socialism with Chinese Characteristics* (special excerpts), Central Party Literature Press, 2002 edition, p. 328.

on for existence, but also the political and theoretical basis to ensure that the people are masters of the country and justify the rationality and legitimacy of the ruling of the Communist Party. In this regard, the socialist China must implement democratic political systems, i.e., the Constitution, because there would be no democracy if the people are not masters of the country, and without democracy there would be no socialism, and the ruling of the CPC. As Mao Zedong pointed out in *The Constitution of New Democracy* in February 1940, the constitution was democratic politics. What is democratic politics then? Mr. Zhang Lan explained it in *China Needs True Democracy*, a long political paper published in 1943. In short, democratic politics refers to the politics in which the people have sovereignty, meaning that the state is governed by the people. Democratic politics in a real sense means that all matters concerning the management of the masses should be managed in the true spirit and good means of the people's sovereignty.[63] In the new democratic revolution period, the belief of communists was to strive for democracy and freedom and implement a new democratic constitution. Otherwise, the country would collapse.[64] In the socialist construction period, the CPC must also implement a socialist constitution for its ruling, which is the fundamental institutional guarantee for realizing the people's democracy and the Communist Party's ruling.

To implement a socialist constitution, all state organs, armed forces, party organizations, social groups, enterprises, and public institutions must safeguard the authority of the constitution and abide by the constitution and the law. For the ruling Communist Party, that is to institutionalize, normalize, and legalize the principle that "the Party acts within the framework of the constitution and the law."

When it comes to the relationship between the ruling party and state organs, we need to be persistent in the Party's leadership and the Party's leadership needs to be reflected[65] and realized through its ruling. On the other hand, we need to improve the constitution and the law, perfect the ruling party's ruling system and criteria, and use the constitution and

[63]Jiang Ping: *The Hundred Years' of Democratic and constitutional Movement in China*, Gansu People's Publishing House, 1998 edition, p. 268.

[64]*Selected Works of Mao Zedong*, Volume 2, People's Publishing House, 1991 edition, pp. 732, 739.

[65]Lu Xianfu: *Several Major Issues Concerning the Building of the Ruling Party*, published on *Selected Lectures of the Party School of the CPC Central Committee: Basic Issues on Marxism* edited by Yu Yunyao, Yang Chungui, Press of the Party School of the Central Committee of the Communist Party of China, 2002 edition, p. 423.

the law to define clearly the ruling party's ruling limits of authority, mode, procedures and responsibilities. Furthermore, we need to guarantee the legitimacy of the ruling party's ruling form. In the meantime, the ruling party's organizations at all levels and relevant party members are required to govern by law.

The ruling party's reports to its 15th and 16th National Congresses made similar statements: the Communist Party's ruling is to lead and support the people to be masters of the country to control and manage the state; broadly motivate and organize the masses to manage national, social, economic, and cultural affairs by law; protect and realize the fundamental interests of the broad masses; realize democratic election, democratic decision-making, democratic management, and democratic supervision; guarantee that the people enjoy broad rights and freedom according to the law; and respect and protect human rights. These statements were declared the Communist Party's ruling purpose and demonstrated the basic relationship between the ruling party and the people's role as masters of the country. Based on the regulations of the constitution of the CPC, the purpose of the CPC, either as a revolutionary party or as the ruling party, is to serve the people wholeheartedly without seeking any private interests. The CPC is trusted and entrusted by the people to control the state political power. It has become the ruling party. Its ruling purpose is to realize the purpose and struggle to achieve the set goals. The objective will not change and could not be changed, no matter what way the ruling party chooses for its ruling to implement the constitutional democracy. Expressing the ruling party's purpose as the legal language of the constitutional system and serving the people are to respect and protect human rights and the fundamental freedoms, realize the people's role as maters of the country, and manage national affairs and undertakings according to the law.

In order to coordinate the relations comprehensively between the Party for one part and the state power and the people's congresses for another, the decision of the 4th Plenary Session of the 18th Central Committee of the CPC further proposed "three unities" and "four adepts" principles. "Three unities" refers to the unity of the rule of law as the fundamental strategy and the basic way of governance by law; the unity of the Party's direction of the overall situation and coordination of all aspects for one part and the performance of functions and powers and conduct of works by the people's congresses, governments, the people's political consultative conferences, judicial organs, and procuratorial organs according to laws and regulations; and the unity of the Party's leadership of the people in enacting and implementing the constitution and the laws for one part and the Party's adherence to act within the framework of the constitution and the laws. The "four adepts" refers to being adept in turning the Party's proposals into the will of the state through legal procedures; being adept in making the candidates recommended by Party organizations become leaders of organs of state power through legal procedures; being adept in leading the state and society through organs of state power; and being adept in applying the principle of democratic centralism to maintain the central authority and the unity and solidarity of the whole Party and the whole nation.

Under the framework of a socialist constitution, democratic politics refers to the values and institutional forms integrating the people, the ruling party, and the state (the rule of law). For the people, democratic politics is the process to present and pool their wills, making decisions by the majority of them. For the ruling party, democratic politics is the process to understand the will of the people, representing the interests of the people, uniting the people, and obtaining the legitimacy of its ruling. For the state, democratic politics is the symbol of modernization and civilization, the basis of justice and legitimacy, and the political guarantee for greatness, prosperity, long-lasting peace, and stability. In a country with a large territory and population but not highly developed transportation and communications, the institutional form of democratic politics is still the representative system.[66] In China, the specific form of representative system is the people's congress system.

The CPC should better handle its relationship with the representative organs of the people for its ruling. This is because the CPC is the party organization comprised of advanced elements of the working class and representing the fundamental interests of the overwhelming majority of the people. This is also because the people's congress is the organ of state power that is comprised of the representatives elected by Chinese people

[66]John Mill, a famous British philosopher in the 19th century, observed that the representative system was the optimal form of government because: (1) it could mobilize and attract the people's wisdom and virtue to manage public affairs, supervise government works and cultivate and promote the development of the people's wisdom and virtue; (2) the supreme power of the representative system belongs to the entire society and every citizen and can best demonstrate the principle of popular sovereignty; and (3) the representative system is the form of government under which the people realize self-insurance and self-service. Refer to [Britain] John Mill: *Representative Government*, translated by Wang Xuan, The Commercial Press, 1982 edition, p. 38 ff.

of all ethnic groups. The people's congress represents the will and interests of the people across the nation. When it comes to the relationship with the people, both the CPC and the people's congress undoubtedly represent the interests and will of the people. The difference is that the CPC, representing the overwhelming majority of the people, is mainly determined by its nature, mission, and task. We say the people's congress has represented the overwhelming majority of the people besides its innate nature and task, because it is the reflection of the institutional democratic election held once every 5 years. If in China it is believed that the institutional arrangement of procedural democracy is more important, once the value connotation of socialist constitutional democracy has already been determined, then it seems that, in terms of representativeness of the people, the people's congress system is stronger in procedural explanatory power, and the ruling party plays a more important role in value judgment. In fact, both are indispensable and complementary to each other.

One of the solutions is to require the CPC members as the people's representatives to participate in the process so as to be elected as deputies to people's congresses at all levels, under the institutional arrangement of "Identification of Party and Government":

- First, embody the value requirement that the ruling party represents the people, so as to realize procedural examination and specific recognition of the individual representativeness of party members by the people.
- Second, realize the people's judgment of the value requirement and political promise of party organizations representing the people and realize the verification and supervision of the representativeness of party organizations by the people in local areas, departments, industries, and units. It's to ensure that party organizations at all levels attach more importance to their responsibilities to the masses and the voters, while guaranteeing their responsibilities to higher-party organizations.
- Third, organically unite the ruling party's political advancement and value representativeness with the democratic rationality and procedural representativeness of the people's congress system. In this way, the political party could always maintain its close relationship with the people and guarantee its legitimacy in form through institutionalized, procedural, and specific processes.

The NPC is the supreme organ of state power and the top legislative body of China. The NPC exercises the national legislative power, decision-making power, power of appointment and removal, and supervision power. The State Council, the Supreme People's Procuratorate, and the Supreme People's Court are elected by, responsible to, and supervised by the NPC. This subordinate relationship between the three organs and the NPC has demonstrated the principle of democratic centralism, which is comprised of the Chinese government and reflected in the people's constitutional relationship with administrative organs, procuratorial organs, and judicial organs through the NPC, i.e., the NPC is elected by, responsible to, and supervised by the people. The relationship between the State Council, the Supreme People's Procuratorate, and the Supreme People's Count for one part and the NPC for another is the people's institutional replication of this kind of relationship. The State Council, the Supreme People's Procuratorate, and the Supreme People's Court have an indirect connection with the people in the political system through their election and supervision by and their responsibility to the NPC. They also have an indirect relationship with the people legally through implementing the constitution and laws. These form all the basic characteristics of the indirect democracy of the representative system. The law as the reflection of the people's will, the ruling party's will and the state, will grant the necessary powers and functions to the State Council, the Supreme People's Procuratorate, and the Supreme People's Court to serve the people, the country, and the society. The law also requires these organs to act in strict accordance with the law and accept the supervision and restriction of the law.

The core of "identification of party and government" means integration of the ruling party's political ruling behaviors, the legitimate authority, and behaviors of the people's congress. In this sense, the ruling party can turn most of the pursuits representing the interests of the overwhelming majority of the people into the will of the state, into laws and policies and other systems, through legislative procedures in the state machine and political systems such as the people's congress. On the one hand, administrative organs are required to administer by law. Judicial organs are required to exercise procuratorial powers and judicial powers independently and impartially so as to ensure their loyalty to the people, the ruling party, and the state through loyalty to the law. On the other hand, the NPC guarantees that the key personnel of the State Council, the Supreme People's Procuratorate, and the Supreme People's Court could be qualified for their legal positions by exercising the decision-making power, power of appointment, and removal and supervision power. The NPC supervises their administrative behaviors, procuratorial behaviors, and judicial behaviors to ensure they are compliant with the constitution and the law. As such, the will of the ruling party to lead and support the people to rule the country by law could be implemented in various kinds of social relations regulated by laws. The people then could truly control the state power and become masters of the country.

"Identification of Party and government" is by no means to "rule the country by the Party." Moreover, there is a need to prevent "ruling the country by the Party." On April 15, 1941, Deng Xiaoping pointed out in his article *The Party and the Anti-Japanese Democratic Government* that the Party's leadership of the political power must be guaranteed in the joint dictatorship of several revolutionary classes implementing "the three-three system."[67] The "three-three system" is the policy on personnel assignment in the anti-Japanese democratic government. According to the system, the Party members, non-Party left progressives, and centrists, respectively, account for one-third of the total. This is the guarantee for China to consolidate the Anti-Japanese democratic government and to win the victory. However, the ruling party's principle to lead the anti-Japanese democratic government was mainly reflected through the guidance and supervision policy and the reliance on its correct propositions that can be accepted, supported, and trusted by the masses. The Party's leadership responsibility is performed based on political principles other than monopolizing everything and the supremacy of the Party's power. This policy is totally opposite to "the rule by the Party."[68] Deng Xiaoping hated "the rule by the Party." He stated that it was the evil legacy of the Kuomintang. It was the most effective way to paralyze, corrupt, and destroy the Party and break the Party from the masses.[69] This evil legacy can be mirrored by some leading comrades as follows. First, these comrades misunderstood the Party's advantages. They thought that party members enjoyed the absolute advantage to monopolize everything. They did not understand that the true advantage should be reflected by the support of the masses. It is unreliable to build the advantage above the power. Second, these comrades misunderstood the Party's leadership by interpreting the leadership as "Party power above all else," interfering in government affairs and changing the order of the superior government. They misunderstood that the Party could randomly transfer cadres working in the government

[67] *Selected Works of Deng Xiaoping*, Volume 1, People's Publishing House, 1994 edition, p. 16.
[68] *Selected Works of Deng Xiaoping*, Volume 1, People's Publishing House, 1994 edition, p. 12.
[69] *Selected Works of Deng Xiaoping*, Volume 1, People's Publishing House, 1994 edition, p. 12.

without administrative procedures. In some areas, government decrees will not work without the notice of the Party. They even developed "Party power above all else" into "Party members above all else." Party members could commit crimes and obtain a pardon. As a result, the masses believed that the government was useless and everything was up to the Communist Party. All mistakes of the government are mistakes of the Communist Party. When the government lost its authority, the Party would break away from the masses. This is truly the most stupid deed.[70]

Implementing the political system identification of party and government is not likely to result in the structure of "ruling the country by the Party." There are a number of reasons for this. First, "identification of party and government" requires the ruling party's members to enter into the people's congresses at all levels by election by the people to realize specific ruling. The people and the democracy elected by them represent the key to determining whether a party member could specifically represent the people's will and interests. Second, the ruling party's will and decisions should reflect the fundamental interests of the people and should be recognized by the people through legislative procedures. In doing so, the ruling party could represent the people's will in the sense of the unity of the form and the essence. Third, the ruling party rules based on the law is to turn the people's will, the ruling party's will, and the state will into common consensus and laws to govern and rejuvenate the country. It also means to exercise its ruling powers in national government within the framework of the constitution and the law. At the same time, the ruling party supervises the State Council, the Supreme People's Court, and the Supreme People's Procuratorate through people's congresses at all levels and their standing committees in order to ensure their actions by law. Fourth, members of the ruling party in the state power system have a dual identity: both as party members and the subjects of some public power. As party members, they must accept the leadership and instruction of party organizations and implement the decisions made based on the will of party organizations when exercising their public powers. As the subject of some public power, they must abide by and comply with the ruling party's will and the people's will reflected as laws. If the decisions of a party organization are inconsistent with the law representing the people's interests and the ruling party's will, the law should prevail according to the ruling

[70] *Selected Works of Deng Xiaoping*, Volume 1, People's Publishing House, 1994 edition, pp. 10–11.

party's organization principle—"the subordinate obeys the superior," and the constitutional principle—"lower-level laws comply with upper-level laws." These principles and institutional arrangements, reflecting constitutional democracy and the rule by law, can differentiate in essence "the integration of the Party and the government" from "the rule by the Party." In addition, these principles and institutional arrangements could also prevent in mechanism the emergence of the malpractice of "the rule by the Party."

Identification of Party and government is by no means to substitute the Party for the government. There is also a need to prevent substituting the Party for the government in system. Based on general understandings, the Party's substitution for the government means that the political party's organizations, institutions, and members directly exercise the functions and powers of state organs, act as a political party to replace state organs to exercise their statutory functions and power, and perform their statutory responsibilities. In this case, state organs would exist in name only. The main conditions for "the rule by the Party" are that party power is above all; the political party is above the constitution and the law; the political party could act beyond the framework of the constitution and the law; party organizations and institutions have the same state with the setup of state organs in major aspect; powers are too concentrated; and some party leaders advocate "the patriarchal system," and "one person alone has the say," among others. The fundamental feature of "the rule by the Party" is the rule of man and the centralization of power. It actually denies the rule of law and democracy. China advocates "the integration of the Party and the government" based on the democratic constitution. "Identification of Party and government" is incompatible with "the Party's substitution for the law" in essence.

At present, many places adopt the party-government integration mode, in which the director of the standing committee of a local people's congress concurrently serves as the secretary of the Party committee. This suggests seemingly that the ruling party attaches importance to the works of the people's congresses. It also represents an institutional measure for the ruling party to strengthen its leadership and support for the works of the people's congresses. But looking from the practical effect, a party secretary usually has no time for work of the people's congress. So it is difficult for the people's congress to make decisions about performing functions and responsibilities, if he or she takes the important position. It thus causes much inconvenience. In fact, the cause for this backfired situation is not the integration of party and government in state organs. Rather, it is the party authority's consideration to the state political power. In this case, the Party and the government are not truly integrated but separated with unequal status. A party secretary "commandingly" and "concurrently" serve as a "full-time" and "part-time" director of the people congress at local levels. As a result, it is hard to avoid the dislocation of the role as both the party secretary and the director of the people's congress, due to the lack of legal definitions and institutional norms. A party secretary may be easily delinquent in performing its duties (fail to fulfill obligations and duties) as the director of the people's congress, due to the limit of their time, spirit, and attention. Alternatively, a party secretary may easily act beyond its authority while performing their duties as the director of the people's congress due to its political powers. The basis for "identification of party and government" proposed here is the ruling party's behavior attribute. The behaviors of the ruling party are divided into intraparty behaviors and ruling behaviors. The ruling party's ruling behaviors should be executed through state organs in the government. However, its intraparty behaviors are not subject to this requirement.

Can the principle of "identification of party and government" be extended to state-owned enterprises? The answer is no. The ruling party must play a key political role in state-owned enterprises to mobilize the enthusiasm of employees and workers by strengthening ideological and political work. This is China's political advantage. It should not be abandoned at any time. The ruling party's role as the core of leadership of state-owned enterprises should not be weakened. That is to say, state-owned enterprises are economic organizations that should follow the rules and principles of the market economy. In addition, state-owned enterprises should build the enterprise leadership system and modern enterprise system as required by the market economy. They should reflect the basic requirements for a clear definition of property rights, well-defined powers and responsibilities, separation of the functions of the Party from enterprise management, separation of government functions from enterprise management, and scientific management. It is inappropriate to implement the principle of "identification of party and government."

Can the principle of "identification of party and government" can be extended to the society? The answer is no. The socialist market economy has its own operation laws. The government takes a moderate stance on the market. Most frequently, the government applies the rule of law to regulate the behaviors of major market players and to control market relations. The corresponding social market has its own laws. Intermediate social organizations should manage and operate based on the principle of social autonomy. The government and the ruling party may realize an indirect regulation and control of the market through the rule of law and appropriately contract from social fields, especially from the third sector. The government and the ruling party should try to reduce or weaken their interference in social fields and the third sector. The ruling party could then concentrate on its self-building and construction of the political power. Also, the ruling party could make better decisions, fully and effectively exercise its ruling power by law, and try to decrease the possibility of corruption committed by party members. On top of that, social capitals could be saved, social democracy could be promoted, and the enthusiasm of social fields and the third sector could be mobilized and given play to, and finally social autonomy could be realized over time.

4.5 CONSTITUTIONAL DESIGN FOR THE IDENTIFICATION OF THE PARTY AND THE GOVERNMENT

Through constitutional ways of thinking and modes of behavior, the requirements of the ruling party and the institutionalization, normalization, and legalization of its ruling by law will be equipped with institutional norms, legal guarantee, and practical operability. Accordingly, the ruling party's exercise of state power could be more legitimate in essence and rational in form. Consequently, rule by law, ensuring that people are masters of the country and upholding the Party's leadership, could be united in an organic and dialectical manner.

4.5.1 Party Members Enter into the National People's Congress and Local People's Congresses through Democratic Election

Democratic election closely links the people and the state through national representative organs and the ruling party in an institutionalized and procedural way. People have formed a fontal political relationship with the state and the ruling party. Marxism never denies the value and function of democratic election for people's democracy. Marx deeply criticized the hypocrisy of the electoral system of the bourgeoisie, but he acknowledged the significance of suffrage, the mode of election as well as the electoral mechanism for democratic politics. He said that elections reflected the true relations between the true civil society, the legislative civil society, and the representative elements. He also said that elections had constituted the most important political interests of the civil society. In his opinion, the civil society had for the first time broken away from the abstraction of itself and become politically a true, universal, and essential political existence due to the unlimited right to vote and the right to be elected.[71] In the *First Draft of the Civil War in France*, Marx spoke highly of the system of universal suffrage of the Paris Commune. He pointed out that the universal suffrage had been abused previously but now had been applied for its true purpose, which was to elect civil servants by the commune for administration and make laws.[72] Undoubtedly, election as the starting point of vertical democracy is one of the most important form of people's democracy.

In 1965, the US President Johnson made a classic speech when signing the *Voting Rights Act*: "This right to vote is the basic right without which all others are meaningless. It gives people, people as individuals, the right to control over their own destinies The vote is the most powerful instrument ever devised by man to break down injustice and destroy the terrible walls which imprison men."[73] Generally speaking, the power to vote has two very important functions. First, the power to vote bestows legitimate status upon the government. All modern political systems adopt the power to vote because all governments wish to attract the public through this symbolic form and add a legitimate halo to their ruling. Civil servants elected through a democratic process could declare that their behavior and the laws are legitimate due to involvement of voters. Second, the power to vote can determine civil servants and in particular evaluate their political behaviors. The power to vote does not empower voters to determine the future, but voters could thereby evaluate their past political behaviors,[74] and enable the public to have the opportunity to evaluate the behaviors of elected officials.

In China, a democratic election is the process by which people elect members of the ruling party, and is also an important way for members of the ruling party to obtain legitimacy in form. The CPC should stand

[71] *Karl Marx and Frederick Engels*, Volume 1, People's Publishing House, 1956 edition, p. 396.
[72] *Karl Marx and Frederick Engels*, Volume 2, People's Publishing House, 1972 edition, p. 414.
[73] Quoted from [US] Thomas Dye, Harmon Zeigler: *The Irony of Democracy*, translated by Sun Zhanping *et al.*, World Affairs Press, 1991 edition, p. 228.
[74] Thomas Dye, Harmon Zeigler: *The Irony of Democracy*, translated by Sun Zhanping *et al.*, World Affairs Press, 1991 edition, pp. 225–226.

the test for its ruling, which means that party members are subject to the people's judgment and selection under new ruling conditions and to the people's democratic electoral procedures in law. Article 47 of the *Electoral Law of National People's Congress and Local People's Congresses of the People's Republic of China* formulated in 1953 notes that the CPC, the democratic parties, and mass organizations should jointly or individually propose a list of candidates through the electoral areas or electoral units. Deng Xiaoping made a special statement on the clause of election in his instructions on this draft law given to the 22nd meeting of the Central People's Government Commission. He pointed out that it should and could be that candidates of local people's congresses are jointly nominated by the Communist Party, democratic parties, and mass organizations.[75] This indicates that there are institutional channels for members of the ruling party to enter into the people's congresses through election. Practices have also proved many times that this is effective.

Democratic election is specific. It targets at individual members of the ruling party and their party organizations. Members of the ruling party need to stand the test for governance in the new era. Under the constitutional system, one of the biggest tests for members of the ruling party is the people's democratic election. Stalin used to express this in his *Speeches Delivered at Meetings of Voters of Stalin Electoral District, Moscow* on December 1937. The election campaign is the court to judge the CPC as the ruling party by voters. The election result is the judgment made by voters. The CPC would have little value if it ware afraid of being criticized and examined. The CPC is ready to accept the judgment of voters.[76] This is the best way for individuals of the ruling party to obtain specific governing powers, an effective channel to implement the "Important Thought of Three Represents" at the current stage, and the process of electing party members as deputies to people's congresses by the people. The formal legitimacy of the ruling party in procedure could be proved. Of course, individual party members could not represent the entire ruling party, nor could they represent some party organization. But if the number of individual party members and candidates recommended by party

[75] Deng Xiaoping: *Instruction on the Draft of the Electoral Law of the National People's Congress and Local People's Congresses of the People's Republic of China*, Published on the *Pandect of Works of People's Congresses*, edited by Liu Zheng *et al.*, China Legal Publishing House, 1999 edition, p. 111.

[76] *Collected Works of J. V. Stalin*, People's Publishing House, 1962 edition, p. 453.

organizations who fail to be elected keeps increasing or shows drastic changes, it may be regarded as "a barometer of public opinion," a thermometer for understanding and judging the fundamental changes of the ruling party's governance.

Candidates will be elected or vetoed during the election. How do we correctly judge party members' victory and failure in the election as deputies to people's congresses? Zhou Enlai gave an answer to this question in a scientific way even before the first nationwide general election in 1953. As he said, China should examine the works and test the cadres through elections. The people's attitude determines the election. If you do a good job, people will certainly elect you. Some people believe that only party members can win an election, but that is wrong. Even a party member can not be elected without the trust from the people.[77] Stalin correctly emphasized when speaking about the voter's supervision on deputies when he said a deputy should know his identity as the servant of the people and the envoy sent by the people to the Supreme Soviet. Therefore he should follow the path directed by the people. If he left the right path, the voters had the right to ask for reelection and make him lose the power.[78] The ruling party's organization could nip evil in the bud beforehand and maintain the ruling party's legitimacy in form if it could regularly, actively, and incisively observe the people's will and common aspiration, timely analyze the cause, and make reviews and corrections in the democratic election of deputies to people's congresses.

Unrestricted power is bound to trigger corruptions. Using democratic election to supervise and restrict powers, prevent power abuse can help guarantee that people are masters of the country, eradicate or prevent the basis for the ruling party' legitimacy from being eroded. The number of communists being elected through democratic, open, free, and competitive elections as deputies to people's congresses by the people according to the law represents not only the test of and supervision of the governance of individual party members but also a specific assessment of party members' implementation of their pledges. There is no need to fear that individual party members may lose the election of deputies to people's congresses. This is because Chinese party members, especially party cadres, should be public servants serving the people wholeheartedly, as required by the Party

[77] *Selected Works of Zhou Enlai on United Front*, People's Publishing House, 1984 edition, p. 245.

[78] *Collected Works of J. V. Stalin*, People's Publishing House, 1962 edition, p. 163.

constitution, and firm practitioners of socialist reform. An overwhelming majority of party members would definitely win the support of the people and the democratic election of deputies to people's congresses. On the contrary, it's normal for individual or a few party members to lose the election. At least this demonstrates that the people have truly supervised Chinese party members in institutional and constitutional aspects.

4.5.2 The Ruling Party Holds Power in the National People's Congress and Local People's Congresses

The ruling party should hold power in the NPC and local people's congresses. This is because after the founding of the PRC, the Chinese Communist Party as the ruling party changed its mode of leadership from that in war times. The realization of its leadership relies not only on its policies but also on the legal system. The Party should make decisions and enact laws for all big events concerning both the state and the people. The Party's leadership is consistent with its actions by law.[79] We need to guarantee in institutional arrangement that the ruling party is always the leader and core of national government in order to swiftly turn the ruling party's will into the will of the state and the will of the people and turn the ruling party's political behaviors into legal acts.

As an institutional arrangement, the ruling party may take the following points into consideration when holding power in the NPC and local people's congresses.

First, guarantee that the number of members of the ruling party in the NPC and local people's congresses is no fewer than half of the total number of deputies. The number of members of democratic parties as participatory parties should not be more than a quarter of the total number of deputies. Therefore the number of the ruling party is always more than that of other participatory parties. The system of multiparty cooperation and political consultation led by the CPC is the fundamental political system of China. Democratic parties as the political parties having long-term cooperation with the CPC inevitably constitute the political leading force of local people's congresses led by the ruling party.

The position and function of the ruling party in the NPC and local people's congresses should be based on the number—at least more than

[79] *Jiang Zemin's Thought on Socialism with Chinese Characteristics* (special excerpts), Central Party Literature Press, 2002 edition, pp. 307–308.

half of the total number,[80] and the quality condition. We should look at the number and quality of deputies to people's congresses in a dialectical manner. The number of Party members as deputies to people's congresses is typically determined by their quality. The communists who can best represent the fundamental interests of the people would win most applauses and support from people. If there is no limit of the quota, the number of communists being elected as deputies would increase.[81] In the anti-Japanese war period, anti-Japanese bases implemented the "three-three system," under which communists accounted for one-third of the total members of the democratic political power, the leftists accounted for one-third, and middle-of-the-roaders accounted for one-third. How do we guarantee the leadership of the CPC in political power and make sure the CPC plays its leading role under this circumstance? In November 1941, Xie Juezai delivered a speech at the meeting of high-level cadres of the CPC Northwestern Bureau. He pointed out that the so-called leadership was to turn the Party's propositions into that of the masses through party members' activities and turn these propositions into reality. This relied on correct policies of the Party and the model of party members. So long as the Party's policies met the interests of the masses, the masses

[80] In October 1949, the CPC Central Committee Northwest Bureau issued the *Decisions on Establishing People's Congresses of Village, District and County Levels and of All Circles*. The Decisions pointed out that party members should not take up a large proportion of deputies to people's congresses or people's representative conferences of all circles in order to avoid the formation of a meeting of party members and party representatives. As long as party members and progressives are dominant in number, the Party's policies and resolutions could be adopted accordingly. The Party should send best party members and cadres to state organs. See *The Instructions of the Central Committee of the Communist Party of China on Guaranteeing Practical Implementation of Criminal Law and Criminal Procedural Law*, published on *The Compilation of Documents of the National People's Congress of the People's Republic of China 1949–1990* compiled by the research office of the General Office of the Standing Committee of the National People's Congress, China Democracy, and Law Press, 1991 edition, p. 365. Certainly, it is worth studying whether the experiences of China in grassroots organs of power building in the early stage of its founding could be promoted and applied to national political power building and to today's historical condition. But this type of attempt indicates that it is totally necessary for the Party's outstanding members to enter into organs of political power. This mode can contribute to the Party's leadership and ruling in state organs of power.

[81] However, China's state organs, public institutions and mass organizations should not just include party members in any time. The idea of only having party members in these organizations is completely wrong. See *Instructions of the Central Committee of the Communist Party of China on Works of the United Front* issued on January 17, 1955.

would become the followers. If party members accounted for the majority, it would mean its monopolization of everything rather than the leadership. This was because no one was being led, and it is just the CPC led by the Communist Party.[82] The ruling party realized its leadership in the anti-Japanese power by relying on its quality but not on its number. Mao Zedong noted that communists accounting for one-third of the total number of deputies must be superior in quality. So long as this condition is there, the ruling party could guarantee its leadership without more members. The so-called leadership is neither to shout the slogan all day long nor to require others to submit to China. Instead, it is to use the Party's correct policies and its model works to persuade and educate non-Party members to willingly accept China's advices.[83] In the harsh environment of war times, the CPC won the true leadership of political power by relying on its quality—advancement, exemplary, and vanguard role. Under the Communist Party's ruling, the ruling party combines its leadership with the principle of ensuring people are masters of the country and realizes its leadership and ruling by relying on its quality.

Second, guarantee that the membership of the ruling party in the Standing Committee of the NPC and the standing committees of local people's congresses accounts for over half of the committee members. The standing committees of China's people's congresses gather once every 2 months. Their membership accounts for 1/20 of the total number of deputies to people's congresses. In this case, the institutional design is convenient for official discussions and decision-making. It can greatly improve the efficiency of the exercise of legislative powers. In practice, decisions of people's congresses are made by their standing committees. In addition, the standing committees assume above 80% of the legislative responsibilities, decide most personnel appointments and removals, and take charge of legislative explanations of the constitution and the law and democratic supervision. The decision-making and voting of the standing committees should be generally approved by over half of the total members. Therefore the ruling party must guarantee that its members account for more than half of the total members of the standing committees of people's congresses.

[82] Xie Juezai: *Issues on Democratic Election* (excerpt), published on *On Democracy and Legal System* compiled by Wang Dingguo *et al.*, Law Press China, 1996 edition, p. 108.

[83] *Selected Works of Mao Zedong*, Volume 2, People's Publishing House, 1991 edition, p. 742.

Third, one of the basic units for the people's congress to perform functions and powers is its special committees. The ruling party should strengthen its leading position in various committees of the people's congress. On the one hand, it should set up several more special committees based on the existing nine committees of the people's congress. This is to further refine their division of labors and expand their coverage. In so doing, the ruling party could realize its coverage in all institutions set up for its ruling and government administration. On the other hand, the ruling party should try to combine its institutions and organizations that manage national living matters, such as diplomacy, finance, politics and law, comprehensive treatment, publicity, and state-owned enterprises with relevant committees of the people's congress to form the organizational system of "the same people with two identities."

Fourth, under the constitutional system of rule by law, it is essential to safeguard the authority of the constitution and supervise the implementation of the constitution and the law. In western countries under the rule of law, constitutional review is one of the most important and cost-efficient institutional arrangements and mechanisms to peacefully dissolve political contradictions, rationally resolve major conflicts, and guarantee national stability. For instance, the disputes between Bush and Gore in the US presidential election in 2000 were resolved through the constitutional review mechanism of the Federal Supreme Court and State Supreme Court. Just as Tocqueville wrote in *Democracy in America*, few issues in the United States did not turn into judicial issues, and they will sooner or later become judicial issues. Therefore all political events have been solved through judges in the United States.[84] The political crisis that happened in the Ukraine in the 2004 presidential election was finally solved through the form of action by the Central Electoral Committee and the Supreme Court. There are many more similar cases. China should refer to and draw upon this constitutional review mechanism and build a system similar to the Constitutional Council of France and German Constitutional Court in the NPC. China should also set up a higher standard of constitutional committee (or "constitutional and legal supervision committee") and perform its function to review to supervise the constitutionality of the implementation of the constitution and the law.

[84]Tocqueville: *Democracy in America*, Volume I, translated by Dong Guoliang, The Commercial Press, 1988 edition, p. 109.

4.5.3 The Ruling Subject of the Ruling Party Holds Most of the Important Posts of Organs of State Power

The ruling party needs to respect and support the people's congresses to exercise its powers and attach importance to and give play to the role of the people's congresses and their standing committees. The people's congresses are organs of state power, and a crucial channel for the ruling party to contact the people.[85] The ruling party should make its excellent personnel (elites) hold most of the essential posts of the NPC and local people's congresses if it wants to put in place the system of identification of party and government in designing the form of government and system. In this way, the ruling party could combine its leadership and ruling with the principle of making people masters of the country effectively in institution.

First, realize the identification of the Party and government between key personnel of the party committees and principal leaders of the people's congresses and between top leaders of party committees at all levels and top leaders of the standing committees of people's congresses of the same level. The Party secretary simultaneously rather than concurrently serves as the director of the standing committee of the people's congress of the same level. When the condition is mature, top leaders of local party committees should be firstly elected as top leaders of the standing committees of the people's congresses of the same level by deputies to the people's congresses of the same level. The selection of the people should be taken as the prepositive and prioritized procedure. This is good for consolidating the Party's ruling status and giving full play to the role of the people's congresses. At the same time, it can help party secretaries get rid of abundant routine works and concentrate on major policies.[86] In the Central Committee, the political power center of the ruling party should be combined with the supreme power of the state. The ruling party's top leaders serve at the same time top leaders of organs of state power, making the supreme power of the ruling party combine with the supreme power of the state. This arrangement can help advance the rule by law and guarantee an authoritative, unified, and democratic will of state on the basis of democratic constitution. This arrangement contributes to a high efficiency

[85] *Jiang Zemin's Thought on Socialism with Chinese Characteristics* (special excerpts), Central Party Literature Press, 2002 edition, p. 305.

[86] Hou Shaowen: *The Rule by Law and the Party's Leadership*, Zhejiang, People's Publishing House, 1998 edition, p. 205.

of state governance; it helps strengthen the ruling party's leadership, consolidate the ruling party's ruling status, and provide a strong institutional guarantee for the guidelines, and policies of the ruling party for governing and rejuvenating the country; and it helps realize, in institution, organic unity of the three principles (namely upholding the ruling party's leadership, ensuring that people are masters of the country, and ruling the country by law).

Second, further intensify the building of the ruling party in the NPC and local people's congresses and firmly establish the concept of building the Party to serve the interests of the people and govern for the people. We must make sure that: (1) the leading Party groups at the NPC and local people's congresses should try to do a good job in leading the legislation, implementing the Party's decisions, and acting in strict accordance with legal procedures; (2) Party groups of people's congresses should report to the party committees of the same level, establish and improve the system of requesting instructions from and submitting reports to party committees of the same level, and guarantee the implementation of the guidelines and policies of the Party during work of the people congresses; (3) the Party could reinforce its work in people's congresses of all levels, have extensive knowledge of the requirements of the masses through deputies to people's congresses, and listen attentively to the voice and criticism of the people; and (4) Party members working in people's congresses should implement the resolutions of the Party and accept the supervision of the Party.[87] Under the system of "identification of party and government," leading party groups of people's congresses should strengthen the supervision over Party cadres working in people's congresses and deputies to people's congresses in accordance with the law.

Third, the ruling party should clearly regulate within the party. Party members should be consistent with the party committees of the same level in voting at people's congresses. Without approval from the leading party groups, they should not vote with personal will. In some countries, political parties allow their members and parliamentarians to vote with their own free will in parliament. In other countries, political parties require their members to vote based on the decisions of their own parties or on the will of the voters. In the parliamentary system, the party discipline is very strict and councilors must follow the will of their respective political

[87] *Jiang Zemin's Thought on Socialism with Chinese Characteristics* (special excerpts), Central Party Literature Press, 2002 edition, pp. 305, 306, and 598.

parties. Members of legislative organs are rarely moved by speeches or arguments to vote against their parties. Otherwise, they would lose the recognition of their parties. Their names would be expunged from the list of their parties in the next election. This actually means they are expelled from the parliament. A successful British politician made a conclusion that he always voted based on the call of his party and never considered himself.[88] All political parties of western countries could ensure that their members maintain consistency with their requirements in parliament. It is a matter for the CPC to require its members to vote based on its will.

Fourth, when exercising its power to appoint and remove the personnel of national administrative organs, procuratorial organs, and judicial organs through election, the people's congresses should follow the ruling party's principle of "placing cadres under party supervision" and try to make the personnel recommended or determined by the ruling party hold corresponding positions according to legal procedures. This is not only a principal measure for the ruling party to control state administrative power, procuratorial power, and judicial power in staff assignment according to the law, but also an important part of the ruling party's governance. According to constitutional and legal provisions, people's congresses have the power to appoint and remove public servants for government administration, while the ruling party typically realizes its ruling through integrating with people's congresses. This guarantees that the ruling party's will of appointing and removing relevant cadres could turn into the will of state through legal procedures of people's congresses.

4.5.4 The Ruling Party Takes the Lead in Acting by Law, Governing by Law, and Supervising Administrative and Judicial Organs' Performance

In the system of identification of party and government, it is not scientific to replace the government (administrative organs) by the ruling party, nor replace the ruling party by the government. People's congresses have the right to appoint and remove government staff and supervise government behaviors of the same level, while the ruling party cannot perform the functions on behalf of the organs of state power.[89] When it comes to

[88] Michael Roskin *et al.*: *Political Science* (edition 6), Huaxia Publishing House, 2001 edition, p. 295.

[89] Wang Bangzuo *et al.*: *Chinese Social Ecology of Political Party System*, Shanghai People's Publishing House, 2000 edition, p. 166.

the arrangement of China's constitutional systems, the State Council, the Supreme People's Court, and the Supreme People's Procuratorate are created by, supervised by, and answer to the NPC. In essence, they are created by, supervised by, and should report to the ruling party. The ruling party's will has been reflected as the law representing the interests of the people, while the law is the behavioral standard and norm with clear and specific regulations on what the action subject should do and should not do, and how they should behave. In this sense, the law is irreplaceable in normativity and operability. Therefore the relationship between the State Council, the Supreme People's Court, and the Supreme People's Procuratorate can be summed up from the following aspects. First, the former answers to the law and the ruling party through acting by law accepts supervision by the ruling party through the law. Second, the former answers to the NPC and the ruling party, subject to the supervision by the NPC and the supervision by the ruling party. Third, the ruling party realizes its governance by law, and political leadership, organizational guarantee, and party democratic supervision through its leading party groups in the State Council, the Supreme People's Court, and the Supreme People's Procuratorate. Moreover, Party members take the lead so as to guarantee the ruling party's leadership and control of the State Council, the Supreme People's Court, and the Supreme People's Procuratorate.

First, the ruling party should be clearly differentiated from the State Council, the Supreme People's Court, and the Supreme People's Procuratorate in specific functions. The ruling party's requirements to the State Council, the Supreme People's Court, and the Supreme People's Procuratorate have been clearly and specifically regulated in the form of law (power, responsibility, and obligation). Therefore the latter acts in strict accordance with the law and demonstrates implementation of the ruling party's guidelines and policies. The ruling party and its organizations at all levels have no need to and are not allowed to exceed their duties and meddle in others' affairs. According to democratic constitution theory, legislative power is to express and collect people's will (usually behave as the stipulation of laws) while administrative power and judicial power refer to implementation of the people's will (usually as implementation of laws). The CPC as the ruling party always represents the fundamental interests of the overwhelming majority of the people. The ruling party, the people, and the state should act as a whole to organically integrate the ruling party and the people's congress system when expressing and collecting the people's common will. They should reach a consensus in interests and consistency in will under the institutional form of identification of party and government. But when the administrative authority and the judicial authority implement the will (laws) of the people and the ruling party, the representative democracy does not directly implement the principle of "combining legislative powers with executive powers." Instead, the people's ruling and the ruling party's governance are realized through applying abstract and universal legal rules to specific objects and behaviors. The leadership of the ruling party is mainly the leadership in politics. The governance of the ruling party is principally the governance with law and governance by law, but not the implementation of laws reflected as the will of the people and the ruling party. Therefore the ruling party needs to draw a clear line with the State Council, the Supreme People's Court, and the Supreme People's Procuratorate in specific functions. The ruling party also needs to manage its own affairs and refrain from meddling in the affairs of the State Council, the Supreme People's Court, and the Supreme People's Procuratorate. They should perform their own functions and fulfill their own duties.

Second, the ruling party should improve supervision for government administrative actions through the people's congress at all levels and legal procedures. The Inter-Parliamentary Union upholds that the supervision of parliament over government originated from a basic principle under which parliament is the embodiment of the people's will, and parliament can supervise all political and administrative activities of the government to ensure its consistency with the will of the entire state.[90] The government's abstract administrative behaviors should be completely included in the constitutional review procedures. A special agency (the Constitutional Council) of the people's congress is in place to review whether government administrative regulations, laws, rules, decisions, and orders are inconsistent with the constitution and the law through the prior register system, constitutional controversy and explanations as well as litigations, among other institutions or procedures. Those inconsistent ones should be altered or abolished. Specific administrative behaviors of the government should be examined through administrative examination procedures and administrative litigation procedures. The ruling party does not examine government behaviors directly through the NPC. Rather, it mainly supervises

[90] *Overview of Parliamentary Systems of Different Countries*, Compiled by the Commission of Legislative Affairs of the National People's Congress *et al.*, Jilin People's Publishing House, 1991 edition, p. 175.

and guarantees the administration of administrative review organs in accordance with the law and supervises and guarantees that the people's courts implement laws in an impartial and independent manner. For the ruling party and the people's congress, this is a kind of indirect supervision through the law in general. The ruling party's supervision over the government through the people's congress is most important to make the people's congress (the ruling party) exercise the financial power and the compilation power for budgeting and final settlement adjudication. This is a general rule in constitutional states. The purpose is to guarantee in institution that these two powers are always under control of the people (through their deputies and representative organs) and that people are masters of the country in economy and personnel arrangement.

Third, improve the system for the ruling party to supervise judicial organs through the people's congress and legal procedures. When it comes to the supervision of the ruling power over judicial organs (courts and procuratorates), the key is to guarantee independent and impartial exercise of judicial and procuratorial powers, rather than replace them or require them to fulfill their duties based on policies, instructions, orders, and decisions. In comparison, when it comes to supervision over government through the NPC and legal procedures, the ruling party could make some necessary instructions, policies, decisions, and orders in institution. This conforms to the so-called government system principle of "administration by law" rather than "independent administration by law." However, the statutory independence of judicial organs should be guaranteed as long as they exercise powers according to the law and live up to the legitimacy in procedure and entity. Only courts and procuratorates could judge independently whether judicial organs legally exercise their powers. Only judicial organs could independently correct their illegal actions under the supervision of the people's congress. If the ruling party, the people's congress, or other organizations, institutions, and parties involved believe that judicial organs fail to make final judgments impartially, or their judicial interpretations are improper and unconstitutional, they could initiate the constitutional review mechanism controlled by the ruling party and the people's congress, acting as the "safety valve" in solving disputes and conflicts. Therefore the best institutional arrangement for the ruling party to supervise judicial organs through the people's congress and the law is to guarantee their independent exercise of powers in the first place and initiate the supervision machine when they act beyond their authority or show misconduct in office.

Fourth, intensify the supervision or mechanism of the Law of Supervision. The Law of Supervision is an important basic law representing the people, the ruling party, and the state to guarantee effective implementation and observation of the constitution and the law. The Law of Supervision should be implemented by a strong authority, mechanism, and means. (1) The Law of Supervision should be positioned as a constitutional law. The authority should rank only second to the constitution. All political party organizations, armed forces, state organs, and civil servants should be subject to the Law of Supervision. All public powers are under supervision. (2) The Law of Supervision shall try to solve the issue as how to supervise the supervisors at the lowest cost. Irrational power structure and unscientific power allocation would inevitably result in the deviation of power execution from the set purpose and target. This is a kind of original drawback and an internal cause for power abuse, power corruption, and power failure.[91] (3) The Law of Supervision should be established with an impeachment system, an ombudsman system,[92] an administrative civil servants' information and property disclosure system, and an amnesty and special pardon system. In addition, there is a need to improve the existing inquiry system, the special investigation system, the budget, and settlement review system. This is to prevent the law from existing in name only.

China's constitution and laws represent the fundamental interests of the overwhelming majority of the people, and reflects the unity of the people's will, the ruling party's will, and the state will. China's constitution and laws are the embodiment of the ruling party's governance for the people as well as the basic behavioral norms for governing and rejuvenating the country. In this connection, that the ruling party's organizations at all levels and its entire members abiding by the constitution and the law is to safeguard the people's interests wholeheartedly, respect the will of the people, and follow the ruling party's leadership. The words and deeds of all party organizations, party members, and especially responsible cadres should not collide with the constitution and the law.[93] Under the

[91] Zheng Keyang and Li Zhongjie: *Study on the Important Thought of Three Represents*, Sichuan People's Publishing House, 2002 edition, p. 331.

[92] The Swedish Ombudsman System, established more than 200 years ago, can be copied or learned for relevant contents. Refer to [Sweden] Bengt Wieslander: *The Parliamentary Ombudsman in Sweden*, translated by Cheng Jie, Tsinghua University Press, 2001 edition.

[93] Jiang Zemin: *On Adhering to and Improving the People's Congress System*, published on *Selected Important Documents Since the Thirteenth Party Congress*, Volume II, pp. 943–944.

system of identification of party and government, the ruling party should take the lead in acting by law, exercise the decision-making power, the legislative power, the power to appoint and remove personnel, and the supervision power according to the law. The ruling party should make sure that administrative organs administer by law, judicial organs exercise powers independently, and the people manage national, social, economic, and cultural affairs according to the law. Party committees and governments at all levels should set an example in implementing the constitution and the law, prevent and correct the misconducts to use words to replace the law, use power to suppress the law, and interfere in law enforcement. In the meantime, there is a need to firmly correct the behaviors that are noncompliance with the law, slack law enforcement and unpunished law breakers.[94] The power of the ruling party is bestowed by the people. Party cadres at all levels are servants of the people no matter what positions they are holding in national government. Therefore they must be subject to the supervision of the people and the law. It is necessary to establish and improve the restriction mechanism and supervision mechanism to strengthen inner-party supervision, legal supervision, and the supervision by the masses, so as to exercise power in accordance with the law.[95]

Of course, "identification of party and government" is always relative, conditional, and diversified. It is only an optional idea and institutional mode but not a panacea to solve all issues related to relations between the Party and the government. It is just a kind of exploration and interpretation. It has to be tested. It needs modification and improvement in practices. So long as we act upon China's national conditions, the standard of "three helps," and the dynamic balance to maintain the coordination of reform, stability, and development, we could build a new type of relationship between the Party and the government of China's socialist political civilization when stick to an organic unity of upholding the Party's leadership. The purpose is to ensure that the people are masters of the country and rule the country by law under the organic unification of ruling the country by law and the ruling style of the ruling party.

[94] *Jiang Zemin's Thought on Socialism with Chinese Characteristics* (special excerpts), Central Party Literature Press, 2002 edition, pp. 332, 333.

[95] *Jiang Zemin's Thought on Socialism with Chinese Characteristics* (special excerpts), Central Party Literature Press, 2002 edition, p. 429.

4.6 SOME PROBLEMS AND THE NEED FOR SOLUTIONS IN ADVANCING GOVERNANCE BY LAW IN CHINA

The ruling party has proposed to insist on ruling by law and keep improving the capacity for and level of governance by law. But there are still many difficulties, obstacles, and challenges to truly realize administration by law. At this point, the following three issues need to be studied and solved.

4.6.1 The Subject of Ruling by Law

Ruling by law will not only induce profound changes of the Party's leading system and style, but also exert great influence on construction of the rule of law in China. For the rule of law, legal subject, legal act, and legal liability represent the three inevitable major elements for study of law and legal practice. Therefore China must study issues related to the subject of governance by law.

The subject is the basic element of ruling by law. Without the subject, there would be no ruling by law. The broad masses are the subjects of rule by law. State administrative organs at all levels are the subject of administration by law. Judicial organs at all levels are the subjects of impartial judicature. So, what is the subject of ruling by law? It seems to be an undisputed question, but it may cause confusion in theory and damage practice without a clear answer. In modern party politics, the subject of ruling by law is certainly the ruling party, which is the political party controlling state political power and implementing, promoting, and realizing its programs, guidelines, policies, and propositions through daily activities of the state organs. In western countries, the ruling party usually refers to the political party controlling the supreme administrative power of the state, no matter whether it is the majority of the representative institution, whether it has completely controlled the legislative power of the parliament, or whether it has controlled other state organs and local government agencies. In western countries, a political party's ruling status is neither formed in history nor changeable. Instead, the ruling status is determined by general election held every few years. The political party that wins the election obtains the legal status as the ruling party. In western countries adopting the parliamentary system, the political party or the alliance of political parties securing the majority of seats in the parliamentary election has the right to form the cabinet, and will become the ruling party when it has all or the main seats of the cabinet. In countries adopting the presidential system, the political party or the alliance of political parties of the president elected in the general election is the ruling party. In contemporary China, determination of the status of the CPC as the ruling party is different from that of western countries. The rationality and legitimacy of the CPC in ruling is formed in history, and determined by the practical needs, nature, and purpose of the Communist Party. This is the system that has already been recognized and fixed by the constitution and the law of China.

It is undoubted in theory that the CPC is the subject of ruling by law, but more discussions are needed on some specific issues. Some say that the subject of the governance of the CPC by law is the entire party members. Others believe that the subject of ruling by law is the representatives of party members assigned by the committee of the ruling party to the organs of state power to assume leading positions. Some others argue that the subject is party organizations of the organs of state power at all levels, and some others observe that the subject includes all party organizations. The CPC has a total of 87 million members. If the subject of ruling by law is the entire party members, then China would have 87 million governing subjects. Apparently, it seems that every party member is a subject of governance, but actually everyone is not the subject of governance. Therefore China believes that the subject of ruling by law should not be all the party members. According to the provisions of *The Constitution of the CPC*, the main task of the state organs' party groups is to implement the Party's guidelines and policies, discuss and determine major issues of the unit, and do a good job in cadre management. But party groups of state organs should not and could not exercise administrative functions and powers in their own names. As such, party groups of state organs at all levels should not become the subject of governance. A party group should be established in Chinese enterprises, schools, scientific research institutions, social organizations, social intermediary organizations, city communities, and villages, among other units, when the number of party members reaches a certain amount. These party groups are not the leading-level institutions of state power. They are obviously not the subject of governance. Also, we could not say that the subject of governance is the representatives of party members assuming leading posts in the organs of state power. This is because the CPC is the only political party that governs directly and steadily in the long run. This is different from the indirect ruling, backstage ruling, and rotator ruling in western countries' political systems. Ruling party has a broader meaning compared than that of western countries. The CPC as the ruling party should not only lead the supreme organ of state power—the NPC—but also lead the supreme administrative organ of the state—the State Council. At the same time, the ruling party directly leads the Supreme

People's Court and the Supreme People's Procuratorate. The representatives of party members sent by the Party Committee to state organs to assume leading posts are only members of the ruling party. They could only represent the ruling party to exercise part of the ruling power. Thus it is improper to take them as the subject of governance. The subject of the ruling by law advocated by China is the CPC, the Central Committee of the Party, and local party committees as a whole. The Party's NPC and its Central Committee exercise the supreme ruling power. The supreme ruling power would be exercised by the Political Bureau of the Central Committee and its Standing Committee when the congress is not in session. Local party committees exercise the governing power of local areas under the unified leadership of the Central Committee. In order to guarantee the Party's ruling by law, it is necessary to use legal forms and the Party constitution to determine the subject of governance and clearly define the specific ruling authority of the Central Committee and local committees.

4.6.2 The Mode of Ruling by Law

What is the nature of the ruling party's governing behavior and power? What should be the governing style? These questions need to be analyzed and studied seriously. In western countries using the presidential system or the parliamentary system, only the political party that wins the general election can control the state power and become the ruling party. The principal way of controlling the state power is to control the administrative power, the legislative power, the judicial power, and the military power to different degrees. Taking the United States as an example, the president winning the presidential election is entitled to the nomination and direct appointment of nearly 4000 political officials loyal to his or her party. The ruling party in western countries only controls the administrative power because all acts, government budgets, major decision-making, government organizations, and crucial personnel appointment and removal shall be presented to the parliament. They can only be adopted and implemented with the approval and recognition of the parliament. The ruling party can not necessarily control the parliament. Judicial organs are independent from not only administrative and legislative organs but also political parties. Judges, no matter if they are appointed, elected, or examined, are not allowed to join in any political party nor participate in their activities. Political party organizations are not allowed to give orders to courts and judges. Even the president, the prime minister, and ministers find it difficult to control the judges they appointed. So the control of the ruling party over judicial power is limited. Of course, the ruling party needs to try its utmost to influence the legislative power and the judicial power. The CPC has been holding power directly for a long time. Its holding of power is overall leadership of the state and the society. Its holding of power is broad in content and range. Therefore the ruling party must adopt a scientific, rational, and legitimate ruling mode.

The ruling power of the CPC is one with Chinese characteristics and different from that of the countries implementing the "tripartite" political system. The ruling power of the CPC is also different from the national public power, which has direct coercive power toward citizens and legal persons in a traditional sense. The ruling power is a special public power that can directly control state powers including the legislative power, administrative power, judicial power, military power, and legal supervision power. The way of exercising this kind of power over the past several decades is rarely regulated by laws. For instance, in China's ruling practice, state leaders are all nominated by the Central Committee of the CPC and elected or determined by the NPC, including the Chinese chairman, vice-chairman, chairman, and vice-chairman of the Standing Committee of the National People's Congress, premier and vice-premier of the State Council, state councilor, chairman and vice-chairman of the Central Military Commission, president of the Supreme People's Court, and chief procurator of the Supreme People's Procuratorate. But there are no provisions on the nomination of the ruling party in China's constitution and relevant laws. This phenomenon also exists extensively in the formation process of local organs of political power. There is a need to reform the governing style.

First, regulate the specific ruling scope of the CPC in accordance with the law. It is the premise for reforming and improving the governing style. The ruling power of the Party is the Party's leadership in politics, organizations, and thoughts of the country and society. Specifically speaking, it includes the power to develop policies, to lead the legislation, to guarantee the supervision over law enforcement, judicature and the law, to direct military affairs, to recommend and manage cadres, to guide the propaganda and ideology, and to make decisions in macro-economic and social affairs. This is the general sense of the ruling power. In-depth studies are required for specific scope and areas. We could only adopt the practical and effective mode of ruling after a scientific definition of the scope of the ruling power.

Second, a primary and tough task for realizing ruling by law is to make the mode of ruling more scientific, normative, and legalized. A more scientific mode of ruling means that the CPC must adopt and choose the mode of ruling that adapts to China's social conditions. The ruling party's leadership over the state power is realized through the leading and core role in the state power rather than beyond the state power or above the state power.[96] At present, the Party is working to transform its ruling from mainly relying on policies to mainly relying on the law; from strictly emphasizing the abidance by the law to not only strictly abiding by the law but also actively creating and applying the law; and from a separate implementation of strengthening its own institutional improvement and leading the country to building the rule of law to their synchronized advancement, united in ruling the country by law and building a socialist country under the rule of law.[97] The mode of ruling of the CPC is diversified in form, including formulating fundamental policies, proposing legislative proposals, recommending important cadres, carrying out ideological publicity, and giving play to the representative role of party members. So there is a need to regulate the specific mode of ruling. Making the mode of ruling under the rule of law means making all ruling behavioral processes and other activities leading the state strictly conform to the standard set by the law, the normative spirit, and value of the law. The mode of ruling is brought under the rule of law in three links. First is the obtaining of the ruling power. Second is the application of the ruling power. Third is the supervision of the ruling power.[98]

4.6.3 The Liability for Breaking the Law in Ruling

Legal liability generally refers to the compulsory and adverse legal consequences assumed by the people for their illegal acts. Legal liability is closely linked with illegal acts. They have a causal relationship. There would be no legal liability without illegal act. Only legal persons and organizations who have conducted illegal acts would assume corresponding legal consequences, i.e., legal liabilities. The main features of legal liability includes: first, there must be clear and specific requirements and regulations in law; second, there must be coercive force of the state to guarantee the realization of legal liability; and third, there must be statutory state organs to investigate, affix legal liabilities, and implement legal sanctions in accordance with the law. No other organizations or individuals have the right to exercise the power.

[96] Shi Taifeng, Zhang Hengshan: On the Exercise of State Power by the Communist Party of China, *Social Sciences in China*, 2003, Issue 1.

[97] Yuan Shuhong: Major Theoretical and Practical Questions of the Party's Ruling by Law, *Journal of Chinese Academy Of Governance*, 2006, Issue 1.

[98] Qing Hong: Nomological Analysis of the Elements of Ruling by law, *Journal of Sichuan Administration College*, 2004, Issue 4.

Legal liability is the life of the rule of law. There would be no rule of law without legal liability. Ruling by law is a major issue of the rule of law. So there is a need to implement ruling responsibilities in order to realize the ruling by law. Otherwise, the ruling by law would be a meaningless term. It would not be implemented in the right place.

The constitution of China clearly stipulates that all state organs, armed forces, political parties, social organizations, enterprises, public institutions, and organizations must abide by the constitution and the law. All acts violating the constitution and the law must be investigated and prosecuted.

The CPC has put in place the system under which the Political Bureau of the Central Committee of the CPC reports to the Plenary Session of Central Committee of the CPC. The CPC has also formulated *The Inner-party Supervision Regulations* and *The Regulation of the CPC on Disciplinary Actions*, which clearly regulates leading party organs and leading party cadres at all levels as the key supervision objects inside the party, especially the person in charge of leading groups at all levels. The CPC has also established critical supervision systems for reporting the work and anticorruption performance, making inspection tours, having talks, persuading and cautioning, removing and replacing of posts.

Ruling responsibility is a new and important question that merits in-depth studies. Both the subject and form of responsibility have demonstrated the complexity and specificity, involving not only party organizations at all levels, party members, as well as leading cadres, but also political responsibility, moral responsibility, party discipline responsibility, and legal liability. China should attach importance to implementation of the Party's guidelines and policies by local party committees, their abidance to the constitution and the law, and major policy decisions. China should also value the ruling responsibility in appointing cadres and building of an incorruptible government. On top of that, China should highlight the ruling responsibility of the Party's leading cadres, especially senior cadres and principals of leading groups.[99] For that matter, in-depth research must be conducted on the responsibility in ruling by law, including the subject of responsibility, specific responsibility form, and the subject and procedure of accountability. Only when the responsibilities are clearly defined could the ruling by law be realized.

[99]Yuan Shuhong: Major Theoretical and Practical Questions of the Party's Ruling by Law, *Journal of Chinese Academy Of Governance*, 2006, Issue 1.

CHAPTER 5

Uniformity of the Party and the Law

After the founding of the New China, how to deal with the relations between the Party and the law became an important theoretical and practical question that was unevadable. In the past when class struggle was taken as the core, the relations between the rule of law and the Party's leadership and between the law and the Party's policy were usually understood as antagonistic and separate. Advocating for the rule of law was taken as denying the Party's leadership. Independently holding cases according to the law by the people's courts and the people's procuratorates was taken as "seeking independence from the Party." State organs and civil servants' acting by law was regarded as the policy of using the law to suppress the Party. These resulted in the tragedy of the 10-year Cultural Revolution, during which the legal system was sabotaged and democracy was trampled. Cases in point were "thoroughly smashing the public security bureaus, the people's courts, and the people's procuratorates" and "respecting no law and order." After the implementation of the reform and opening up program in 1978, the Communist Part of China (CPC) put wrongs to rights in the democratic and legal systems, identified the basic principle of developing socialist democracy and improving the socialist legal system, and set out the basic principle that the Party must act within the framework of the constitution and the law. The CPC also specified the basic mutually supplementary relations between the Party's policy and the law and abandoned the practice of reviewing and approving cases by Party committees. In particular, after establishing the rule of law as the fundamental strategy at the 15th National Congress of the CPC, the CPC proposed that sticking to an organic unity of the Party's leadership, the people's role as masters of the country, and the rule of law is an intrinsic requirement and essential feature of the socialist democracy with Chinese characteristics. The CPC also put forward a host of new principles, new ideas, and new measures for strengthening the building of the Party and the state under the rule of law, such as adhering to democratic governance, scientific governance, governance by law, taking the lead in legislation and

Building the Rule of Law in China.
DOI: http://dx.doi.org/10.1016/B978-0-12-811930-3.00005-2

law observation, guaranteeing law enforcement and supporting judicature, and preserving in the common advancement of the rule by law, governance by law, and administration by law. In this way, the CPC has well interpreted and straightened out the important relations between the ruling party and the law, between the Party's policy and Chinese constitution and laws, between the Party's leadership and the rule by law, and between the Party's leadership and handling of judicial cases. The CPC has also guided, guaranteed, and propelled smooth progress of the building of the rule of law in China and the cause of ruling the country by law.

In the development process of China's socialist democracy and rule of law, there are unceasing arguments about the relations between the Party (mainly refers to the CPC, the leadership of the CPC, etc.) and the law (chiefly refers to the constitution and the laws, socialist rule of law, the rule by law, the building of the rule of law, etc.). In China, the question regarding the relations between the Party and the law, or the question of "whether the Party or the law is superior," is not only a question about the rule of law but also a political issue; it is not just a theoretical problem, but also a practical problem. General-Secretary Xi Jinping pointed out that the relationship between the Party and the law is a fundamental issue. Properly handling the issue will lead to the development of the rule of law, the Party, and the state; otherwise, it will result in the recession of the rule of law, the Party, and the state. The Party's leadership is the spirit of the socialist rule of law with Chinese characteristics.

The relationship between the CPC and the socialist rule of law is the core of the building of the rule of law. The key to comprehensively advancing the rule by law is determining whether the direction is right and the political guarantee is strong. Specifically speaking, we need to keep to the Party's leadership, adhere to the socialist system with Chinese characteristics, and implement the theory of socialist rule of law with Chinese characteristics. The Party's leadership is the most essential feature of socialism with Chinese characteristics and the most fundamental guarantee of the socialist rule of law. The socialist system with Chinese characteristics is the fundamental institutional foundation of the system of socialist rule of law with Chinese characteristics and the fundamental institutional guarantee of comprehensive advancement of the rule by law. The theory of socialist rule of law with Chinese characteristics is theoretical guidance and scientific support of the system of socialist rule of law with Chinese characteristics and the guide to action for a comprehensive advancement of the rule by law. These three aspects are in essence the core idea of the path of socialist rule of law with Chinese characteristics and have stipulated and ensured the institutional attribute and direction of the system of socialist rule of law with Chinese characteristics.

In China, keeping to the leadership of the CPC is the fundamental requirement of the socialist rule of law, and is essential to the Party and the state. Keeping to the leadership of the CPC is related to the interests and happiness of the Chinese people of all ethnic groups, and is the main idea of comprehensively advancing the rule of law. The leadership of the CPC and the socialist rule of law are consistent in essence and unified in theoretical logic and practical process. The socialist rule of law must adhere to the leadership of the Party while the leadership of the Party must rely on the socialist rule of law. This is the fundamental feature of the road of socialist rule of law with Chinese characteristics.

To comprehensively advance the rule by law, build the system of socialist rule of law with Chinese characteristics, and build a socialist country under the rule of law, we must give a direct answer to the question about the relations between the Party and the law based on the combination of theories and practices, history, and realities. As such, we could more consciously keep to a high degree of uniformity of the Party and the law in specific practices of comprehensively advancing the rule of law.

5.1 CONCEPTUAL CATEGORIES OF THE PARTY AND THE LAW

In the Chinese context, we should make clear the conceptual categories of the Party and the law and the main relations involved before discussing the relations between the Party and the law, answering the question about "whether the Party or the law is superior," and sticking to a high degree of unity of the Party and the law.

5.1.1 Conceptual Category of the Party

First, from the perspective of the full name, the "Party" herein refers to the Communist Party of China, excluding other party organizations or social groups. According to *The Constitution of the Communist Party of China*, the Party is the vanguard of the Chinese working class, the Chinese people, and the Chinese nation; the Party is the core of leadership of the socialist cause with Chinese characteristics; and the Party has no special interests of its own except for the interests of the working class and the overwhelming majority of the people. According to *The Constitution of the People's*

Republic of China, the Party is the leading party of the state power of the People's Republic of China, and the Party must act on the basis of the constitution. Also, the Party is the ruling party responsible for maintaining the dignity and guaranteeing the implementation of the constitution.

Second, from the perspective of the subject, the "Party" herein is a collective concept including such main parts as all members of the CPC, Party leaders, Party organizations of all levels, and Party organs of all kinds, which means an individual entity is only part or a member of the Party, and should not be simply equalized to the Party. Their words and deeds may represent the image, authority, and will of the Party in a limited sense, but cannot be simply equalized to that of the Party.

Third, from the perspective of leading and governing behaviors, the Party herein sometimes has a transferred meaning, such as the Party's leadership, the Party's governance, the Party's policy, the Party's decision-making, the Party's document, the Party Committee's decision, organization opinion, a leader's speech, a party secretary's instruction, or an order of the superior. All these are important methods for the CPC and its organizations and leading cadres of all levels to fulfill the Party's purpose, implement the Party's leadership, carry out governing activities, and lead the masses to rule the state and deal with government affairs. However, their individual activity cannot be simply equalized to the will and collective behavior of the entire Party.

5.1.2 Conceptual Category of the Law

The law herein firstly refers to the code of conduct system developed by the state and implemented under the guarantee of the coercive force of the state. The law regulates citizens' rights and obligations and adjusts social relations. In China, the law refers to the socialist system of law with Chinese characteristics. The system of law mainly includes the constitution, basic laws, laws, administrative laws and regulations, local laws and regulations, autonomous regulations, specific regulations, etc. Second, the law refers to the legal system, the rule of law, the rule by law, governance by law, administration by law, acting by law, scientific legislation, strict law enforcement, impartial judicature, and law observation by all people, among other concepts and activities. Third, the law has transferred meanings, referring to legislators' legislative actions, law enforcers' acts of enforcement, judges and procurators' judicial acts, law-abiding conducts of all the citizens and social organizations, etc.

5.1.3 Relations between the Party and the Law

In the Chinese context, the relations between the Party and the law basically can be interpreted as follows:

(1) It is the relation between the CPC and state laws.

(2) It is the relation between the Party's leadership and the state's rule of law and rule by law; the relation between the Party's leadership for one part and scientific legislation, strict law enforcement, impartial judicature, and law observation by all the people for another.

(3) It is the relation between the Party's line, principles, and policies for one part and the constitution, laws, and regulations of the state for another.

(4) It is the relation between the Party's leading and governing style for one part and the rule of law and the rule by law for another.

(5) It is the relation between the powers and behaviors of specific party leaders, civil servants, law enforcers, and judicial personnel for one part and the rule of law, administration by law, and acting by law for another.

(6) It is whether the Party and the law have extrajudicial privileges and make everyone equal before the law.

Due to people's different interpretations of the concept of and relations between the Party and the law, in reality, the relations between the two have evolved into such questions as "which one is applicable, the Party's documents or state laws," "which one shall be followed, leaders' instructions or the state's rule of law," "which one should be followed for courts to handle cases, the law or leaders' instructions," "which one has the final say, leaders or the law," "which one is superior, party secretaries or the law," and so on and so forth. In most cases, leaders' words are taken as the law; specific words and deeds of some Party members, civil servants, Party leaders, and even Party secretaries are taken as the Party; specific behaviors of legislative, administrative, and judicial organs are taken as activities of the Party; and acts of some leading cadres, law enforcers, and judicial personnel violating the law or breaking the principles of the rule of law are even taken as the acts of the Party. In this case, the question of "whether the Party or the law is superior" has been raised.

General-Secretary Xi Jinping noted that the question of "whether the Party or the law is superior" is a pseudo-proposition, because we will fall into a dilemma no matter how we answer the question. If we say the Party is superior, someone would attack us by saying that we put the

Party above the law, replace the law with the Party, and rule the country by the Party; if we say the law is superior, someone would ask why we need the Party's leadership if the law is superior. Theoretically speaking, the question of "whether the Party or the law is superior" is indeed a pseudo-proposition, but this question and the question about the relations between the Party and the law have been answered emphatically by combining the legal theory with the system and the Party constitution with the constitution. However, from the perspective that the masses have observed and felt a variety of malpractices and insufficiencies in building the rule of law in China,[1] they look forward to realizing good law and proper governance, which means "there must be laws for the people to follow; laws must be strictly observed and enforced; law-breakers must be brought to justice; powers are administered according to law; and all people are equal before the law," the questions about whether the Party

[1] *The Decisions* of the Fourth Plenary Session of the 18th Central Committee of the CPC pointed out that while highly affirming the historical achievements in building the rule of law in China, we "must clearly realize that, some adaptable and incompatible issues still exist in building the rule of law compared with the requirement for national development, the expectation of the masses and the modernized target of state governance system and governance ability, and these issues can be manifested as: some laws and regulations fail to comprehensively reflect objective laws and the people's will, and are narrowly targeted and less operable; the trend of departmentalization and the phenomenon of fighting for power and evading responsibility remain salient in legislation; the phenomenon of failure to abide by the law, slack law enforcement, impunity of law breakers is very serious; the phenomenon of separated power and responsibility, duplicated law enforcement and selective law enforcement still exist in the law enforcement system; unregulated, relaxed, nontransparent, uncivilized phenomenon remains outstanding; the masses react strongly to impartial judicature and law enforcement as well as corruption; some social members do not have strong awareness of respecting, believing, observing and using laws and the consciousness of rights safeguarding; some national staff, especially leading cadres do not have a strong sense of acting by law and a strong capacity, and the phenomenon of deliberately breaking the law, replacing the law by words, suppressing the law by power and bending the law for personal gain still exist. All these issues violate the principles of socialist rule of law, damage the interests of the masses, and hamper the development of the cause of the Party and the state, so they must be solved energetically." General-Secretary Xi Jinping further pointed out in *The Instructions on the Decision of the Central Committee of the Communist Party of China on Major Issues Concerning Comprehensively Advancing the Rule of Law* that the principal issues existing in judicial areas are that denial of justice and lower judicial credibility remain extremely salient; some judicial personnel fail to form a good style of work and to be honest in handling cases, sometimes handle cases for money, relationship, and favor, and even take bribes from both plaintiffs and defendants, and so on and so forth.

or the law is superior and the relations between the Party and the law are not only a theoretical and ideological issue but also a practical issue. In other words, if the theory of the socialist rule of law with Chinese characteristics cannot, in the practice of building the rule of law, practically address issues like replacing law by power, suppressing law with power, abolishing law by words, failing to abide by the law, slacking law enforcement, refraining from punishing law-breakers, failing to handle judicial cases impartially, and perverting justice for a bribe existing in some local areas and departments or committed by some leading cadres, then the words and deeds of these local areas, departments, and individuals violating the rule of law would be blamed on China's political system, the Communist Party's leadership, and the socialist rule of law. As such, the question about whether the Party or the law is superior would not easily fade out in our real life. Therefore under the precondition of clearly explaining a high degree of uniformity of the Party and the law and answering the question of whether the Party or the law is superior, there is a need to redouble the effort to address a host of institutional and practical issues related to administering power by law, governing officials by law, and practically controlling power by law and institution.

5.2 RELATIONS BETWEEN THE RULE OF LAW AND POLITICS

A high degree of identification of the Party and the law is determined in the final analysis by the correlation between the science of law and political science as well as the uniformity of the rule of law (the law) and politics. Speaking from the origin, in early western society (such as in ancient Greece), the science of law was included in political science, or the science of law was combined with political science. Today, the science of law and political science are more often than not inseparable "politics and law" or "law and politics" subjects, and law and politics have become interdependent, inseparable, and a highly unified ruling (governing) art, so the rule of law and politics are bound to be highly unified in core values and essential functions. The intersection, integration, and scientific consolidation of the science of law and political science have shaped the politics of law. The politics of law focuses on studying the social phenomenon with dual attributes, namely, politics and law. The politics of law studies the interdiscipline of the science of law and politics of related social phenomenon by adopting the research method of political science and the science of law.[2]

The Oxford Companion to Law of the Britain pointed out that just as the theoretical studies of jurisprudence are always closely connected with political theories, more practical legal rules and realistic politics are always closely connected. Legal rules are formulated or abolished by politicians and political organizations for the purpose of realizing some political theories, political beliefs, and political objectives. The entire field of public management is filled with the mutual influence of legal needs and political needs, legal means and political means, legal functions and political functions.[3] Lenin pointed out straightly and precisely that "law is a political measure, a policy."[4] In this connection, the constitution and laws are sometimes called "codified politics." Under the constitutional control, politics is sometimes called "constitutionalism" for short. Questions about the legitimacy, legality, and legalization of political power, political system and political behavior, and questions about political orientation, political attribute and state, features of the legal system, rule of law procedure and judicial power are undoubtedly the major issues that should not and cannot be avoided by current science of law and political science as well as the rule of law and politics. In the sense of politics of law, state law and legislation are inseparable with party politics, political party election, ruling party theory, ruling party objective, and ruling party policy; state law is inseparable with people's democracy, sovereignty, interests, and rights; national constitution is inseparable with legislative power, administrative power, judicial power, and civil rights; and state politics and judicial power, politics and judicial independence, political principle and judicial activity, political system and judicial system, and political system restructuring and judicial system reform are all inseparable. Looking from a macroperspective, politics, the rule of law, and the rule of virtue are actually methods and institutional arrangements of humanity to govern the state and the society, are different theories and methods of humanity to settle for "heteronomy, autonomy, and shared governance," and are aimed at realizing scientific, law-based, and democratic human governance ultimately.

From a value perpective, the rule of law involves not only abstract values like existing rationality, justice, fairness, will, good and evil, happiness, equality and freedom, but also concrete values like interest, right,

[2]Zhuo Zeyuan: *Politics of Law*, Law Press China, Beijing, 2005 edition, p. 5.

[3]Walker: *The Oxford Companion to Law*, translated by Deng Zhenglai *et al.*, Guangming Daily Press, Beijing, 1989 edition, pp. 520–521.

[4]Vladimir Lenin: *A Caricature of Marxism and Imperialist Economism*, *The Collected Works of Lenin*, Volume 28, People's Publishing House, Beijing, 1990 edition, p. 140.

democracy, order, benefit, safety, peace, and development. These value criteria can be generalized as four relation structures: consistent, opposite, hypotactic, and discrete relations.[5] The value of law depends on legal norms and is realized through the implementation of laws. The value of law is highly political in essence, and its political nature of judicature is self-evident as it takes fairness and justice as the mission. Compared with legislation and administrative function, judicial activity has been a strong political function since ancient times; a country may not have parliament. It may have the minimum administrative organs in number, but it must have stronger judicial organs; judicial function is one of the most fundamental political functions of a state, and it would be impossible for a state to survive without judicature.[6] Law and judicature are obviously political. Under the condition of party politics, the values of law and judicature necessarily demonstrate the political orientation and policy tendency of the ruling party. In other words, the ruling party would certainly transfer and implement its basic governing ideas and policy requirements into some content of the law and implement them in specific judicial procedures through various channels and ways.

The United States is a country that attaches great importance to judicial independence, and even upholds the philosophy that judicature has nothing to do with politics. However, in American judicial life, judicial independence as a principle is bound to be distorted to a certain degree in real political life.[7] In the United States, the judge-selecting process is highly political. No matter how honest and unimpeachable the judge of the Supreme Court is, the Supreme Court is generally and will undoubtedly maintain its distinct political nature, which reflected the features of their times. And most of its members were selected from that era.[8] Former democratic President Roosevelt appointed 203 democrats and 8 republicans as federal judges; former republican President Eisenhower appointed 176 republicans and 11 democrats as judges; former democratic President Kennedy appointed 169 democratic judges and 11 republican judges; former republican President Nixon appointed 198 republican judges and 15 democratic judges; and

[5] Refer to Zhuo Zeyuan, *Axiology of Law*, Law Press China, Beijing, 2006 edition.

[6] Hu Wei: *Judicial Politics*, chiefly edited by Wang Huning, Joint Publishing (Hong Kong) Company Limited, 1994 edition, p. 34.

[7] Hu Wei: *Judicial Politics*, chiefly edited by Wang Huning, Joint Publishing (Hong Kong) Company Limited, 1994 edition, p. 63.

[8] Woodrow Wilson: *Congressional Government*, translated by Xiong Xiling, Lyu Deben, The Commercial Press, Beijing, 1986 edition, p. 24.

former republican President Ford appointed 52 republican judges and 12 democratic judges.[9] Almost without exception, those "great" or "nearly great" judges in the United States always show a political rather than judicial style. From John Marshal to Earl Warrant, most influential judges of the United States used to be elected or appointed for political post, and they were politicians with strong partisanship in most cases. Once entering the Supreme Court, this kind of political experience influenced their working style.[10] As a matter of fact, the Supreme Court of the United States is not an independent institution that is free from politics. Instead, it usually plays a critical role in the political life of the country. The Supreme Court has indeed become involved in politics, and some major decisions in American political history were made by the Supreme Court rather than the President or the Congress.[11] At the same time, the Supreme Court has many advantages and disadvantages as a result of its legal, political, and human features.[12] Tocqueville described the relations between American politics and judicature from another perspective in *Democracy in America*. He wrote, "Scarcely any political question arising in the United States will not turn, sooner or later, into a judicial question. As such, a kind of litigation has usually ended up before the highest bench."[13] It's therefore easy to understand why the former US President Roosevelt proposed the court-packing plan in the 1930s in order to reshuffle the party structure in the Supreme Court.

In the autonomous law society highly praised by American scholars Philippe Nonet and Philip Selznick, the separation between law and the politics is also relative. In the autonomous law society, law is the guarantee of sticking to the existing political order, performs its political functions consistently with the state, and endeavors for order, control, and obedience. In the autonomous law society, legal institutions (courts, etc.) exchange entity obedience for procedural autonomy, and exchange the

[9] Refer to *Judicial Politics* by Hu Wei, chiefly edited by Wang Huning, Joint Publishing (Hong Kong) Company Limited, 1994 edition, p. 63. Also refer to [US] Abraham Lincoln: *A Political History of Appointments to the Supreme Court*, translated by Liu Taixing, The Commercial Press, 1990 edition, pp. 39–61.

[10] Peter Woll: *Behind the Scenes in American Government: Personalities and Politics*, translated by Li Hong *et al.*, Social Sciences Academic Press, Beijing, 1992 edition, p. 355.

[11] M.J.C. Vile: *Politics in the USA*, translated by Wang He *et al.*, The Commercial Press, Beijing, 1981 edition, p. 211.

[12] Abraham Lincoln: *A Political History of Appointments to the Supreme Court*, translated by Liu Taixing, The Commercial Press, Beijing, 1990 edition, p. 270.

[13] Alexis de Tocqueville: *Democracy in America*, Volume I, translated by Dong Guoliang, The Commercial Press, Beijing, December 1988 edition, p. 109.

consistency with politics in entity for its relative independence from politics in procedure, instead of the separation between law and politics in a real sense.[14]

Marx pointed out that everything people strive for is related to their interests.[15] Interests are a social principle. As a branch of western sociology of law, jurisprudence of interests sticks to the theoretical basis and emphasizes that judges should pay attention to balancing various conflicting interests, and hold that law is the principle formulated by legislators to solve various conflicting interests. Therefore judges must firstly determine what interests legislators want to protect in order to make fair judgment. Judges should by no means be an autonomous law vending machine running according to logic mechanical rules, but an assistant to legislators thinking independently. Judges should not only pay attention to the words and expressions of legal provisions, but also control the intention of legislators through observing related interests in person. Western jurisprudence of interests advocates that "social benefit" is an important objective of judge to make a judgment, and emphasizes the political function to which the law is applicable, i.e., the relations among science of law, practice of court, and politics.[16] The epoch-making contribution of western jurisprudence of law is its consideration of social and political reality and the purpose of science of law under the law.[17] In short, it is impossible for a court to act purely upon legalism and emphasize the one-sided principle of the supremacy of the constitution and the law and the provisions of laws, without considering complex factors such as politics, society, morality, interests, folk customs, and culture when making a judgment according to the law.

Even some western jurists have to admit the existence value of Marxist jurisprudence as a school of academic principle and admit the following standpoints of Marxist jurisprudence: any law is in favor of the ruling class party; it forms, cultivates, and builds consciousness and protects existing ruling relations from being attacked by hostile forces; socialist law

[14] Philippe Nonet and Philip Selznick: *Law and Society in Transition*, translated by Zhang Zhiming, China University of Political Science and Law Press, Beijing, 1994 edition, pp. 63–66.

[15] *Karl Marx and Frederick Engels*, Volume 1, People's Publishing House, Beijing, first edition in 1956, p. 82.

[16] Bernd Ruthers: *Jurisprudence*, translated by Ding Xiaochun *et al.*, Law Press China, Beijing, 2003 edition, p. 241.

[17] Bernd Ruthers: *Jurisprudence*, translated by Ding Xiaochun *et al.*, Law Press China, Beijing, 2003 edition, p. 247.

is the tool for the working class to obtain the state power under the leadership of the Marxist–Leninist party; and the primary task of socialist law is to protect the independent ruling of the socialist society and Marxist–Leninist party from being sabotaged by hostile forces externally and by counter-revolutionary hostile forces internally, and the second task is to build socialism and guide the establishment of the communist society by means of law.[18] Judicature is the tool for state activities in nature, and realizes various judicial functions through effective supplement to the ruler's legitimacy, ideology, and morality.[19]

The Marxist viewpoint of the rule of law holds that the rule of law (legal system) in a class society has political, class, and legal nature. The political nature of the rule of law (legal system) is an important attribute determined and reflected by the guiding principles, line, and policies of the ruling party or the governing group. The class nature of the rule of law (legal system) is an important attribute determined and reflected by the interests, will, and essential requirements of the ruling party and its alliance class. The legal nature is an essential technical feature and cultural attribute of the rule of law (legal system). Just as Xie Juezai, who used to be the Chief Judge of the Supreme People's Court, clearly and directly pointed out in *Marxist–Leninist Theory of Law*, "Our law is subject to politics, and there is no law independent from politics. Our judicial practitioners must understand politics. Otherwise, they would never understand the law. Judicial practitioners would not administer justice without understanding politics." The most important work of the people's courts is to make adjudications. Adjudication is not only highly professional but also strongly political. A "trial" is intended to investigate the facts of a case while "judgment" is used to make a judgment on the basis of the facts. "Trial" is an objective fact but not what a judge thinks. "Judgment" means to consider the extent for measurement of punishment within a certain scope of law-based on the Party's principles and policies. Objective fact is the object of judgment, and figuring out the facts is the first step of works. Based on the facts figured out, the second step is to make a judgment according to the Party's policies and laws.

Under the condition of socialism with Chinese characteristics, the political nature of socialist rule of law has intensively demonstrated the

[18] Bernd Ruthers: *Jurisprudence*, translated by Ding Xiaochun *et al.*, Law Press China, Beijing, 2003 edition, pp. 226–228.

[19] *Introduction to Contemporary Law Philosophy and Law Theory*, chiefly edited by Kaufmann and Hassemer, translated by Zheng Yongliu, Law Press China, Beijing, 2002 edition, p. 443.

CPC's nature, purpose, basic task, and struggle objective, among other undertaking requirements. The political nature of the socialist rule of law has also embodied the institutionalization, normalization, and legalization of the Party's guidelines, principles, and policies. The class nature of the socialist rule of law is intensively reflected by its affinity to the people and democracy because class contradictions have no longer been the principal contradictions of the Chinese society; citizens as the absolute majority of social members belong to the people category; people are masters of the country and control the state political power; and the affinity to the people of the rule of law has replaced the class nature of the rule of law. The legal nature of the socialist rule of law is intensively manifested in two aspects: first, it is the inherent and deserved objective, normative, compulsory, predictable, clear, procedural, and technical nature of the law and the rule of law; second, it is the Chinese traditional legal culture and its modern features of the law and the rule of law, and the Chinese characteristics of all beneficial achievements from human civilization of rule of law.

Of course, we must admit the obvious distinctions and major differences between the science of law and political science and between the rule of law (law) and politics while demonstrating their close correlation and uniformity. Their distinctions and differences in subject division, research object, conceptual category, practice and operation, and institutional mechanism are just the premise and basis for us to discuss their correlation and uniformity.

5.3 UNIFORMITY OF THE PARTY AND THE LAW

Under western political philosophy and the constitutional mode of multiparty system and "tripartite" political system (checks and balances of legislative, executive, and judicial power), political parties and the rule of law of western countries usually have diversified, staggered, and even separated relations because western political parties represent different interests with the different roles of the ruling party, parties out of power, and the opposition party. Western political parties represent different classes, stratums, and interest groups, and western rule of law claims to represent the will of the entire people reflected as the will of the state. This kind of political system based on multiplicity of interests is bound to have contradictions and conflicts with the neutrality, equality, and impartiality publicized by its rule of law. In essence, it is certainly difficult to unify western political parties and their rule of law.

The relationship between the CPC for one part and the people, the state, and the rule of law for another is not contradictory but harmonious and highly unified under the socialist system and political system led by the CPC; under the economic system based on public ownership and the political system with the people as masters of the country confirmed and safeguarded by Chinese constitution and laws; under the essential stipulation of the nature, purpose, and historical mission of the CPC; and under the condition that the socialist law is the unity and inherent consistency between the proposition of the Party and the will of the people.

5.3.1 The Uniformity of the Party and the Law from the Perspective of the Essence of the Party's Leadership and the Socialist Rule of Law

In a sense, sticking to and improving the Party's leadership, implementing the socialist rule of law and advancing the rule by law are all means, methods, measures, and procedures. They are serving the people wholeheartedly in essence, and their purposes are all to realize the Chinese dream of national prosperity, people's happiness, the great rejuvenation of the Chinese nation, and the ambitious goal of socialist modernization. The CPC represents the fundamental interests of the overwhelming majority of the Chinese people. With the exception of representing the interests of the working class and the overwhelming majority of the masses, the CPC does not have any special interests and powers of its own. The CPC puts the people's interests in the first place at any time, and shares weal and woe and keeps the closest contact with the masses. The CPC adheres to functioning by the mandate of the people, empathizing with the feelings of the people and working for the well-being of the people. The CPC does not allow any party member to stand apart from and place themselves above the masses. The socialist rule of law is the rule of law for the sake of the people, relying on the people, bringing benefits to the people, and protecting the people. The socialist rule of law guarantees that the people enjoy extensive rights and freedom, safeguards social equity and justice, and promotes common prosperity by taking the people as the subject, with administering power by law and governing officials by law as the means, and safeguarding the people's fundamental interests as the initial and ultimate goal. The CPC and the law, the Party's leadership and the socialist rule of law take, in the final analysis, the people's interests as the fundamental interests, the people's will as the lofty will, the people's happiness as the highest pursuit, the people's satisfaction as the highest praise, the people's support as the political basis, and the people's democracy as the source of life. The CPC and the law, the Party's leadership and the socialist rule of law are, in the final analysis, highly united under the essential attribute of and internal requirement for serving the people wholeheartedly.

5.3.2 Look at the Uniformity of the Party and the Law from the Constitution of the PRC

The constitution as the fundamental law of China has the highest legal effect and authority of the rule of law and represents the general regulations of the CPC to lead the people, run the country, and bring peace to the country. The constitution of China has affirmed the leading position and role of the CPC in guiding the people to carry on revolutions and constructions and in the reform process in the form of the fundamental law. The constitution of China has also affirmed that the CPC is the core of leadership for building China into a rich, strong, democratic, and civilized socialist country. The constitution of China has stipulated that China shall implement the principles of ruling the country by law, safeguarding the unity and dignity of the socialist legal system. The constitution of China requires that all political parties including the CPC must take the constitution as the fundamental rule for activities and bears the responsibility for upholding the dignity of the constitution and guaranteeing the implementation of the constitution. The constitution of China requires that all political parties including the CPC abide by the constitution and the laws, and all acts violating the constitution and the laws must be investigated. The constitution also stipulates that no organization or individual has the privilege to stand above the constitution and the laws. All these provisions of the constitution have provided a constitutional basis and foundation for a high degree of uniformity between the CPC and the laws in the form of the fundamental law of the state. All these provisions of the constitution have created a new type of Party-law relationship with Chinese characteristics that is different from the western "tripartite" system and the multiparty system.

5.3.3 Look at the Uniformity of the Party and the Law from the Constitution of the CPC

The constitution of the CPC is the highest criterion for inner-party system and behaviors, the general rule for running the Party strictly by regulations, and the fundamental inner-party laws and regulations guaranteeing a high degree of unity of the CPC and the law. While clearly stipulating that the CPC is the core of leadership of the socialist cause with Chinese characteristics, the Party constitution explicitly requires to stick to an organic unity of the Party's leadership, the people's role as masters of the country and the rule by law, and to follow the development path of socialist politics with Chinese characteristics. The Party constitution explicitly requires expanding socialist democracy, improving the socialist legal system, and building a socialist country under the rule of law. The Party constitution explicitly requires improving the socialist system of law with Chinese characteristics, strengthening law enforcement and bringing all works of the state under the rule of law. In order to guarantee a high degree of uniformity of the Party and the law as well as the Party's leadership and the state's rule of law, the Party constitution stipulates that the leadership of the CPC is mainly the leadership in politics, thought, and organization. The Party constitution also stipulates that the CPC must act within the framework of the constitution and the laws and persist in scientific and democratic governance by law; the CPC must ensure that the state's legislative, judicial, and administrative organs and economic, cultural, and mass organizations work actively, independently, responsibly, and coordinately; except for the individual interests and job-related power within the scope stipulated by laws and politics, no Party members shall seek any private interests and privilege and must play an exemplary role in abiding by state laws and regulations. These stipulations of the Party constitution are more concrete, stricter, and pertinent compared with related provisions of the constitution, and represent the fundamental norms and institutional guarantee for a harmonious relationship between the Party and the law.

5.3.4 Look at the Uniformity of the Party and the Law from Documents of the CPC National Congress

Properly handling the relationship between the Party and the law and building a new type of relationship between politics and law featuring a high degree of unity of the CPC and the rule law as well as the Party's leadership and the rule by law have always been important theoretical and practical issues highly valued by the CPC in leading the people to develop socialist politics with Chinese characteristics and advance the rule by law. The report of the CPC to its 15th National Congress officially established the rule by law as the fundamental strategy for the Party to lead the people to govern the state. The report emphatically pointed out that the Party leads the people to establish the constitution and laws and acts within the framework of the constitution and the laws. The rule by law upholds the unity of three principles, namely sticking to the Party's leadership, promoting people's democracy, and acting strictly by law. The rule by law guarantees the implementation of the Party's basic line and principles in constitution and law. The rule by law guarantees that the Party always plays a leading role in directing the overall situation and coordinating the efforts of all quarters. The report put forward the proposition of and requirement for uniting the Party's leadership, the people's democracy, and acting by law for the first time in the form of the political documents of the CPC National Congress. The report also clearly answered the question of how to build the relationship between the Party and the law in the context of ruling the country by law. The report of the CPC to its 16th National Congress clearly stated the essential features and intrinsic requirements of the socialist democratic politics with Chinese characteristics: "the essential requirement for developing socialist democracy is to organically unite the Party's leadership, the people's role as masters of the country and the rule by law." The report identified officially for the first time the basic political principle of "an organic unity of the three." The CPC's report to its 17th National Congress made it clear that there is a need to stick to the Party's leadership in directing the overall situation and coordinating the efforts of all quarters, improve the Party's scientific and democratic governance by law, and guarantee that the Party leads the people to govern the state effectively on the basis of adhering to "an organic unity of the three."

The report of the CPC to its 18th Central Committee put more emphasis on the role of the rule by law and the rule of law in the relationship between the Party and the law. The report reiterated that the rule by law is the basic strategy for governing the state and proposed for the first time that the rule of law is the basic way for the CPC to run the state and deal with politics. The report placed more emphasis on bringing the rule of law into full play in state governance and social management. The report also stressed that no organization or individual has privilege over the constitution and the law, and no organization or individual is allowed to put personal views above the law, suppress the law by power, or bend the law for personal gain.

The 4th Plenary Session of the 18th CPC Central Committee systematically answered, for the first time, the question of how to correctly understand, in theory, the relationship between the Party and the law and unite the Party's leadership with the rule by law in top design and institutional arrangement. *The Decision* of the 4th Plenary Session explains the new type of relationship between the Party and the law of socialism with Chinese characteristics from the following six aspects. First, the essential feature—the constitution of China has established the leader status of the CPC. The CPC's leadership is the most essential feature of socialism with Chinese characteristics and the most fundamental guarantee for the socialist rule of law. Second, the basic experience—implementing the CPC's leadership in the entire process of the rule by law and in other aspects is a basic experience in building the socialist rule of law in China. Third, the fundamental requirement—sticking to the CPC's leadership is the fundamental requirement for the socialist rule of law and an essential part of comprehensively advancing the rule of law. Fourth, the correlation—the CPC's leadership and the socialist rule of law are consistent; the socialist rule of law must stick to the CPC's leadership; and the CPC's leadership must rely on the socialist rule of law. Fifth, the governance by law—the CPC's running of state and dealing with politics according to the constitution and the laws and the administration of the Party according to inner-party laws and regulations must persist in the CPC's leadership in legislation, guarantee law enforcement, support judicature, and take the lead in abiding by the law. Sixth, the top design of a high degree of unity of the Party and the law includes "three unites": unite the rule by law as the fundamental strategy with the governance by law as the basic mode; unite the CPC's direction of the overall situation, coordination of all quarters with the performance of functions and conduction of works of the people's congresses, governments, the political consultative conferences, judicial apparatuses, procuratorial organs to perform functions according to laws and regulations; and unite the CPC's leading of the people to formulate and implement the constitution and the laws with the Party's act under the framework of the constitution and the laws. The top design of a high degree of unity of the Party and the law also includes "four adepts": being adept in making the CPC's proposition turn into the will of the state through legal procedures; being adept in making the candidates recommended by the CPC organizations leading members of organs of state political power through legal procedures; being adept in making the CPC lead the state and the society through organs of state political power; and being adept in safeguarding the authority of the Central Committee and the unity of the entire Party and the entire nation through applying the principle of democratic centralism.

5.3.5 Look at the Uniformity of the Party and the Law from the CPC's Line, Principles, and Policies

In the last 60-plus years since the founding of the New China, the relationship between Party policies and state laws has experienced a historical transition period from having to handle affairs by relying on policies due to the lack of laws (or few laws) to handling affairs entirely by law for sticking to and implementing the rule by law. Under the new situation that the system of socialist rule of law with Chinese characteristics has taken shape and that we adhere to integrated development of a law-based state, law-based government, and law-based society and common advancement of the rule by law, governance by law and administration by law, the Party's basic line and major principles and policies have become mature and improved over time after 30 years of explorations and practices. The development process of the past 3 decades fully demonstrates that the constitution is a good constitution suitable to China's national condition, actuality, and development requirements of the era; a good constitution fully reflecting the people's common will, fully guaranteeing the people's democratic rights, fully safeguarding the people's fundamental interests; and a good constitution facilitating national development and progress, guaranteeing the people's happy life, and safeguarding the great rejuvenation of the Chinese nation. Under this condition, there is a need to keep to the principles of the supremacy of the constitution and the laws, adhere to law-based ideas, law-based modes, and the principle that Party policies are not allowed to contradict the constitution and the laws without special reasons while properly understanding and handling the relationship between Party's policies for one part and the constitution and the laws for another. When the Party's major decision-making is inconsistent with the provisions of the constitution and laws due to some specific reasons, there is a need to revise and improve the constitution and laws as soon as possible or revise and improve Party policies as soon as possible so as to eliminate the gap and even conflict between the two. When Party policies need to be implemented in the entire society, especially reform and development policies on boosting economic, political, cultural, social, ecological, and civilization development, there is a need to make as many of these policies legalized and stipulated as possible and as soon as possible based on the conditions of continuous and practical development, and experience summarization and improvement. Very important policies should be constitutionalized as soon as possible. China's constitution and laws are the finalized, documented, and legalized line, the principles and policies of the CPC. This has maximally guaranteed consistency and coordination between the CPC's major decisions on reform and development stability and state legislation in the form of laws and legal norms. This has also organically united the Party and the law in the national system of law. On the one hand, legal means are used to institutionalize, legalize, and nationalize the Party's mature and finalized line, principles, and policies; state laws are used to guide, advance, and guarantee the comprehensive implementation of the Party's mature and finalized line, principles, and policies. On the other hand, the successful practice of the Party's line, principles, and policies has also guided and driven the continuous improvement of state laws and propelled the innovative development of the national system of law.

5.3.6 The Uniformity of the Party and the Law in National Democratic Legislation

Legislation is in essence the combination of the CPC's propositions and the people's will that have been transformed into the state will through legislative procedures. On the basis of fully promoting democracy, national legislative bodies transform the CPC's propositions reflecting the people's overall will and fundamental interests and pursuits into the will of the state in a timely manner through democratic and scientific legislative procedures. National legislative bodies also give legal effects to this will of state implemented with the guarantee of the coercive force of the state. All social members are required to follow this will of state. In this way, the CPC's propositions and the people's will are transformed into the will of the state through legislation. Also, the Party and the law have realized legalized combination, and the CPC's leadership and the rule by law have realized organic unity.

5.3.7 Look at the Uniformity of the Party and the Law from Sticking to the CPC's Leadership and Judicial Organs' Independent and Impartial Exercise of Powers by Law

In China, keeping to the CPC's leadership is united and consistent with the courts and procuratorates' independent and impartial exercise of judicial powers by law. First, the constitution and the laws are the concentrated reflection of the unity of the CPC's propositions and the people's will and the legalization of the CPC's line, principles, and policies. This has realized organic unity of the CPC's leadership and the rule by law in legislation and guaranteed the uniformity and consistency of the CPC's policies and state laws. On this basis, judicial organs' compliance with law-based principles and independent and strict exercise of judicial and procuratorial powers according to the law are their judicial responsibilities according to the CPC's propositions and the people's will. This has reflected the unity of sticking to the CPC's leadership and independently exercising judicial powers according to the law. From the perspective of the actuality of China as a socialist country, Liu Shaoqi explained the meaning of the people's courts and people's procuratorates' independent exercise of powers as follows: it is right for the courts to implement independent adjudication as stipulated by the constitution, so Party committees and governments shall not intervene in their adjudication. The people's procuratorates should fight against all phenomena violating laws and disciplines, no matter what organ or who is involved. We should not propose absolute obedience of judicial and public security organs to the leadership of Party committees of all levels. Judicial and public security organs shall not be followed as long as they violate the law. If local Party committees' decisions are inconsistent with the laws and policies of the Central Committee, which one shall be followed? Under this circumstance, the laws and policies of the Central Committee shall prevail.[20] Judicial organs' obedience to the law is to obey the decisions of the leadership of the CPC Central Committee and the supreme organ of state power and obey the whole nation.[21] Second, under the background that China's system of law has taken shape as expected, that most contents of the Party's line, principles, and policies and the Party's practices of political and organizational leadership have been brought under the rule of law, and that most strategic plans of the CPC on advancing economic, political, cultural, social, and ecological civilization development have been legalized, judicial organs' strict action by law and practical, impartial and independent exercise of judicial powers are to stick to the Party's leadership, fulfill the Party's will, and safeguard the Party's authority. Furthermore, more independent and impartial exercise of judicial powers by judicial organs means that the people could feel equity and justice of the rule of law in every case. On top of that, if judges and procurators only uphold the fact and the laws and always exercise judicial powers impartially and incorruptibly, this would give more embodiment to the Party's tenet, the implementation of the Party's principles and policies, and the fundamental adherence to the Party's leadership. Third, the CPC is the ruling party that supports and guarantees judicial organs' independent and impartial exercise of judicial powers by law.

[20] *Selected Works of Liu Shaoqi*, Volume II, People's Publishing House, Beijing, 1985 edition, p. 452.

[21] Peng Zhen: *Political-Legal Work in the New Era*, Central Party Literature Press, Beijing, 1992 edition, p. 178.

That is, in essence, to consolidate the foundation of the rule of law under the leadership and governance of the CPC and to use law-based thinking and methods to practically and effectively uphold and maintain the Party's leadership. Judicial independence and procuratorial independence stipulated by China's constitution and laws for one part and sticking to the Party's leadership for another are organically united in theoretical logic and completely consistent in judicial system design. Judicial independence and procuratorial independence and sticking to the Party's leadership develop interactively in judicial practices.

What needs to be particularly noted here is that sticking to a high degree of unity of the Party and the law is by no means to "uphold no separation between the Party and the law," "replace the law with the Party," "replace government with the Party," or even "rule the country by the Party." Deng Xiaoping pointed out in his article *The Party and the Anti-Japanese Democratic Government* that the Party's leadership over the state power must be guaranteed.[22] The Party's leadership is in political principles rather than monopolizing everything, intervening in everything, or acting above everything. This policy is completely opposite to "ruling the country by the Party." This is because the evil legacy of the Kuomintang that ruled the country by itself is the most effective method to paralyze, corrupt, and destroy the Party and break the Party from the masses.[23] This kind of evil legacy exists in some leading cadres, which can be reflected by their misunderstanding of the Party's leadership and their misinterpretation of the Party's power as above everything. They meddle in government works and randomly change the decree of the superior government. They randomly redeploy some cadres in the state government without administrative formalities. In some local areas, government decrees are impractical without Party notifications. They have even developed the "Party's power above all" into "Party members above all," and Party members can commit crimes and be pardoned from breaking the laws. Consequently, the masses think the government is useless and everything is determined by the CPC. All mistakes of the government are the mistakes of the CPC, and the government has lost its credibility and the Party has certainly broken away from the masses. This is most stupid![24]

[22] *Selected Works of Deng Xiaoping*, Volume 1, People's Publishing House, Beijing, 1994 edition, p. 16.

[23] *Selected Works of Deng Xiaoping*, Volume 1, People's Publishing House, Beijing, 1994 edition, p. 12.

[24] *Selected Works of Deng Xiaoping*, Volume 1, People's Publishing House, Beijing, 1994 edition, pp. 10–11.

"No separation between the Party and the law," "replacing the law with the Party," "replacing the government with the Party," or "ruling the country by the Party" actually deny the state's rule of law and the people's democracy, which completely deviates from the principle of a high degree of unity of the Party and the law.

5.4 KEEPING TO THE UNIFORMITY OF THE PARTY AND THE LAW

Sticking to the leading status of the CPC and giving full play to the Party's leading and core role have always been key to the success of China's revolution, construction, and reform. However, China has gone through the development process from the rule of man to the rule by law, from the rule by law to the rule of law, and then to ruling the country by law in the following endeavors: sticking to the socialist rule of law and taking the rule of law as the basic mode for the CPC to run the state and deal with politics; sticking to the rule by law and taking the rule by law as the basic strategy for the CPC to lead the people to govern the state and the society; sticking to governance by law and taking governance by law as the basic method for the CPC's governance; and highly uniting the Party and the law. In this historical development process, the relationship between the Party and the law and between the Party's leadership and the rule of law have consistently shown a dynamic, coordinated, and highly united feature with the continuous strengthening of socialist rule of law, unceasing advancement of ruling the country by law, and consistent improvement of law-based ideas.

In the new-democratic revolution period, the CPC as the revolutionary party on a mission to seize the state power mainly relied on politics, orders, decisions, and resolutions to organize and lead the revolution. The process by which the CPC led the people to seize the state power was the process used to break old laws and abolish the old legally constituted authority. The revolution of the working class denied the constitution and law of the Kuomintang authority. If the law would have been emphasized, there would not have been a revolution, and thus the ruling order of the three major enemies (imperialism, feudalism and bureaucrat-capitalism) would have been maintained. Then, the reactionary class would be lawless, so policy was the focus among the people.[25] The CPC overturned these

[25] *Selected Works of Peng Zhen*, People's Publishing House, Beijing, 1991 edition, p. 491.

three mountains by relying on policies. At that time, the CPC could only rely on policies.[26] Revolutionary laws were only an assistant mode for the CPC to lead mass movements and carry out armed struggles.

Just before the founding of the New China, the Central Committee of the CPC issued the *Instructions Concerning Abolishing the Six Codes of the Kuomintang and Determining Judicial Principles for the Liberated Areas. The Instructions* clearly stated that, under the people's democratic dictatorship with the worker-peasant alliance as the main body under the leadership of the proletariat, the "Six Codes" of the Kuomintang should be abolished and the people's judicial works should no longer be carried out based on the "Six Codes" of the Kuomintang but on the people's new laws. At the same time, *The Instructions* also required the people's judicial organs to educate and transform judicial leaders with the spirit of scorning and criticizing the "Six Codes" and all other reactionary laws and decrees of the Kuomintang as well as all laws and decrees of imperialist countries like the United States and Japan against the Chinese people. *The Instructions* also required the people's judicial organs to educate and transform judicial leaders through learning and grasping Marxism–Leninism—the national outlook and the view of law of Mao Zedong Thought—and new democratic policies, programs, laws, orders, regulations, and resolutions. *The Instructions* made it clear that the majority of judicial leaders should realize that our law is the law of the people and courts are tools of the people; our law should follow politics; the law would provide what politics need, so judicial workers must understand politics, otherwise they would not understand the law; and judicial staff must administer justice from the political perspective and put cases into various aspects that require political knowledge.

The CPC led the people to establish the political authority in 1949, which opened a new historical chapter for the people's legal system. The formulation of the *Common Programme*, the constitution of 1954, and a batch of important laws and decrees laid a legal foundation for building of the political authority of the New China. The CPC started to transit from acting by relying on policies to acting by not only relying on policies but also by establishing and improving the legal system. After the founding of the New China, the CPC as the ruling party changed its style of leadership that was different from that in war times. The CPC relied not only on its policies but also on the legal system. All major affairs having a bearing

[26] *Biography of Peng Zhen*, Volume IV, Central Party Literature Press, Beijing, 2012 edition, p. 1570.

on the state and the people were decided by the Party and national laws were enacted. The Party's leadership was consistent with acting by law.[27]

However, in the second half of 1957, the "antirightist struggle" started, and national political, economic, and social life begun to show abnormalities. Should we should settle for the rule of man or the rule of law? Some principal leaders of the Party have argued that law is a must. But we have our ways. We generally do not depend on laws but on our ways. We typically depend on resolutions and meetings but not on the civil law and the criminal law to maintain the order. The people's congresses and the State Council have their ways, but we have our ways. So should we choose the rule of man or the rule of law? It seems that we could only choose the rule of man while the law could only be taken as a reference.[28] During the Cultural Revolution, class struggle was taken as the guiding principle; the "great democracy" mass movement became a main governing way; local people's congresses and governments were replaced by "revolutionary committees"; public security bureaus, courts, and procuratorates were smashed; the democratic legislative system established by the New China was completely destroyed; and the socialist legal system was severely damaged.

Why did these tragedies happen? A primary cause was that the national legal system was seriously damaged, and both the Party and the state fell into lawlessness and disorder. In the special period when class struggle was taken as the guiding principle and "great democracy" was advocated, a small number of people acted above the CPC and the national leading system, replaced laws with their words, abolished laws with their powers, and acted without regard for the authority. Under this abnormal and special historical condition, some cadres and masses dissatisfied with the words and deeds of Lin Biao and the "Gang of Four" (Jiang Qing, Zhang Chunqiao, Yao Wenyuan, and Wang Hongwen) who destroyed inner-party laws, regulations, and systems, trod on the constitution, violated human rights, and undermined the legal system under the guise of the name of the CPC. These cadres and masses questioned whether the Party or the law is superior with the purpose of fighting against the retroactions of Lin Biao and the "Gang of Four." In effect, they required adherence to the collective leadership of the CPC and maintaining the people's democracy and order of the state's legal system.

[27] Jiang Zemin's *Thought on Socialism with Chinese Characteristics* (special excerpts), Central Party Literature Press, Beijing, 2002 edition, pp. 307–308.

[28] *Biography of Peng Zhen*, Volume IV, Central Party Literature Press, Beijing, 2012 edition, p. 1572.

Deng Xiaoping profoundly pointed out in *The Reform of the Party and State's Leadership System* that it is no doubt that the mistakes we made before have something to do with some leaders' way of thinking and behaviors; however, problems in the organizational system are more serious. Bad people cannot run amuck if these systems are good, and good people may fail to do enough good and may even go over to the opposite side if these systems are bad. Institutional issues have more fundamental, comprehensive, stable, and long-term natures.[29] Practices have shown that running the state and dealing with politics by adopting the rule of man in a socialist country led and governed by the CPC is bound to cause double damage to the CPC's leadership and the state's legal system: damage to the collective leadership of the CPC, weakening of the CPC's political authority, trampling upon the people's democracy, undermining the socialist legal system, and bringing grave disasters to the CPC, the state, the people, and the society. After crushing the "Gang of Four" and ending the "Cultural Revolution," the CPC profoundly summarized the painful lesson of the "Cultural Revolution" that had sabotaged the democratic legal system. The CPC also analyzed the fundamental disadvantages of the rule of man in running the state and dealing with politics, and resolutely chose the political development path featuring the development of the socialist democracy and the improvement of the socialist legal system. Just as *The Decision* of the 4th Plenary Session of the 18th CPC Central Committee pointed out, since the 3rd Plenary Session of the 11th CPC Central Committee, our Party has profoundly summarized the successful experiences and profound lessons in building the socialist rule of law in China and proposed that there is a need to strengthen the rule of law and institutionalize and legalize the democratic legal system in order to guarantee the people's democracy. It is inevitably the choice for the practice of building China's socialism and the necessary requirement for the reform and opening up in this new era that we should unswervingly take the road of the socialist rule of law under the leadership of the CPC and keep to a high degree of unity of the Party and the law.

Over the past 30-plus years since the reform and opening up, the CPC has given top priority to correct recognition and understanding of the relations between the Party and the law, the core of building the socialist rule of law in the practice of leading the people to strengthen the rule

[29] Deng Xiaoping: *The Reform of the Party and State's Leadership System*, *Selected Works of Deng Xiaoping*, Volume 1, People's Publishing House, Beijing, 1994 edition, p. 293.

of law and advance the rule by law. In December 1978, Deng Xiaoping pointed out in *Emancipating the Minds, Seeking Truth from Facts, and Looking Forward in Unity* that the legal system must be strengthened in order to guarantee the people's democracy, and the democratic system must be institutionalized and legalized so that these systems do not change with the alteration of leaders or with the change of leaders' views and priorities. He also said that the issue at that moment was that the law was not yet perfect and there were still many laws to be enacted. More often than not, what leaders said would be taken as "laws," and disagreeing with what leaders said would be considered a "violation of the law." Thus alteration of leaders' words meant alteration of "laws." Since leaders were usually taken as the representative of the Party,[30] some masses raised the question of whether the Party or the law was superior, which was in effect to accuse the practice of the rule of man under which individuals or a few people made final decisions in the past political life of the Party and the state and to lash out at bureaucracy featuring power over law. Given this phenomenon, Deng Xiaoping made it clear in the early stage of the reform and opening up that considering leaders' words as laws and disagreeing with those words being considered a violation of law should no longer exist.[31]

Peng Zhen clearly answered the question of whether the Party or the law is superior when speaking of the CPC's leadership and the people's courts and the people's procuratorates' independent exercise of powers only by law in July 1979. He said, "Some comrades raised the question of whether the law, a leading cadre, or a local party committee is superior.

[30] Deng Xiaoping pointed out that bureaucratism featuring excessive concentration of power indeed existed within the Party due to the destruction of democratic centralism, and this kind of bureaucratism usually appeared as the Party's leadership, the Party's instructions, the Party's interests, and the Party's discipline. Deng Xiaoping: *Emancipating the Minds, Seeking Truth from Facts, and Looking Forward in Unity, Selected Works of Deng Xiaoping*, Volume 2, People's Publishing House, 1994 edition. Deng Xiaoping also said that "centralized Party leadership" often turned into leadership by individuals. Powers were excessively concentrated in the hands of individuals or the minority, most people handling affairs had no decision-making powers, and a small number of people with powers had heavy burdens and would definitely become bureaucrats, make all kinds of mistakes, bring harm to the democratic life, collective leadership, democratic centralism, the system of division of responsibility of individuals of the Party, and the government at all levels. Deng Xiaoping: *Reform of the Party and State's Leadership System, Selected Works of Deng Xiaoping*, Volume 2, People's Publishing House, 1994 edition.

[31] *A Chronicle of Deng Xiaoping*, Central Party Literature Press, Beijing, 1998 edition, p. 84.

For my part, the law is superior... No matter who you are, you shall be subject to the law. No one shall have the privilege before the law. Being subject to the law is to follow the leadership of the Central Committee of the Party and comply with the decision of the supreme organ of state power that is amenable to the entire nation."[32] In March 1984, Peng Zhen further explained the relations between the Party and the law in *Not Just Depending on the Party's Policy but also Acting by Law*. He said, "The Party's leadership is consistent with acting by law. The Party not only leads the people to enact the constitution and the laws but also leads the people to abide by and implement the constitution and the laws. *The Party Constitution* clearly stipulates that Party organizations and Party members must act within the framework of the constitution and the laws. This sentence was finally put forward after 10 years of miserable civil strife... Would it be fine if the Party did not act within the framework of the constitution and the laws? No, it would definitely not be! This has been shown by the 10 years of civil strife. *The Party Constitution* and the constitution have clear stipulations on this."[33] From the classical explanations of Peng Zhen on whether the Party or the law is superior and on the relations between the Party and the law, we can conclude that: (1) the "law" herein, no matter whether it is an abstract concept or a concrete concept, is the reflection of the authority and will of the state, and all organizations and individuals must abide by the law; (2) the "Party" herein does not abstractly refer to "the CPC;" but specifically to some leading "cadre," or "some local party committee," so we do not equalize or confuse an individual leading cadre of the Party or some organization or institution of the CPC with "the CPC;" (3) all people are equal before national laws, and leading Party cadres (even a leading cadre with a high position), or some organization or institution of some level of the CPC must be subject to national laws and act within the framework of the constitution and the laws; (4) National laws are always supreme before all leading Party cadres, or some organization or institution of the CPC at some level; and (5) the Party members and cadres, the Party organizations and institutions following laws means the same as to follow the leadership of the CPC Central Committee, the decision of the supreme organ of state power, the

[32] Peng Zhen: *On Political and Legal Works in New China*, Central Party Literature Press, Beijing, 1992 edition, pp. 176–177.

[33] Peng Zhen: *On the Establishment of Socialist Democracy and a Legal System in the New Era*, Central Party Literature Press, Beijing, 1989 edition, pp. 220, 221.

entire nation. The Party and the law, and the Party's leadership and the state legal system are completely unified.

While serving as General-Secretary, Jiang Zeming expressed his point of views on the relations between the Party and the law many times. When answering a question raised by a reporter of the *New York Times* on September 26, 1989, he said that the Party should never replace the government or the law, which was also a question about the rule of man and the rule of law talked about by the media. In 1998, he emphasized at the working conference on studying Deng Xiaoping Theory that advancing the socialist democratic political development requires better handling the relations among the Party's leadership, carrying forward the democracy, and acting by law. He also said that the Party's leadership was the key and carrying forward the democracy was the foundation while acting by law was the guarantee. These three should by no means be separated and antagonistic to each other. He also pointed out that sticking to the Party's leadership was completely consistent with ruling the country by law. The propositions of the CPC and national laws all represent and reflect the people's will and interests. The Party leads the people to formulate the constitution and laws and turns its propositions into the will of the state through organs of state power. The Party acts within the framework of the constitution and the laws, and governments at all levels administer the governmental affairs by laws. As such, the Party's leadership is united with ruling the country by law.

While also serving as General-Secretary, Hu Jintao also clearly noted that the essence of developing socialist democratic politics is to organically unite the Party's leadership, the people's role as masters of the country, and the rule by law. The Party's leadership is the fundamental guarantee of enabling the people to be masters of the country and ruling the country by law. Enabling the people to be masters of the country is the essential requirement of the socialist democratic politics. Ruling the country by law is the basic strategy for the Party to lead the people to govern the state. Correctly understanding and handling the relations among the three could further synergize the will and force of the entire Party and the Chinese people of all ethnic groups.

Since the convocation of the 18th Central Committee of the CPC and at a new starting point of comprehensively advancing the rule by law and accelerating the building of the socialist country under the rule of law, General-Secretary Xi Jinping has attached more importance to understanding the relations between the Party and the law from the perspective of the Party and the nation's overall working strategic situation. In the important speech delivered at the central political and legal work conference held in January 2014, General-Secretary Xi Jinping required political and judicial organs to insist on the supremacy of the Party's cause, the supremacy of the people's interests and the supremacy of the constitution and the laws in political and legal works, and proper handling of the relations between Party policies and national laws. Party policies and national laws are consistent in essence because they are all the reflection of the people's fundamental will. The Party not only leads the people to enact the constitution and the laws but also leads the people to implement the constitution and the laws. In the introduction to *The Decision* of the 4th Plenary Session of the 18th Central Committee of the CPC made in October 2014, General-Secretary Xi Jinping profoundly pointed out that the relationship between the Party and the rule of law is the core of building the rule of law. Organically uniting the Party's leadership, the people's role as masters of the country, and the rule by law is a basic experience of China in building the socialist rule of law. The key to comprehensively advancing the rule by law is to ensure the right direction and strong political guarantee. Specifically speaking, it is to keep to the Party's leadership, adhere to the socialist system with Chinese characteristics, and implement the theory of socialist rule of law with Chinese characteristics. In the important speech delivered at the opening ceremony of the special seminar for leading cadres at provincial and ministerial levels in February 2015, General-Secretary Xi Jinping re-emphasized that sticking to the Party's leadership was an important feature of the road of socialist rule of law with Chinese characteristics and the most fundamental guarantee for building the system of the socialist rule of law with Chinese characteristics. Therefore the direction should be right and the political guarantee should be strong in order to comprehensively advance the rule by law. The socialist rule of law must stick to the Party's leadership while the Party's leadership must rely on the socialist rule of law. The law is the proposition of the Party and the unified embodiment of the people's will. The Party leads the people to enact and implement the constitution and the laws. The Party must act within the framework of the constitution and the laws. In order to implement its leadership in the entire process and all aspects of the rule by law, first the Party needs to lead legislation that conforms to its propositions, respecting the people's will and satisfying the realistic needs based on the Party and the state's overall situations and the will of the masses; second, the Party needs to guarantee law enforcement and establish law-based governments featuring scientific functions, statutory rights and liabilities, strict and impartial law enforcement, openness and fairness, honesty and high efficiency, and law-abiding integrity, and statutory duties must be fulfilled and national public powers must be exercised with authorization; third, the Party needs to support judicature, provide a strong guarantee for judicial organs to independently and impartially exercise powers by law, improve the institutional mechanisms supervising and constraining judicial activities, and guarantee judicial powers are exercised within the framework of institutions; fourth, the CPC needs to take the lead in abiding by the laws, and every leading cadre must be subject to and abide by the constitution and the laws and shall not take the Party's leadership as the shield for replacing the law by individual's words, suppressing the law by power, and bending the law for personal gain but be the example for respecting, studying, abiding by, and using the law.

In short, from the perspective of the theory of socialist rule of law with Chinese characteristics, the road of socialist rule of law with Chinese characteristics after the 16th Central Committee of the CPC has always stressed sticking to an organic unity of the Party's leadership, the people's role as masters of the country, and the rule by law, and understanding the highly united relations between the Party and the law-based on this political philosophy. This political philosophy believes that the CPC's leadership is the fundamental guarantee of the rule by law while the rule by law is the basic strategy of the Party to lead the people to govern the state and the basic mode for the Party to run the state and deal with politics. In the practice of building the socialist rule of law with Chinese characteristics, the relations between the Party and the law have been experiencing a long-term exploration process featuring continuous development and transformation from policy guidance to legal guidance, from the rule of man to the rule by law, and from the rule by law to the rule of law. It is also a long-term process of exploring the mutual supplement and a high degree of unity of the Party and the law, of politics and the rule of law, and of the Party's leadership and the rule by law. In the development process of the socialist law-based civilization with Chinese characteristics, the so-called "question" of whether the Party or the law is superior has become a past tense historical concept with the continuous implementation and comprehensive advancement of the rule by law as the basic strategy. Keeping to a high degree of unity of the Party and the law has become the common consensus of the entire Party and the whole nation and has become a basic feature and political advantage of the socialist rule of law with Chinese characteristics.

CHAPTER 6

Advancing the Building of the Rule of Law in China

The 18th National Congress of the Communist Party of China (CPC) was convened in 2012. The ruling party made the decision on "comprehensively deepening the reform" in 2013 and on "comprehensively ruling the country by law" in 2014. These major strategies were the call for a new advancement of China's economic, political, social, cultural, and ecological civilization. The convocation of the 18th National Congress and these major strategies also announced that China had entered into a new development era for the great cause of ruling the country by law and building the rule of law in China. The convocation of the 18th National Congress and these major strategies also signaled that China had entered into a new development stage for the great practices of comprehensively deepening the reform, trying to promote development, building a moderately prosperous society across the board, and achieving the great rejuvenation of the Chinese nation.

At this new historical starting point, an important consensus was reached for building the rule of law in China including: Ruling the country by law is the fundamental strategy for state management and social governance; the rule of law is the basic mode of ruling the country and dealing with politics; and building the rule of law in China is an indispensable and important part of the great China dream. In order to build China into a country under the rule of law and realize the China dream of building the rule of law at an early date, there is a need to comprehensively deepen the reform of the legal system, vigorously promote the process of ruling the country by law, and adhere to an organic unity of upholding the party's leadership, ensuring that the people are masters of the country and ruling the country by law. There is a need to stay committed to scientific legislation, strict law enforcement, impartial judicature, and law abidance by all the people. There is also a need to adhere to a common advancement of the rule by law, governance by law, administration by law and an integrated promotion of law-based state, law-based government, and law-based society.

Building the Rule of Law in China.
DOI: http://dx.doi.org/10.1016/B978-0-12-811930-3.00006-4

6.1 DEEPENING POLITICAL RESTRUCTURING THROUGH COMPREHENSIVELY PROMOTING THE RULE BY LAW

To persist in the socialist political development path with Chinese characteristics, there is a need to actively and steadily deepen political restructuring, comprehensively promote the rule by law, and accelerate the building of a socialist country under the rule of law. The ruling party proposed at its 3rd Plenary Session of the 18th National Congress to deepen political restructuring by firmly centering on an organic unity of upholding the party's leadership, ensuring that the people are masters of the country and ruling the country by law. Political restructuring is the basic policy that has always been upheld by the party and the state since the 3rd Plenary Session of the 11th Central Committee of the CPC. Political restructuring is the self-improvement of the socialist political system with Chinese characteristics and a sound development of the legal system.

6.1.1 Comprehensively Advancing the Rule by Law is Political Restructuring in Essence

The rule by law is the basic strategy for the party to lead the people to rule the state and deal with politics. From the perspective of developing democratic politics, the rule by law means to make the people masters of the country and manage national, social, economic, and cultural affairs based on the constitution and the law. From the perspective of strengthening and improving the party's leadership and ruling, the rule by law means that the party acts within the framework of the constitution and the law, rules the state, and deals with politics based on and by applying the constitution and the law, i.e., to exercise the state power according to the constitution and the law. From the perspective of the internal functions and values of the rule of law, the rule by law is to administer powers and officials according to the law, respect and guarantee human rights, and bring various kinds of state works under the rule of law. From the perspective of boosting the modernization of the national governance system and governance capacity, the rule by law is used to consistently improve the national system of law and the legal system, and at the same time make these laws and systems operate properly and effectively so as to realize good laws and proper governance.

The Decision of the ruling party at its 3rd Plenary Session of the Central Committee clearly required organic unity of the party's leadership, the people's role as masters of the country, and the rule by law to deepen the political restructuring. Thus it is clear that the rule by law has the nature of political restructuring in its final analysis. General-Secretary Xi Jinping further pointed out that comprehensively advancing the rule by law is a systematic project and an extensive and profound revolution in state governance.[1] This "revolution" with the nature of political restructuring in modern China is different from China's past economic system reform, social system reform, educational system reform, and health system reform in many aspects, such as in the guiding thought, the basic principle, the leading mode, and the reform action. Comprehensively promoting the rule by law requires resource coordination in politics, economy, culture, and society, among other aspects, and the synergy of education, administration, economy, morality, discipline, and customs, among other means. However, looking from the institutional aspect of the national governance system, political reform is reformation, or political system reform. Comprehensively promoting the rule by law is the deepening reform and self-improvement of China's political system in a sense.

To comprehensively promote the rule by law and try to build the rule of law in China, there is a need to keep to an organic unity of upholding the party's leadership, ensuring that the people are masters of the country and ruling the country by law. Also, there is a need to adhere to comprehensive enhancement of scientific legislation, strict law enforcement, impartial judicature, and all people's abidance by the law. There is a need to insist on a common advancement of the rule by law, governance by law and administration by law, and integrated development of a law-based state, law-based government, and law-based society. Implementing all these requirements for comprehensively promoting the rule by law and building the rule of law in China in modernized systems and mechanisms of the state governance system is bound to touch or trigger issues related to political system reform and improvement. Therefore China needs to be soberly aware of and fully prepared for this.

Undoubtedly, the institutional form featuring "an organic unity of the three" is the democratic political system of socialism with Chinese characteristics, and the core is the political system of sticking to the leadership and ruling of the Communist party and the people's congress system as China's fundamental political system. Promoting the reform measures

[1] Xi Jinping: *Speech at the Opening Ceremony of the Special Seminar on Implementing the Spirit of the Fourth Plenary Session of the 18th Central Committee of the CPPCC for Leading Cadres at Provincial and Ministerial Levels*, *People's Daily*, February 3, 2015.

for the rule by law and implementing various reform designs and suggestions for the rule by law as the fundamental strategy will inevitably have a direct and indirect bearing on the party's leadership system and the people's congress system and on China's political system. Promoting scientific legislation involves structural and mechanistic issues, such as how to improve the legislative system, the legislative procedure, legislative technology, legislative quality and legislative effect, and the system of law. Moreover, promoting scientific legislation involves deep-seated structural and mechanistic issues, such as how to further improve the quality of deputies to the people's congress, implement the constitutional power of the people's congress, strengthen the supervision of the people's congress, and develop the democracy of the people's congress. Promoting strict law enforcement involves issues like how to reform and improve the administrative law enforcement system, mechanism, and mode, and strengthen the regulations and restrictions on the discretionary power of administrative law enforcement. In addition, promoting strict law enforcement involves issues like how to deepen administrative system reform, transform government functions, boost administration by law, build law-based government, and a series of deep-seated structural and mechanistic problems. Promoting impartial judicature inevitably requires comprehensive reform of the judicial system and even takes the reform of the judicial system as the breakthrough of the political system reform. Promoting governance by law and implementing in institution the principles of ensuring the party's leadership in legislation, guarantee of law enforcement, safeguard of judicature, and leadership in law abidance are a revolution transforming the revolutionary party to a ruling party, i.e., the reform of the Communist Party of China.

Determining the nature of comprehensive advancement of the rule by law as China's political system reform is the requirement for an active adaption of China's political system to social and economic development and for a comprehensive and deepened reform of the legal system under the new situation. The determination is the self-improvement and optimized development of political systems and mechanisms under the constitutional framework and on the law-based track. Determining the nature of comprehensive advancement of the rule by law as the political system reform is a reliable path for boosting the political restructuring in an organized, guided, active, steady, and progressive manner after the exploration of China and its party over the past six decades, especially after their continuous practices in the past more than three decades since the reform and opening up. Determining the nature of comprehensive advancement of the rule by law as the political system reform is the only road for continuously developing and improving the socialist democratic politics with Chinese characteristics. This road conforms to China's national conditions.

It's of great significance to comprehensively press ahead with the rule by law and use law-based thinking and methods to advance political restructuring in an active and steady way. First, the existing explorations in political restructuring can be formally put on the agenda of the party and the state to further the reform under the precondition of keeping to the party's leadership and guaranteeing national and social stability and ethnic solidarity. Thus the political restructuring could enjoy a harmonious, orderly, perfectly justifiable, and good social environment and atmosphere. Second, reasonable demands of the people for the reform of institutional mechanisms (political system reform in particular) could be included in the concept of the rule of law through making, revising, annulling, and interpreting the law. Broad consensuses can be formed through legal rationality. These broad consensuses can be translated into legal forms through democratic legislation and other procedures. In so doing, the results of political restructuring and other reforms can be presented and consolidated by the legal system, and radical reform can be avoided. Third, the implementation of the constitution and the law can be effectively guaranteed, and social equity and justice, basic human rights, and freedom could be fully safeguarded through constant improvement of the system of law with Chinese characteristics and through the rather robust legal system and procedural mechanisms in legislation, law enforcement, judicature, law abidance, and law protection. Consequently, we can move forward with the modernization of the national governance system, keep bringing the national governance system under the rule of law, and make the superstructure of China's political laws better meet the needs of social and economic reform and development. Fourth, the significance is to firmly hold the right to speak and lead in the political restructuring and respond to reasonable demands of the people for political restructuring and development. The significance is to fight back at the slander and misrepresentation of China's democratic politics and political restructuring by western hostile forces and elements. Therefore we can righteously declare to the world that China's reform is an all-round and profound reform in all areas, including not only the reform of the economic system, social system, and cultural system but also the political system, all of which firmly center on "an organic unity of the three" and rely on the path of comprehensively advancing the rule by law.

The essence of comprehensive advancement of the rule by law is the reform of the political system, so China must not take it lightly. Rather, China needs to pay attention to it and strengthen the leadership over it. China also needs to prevent Chinese and foreign hostile forces from using the reform of legal system, especially the opportunity to deepen the reform of the judicial system, to disseminate democratic values and judicial models of the West and cause these values and models to infiltrate into China's legal system reform. At the same time, there is a need to intensify the positive guidance of domestic theoretical circle and media circle in theoretical studies and public opinion propaganda. There is also a need to pay attention to the interest demand of the people for political restructuring and prevent some people with ulterior motives from utilizing the political restructuring by comprehensively advancing the rule by law to instigate street politics, large-scale mass incidents, and other activities violating the rule of law.

6.1.2 Comprehensively Advancing the Rule by Law is the Way to Deepen the Reform of the Political System

In a peaceful and rational society, "political reform" is usually the way to manifest and implement political restructuring. The Reform of Li Kui, Reform of Wu Qi, Reform of Shang Yang, Reform of Wang Anshi, and Hundred Days' Reform in China history are all examples of "political reform." These political reforms were actually meant to improve the political system by changing the laws and systems at the time. Political reform as the carrier to implement political restructuring is neither a stormy revolution nor a reaction for changing the rule. Reform equals change, improvement, and reformation. It is to actively change and improve national laws and the political system under the premise of maintaining the existing power base and political rule. The purpose of political reform is to make the political system better meet the needs of social and economic development. A revolution involves profound changes of a social and political system. The aim of a revolution is to overturn the existing state power and realize political changes through rebellions, uprisings, and other extreme and violent means. All laws and systems of the existing state power are included in the list for reformation.

Under the constitutional system, comprehensively advancing the rule by law and accelerating the building of the rule of law in China are not only an important part of and a main approach for political restructuring, but also a legal guarantee for deepening the political restructuring in an active and steady way. An effective way to realize orderly political restructuring through reforming the legal system and improving the laws is to comprehensively advance the rule by law and realize the aim of administering power by law, governing officials by law, and governing according to the law. It is to fully safeguard the people's democracy and to respect and protect human rights. It's to actively and steadily deepen the political restructuring on a law-based track. The constitution is the top-level design and concentrated expression of a state's political system. Good operation of a political system should be demonstrated in the following aspects: Earnest implementation of the constitution, ruling the country and holding the power in accordance with the constitution, and safeguarding the authority of the constitution. Revising and interpreting the constitution means to actively and steadily deepen the political restructuring from the perspective of the fundamental legal norms of the state. In particular, modern democratic politics is the law-based politics regulated and guaranteed by laws and systems on the basis of the constitution. In effect, adhering to the institutionalization and legalization of democracy and advancing the rule by law, governance by law, and administration by law are in essence the self-improvement, self-reform, and self-renewal of the political system under the constitutional framework, which also includes building the country, the government, and the society according to the rule of law, promoting the making, revision, annulment, and interpretation of laws, advancing judicial system reform, and reinforcing power supervision.

After over 30 years of exploration and practice since the reform and opening up, people have increasingly realized the necessity to reform the political system simultaneously with reform of economic system, social system, and cultural system. People have also increasingly understood the necessity to better handle relations among reform, development, and stability. People have deepened their understanding and recognition of active, steady, and orderly advancement of political restructuring in line with China's national conditions. History has shown that without political restructuring, it would be difficult to deepen and effectively reform other areas. However, political restructuring is highly risky. To prevent and dissolve the risks evoked by political restructuring and deepen political restructuring in an active, orderly, and highly effective way, the most fundamental principle is to keep to an organic unity of upholding the party's leadership, ensuring that the people are masters of the country and ruling the country by law. The most fundamental strategy is to beat the targets of political reform through pressing ahead with the rule by law and building the rule of law in China within the constitutional framework and on a law-based track.

The only road for China to promote democracy, the rule of law, realize self-improvement, and deepen the political system reform under the new situation is to comprehensively advance the rule by law and deepen the political restructuring when building the rule of law in China.

First, comprehensively advancing the rule by law is a major reform of the political system. Ruling the country by law means the people manage national, social, economic, and cultural affairs under the guidance of the party and in accordance with the constitution and the law. All works of the state should be under the rule of law. The process of ruling the country by law is the process in which the people exercise democratic and political rights and act as masters of the country. It's the process to enjoy, regulate, and exercise national political powers under the law; the process to build, operate, and improve the national political system under the law. Since 1978, China has witnessed the process from the rule of man to the rule by law, from the rule by law to the rule of law, and then to ruling the country by law. The party has led the people to make major reforms in state governance. China's political system is also deeply reformed to be more democratized, scientific, and legalized. Comprehensive advancement of the rule by law, adherence to the party's leadership, and ensuring that people are masters of the country in a law-based thinking and law-based way could guarantee orderly and effective operation of state machines and political system, and guarantee to exercise the powers bestowed by the people for the people, seek the interests of the people, feel for the people, and realize governance for the people.

Second, there would be no democratic politics without the rule of law. The rule of law is the institutionalization and legalization of democracy, the institutional guarantee for democratic politics. China has established its system of law. In China, laws are available in various aspects of life, such as national economic, political, social, and cultural lives, signifying that the socialism with Chinese characteristics has been established and under constant improvement. China's political systems (the system led by the Communist Party, the system of people's democratic dictatorship, the system of people's congress, the system of regional and national autonomy, the system of grassroots democratic autonomy, the system of democratic election and democratic consultation, the state administrative system, and the judicial system) are regulated and guaranteed by the constitution and the law, and built, operated, and changed according to the law. On the one hand, comprehensive advancement of the rule by law and constant improvement of China's constitutional system, legal system, legal norms, and the system of law could speed up the process to build the political system under the rule of law in a normalized manner. In this way, political powers and behaviors could be incorporated into law-based regulation, control, and guarantee. On the other hand, this can help realize the reform, improvement, and development of relevant institutions, procedures, and norms in China's political framework on a law-based track, and as a result, deepen political restructuring by law-based means during the practical process of ruling the country by law.

Third, promoting scientific legislation is "political reform." Strengthening legislative works and constantly improving the system of law and the foundation for the rule of law, which are indispensable for the political system, are "political reform." In an orderly way we can boost continuous development of China's political civilization by the rule of law, constantly promote regulation of political behaviors, and improve the political system. Revision of China's constitution, and the making, revision, annulment, and interpretation of laws and regulations will certainly promote the setup, improvement, alternation, and even annulment of some or some kind of political systems. For instance, the formulation of the administrative procedural law has induced the administrative litigation system, under which ordinary people could sue government officials. The revised electoral law stipulates that the urban and rural areas elect deputies to people's congresses based on the same proportion. This has improved China's electoral system. Obviously, the making, revision, annulment, and interpretation of Chinese laws and regulations in the process of ruling the country by law is not only the continuous improvement and self-development of the legal system but also the reform and perfection of China's various systems including the political system.

6.1.3 Deepen Political Restructuring in the Process of Comprehensively Advancing the Rule by Law

China's political restructuring is not a great disaster under the current national, political, social, and cultural conditions. The political wisdom and rational intelligence enable the Chinese people to taking absolute control of the reform. Therefore there is no need for China to be afraid of "political reform." Political restructuring is not a go-as-you-please move. The socialist institutional system with Chinese characteristics, ruling the country by law, and ruling the country by the constitution are the premise, boundary, criterion, and guarantee for this reform. No force is allowed to take advantage of the "political reform."

Looking from the essence of political restructuring, deepening political restructuring through comprehensively advancing the rule by law means readjusting and reallocating a series of vital interests guaranteed by the rule of law and oriented with equity and justice within the constitutional framework. The law is a distributor of social interests. For all kinds of public powers, reforming the political system through the rule of law and using the rule of law to break the fence of interest solidity actually decrease private interests brought by public powers and increase responsibilities and services. In addition, it is unfair to decrease go-as-you-please behavior and increase supervision and restriction; decrease corruption opportunities and increase integrity and self-discipline; and decrease malpractices and negligence and increase democracy and efficiency. For the subjects of private rights and social rights, such as citizens, enterprises, and general social organizations, political restructuring will not damage any of their vital interests in essence but empower them with more freedom, equality, democracy, the rule of law, justice, fairness, integrity, and efficiency. In China, the people are masters of the country, the society, and themselves. Orderly deepening the political restructuring through ruling the country by law conforms to the fundamental and long-term interests of the masses. The broad masses will not be suppressed and exploited by bureaucracy and privilege; on the contrary, they gain fairness, justice, democracy, and the rule of law in this process. Consequently, they are advocators, supporters, players, and beneficiaries of political restructuring, the force on which the political restructuring firmly relies. Those who are afraid of, oppose, or obstruct political restructuring are only a few people with vested interests, or departments and places of vested interest. The political restructuring in the process of ruling the country by law aims to make the powers bestowed by the people serve the people, returning the benefits and achievements created by the people to the people.

Looking from the perspective of political restructuring, deepening political restructuring through comprehensively advancing the rule by law needs to adjust and change a series of crucial political and social relations in national and social lives. These relations include the relations among the party, the people, and the state, mainly manifested as the mutual relations of party power, civil power, and political power. It also includes the relations among politics, democracy, and the rule of law, manifested as adhering to "an organic unity of the three;" the relations between the central committee and local committees, manifested as the division of power between the two; the relations between the government for one part and the society and individuals for another, manifested as the relations among administrative powers, social rights, and individual rights; the relations between government and market, manifested as the relations between administrative power and the law of market economy; the relations between the National People's Congress for one part and administrative organs, judicial organs, and procuratorate organs for another, manifested as the relations of mutual division of labor, mutual coordination, and mutual restriction among administrative powers, judicial powers, and procuratorial powers. The law is meant to adjust social relations. Political restructuring in the process of ruling the country by law aims to further straighten and improve relevant political and social relations through law-based thinking and ways. It aims to incorporate a series of basic relations in the political system into constitutional and legal adjustments, regulations, and supervisions; to include the changes of political relations and the improvement of political systems in law-based guidance, regulation, and control; to realize a deep-seated reform and optimization of political systems; and to bring the national governance system under the rule of law.

Looking from the objects of political restructuring, deepening political restructuring through comprehensively advancing the rule by law does not mean giving up the socialist direction and the socialist road. It also does not mean changing China's fundamental political system and basic political system, nor changing China's nature of state and form of government and implementing the western multiparty system and the "tripartite" political system (the legislative power, the administrative power, and the judicial power are controlled by the parliament, cabinet, and court, respectively). Rather, it is to reform and improve some specific political systems, procedures, ways, and mechanisms that are not adaptable to the needs of social and economic development and are unsatisfactory to the broad masses. It has to be done under the precondition to stick to the socialist direction and the socialist road with Chinese characteristics, adhering to China's fundamental political system and basic political system. The political restructuring in the process of ruling the country by law is to use law-based thinking and ways to promote the reform, improvement, innovation, and development of specific political systems and mechanisms (national leading system, legislative system, administrative system, judicial system, electoral system, intra-party democratic system, democratic management system, democratic supervision system, and democratic participation system), according to the regulation and guidance of the constitution and the law. The problems and disadvantages of the above-mentioned systems and mechanisms are the main objects for China to deepen political restructuring, as well as the key issues requiring attention and solutions for comprehensive advancement of the rule by law.

Looking from the perspective of political restructuring, deepening political restructuring through comprehensively advancing the rule by law is not to implement "great democracy" regardless of the law. It is not to practice "cultural revolution" deconstructionism and political movement eradicating the old and fostering the new. It is not to go for stormy political revolutions and struggles. Rather, it is to stay committed to constructivism in the sense of democracy and the rule of law; to reform and improve China's political system in a constructive, active, and steady way in the process of advancing the rule by law; to do a good job in the top design of the political system reform through law-based thinking by fully promoting democracy; to give full play to the innovation and exploration of the spirit of local places, the grassroots, and the people in reform; to guide the good appeal of people for political restructuring to the practice of comprehensively advancing the rule by law; to guide the different recognitions of political restructuring by the broad cadres to the overall layout of accelerating the building of the rule of law in China; and to boost the reform of various aspects of China's political system in an active and steady way on a law-based track and through ruling the country by law.

6.2 THE STRATEGIC TARGET OF RULE OF LAW CONSTRUCTION AND REFORM IN CHINA

It is of great significance to comprehensively promote the rule by law, strive to build the rule of law in China, and constantly deepen the legal system reform, and thus to deepen reform at national and social levels.

On the one hand, the rule of law is an integral part of socialist democratic politics. Promoting the rule by law serves as an important channel for China to implement the political system reform. There would be no socialist democratic politics without the socialist rule of law. In this sense, promoting the rule by law in an all-round way and constantly deepening the reform of the legal system are important for innovations of socialist democracy with Chinese characteristics, which means standardized, institutionalized, and legalized development. Moreover, it is an important channel for deepening political restructuring in an active, steady, and all-round way within the existing constitutional framework and on a law-based track. Under the political system and constitutional framework of China, and determined by the contents, characteristics, and functions of the rule of law, the process to strengthen the development of the rule of law, advance the rule by law, deepen the reform of legal system, and even all practices of the rule of law (legal system), are not limited to improvement of laws, development of the rule of law, and issues related to the law. They are also about political development, political restructuring, and issues related to politics in a broader sense.

Since the reform and opening up, China has scored unprecedented achievements in building the rule of law. The rule by law has been identified by the party and the state as the fundamental strategy, which remarkably enhances the ruling party's capacity of ruling by law and constitution. The socialist system of law with Chinese characteristics has taken shape as scheduled. Human rights and democracy are guaranteed under the rule of law. The legal environment continues to improve, boosting social and economic development. The level of administration by law and impartial judicature keeps improving. The restriction and supervision over powers by the rule of law have been reinforced. Impressive progress has been made in legal publicity, education, and legal services. Local rule of law and industry governance by law keep developing in a new way. The "one country, two systems" policy and the basic law of special administrative regions have been implemented effectively. The concept of the rule of law has been generally enhanced in the entire society. Jurisprudential studies and education have witnessed rapid development.

At the same time, however, we should realize that the rule of law in China still has a long way to go to meet the new expectations of the people. Although China has gained achievements in building the rule of law, it is still fall behind the increasingly improved status of China as a great power. The rule by law as the fundamental strategy has been implemented for many years, but the development remains unbalanced in different areas, different links, and different sectors. Principled requirements have been raised for governance by law, but there is still a lack of specific systems and procedural guarantees. The system of law with Chinese characteristics has taken shape, but it needs to be further improved and developed. Brilliant results have been produced in legislative works. There are laws to regulate people's behavior. However, things are not up to expectations in law enforcement, judicature, law abidance, and legal supervision. Great achievements have been made in legal publicity and education, but the law-based environment has not been improved fundamentally.

At present, there are many deficiencies in the building of the rule of law in China: an imperfect supervision mechanism and specific system for guaranteeing the implementation of the constitution; failure to abide by the law, and slack law enforcement, impunity of law breakers in some local areas and departments; salient issues related to law enforcement and judicature concerning the immediate interests of the public; seriously damaged national legal authority as a result of public servants' power abuse, dereliction of duties, lawbreaking activities, and even crimes of bending the law for personal gain; the constitutional awareness of citizens including some leading cadres needs to be further improved. China must take all these issues seriously and have them solved practically.[2] China must address institutional and mechanical issues existing in the process of building the rule of law and ruling the country by law by comprehensively deepening the legal reform in different areas and links such as legislation, law enforcement, judicature, law abidance, and legal supervision, based on the strategic layout of ruling the country by law in an all-round way. Deepening the reform of the legal system is in itself reform of the political system. Strengthening the development of the rule of law is in itself to promote socialist democracy with Chinese characteristics.

Moreover, the rule of law is an essential guarantee for deepening the reform in an all-round way. It would be impossible to gain success in comprehensively deepening the reform across the nation without comprehensive planning, overall arrangement of what should be encouraged and reformed, guidance, regulation, and guarantee of the rule of law, the making, revision, annulment, and strict enforcement of the law, and impartial judicature and law abidance by all the people nor effective implementation of the constitution and the law. Therefore China must comprehensively promote the rule by law, deepen various reforms in law-based thinking and ways, orderly adjust various kinds of social relations, rationally allocate social resources, effectively regulate social behaviors, and realize social fairness and justice. These are not only the inevitable requirements posed by the new circumstances but also the historical responsibilities and time missions to develop the rule of law in China.

History has shown that more comprehensive and deepened reform will result in fiercer conflict of interests, more uncertainties, and higher unpredictable risks. Therefore there is a need to attach more importance

[2] Xi Jinping: "Speech at the Meeting of All Walks of Life Marking the 30th Anniversary of the Issuance and Implementation of the Existing constitution," *People's Daily*, December 5, 2012.

to the leading role of the rule of law and keep intensifying the development of the rule of law. The people's demand, interest game, relationship adjustment, resource allocation, solution selection, top-level design, path arrangement, implementation process, and supervision guarantee shall be included into the legal order framework for ruling the country by law and building the rule of law in China. In so doing, the goal of comprehensively deepening the reform could be realized in the practical process of legalization.

In December 1978, Deng Xiaoping pointed out that there was a need to continuously develop socialist democracy and improve the socialist legal system. It was the basic policy firmly upheld by the Central Committee since its 3rd Plenary Session. He also said that this basic principle should be upheld unswervingly going forward.[3] In February 1996, Jiang Zemin emphasized that strengthening the development of socialist legal system and ruling the country by law represented not only an essential part of the theory of building the socialism with Chinese characteristics proposed by Deng Xiaoping, but also a principal policy of the party and Chinese government for managing national and social affairs.[4] At the 15th National Congress of the Communist Party of China in 1997, the rule by law was identified as the fundamental strategy for the party to lead the people to rule the state and deal with politics. The 16th National Congress of the party in 2002 made it loud and clear that we must keep to the "an organic unity of the three" in order to implement the rule by law. The National People's Congress adopted the amendments to the constitution in 2004 and included in the constitution ruling the country by law and building a socialist country under the rule of law. Thus the rule by law became a constitutional principle with the supreme legal effects and the supreme authority of the rule of law. The 17th National Congress in 2007 clearly proposed the law-based development strategy—to implement the rule by law as the fundamental strategy in an all-round way and accelerate the building of a socialist country under the rule of law. The 18th National Congress in 2012 further stressed the need to press ahead with the rule by law in an all-round way to speed up the building of a socialist country under the rule of law. In 2014, the 4th Plenary Session of the 18th

[3] Deng Xiaoping: *Implement Adjustment Policy to Ensure Stability and Unity, Selected Works of Deng Xiaoping*, Volume II, People's Publishing House, 1993 edition, p. 359.

[4] Jiang Zemin: *Implement and Adhere to the Rule by Law to Ensure National Long-term Stability and Peace, People's Daily*, February 9, 1996.

Central Committee of the ruling party put forward the overall objective of building the system of socialist rule of law with Chinese characteristics and building a socialist country under the rule of law. All this indicates that facilitating the development of the rule of law, advancing the rule by law, and building the rule of law in China are the basic principles and important strategic goals that China must adhere to in the long run.

The strategic goal of the "Reform to Build the Rule of Law in China" is not groundless. It should match the overall development strategy of China and coordinate with the China dream of the "200-year strategic goals," which include: by 2020 when the well-to-do society is established, realizing a doubled increase of the Gross Domestic Product (GDP) and the income of urban and rural residents compared with that of 2010; and by 2049 when the People's Republic of China has been founded for 100 years, develop China into a prosperous, democratic, and harmonious socialist country. China has made remarkable achievements in building the rule of law, achieved obvious progress in ruling the country by law, and put in place the system of law with Chinese characteristics. Against this background and according to the national "200-year strategic goals," China needs to identify a "two-step" strategy for building the rule of law in China. In so doing, China could, going forward, further strengthen the development of the rule of law, comprehensively promote the rule by law, constantly deepen the reform of the legal system, and transform from the system of law to the system of the rule of law, from a great country under the law to a strong country under the rule of law, and from centering on legislation to focusing on the implementation of the constitution and the laws in building the rule of law.

The first step is basically to realize the goal of building the rule of law in China by 2020 when China has become a moderately prosperous society. The report of the Communist Party of China to its 18th National Congress pointed out that China was still facing important strategic opportunities for development. There was a large room for improvement as analyzed from international and domestic situations. China needs to accurately judge the changes and conditions in the period of important strategic opportunity, and seize the opportunity to respond to challenges. Moreover, China needs to take initiative to develop its competitive edge and win the future. The ultimate goal is to build a moderately prosperous society by 2020. Of cause, the strategic goal to build the rule of law in China (a well-off society under the rule of law) is also a part of the ambitious goal to build a moderately prosperous society by 2020. It means basically buliding the rule of law in China.

The second step is to complete building of the rule of law in China by 2049 when the People's Republic of China celebrates its 100th anniversary. The party's report to its 15th National Congress pointed out that China will basically become a modernized, prosperous, strong, and democratic socialist country by the middle of the century when it celebrates its 100th anniversary. The report further stressed that China is bound to build an all-round well-off society at the time when the Communist Party of China will have been founded for 100 years, provided that China has the ideal, keeps the faith, stands unswervingly, avoids slothfulness and self-inflicted setbacks, and fights relentlessly, painstakingly, and untiringly. By then, China could certainly build a prosperous, strong, civilized, democratic, and harmonious society and a modernized country. The entire party should hold confidence in this development road, theory, and institution. China has clearly identified the "200-year strategic goals," the great objective of the struggle to realize China's dream to rejuvenate the great Chinese nation. The China dream is the dream of the Chinese people as well as the Chinese nation. Undoubtedly, the China dream certainly includes the following: building a prosperous, strong, democratic, civilized, harmonious, and modernized country, realizing great rejuvenation of the Chinese nation, and building of the rule of law in China.

6.3 RULE OF LAW CONSTRUCTION AND REFORM IN CHINA: GENERAL IDEA AND BASIC REQUIREMENTS

6.3.1 General Idea

As driven by the strategic goal to build the rule of law in China and the overall requirements for economic, political, social, cultural, and ecological civilization development, China must keep to an organic unity of upholding the party's leadership, ensuring that the people are masters of the country and ruling the country by law under the unified leadership of the Central Committee of the CPC. China also must deepen the legal system reform in an active and steady way. China must spare no effort to solve issues such as improper legislation, slack law enforcement, denial of justice, disordered law abidance, and weak rule of law. China must comprehensively and in an orderly way advance the rule by law, governance by law, and administration by law. China must strive to build a law-based country, law-based government, and law-based society, and build a modernized China under the rule of law as early as possible.

Comprehensively deepening the reform must include deepening the reform of the legal system in an all-round way. The legal system is the abbreviation of laws and systems, and generally includes the legislative system, the law enforcement system, the judicial system, the legal supervision system, the law implementation system, the legal service system, the system of constitutional law, the system of administrative law, the system of economic law, the civil and commercial legal system, the system of criminal law, the system of social law, the system of litigation and nonlitigation, and the system of international law. The purpose of comprehensively deepening the reform of the legal system is to further advance all-round reform of the legal system in a broad, deep, and vigorous manner. It should be implemented on the basis of the national strategic goal and overall mission of the "200-year strategic goals," the reform of the legal system during the last 30-plus years since the reform and opening up. In so doing, China could continuously improve, innovate, and develop the legal system. Consequently, the legal system could better adapt to socialist modernization with Chinese characteristics and meet the needs of great rejuvenation of the Chinese nation. Moreover, the legal system could better meet needs of comprehensively deepening the reform, opening wider to the outside, and vigorously promoting the development; the legal system could also better meet the needs of the people's ever-increasing requirements for human rights and fundamental freedom, fairness, and justice, and a safe, and a stable and happy life. Last but not least, the legal system could better meet the needs for comprehensively advancing the rule by law and realizing scientific legislation, strict law enforcement, impartial judicature, and law abidance by all the people, as we strive to build the rule of law in China.

Comprehensively advancing the rule by law is a part of China's political restructuring. It is the self-improvement and development of the socialist legal system. In this regard, China must adhere to an organic unity of upholding the party's leadership, ensuring that the people are masters of the country and ruling the country by law. China must keep to the authority of the constitution and the principles of the rule of law, acting upon its national condition and reality to promote the fine tradition of Chinese legal culture. At the same time, China needs to learn from other human political and legal civilizations and adhere to the socialist road with Chinese characteristics.

To comprehensively deepen the reform of the legal system, there is a need to solve various issues like improper legislation in the legislative system, legislative mechanism, legislative proceedings, and legislative process; solve a series of institutional, mechanical, and procedural issues related to duplicated law enforcement, multilevel law enforcement, evading law enforcement, disordered law enforcement, fishing law enforcement, rough law enforcement, rent-seeking law enforcement, restrictive law enforcement, selective law enforcement, campaign-style law enforcement, weak law enforcement, hysteretic law enforcement, and slack law enforcement; solve issues resulted from arbitrary and unfair judicatures, such as difficult and expensive litigation procedures, power abuse of judges, abuse of discretion, seeking personal gain through cases, more unsolved cases, more protracted cases, difficult law enforcement, extorting confessions by torture, presumption of guilt, erroneous judgment; correct the ideas and habits to disorderly observe the law, such as believing in powers, relations, and money rather than the law, believing in the ideas and habits making minor troubles only get minor problems solved, making big troubles could get major problems solved, and making no troubles solves nothing, and believing in the Chinese style of violation of the law, selective use of the law; and solve the weak rule of law. For instance, the constitution has become "an idle law;" some laws and regulations exist in name only; policies are supreme than laws; politics are supreme than the rule of law; privileges are supreme than legal powers; leaders are supreme than laws; leaders break the law; law-enforcement personnel break the law while enforcing the law; and bullying the weak and fearing the strong has become all too common.

6.3.2 Basic Requirements

China needs to understand scientifically and correctly the basic implication of comprehensively advancing the rule by law and accelerate said progress. The so-called "comprehensive" advancing the rule by law means to regard the rule by law as a huge and systematic project, taking into full account all links and elements of the rule of law and achieving comprehensive and effective advancement of the rule by law as the fundamental strategy. It is also to integrate the spirit, value, sense, ideas, and culture of the rule of law into a practical process of ruling the country by law. It means unified ruling of the country by the constitution and the law, governance by law, administration by law, and acting by law. It means realizing the unity of the establishment and the strict and punitive enforcement of the law. It is to realize the unity of scientific law making, strict law enforcement, impartial justice, observance of law by everyone, and effective protection of the law. It is to closely combine the study of law, the education of law, and the publicity of the rule of law with the practices of the rule of law. It is to systematically integrate various elements of the rule by law, comprehensively straighten various links of the rule of law, form a systematic project to build the rule of law in China, and implement the rule by law as the fundamental strategy in an all-round and specific way.

The so-called comprehensively "advancing" the rule by law means that ruling the country by law should only result in progress but not development retrogress. It should be advanced actively rather than passively. The rule by law should only be implemented soundly. It is not empty talk. The rule by law should be carried out without hesitation rather than given up halfway. To "comprehensively" advance the rule by law, there is a need to unswervingly follow the road of socialism with Chinese characteristics, stick to the law-based development orientation of ruling the country by law, and build the rule of law in China. There is a need to resolutely oppose and reject various kinds of rule of man and autocracy, prevent stagnation, backset, deflection, and alienation of the rule by law. At any time, if we give up the rule by law as the fundamental strategy, we would abandon the road of socialist rule of law. As a result, comprehensively advancing the rule by law would be out of the question. Thus Rejuvenation of the Chinese nation would be out of the question.

The so-called "accelerating" the building of the rule of law in China means to speed up the practical process of ruling the country by law to build the rule of law in China as quickly as possible. It would be impossible to realize the target quickly without speeding up the process. It would be impossible to finally accelerate the building of the rule of law in China without steady advancement of the rule by law. Therefore it seems that the term "accelerating" is the requirement to speed up building the rule of law in China, but actually it is the requirement for the practical process of the rule of law development and the rule by law. It's an arduous task. There are a number of requirements for "accelerating" the advancement of the rule by law and the building of the rule of law in China. First, the development strategies and goals to pursue building the rule of law in China should be set up, including the goals and tasks in different times and stages. Second, a specific, clear-cut, and operable indicator system for evaluating the rule by law and the building of the rule of law in China should be established. Third, a specific roadmap, timeline, and assignment book on the targets and tasks of building the rule of law in China should be in place for realizing the development of rule of law. Fourth, we should speed up the progress of the rule by law and the building of the rule of law in China when it is possible, and consequently accelerate realization of the target of building the rule of law in China. The proposition of accelerating the rule by law and building the rule of law in China is conditioned and relative. The word "accelerating" should not break away from the current economic, social, political, and cultural development, nor away from the main track and basic law of the self-improvement and development of the rule of law, nor away from the understanding, recognition, respect, and observation of the rule of law by hundreds of millions of people. Compared to the dynamically ever-changing social and economic conditions during the reforming period, the rule of law is somewhat hysteretic and conservative. In this sense, we must correctly understand the speed and strength of acceleration from a strategic perspective. Otherwise, more haste would result in less speed.

The timeline, roadmap, and task book on comprehensively advancing the rule by law and accelerating the building of the rule of law in China should be prepared in advance. We should try to realize the following "two-step" strategic objectives as the basic requirements of reform in an effort to build the rule of law in China.

By 2020, China will develop into a well-off society in an all-round way, realize scientific legislation, strict law enforcement, and judicial impartiality and law abidance by all the people. By 2020, China will see all-round implementation of the rule by law as the fundamental strategy and more perfect system of law with Chinese characteristics. Also by 2020, China will basically build the government under the rule of law, realize constantly improved judicial credibility, respected, and safeguarded human rights. By 2020, China will bring all work of the state under the rule of law and basically accomplish the building of the rule of law in China. The 4th Plenary Session of the 18th CPC Central Committee further put forward the following objectives and requirements: Under the leadership of the CPC, we should keep to the socialist system with Chinese characteristics; implement the theory of socialist rule of law with Chinese characteristics; put in place a perfect system of legal norms including a highly effective law-based implementation system, a strict law-based supervision system, and a strong law-based guarantee system; shape an impeccable inner-party system of laws and regulations; adhere to a common advancement of the rule by law, governance by law, administration by law and an integrated promotion of law-based state, law-based government, and law-based society; realize scientific legislation, strict law enforcement, impartial judicature, and all people's abidance by the law; and promote the modernization of the national governance system and governance capacity.

Here "a well-off society under the rule of law" is an important part of an all-round well-off society and an important guarantee of the rule of law to successfully build an all-round well-off society. "A well-off society under the rule of law" pursues freedom, equality, democracy, the rule of law, justice, fairness, happiness, charity, harmony, order, and full realization of human rights and human dignity from the perspective of value. From an institutional perspective, it pursues the people's democracy, the supremacy of law, ruling the country by the constitution, governance by law, administration by law, judiciary impartiality, and governing powers by law in a bid to build the rule of law in China. From a practical perspective, it pursues strict and punitive enforcement of the law and act by law, and seeks to realize good law and proper governance. At the same time, "a well-off society under the rule of law" can provide a sound legal environment and effective legal guarantee to build an all-round well-off society through the special institutional arrangement, regulation means, and education compulsory function of the rule by law.

By 2049 when the People's Republic of China will have been established for 100 years, China will have established the tasks of commonly advance the rule by law, governance by law, and administration by law, and targets of building the country, government, and society under the rule of law will be met. The requirements for law-based spirit, authority, and order will be totally satisfied, and China will be a country under the rule of law. People will enjoy freedom, equality, democracy, human rights, fairness, justice, harmony, and civilization.

6.4 SOLVING PROBLEMS IN THE CONSTRUCTION OF BUILDING THE RULE OF LAW IN CHINA

6.4.1 Strengthening and Improving the Party's Leadership in Ruling the Country by Law

The ruling party's leadership is the key to ruling the country by law, building the rule of law in China, and deepening the legal system reform. Therefore there is a need to give full play to the core and leading role of the ruling party in related works. As Xi Jinping emphasized, the Communist Party of China is the ruling party, and it is important to keep to the governance by law when comprehensively advancing the rule by law in an all-round way. In this context, there is a need to adhere to an organic unity of upholding the party's leadership, ensuring that the people are masters of the country, and ruling the country by law. There is a need to uphold the party's leadership in the entire process of ruling the country by law. Party organizations at all levels must persevere in acting within the framework of the constitution and the law. Leading cadres at all levels must take the lead in acting and abiding by the law. Organizational departments at all levels should judge whether the cadres could act and abide by the law and take this as an important index to evaluate the cadres.[5]

Strengthening and improving the ruling party's leadership in ruling the country by law is the fundamental political guarantee for building the rule of law in China. In order to give full play to the core and leading role of the party, the following principles need to be followed as to improving policies, institutions and mechanisms. First, the party needs to practically keep to the constitutional principle of acting within the framework of the constitution and the laws, adhere to governance by the constitution and the laws, and use law-based thinking and ways to lead legislation and law abidance, guarantee law enforcement, and support judicature. The party also needs to keep strengthening its leadership and authority, consolidate its ruling status, and entrench its ruling foundation through comprehensive advancement of the rule by law. Second, the ruling party should set up a leading group of the Central Committee for united leadership, organization, and coordination of the undertakings of the rule by law. The party needs to study and develop a medium- and long-term reform and development plan to comprehensively advance the rule by law and build the rule of law in China and identify the basic tasks for the rule by law and legal reform in the near future based on the 200-year national strategic goals and "four comprehensive" strategic layouts and strategic thoughts. The party needs to study and develop an outline for its governance by the constitution and the laws and lead and guide the entire party and local party organizations in governing works by law. Third, the ruling party should make an in-depth study on the major relations between the party and the law, between the party and the government, and between the party and the people under the new situation. The party needs to implement the principle of an organic unity of upholding the party's leadership, ensuring that the people are masters of the country and ruling the country by law in institutions and procedures. The party also needs to guarantee common advancement of the rule by law, governance by law, and

[5] *Xi Jinping's Speech at the Fourth Meeting for Collective Study of the Political Bureau of the CPC Central Committee*, *People's Daily*, February 24, 2013.

administration by law in leading institutions and management mechanisms and integrated development of law-based state, law-based government, and law-based society. Fourth, the ruling party should do an in-depth study on issues related to the reform of the political and legal committees, based on the new situation and new requirements to build the rule of law in China. The ruling party should stick to the leadership of the political and legal committees in thoughts, politics, and organizations and fully leverage on these committees' political advantages and organizational guarantee functions to ensure courts and procuratorates to exercise functions and powers independently according to the law and eliminate interferences of all kinds.

6.4.2 Advance Democratic and Scientific Legislation and Improve Legislative Quality and the System of Law

Advancing scientific and democratic legislation is the fundamental way to improve the quality of legislation. The core of scientific legislation is to respect and reflect objective laws while the core of democratic legislation is for the sake of the people and relies on the people. As such, there is a need to perfect scientific legislation and democratic legislation mechanisms, innovate the way of public participation in legislative works, and gather advice and suggestions from all circles. China's legislative reform should focus on making legislation more democratic and scientific, improving the quality of legislation, optimizing the system of law, strengthening legislation in key areas, and preventing corruption in legislation.

In order to strengthen legislative works and boost legislative reform, we should first change the passive legislative situation, advance legislation and an all-round deepening of reform in a coordinated way, and provide a legal basis and guarantee for an all-round depending of reform and opening up by creating, revising, and annulling laws. Second, we should use various kinds of forms to boost democratic and scientific legislation, guarantee the public can extensively and effectively participate in legislation, and make laws more regulated and operable. We should also ensure that legislation can truly reflect the people's will and interest appeals. Laws should not represent the interests of some administrative departments or some special groups. In so doing, "distributive justice" of legislation could be realized. Third, we should promote the reform and innovation of legislative works and make breakthroughs in this regard. We need to be brave and good at addressing focal points of conflicts through legislation when problems and conflicts occur during the process to deepen reform. We should not avoid important things and dwell on trivial things. We should not address easy matters and avoid difficult issues. We should avoid making excuses, arguing back and forth, or firmly focusing on department interests. Fourth, we should improve the systems and mechanisms for the people's congresses with legislative powers to dominate legislative works, and give play to the leading role of the people's congresses and its standing committees in legislative works. We should put in place the system under which relevant special committees of the NPC and the Commission of Legislative Affairs of the Standing Committee of the NPC organize competent departments to participate in drafting comprehensive, overall, fundamental, and important legal bills. We should increase the proportion of full-time members of the Standing Committee with practical experience in building the rule of law. We should establish and improve a legislative special committee and a working committee. Fifth, we should actively plan and build the system of law with Chinese characteristics under the guidance of the "one country, two systems" policy, and based on the national condition, "one country, two systems, three law systems (socialist law system, civil law system and Anglo-American law system)," and four territorial legal units (mainland China, Taiwan, Hong Kong and Macao Special Administrative Regions). It provides a more solid legal foundation for the reunification, prosperity, strength, and great rejuvenation of the Chinese nation. Sixth, we should pay more attention to use the functions of the rule of law to create a favorable international environment and surrounding environment. We should attach more importance to leveraging the role of the rule of law to guarantee national interests and boost China's peaceful development. We should use the constitution to regulate clearly the relations between international laws and Chinese laws, and create a more enabling international law-based environment for China's reform and opening up. Lastly, we should better handle the relations between reform and the rule of law, realize major reforms with lawfully recognized evidences, and propel reforms on the law-based track. We should combine major decisions on reform with legislation, revise the law first if needed, and make a law first and then revise it as needed. We should interpret a law in a timely manner if issues need to be solved through interpreting a law, i.e., interpret a law first and then revise the law. We should firmly abolish a law if needed and then revise it as necessary. For a reform pilot indeed requiring a breakthrough of the existing constitutional and legal provisions, if issues cannot be solved through above methods, the mode of authorized legislation of reform experiments can be adopted so as to provide a lawful basis for reform experiments and avoid the occurrence of illegitimate reforms.

6.4.3 Comprehensively Deepen the Reform of the Administrative System and Speed Up the Building of a Law-based Government

The key to comprehensively advancing the rule by law should guarantee strict law enforcement and ensure strict implementation of laws and decrees. Government is the main body of law enforcement. Regarding those prominent problems existing in law enforcement, such as failure of full observation and strict enforcement of laws, allowance of unpunished law-breakers, even suppressing the law by power, power-for-money deal, and crime of bending the law that are extremely hated by the public, more efforts need to be made to address these problems. *The Decision* of a plenary session of the CPC Central Committee put forward that governments at all levels must insist on carrying out works under the leadership of the party and on the law-based track, and step up efforts to build a law-based government featuring scientific functions, statutory rights and responsibilities, strict and impartial law enforcement, openness and fairness, honesty and high efficiency, and law-abiding integrity.

Administration by law is the key to rule by law. Construction of a law-based government is the focus needed to build the rule of law in China. In China, one of the key premises for comprehensively advancing the administration by law and accelerating the building of a law-based government is to comprehensively deepen the reform of the administrative system. Otherwise, irrational administrative systems would be "legalized" and "brought under the rule of law," which would add difficulties in the reform of administrative systems. Relative to administrative powers, administrative systems, administrative functions, administrative institutions, administrative relations, administrative behaviors, departmental interests, and other substantial administrative entities, laws, and regulations, governance by law and law-based government might be the external wrap of the realization of the rule of law, it might be the confirmation of legalization of laws and regulations. If China fails to transform the functions of administrative organs, to reform administrative systems, to break departmental interests, and to avoid the monopoly of administrative powers, then more intensified building of the rule of law, a higher degree of administrative legalization, and irrational administrative functions, administrative systems, and departmental interests might be fixed by laws and regulations and might appear as the legal system or legalization. They are obstacles to the reform. Therefore the reform of administrative systems should be carried out as a priority in order to build a law-based government.

To comprehensively deepen the reform of administrative systems and accelerate building of a law-based government, first, there is a need to deepen the reform of the administrative approval system in an all-round way and minimize government approval matters through extensive democratic participation and supervision by the people's congresses. Second, the government should know what to do and what not to do, better manage issues such as public security, environmental protection, food safety, social security, transportation, education, medical care, and health. At the same time, there is a need to reduce government's interference in and control over the market, society, and enterprises. Return what belongs to the market to the market, what belongs to society to society, and what belongs to enterprises to enterprises. Third, there is a need to comprehensively facilitate large ministry reform, streamline government organs, reduce hierarchies, lay off redundant personnel, improve efficiency, and build a highly effective government. Fourth, there is a need to press ahead with administration by law in an all-round manner based on the unity of the rule of law, to weaken administrative legislation, and to strengthen administrative law enforcement. There is also a need to improve administrative procedures, enhance administrative supervision, and build a law-based government. Fifth, there is a need to effectively restrict administrative powers, make public administrative actions, and strictly punish administrative corruptions in institution and mechanism, especially corruption issues related to state-owned enterprise supervision, government procurement, bidding, and tendering, as the aim is to build a transparent and clean government.

Specifically speaking, we should deepen the reform in the following aspects based on the requirements of the 4th Plenary Session of the Central Committee of the CPC. First, there is a need to keep making institutions, functions, extent of power, procedures, and responsibilities more statutory. There is a need to ensure that administrative organs have no powers beyond the provisions of the laws and cannot make decisions on reducing the interests or increasing the obligations of citizens, legal persons, and other organizations without the basis of laws and regulations. There is also a need to put into force the government power list system and resolutely eliminate the power rent-setting and rent-seeking space. Second, there is a need to establish a legitimacy review mechanism for major decisions within administrative organs, actively put in force a government legal advisory system, and guarantee that legal advisors play positive roles in making major administrative decisions and promoting administration by law. There is also a need to establish a lifelong accountability system and a reversed investigation mechanism for major decision-making. Third, there is a need to move forward with comprehensive law enforcement, straighten out the urban management law enforcement system, and improve law enforcement procedures. There is also a need to set up a recording system to record the whole process of law enforcement, strictly implement the legal review system for major law enforcement, and comprehensively implement and practice the system of administrative enforcement of law. Fourth, there is a need to enhance restrictions on power inside governments, to separately exercise powers to divide power arrangement and hierarchical authorization, to create regular work shift and strengthen internal process control to prevent power abuse in some departments and positions where concentrated powers exist for fiscal fund allocation and usage, state-owned asset supervision, government investment, government procurement, public resource transfer, and public project construction. There is also a need to improve internal government supervision and specialized supervision, and guarantee independent exercise of audit supervision power according to the law. Fifth, there is a need to comprehensively advance the openness of government affairs, promote the openness of decision-making, execution, management, services, and results. There is also a need to focus on the approval and implementation of financial budget, public resource allocation, and government information publicity in social and public welfare undertakings.

6.4.4 Comprehensively Deepen the Judicial System Reform

The reform of the judicial system is an important part of China's political restructuring, a major initiative to advance the rule by law in an all-round way, and also an important basis for comprehensively implementing the constitution and the law. Therefore there is a need for good top-level design and scientific planning of the new round of judicial system reform, in line with the new situation and new requirement of political restructuring and the comprehensive advancement of the rule by law. The new round judicial system reform should practically reflect the orientation of constitutional principles and spirit, law-based thinking and ways, and respecting judicial laws and attributes. The aim is to try to solve issues concerning the politicization, administration, localization, and bureaucratization of judicature; build up judicial authority and judicial credibility; and practically ensure that the people's courts and procuratorates exercise functions and powers independently and impartially.

To comprehensively deepen the reform of the judicial system, first, there is a need to decide whether to walk out of the vicious cycle of "seeking independence first" or "seeking justice first." At present, the dilemma is which one should come first, "independence" or "justice." Some argue that judicial injustice should come first because courts and procuratorates could not independently exercise powers within the framework of the law. Others believe that judicial corruption should come first as analyzed from the fact that courts and procuratorates fail to exercise judicial powers and procuratorial powers independently. This is a thorny issue that has existed ever since the reform and opening up. The realistic choice at the moment is to ensure "justice" while ensuring "independence." We also need to apply law-based thinking and ways to straighten our judicial external relations, in accordance with the provisions of the constitution and the law. That includes the relations between justice and party committee, between justice and political and legal committee, between justice and government, between justice and news media, and between justice and social organizations. In this way, we could prevent adjudication from being interfered with by various powers, money, human feelings, or relationships. Courts and procuratorates could independently exercise judicial powers and procuratorial powers in the division of judicial districts, and reform of institutions and mechanism, human and property management systems. Moreover, we need to comprehensively reform the internal systems of justice according to the provisions of the constitution, and the organizational law and the procedural law of courts and procuratorates. This includes the selection, appointment, assessment, reward, and punishment of judges and procurators, and the regulation, evaluation, supervision, and accountability of judicial acts. We need to ensure that judges and procurators can independently exercise their statutory functions and powers, independently fulfill their legal responsibilities, and independently assume legal liabilities. Lastly, petitions involving litigations and laws should be completely included in the rule of law, given the phenomenon of "believing in petitions but not in laws" and "believing in making troubles but not in laws." The functions of justice as the last straw should be fully leveraged to solve conflicts and disputes. The virtuous cycle mechanism for judicial conflicts and disputes involving laws and litigations should be rebuilt in order to build a legal order featuring long-term peace. Advancing judicial reform needs to follow the following principles. First, reform of the judicial system should be boosted in an organized, leading, guided, active, steady, progressive, legitimate, and orderly manner. Major reforms should be carried out with lawfully recognized evidence and legal authorization. Second, we should stick to the leadership of the CPC and the socialist direction with Chinese characteristics. Third, we need to adhere to the people's dominant role and reform the judicial system for the sake of the people, by relying on the people and to benefit the people. Fourth, we need to persist in proceeding from the actual conditions of the country. The reform of the judicial system must adapt to China's fundamental political system, basic political system, and the social and economic development level. The reform of the judicial system should maintain its own features and advantages and learn from foreign beneficial results of the rule of law but not copy the judicial system of foreign countries. Fifth, we need to comply with the objective laws of judicial activities and reflect the requirements for the integration of powers and responsibilities, openness and fairness, and respecting procedures. Sixth, we need to persevere in making overall plans and coordination and scientific verification to guarantee the advancement of judicial system reform in an active and steady manner.

6.4.5 Rebuild Social Equity and the Justice Mechanism Through the Rule of Law

Currently, society lacks a basic consensus and standard of equity and justice (or impartiality). So there is a need to put more emphasis on rebuilding the mechanism of social equity and justice through the rule of law. It should be noted that the equity and justice of a society under the rule of law is characterized by property of value. There are several reasons behind this. First, people's cognition on equity and justice is a relative term. What is believed to be fair and just by the majority may be objected to by the minority. What is believed to be fair and just by one culture may be objected to by another culture. What is believed to be fair and just at one time may be objected to in another time. What is believed to be fair and just by someone may be objected to by another person. Second, due to the contradictory relations of interests, the equity and justice of the law-based society is mainly reflected in form but not in reality. Procedural equity and justice is usually preset. In a democratic society under the rule of law, procedures need to be discussed by the masses and agreed by the majority first, and then formed into rules for distribution of interests. The procedures would be applied for specific distribution of interests based on the principle that all people are equal before rules (the law). The main features of rules and procedures before formation are the democracy of discussion, the possibility of bargaining and the diversity of interest expression. The main features of rules and procedures after formation are openness and universality, certainty and abstractness, the equality and consistency in application of rules. Third, the precondition of equity and justice does not necessarily result in equity and justice. Injustice can be resulted from injustice or justice. The strong point of the rule of law is not trying to eradicate the differences between this precondition and the result, nor to directly unify the precondition of equity and justice of laws and the fair and just results of laws. Any rule of law will be helpless for this kind of value goal. What the rule of law can do is narrow the gap between them through procedures and rules, by means of prevention and remedy. But it is impossible to make the best of both worlds. For example, when national legislation guarantees the legitimacy and inviolability of private property, then it will not be just for those without property and those with little property, because the law only provides one possibility or a big possibility, whereas in fact, those without property are excluded. It is also somewhat unfair and injustice for those with little property. Under this circumstance, we can leverage the rule of law to achieve a relatively shared justice of social wealth, and meanwhile guaranteeing private property, by means of taxation, social welfare, and redistribution mechanisms. Fourth, the difference in personality and demands determines that people have different and even very different cognitions on the same results. Therefore a law-based society could only guarantee the procedural equity and justice, where all people are equal before the law. However, the law-based society cannot realize fair and just results for everyone.

The equity and justice pursued by a law-based society is equity and justice in a relative sense, as well as the equity and justice of procedures and rules. Law-based society advocates the equity and justice of facts and results, but could not guarantee what it advocates. A law-based society pursues the equity and justice of rights, opportunities, rules, procedures, and processes. As long as we can comprehensively promote practices such as the rule by law, scientific legislation, strict law enforcement, impartial judicature, law abidance by all the people, and enhance good law, proper governance, and human rights protection, we could achieve justice in equity, rights, opportunities, rules, processes, and procedures.

The equity and justice pursued by a law-based society is specific and relative, with legal basis and guaranteed by legal procedures. In a law-based society, no one should advocate equity and justice in an abstract manner, nor break away from legal rules to pursue equity and justice, nor seek equity and justice by destructing the order of the rule of law or damaging the rights or others.

To rebuild the mechanism of equity and justice through the rule of law, first, there is a need to give full play to the rule of law to rebuild the basic judging system for Chinese social equity and justice. Laws are general behavioral norms reflected as the will of the state, the distributors of social interests, the adjusters of social relations, and stabilizers of social order. So we should leverage more on the law to judge social value and social behavioral norms. Second, there is a need to rationally regulate the citizens' rights and obligations, distribute resources and interests, and scientifically allocate powers and responsibilities through fair and just substantial laws in order to realize equity and justice in distribution of substantive matter. Third, there is a need to develop the procedures and rules which can fully reflect the will of the people and can be accepted by the majority through democratic, scientific and effective procedural laws. There is a need to allocate resources, balance interests, coordinate and alleviate conflicts in procedural laws, so as to realize equity and justice in procedures and rules. Fourth, there is a need to solve disputes and conflicts of interests through law-based procedures and mechanisms, including judicial procedures, and realize tangible and procedural equity and justice of the rule of law, at least the equity and justice of law-based procedures.

6.4.6 Constantly Intensify Respect and Guarantee for Human Rights

Human rights are the rights enjoyed by people. They are determined by human natural and social attributes. Statutory human rights are in essence the manifestation of legalized interests and the needs of the people. In a society, a higher degree of legalization of human rights means more sufficient remedies and guarantees for justice for the people and more profound realization of human rights. Accordingly, it will be easier for a society to realize stability, harmony, equity, justice, integrity, and order. In this sense, full respect and guarantee for and realization of human rights are important contents of ruling the country by law and building the rule of law in China.

By 2020, when China completely develops into a moderately prosperous society, it should achieve the goal of practical respect and guarantee for human rights. This is a high requirement and difficult to achieve. But it is a struggle objective and strategic task that are of great significance. To meet this target, we should work harder to promote human rights at this point. To this end, first, we should comprehensively implement the basic principles to respect and protect human rights stipulated by the constitution of the People's Republic of China. We should practically guarantee that citizens enjoy extensive rights and freedom based on the law. We should comprehensively improve various legal provisions and systems to protect human rights protection. We should expand the scope of basic rights and incorporate major rights of the people into the constitution, including the right to environment, to peace, to development, to privacy, and to know. Second, we should continuously promote the legalization of basic rights of the constitution, research and develop laws such as the press law, the combination acts, the law on freedom of religious believe, national compensation law, civil servants' property declaration law, and individual information protection law. We should also comprehensively reform the household registration system. Third, we should further amend criminal law and reduce the number of death penalties (at the current stage, the death penalty for economic crimes such as illegal fund-raising can be annulled) to prepare for the final annulment of death penalty in future. At the same time, we should strictly and prudently apply the death penalty so as to completely eradicate unjust, false, and erroneous cases. Fourth, we should further guarantee citizens' economic, social, and cultural rights and spare no effort to address long-standing and knotty issues common to society, such as inaccessible education, medical care, housing and pension scheme, unfair distribution of income, polarization, and unequally distributed wealth. There is also a need to pay attention to the rights of vulnerable groups, realize social equity and justice, as well as common prosperity through the rule of law. Lastly, we should earnestly implement a new round of *National Human Rights Action Plan (2012–15)*, and beef up our studies on the UN *International Covenant on Civil and Political Rights* to be deliberated and approved by the National People's Congress.

6.4.7 Practically Strengthen and Guarantee Implementation of the Constitution and the Law

What's difficult is not the making of the law but the implementation of the law.[6]

The life and authority of the constitution and the law lie in implementation.

[6] Zhang Juzheng: Qing Ji Cha Zhang Zou Sui Shi Kao Cheng Yi Xiu Shi Zheng Shu.

The socialist system of law with Chinese characteristics has been in place and resolved the issue that there are "no laws to abide by." So, how do we turn written laws into action, and turn propagated articles of laws into beliefs? It requires more emphasis. Moreover, more efforts should be put into place to settle institutional and mechanical issues related to the implementation of the constitution and the law.

At present, the constitution and the law are not authoritative as designed. They are not effectively implemented in practice. Thus we should advance the following reforms to solve these issues. First, when promoting the rule of law and ruling the country by law, we should try to shift the focus from legislation of the constitution and the law to implementation, i.e., to follow the overall objective and requirements of comprehensively advancing the rule by law, accelerating the building of the rule of law in China, and comprehensively deepening the reform of legal system. In so doing, the constitution and the law could play a bigger role in China's reform and opening up and its modernization drive. Second, we should set up and improve the censorship for constitutionality and legitimacy and set up a constitution supervision committee in the National People's Congress. The committee led by the Standing Committee of the National People's Congress will be responsible for examining the constitutionality and legitimacy of the constitution and the law during implementation and will try to solve issues like "fight of laws, fight according to laws, conflict of laws, and illusive establishment of laws." Third, we should propel the reform of large ministries in the judicial field. We can consider merging the Legislative Affairs Office of the State Council and the Ministry of Justice. We can also transfer the power of executing judgment from courts to judicial administrative organs. We should try to peel off or reduce the economic, civil, administrative, and social activities of judicial powers, prevent judicial organs from acting as defendants, and decrease the possibility of judicial corruption in institutional design and procedural arrangement. Detention houses currently managed by public security organs can be managed by the administration of judicial administrative organs. Fourth, we should learn from the World Justice Project as the Rule of Law Index and the Rule of Law Evaluation Index of Hong Kong and summarize the best practices of some places

[7]"The rule of law evaluation index" would be firstly implemented in areas like Yuhang District of Hangzhou, Zhejiang province, Kunming city of Yunnan province, Nanjing and Wuxi of Jiangsu province, and Chengdu city of Sichuan province.

in Mainland China that took the initiative to implement the rule of law evaluation index.[7] We should roll out the rule of law index at the national level, which will be taken to advance the implementation of the rule by law in local areas, departments, and industries. We should boost "the rule of law evaluation project" nationwide as soon as possible, so as to quantitatively evaluate building the rule of law in China. Fifth, we should continuously deepen the publicity and education on the rule of law and make innovations on the methods and mechanisms for publicity and education. We should also promote the law-based spirit, cultivate the culture of the rule of law, build up law-based concepts, and take law-based capacity as the basic capacity for state governance, the evaluation system, and rigid evaluation contents for leading cadres at all levels.

6.4.8 Boost "Anticorruption and Power Governance" Through Law-based Thinking and Ways

Power corruption is a deadly enemy of democracy and the rule of law, the biggest obstacle for building a socialist country under the rule of law. To comprehensively advance the rule by law, build the rule of law in China, and deepen the legal system reform, there is a need to put powers in the cage of the legal system and to use law-based thinking and ways to promote anticorruption and power governance. First, we should admit the "evil human nature" when facing public powers, i.e., remember that no one is a saint before the great temptation of public powers. Everyone has weaknesses, shortcomings, and limits. They may make mistakes and abuse powers. Even great revolutionists and great Marxists like Mao Zedong made mistakes. To admit the "evil human nature" matter-of-factly, we should not blindly trust or indulge any subject of public powers. Instead, we should put in place an effective legal system and law-based mechanism and put all public powers in the cage of laws and systems for the sake of justice. We should supervise and restrict all public powers and every public power holder. Second, we should use laws to control powers, use systems to regulate powers, use democracy to supervise powers, use powers and rights to restrict powers, and use virtue to restrict powers in order to reduce the opportunity of power corruption, while increasing the cost of power corruption. The top priority is to practically address the issues—who will supervise the supervisors, who will supervise top leaders, and who will supervise and control the real controller of people's property. Proper mechanism and law are the best means. We should study the rationality of the internationally-recognized mechanism i.e., "separating legislation, administration, and judiciary and making them mutually check and balance." We should actively introduce the "Rock–Paper–Scissors" cyclic constraint mechanism. Third, we should not only prioritize the top design for anticorruption and power governance, but also emphasize the design of specific institutions, links, procedures, and mechanisms. We should not only focus on educating and punishing the subject of public powers and preventing public powers from committing corruptions, but also try to prevent corruption channels and conditions such as market behaviors, economic behaviors, and social behaviors from eroding public powers. We should fill the institutional, systematic, and mechanical gaps at all levels, all links, all areas, and all aspects, and eradicate corruption on its "soil and hotbed." We should integrate national anticorruption resources, merge the party and national anticorruption institutions, and set up a national anticorruption commission, comprised of members from the party, the government, and the justice. We should use law-based thinking and ways to solve issues related to the legitimacy of "double designation." Lastly, we should give full play to the role of justice in anticorruption and power governance, eliminate various kinds of interventions and interferences, and practically guarantee that judicial organs exercise powers independently within the framework of the law. Judicial organs should exercise power impartially, based on facts and law. All kinds of corruption crimes should be severely punished according to the law. We should adhere to the principle that all people are equal before the law, and implement the principle that all those violating the party disciplines and state laws would be severely punished, no matter who are involved, how powerful they are, or what position they hold.

CHAPTER 7

New Requirements for Comprehensive Rule by Law

The 4th Plenary Session of the 18th Central Committee of the CPC adopted *The Decision of the Central Committee of the Communist Party of China on Major Issues Concerning Comprehensively Advancing the Rule of Law* in October 2014. *The Decision* depicted a blueprint for building the rule of law in China and proposed new requirements for comprehensively advancing the rule by law. The rule by law is a great systematic project involving all links, areas, aspects, and elements of building the rule of law. In this case, a slight move in one part may affect the whole, and a slight system reform may affect the overall situation. Thus we must do a good job in the overall strategic planning and top design by using strategic and systematic thinking and from the perspective of the whole and in advance in an organized, guided, active, steady, comprehensive, and coordinated manner.

7.1 COMPREHENSIVE RULE BY LAW REPRESENTS A PROFOUND REVOLUTION IN STATE GOVERNMENT

When creating the strategic plan on deepening the reform in an all-around way, *The Decision* of the 3rd Plenary Session of the 18th Central Committee of the CPC clearly required deepening the political restructuring by firmly centering on an organic unity of upholding the Party's leadership, ensuring that the people are masters of the country, and ruling the country by law in the field of democratic rule of law. *The Decision* also required speeding up the effort to give socialist democracy an institutional, normalized, and procedural basis, building a socialist country under the rule of law, and developing fuller, more extensive, and improved people's democracy. Obviously, in the strategic decision of the Central Committee on comprehensively deepening the reform, the reform in the rule by law

Building the Rule of Law in China.
DOI: http://dx.doi.org/10.1016/B978-0-12-811930-3.00007-6

is different from that of the economic system, social system, cultural system, ecological civilization system, and the Party's leadership characteristics. Comprehensively advancing the reform in the rule by law belongs to the nature and scope of national political restructuring.

In his speech delivered at the meeting of the Central Committee on political and legal works held in January 2014, General-Secretary Xi Jinping clearly pointed out that the reform of the judicial system is an important part of political restructuring and thus is of great importance for boosting modernization of the national governance system and governance capacity. He also clearly noted that there is a need to strengthen leadership, unite efforts in the advancement, be pragmatic and efficient, and accelerate the building of a fair, efficient, and authoritative socialist judicial system. There is also a need to further keep to the Party's leadership, further make use of the advantages of China's judicial system, and further promote socialist equity and justice. Since the reform of judicial system represents an essential part of China's political restructuring, other reforms like the reform of legislative system, the reform of administrative law enforcement system, the reform of legal supervision system, the reform of the law-abiding system, and institutional reform for the Party's leadership of the rule of law development certainly belong to the political restructuring.

In the important speech delivered at the opening ceremony of the special seminar for leading cadres at provincial and ministerial levels to learn and implement the spirit of the 4th Plenary Session of the CPC Central Committee held in February 2015, General-Secretary Xi Jinping further pointed out that comprehensively advancing the rule by law is a systematic project and an extensive and profound revolution in state governance.[1] Thus it can be seen that ruling the country by law in an all-round way is a revolution. The nature and features of this "revolution" aim to boost the political restructuring in an organized, guided, active, steady, and progressive manner through channels of making, revising, annulling, and interpreting the law and authorization under the framework of the constitution and on the track of the rule of law.

[1] Xi Jinping: Speech at the Opening Ceremony of the Special Seminar on Implementing the Spirit of the 4th Plenary Session of the 18th Central Committee of the CPPCC for Leading Cadres at Provincial and Ministerial Levels, *People's Daily*, February 3, 2015.

How is a state governed? This is a basic question that needs to be answered by the Marxist theory of state,[2] and a core issue that needs to be studied and addressed by politics and the science of law. The Marxist theory of state upholds that issues regarding state and state governance should be analyzed and understood from various perspectives, such as the nature of state, the form of government, the political pattern, and the basic strategy. From the perspective of the nature of state in state governance, there is a need to analyze the nature of the state to judge whether the majority rules the minority or the minority exercise dictatorship over the majority in a state. From the perspective of the form of government in state governance, a question that needs to be answered in regards to the state governance is the adoption of the organizational form of political power and whether it should be the republican form or the constitutional monarchy, the federal system or the unitary system, the head of state responsibility system or parliamentary cabinet responsibility system, or the people's congress system. From the perspective of the political pattern in state governance, it is a question of whether to practice the direct election system, the multiparty system, the "tripartite" political system, the bicameralism, or a combination of the direct and indirect election systems, the combination of one party leadership and multiparty cooperation, the combination of the ruling party's inner-party democracy and the people's democracy, or the democratic centralism system, or other political system for running the state and dealing with politics affairs. This is the issue regarding political pattern that needs to be addressed for state governance. From the perspective of basic strategy in state governance, it is the question of whether to practice the

[2]The Marxist view of the state holds that, "The state is nothing but a machine for the oppression of one class by another, and indeed in the democratic republic no less than in the monarchy" (*Collected Works of Marx and Engels*, Volume 3, People's Publishing House, 2009 edition, p. 111); "The state is a product of irreconcilable class contradictions" (*The Selected Works of Lenin*, Volume 3, People's Publishing House, 2012 edition, p. 114). The special institution systematically using violence and forcing people to obey the violence is called the state (*Special Collected Works of Lenin*, People's Publishing House, 2009 edition, p. 285). Political rule has always taken some social function as the basis and could only be maintained after it has exercised this social function (*Collected Works of Marx and Engels*, Volume 3, People's Publishing House, 2012 edition, pp. 559–560). The state has always been a structure split from the society and an institution consists of people specialized in, virtually specialized in or mainly specialized in management. People are divided into administrators and those being administered (*Special Collected Works of Lenin*, People's Publishing House, 2009 edition, p. 288).

autocracy, the rule of man, dictatorship, or democracy, the rule of law, the republicanism, or other state governance pattern. This is a question of path reliance and state governance strategy that needs to be addressed in state governance.

In the great practices of leading the people to win the revolution, construction, and reform and on the basis of establishing the People's Republic of China and practicing the socialist system, the CPC has identified, through the form of constitution and laws as well as party constitution, the PRC's nature of state, form of government, and political pattern and the Party's basic strategy to lead the people to govern the state and basic mode to run the state and deal with politics. The nature of the state is the people's democratic dictatorship with the worker–peasant alliance as the main body under the leadership of the proletariat. The form of government is the people's congress system. The main contents of the political pattern are the Party's leadership, the system of democratic centralism, the system of people's congress, the system of regional ethnic autonomy, the system of multiparty cooperation and political consultation, and the system of grassroots democratic autonomy. The rule by law is the basic strategy for the Party to lead the people to govern the state. The rule of law is the basic mode for running the state and dealing with political affairs.[3] The CPC has also identified the road of continuously developing the

[3]At the First Meeting of the Fifth CPPCC held in February 15, 1978, Liang Shuming said, "We now again have the chance to discuss and take part in enacting the constitution, which is a delighted thing. … My experience is that constitution is usually a mere scrap of paper as state governance mainly relies on the rule of man but not on the rule of law. 30 years passed after the founding of the New China, we have enacted our own constitution. However, is the constitution the most authoritative? Does everyone must abide by the constitution? Looking from the several major periods in these three decades, what I said is not groundless. But, I want to seriously point out that the rule of man seems to have come to an end since China's historical development begun. Prestigious leaders like Chairman Mao Zedong have passed away, and there would be no more people like them in the near future. Even someone wants to practice the rule of man, it would be very difficult. Besides, we have personally experienced the disasters brought by the rule of man, especially the lesson of the ten-year 'Cultural Revolution', so people have an instant anticipation of and demand for the rule of law. In this case, it's quite necessary and important for us to discuss the constitution today, and we should be very serious and careful about this big issue. China has gradually entered into the stage of the rule of law from the rule of man, and now we are standing at a turning point. Going forward, we need to gradually depend on the authority of the constitution and the laws and govern the state by law. This is the trend of historical development, the future of China, and no one could stand in the way." Wang Donglin: *The Liang Shuming's Questions and Answers*, Hubei People's Publishing House, 2004 edition, pp. 297–298.

socialist democracy with Chinese characteristics and advancing the modernization of the rule by law and state governance.

State governance[4] is the institutional arrangement and activity used to make the people masters of the country, control and exercise state powers, and manage state affairs through the National People's Congress and local people's congresses at all levels. State governance is the institutional arrangement and activity process in which people of all ethnic groups, all state organs, armed forces, political parties, social groups, enterprises, and public institutions, among other social subjects under the leadership of the ruling party, jointly participate in the state's political life, economic life, and social life, jointly manage state, social, economic, and cultural affairs, and jointly promote comprehensive development of politics, economy, society, culture, and ecological civilization. State governance means the ruling party runs the state and deals with politics by keeping to governance by the constitution and the laws, directing the overall situation, coordinating all aspects, supporting state organs to perform functions and powers independently and leading and supporting various social subjects to conduct systematic, comprehensive, and source state and social governance according to the law.

The rule by law is the basic strategy for the Party to lead the people to rule the state and deal with politics. From the perspective of developing

[4]At present, Chinese theoretical circle does not share the same understanding of the concept of "state governance." Theorists have different views and definitions of the concept of "state governance." *Seeking Truth* published an article arguing that state governance is that the Party leads the people to manage national, economic, cultural and social affairs through various channels and in various forms in accordance with the laws. Refer to Qiu Shi: *State Governance Modernization Will Move from the Rule of Man towards the Rule of Law*, published on *Seeking Truth*, Issue 1 of 2014. According to Professor Wang Puqu of Peking University, "state governance" is actually the system and process under which the CPC represents and leads the people to control and run the state power under the precondition that the state power belongs to the people; is to scientifically, democratically and effectively carry out national and social management under the premise of keeping to, consolidating and improving China's fundamental and basic political and economic systems; is to run the state and deal with politics in the layout of keeping to the CPC's direction of the overall situation and planning as a whole. See Wang Puqu's *Scientifically Understand the Meaning of "State Governance,"* published on *Guangming Daily* on June 18, 2014. The writer believed that, in Chinese context, describing and defining the concept of "state governance" should firmly center on an organic unity of upholding the Party's leadership, ensuring that the people are masters of the country and ruling the country by law. This is the essential feature of the socialist democracy with Chinese characteristics and the key to understanding "state governance."

democratic politics, the rule by law is to make the people masters of the country and manage national, social, economic, and cultural affairs based on the constitution and the laws. From the perspective of strengthening and improving the Party's leadership and ruling, the rule by law means that the Party acts within the framework of the constitution and the laws, rules the state, and deals with politics based on and by applying the constitution and the laws, i.e., to exercise the state power according to the constitution and the laws. From the perspective of the internal functions and values of the rule of law, the rule by law is to administer powers and officials according to the law, respect and guarantee human rights, and bring various kinds of state works under the rule of law. From the perspective of boosting the modernization of the national governance system and governance capacity, the rule by law is to consistently improve the national system of law and the legal system, and at the same time make these laws and systems operate properly and effectively so as to realize good laws and proper governance. General-Secretary Xi Jinping has given incisive expositions on the nature and significance of comprehensively ruling the country by law from strategic and multiple perspectives of the Party and the state. In the report on the work of the Political Bureau of the Central Committee delivered at the first meeting of the 4th Plenary Session of the 18th Central Committee of the CPC, General-Secretary Xi Jinping also profoundly pointed out that the rule by law is an essential requirement and important guarantee for keeping to and developing the socialism with Chinese characteristics and an inevitable requirement for realizing the modernization of national governance system and governance capacity. He also pointed out that the leading and normative role of the rule of law must be brought into full play if China wants to realize economic development, clear and bright politics, cultural prosperity, social fairness, and a good ecological environment.

In the introduction to *The Decision of the Central Committee of the Communist Party of China on Major Issues Concerning Comprehensively Advancing the Rule of Law*, General-Secretary Xi Jinping further clarified that comprehensively advancing the rule by law has a bearing on the Party's efforts to govern and rejuvenate the country, on the people's happiness and health, and on the Party's major strategy of building a long-term peace and order. Comprehensively advancing the rule by law is an important aspect of improving and developing the socialist system with Chinese characteristics and boosting the modernization of the national governance system and governance capacity. Comprehensively advancing the rule by law is the fundamental requirement for addressing a series of major issues faced in the development of the Party and national undertakings, and for emancipating and strengthening social vitality, promoting social fairness and justice, maintaining social harmony and stability, and ensuring the long-term peace and stability of the Party and the country.

In China, the rule by law is ultimately the political reform or change of the superstructure of law and "the revolution of law." The rule by law has a strong feature and nature of political restructuring. This revolution of law with the nature of political restructuring in modern China is different from China's past reforms of the economic system, social system, educational system, and health system in guiding thought, leadership style, and reform measures. Comprehensively promoting the rule by law requires resource coordination in politics, economy, culture, and society, among other aspects, and the synergy of education, administration, economy, morality, discipline, and customs, among other means. However, looking from the institutional aspect of national governance system, political reform is reformation, or political system reform. Comprehensively promoting the rule by law is deepening reform and self-improvement of China's political system in a sense.

To comprehensively promote the rule by law and try to build the rule of law in China, there is a need to keep to an organic unity of upholding the Party's leadership, ensuring that the people are masters of the country and ruling the country by law. There is also is a need to adhere to comprehensive enhancement of scientific legislation, strict law enforcement, impartial judicature, and all people's abidance by the law. There is a need to insist on common advancement of the rule by law, governance by law and administration by law, and integrated development of law-based state, law-based government, and law-based society. Implementing all these requirements for comprehensively promoting the rule by law and building the rule of law in China in modernized systems and mechanisms of the state governance system is bound to touch or trigger issues related to the political system reform and improvement. Therefore, China needs to be soberly aware of and fully prepared for this.

Undoubtedly, the institutional form featuring "an organic unity of the three" is the democratic political system of socialism with Chinese characteristics, and the core is the political system of keeping to the leadership and ruling of the Communist Party and the people's congress system as China's fundamental political system. Promoting the rule by law and implementing various reform designs and suggestions for the rule by law as the fundamental strategy will inevitably have a direct and indirect bearing on the Party's leadership system and the people's congress system and on China's political system. Promoting scientific legislation involves structural and mechanistic issues, such as how to improve the legislative system, the legislative procedure, legislative technology, legislative quality and legislative effect, and the system of law. Promoting scientific legislation also involves deep-seated structural and mechanistic issues, such as how to further improve the quality of deputies to the people's congress, implement the constitutional power of the people's congress, strengthen the supervision of the people's congress, and develop the democracy of the people's congress. Promoting strict law enforcement involves issues like how to reform and improve the administrative law enforcement system, mechanism and mode, and strengthen regulations and restrictions on the discretionary power of administrative law enforcement. In addition, promoting strict law enforcement involves issues like how to deepen administrative system reform, transform government functions, boost administration by law, build law-based government, and a series of deep-seated structural and mechanistic problems. Promoting impartial judicature inevitably requires comprehensive reform of the judicial system and even takes the reform of the judicial system as the breakthrough of the political system reform. Promoting governance by law ensures the Party's leadership in legislation, guarantee of law enforcement, safeguard of judicature, and leadership in law abidance. This is a revolutionary transformation from a revolutionary party to the ruling party; it is the reform from the Communist Party of China itself and the most profound one in the political system.

Determining the nature of comprehensive advancement of the rule by law as China's political system reform is the requirement for active adaption of China's political system to the social and economic development and for a comprehensive and deepened reform of the legal system under the new situation. The determination is the self-improvement and optimized development of political systems and mechanisms under the constitutional framework and on the law-based track. Determining the nature of comprehensive advancement of the rule by law as the political system reform is a reliable path for boosting the political restructuring in an organized, guided, active, steady, and progressive manner after the exploration of China and its party over the past six decades, especially after their continuous practices in the past more than three decades since the reform and opening up. Determining the nature of comprehensive advancement of the rule by law as the political system reform is the only road for continuously developing and improving the socialist democratic politics with Chinese characteristics. This road conforms to China's national conditions.

It is of great significance to comprehensively press ahead with the rule by law and use law-based thinking and methods to advance political restructuring in an active and steady way. First, the current political restructuring can be formally put on the agenda of the Party and the state for deepening the reform in an all-round way under the precondition of keeping to the Party's leadership and guaranteeing national and social stability and ethnic solidarity. Thereby, the political restructuring could enjoy a harmonious, orderly, perfectly justifiable, and good social environment and atmosphere. Second, reasonable demands of the people for the reform of institutional mechanisms (political system reform in particular) could be included in the concept of the rule of law through creating, revising, annulling, and interpreting the law. Broad consensuses can be formed through legal rationality. These broad consensuses can be translated into legal forms through democratic legislation and other procedures. In so doing, the results of political restructuring and other reforms can be presented and consolidated by the legal system and radical reform can be avoided. Third, the implementation of the constitution and the law can be effectively guaranteed, and social equity and justice, basic human rights, and freedom could be fully safeguarded through constant improvement of the system of law with Chinese characteristics and through the rather robust legal system and procedural mechanisms in legislation, law enforcement, judicature, law abidance, and law protection. Consequently, we can move forward with the modernization of the national governance system, keep bringing the national governance system under the rule of law, and make the superstructure of China's political laws better meet the needs of social and economic reform and development. Fourth, the significance is to firmly hold the right to speak and take lead in the political restructuring and respond to reasonable demands of the people for political restructuring and development. The significance is to fight back at the slander and misrepresent of China's democratic politics and political restructuring by western hostile forces and elements. Therefore we can righteously declare to the world that China's reform is an all-round and profound reform in all areas, including not only the reform of the economic system, social system, and cultural system but also the political system reform firmly centering on "an organic unity of the three" and relying on the path of comprehensively advancing the rule by law.

The essence of comprehensive advancement of the rule by law is the reform of the political system, so China must not take it lightly. Rather, China needs to pay attention to it and strengthen the leadership over it. China also needs to prevent Chinese and foreign hostile forces from disseminating the western democratic values and judicial modes and infiltrating our legal system reform when we are advancing and deepening our legal and judicial system. At the same time, there is a need to intensify the positive guidance of the domestic theoretical circle and media circle in theoretical studies and public opinion propaganda. There is also a need to pay attention to the appeal of people's interest in political restructuring and prevent certain people with ulterior motives from instigating street politics, large-scale mass incidents and other activities violating the rule of law when the comprehensive advance of political restructuring is being undertaken.

7.2 SIGNIFICANCE OF COMPREHENSIVELY ADVANCING THE RULE BY LAW FROM THE STRATEGIC LAYOUT OF "FOUR COMPREHENSIVE OBJECTIVES"

Since the convocation of the 18th National Congress of the CPC, the Central Committee with Xi Jinping as the General-Secretary has acted upon the overall situation of upholding and developing the socialism with Chinese characteristics and proposed and formed the strategic thinking and layout of comprehensively building a well-off society, comprehensively deepening the reform, comprehensively ruling the country by law, and comprehensively and strictly governing the Party. Comprehensively ruling the country by law is not only an important part of the strategic layout of "four comprehensive objectives" but also an important institutional foundation and law-based guarantee for coordinately propelling the "four comprehensive" strategic layout.

In November 2014, General-Secretary Xi Jinping noted in his *Speech at the Federal Parliament of Australia* that at present, the Chinese people are making unremitting efforts to realize the Chinese dream of great rejuvenation of the Chinese nation. The Chinese dream is meant to make the country prosperous and powerful, the nation revitalized and the people happy. Our development goal is to, by 2020, realize a doubled increase of the GDP and the income of urban and rural residents compared with that of 2010, build a moderately prosperous society, and by the middle of the century, build China into a strong, prosperous, democratic, civilized, and modernized socialist country. In order to realize the Chinese dream, we will comprehensively deepen the reform and opening up, comprehensively advance the rule by law, and keep boosting the modernization drive and improving the people's living standards. In February 2015, General-Secretary Xi Jinping further and clearly put forward that there is a need to understand the comprehensive rule by law from the strategic layout of "four comprehensive objectives," profoundly understand the relations between the comprehensive rule by law and the other three "comprehensive objectives," and seek to make the "four comprehensive objectives" supplement, promote, and bring out the best in each other.

The Decision of the 4th Plenary Session of the 18th Central Committee of the CPC pointed out that there is a need to comprehensively advance the rule by law in order to build a moderately prosperous society, realize the Chinese dream of great rejuvenation of the Chinese nation, comprehensively deepen the reform, improve and develop the socialist system with Chinese characteristics, and enhance the Party's governing capacity and ruling level. Building a moderately prosperous society is a periodic objective of struggle and plays a strategically leading and objectively guiding role. Comprehensively deepening the reform is fundamental to realizing the periodical objectives of struggle and advance the rule by law. Comprehensively advancing the rule by law is the fundamental mechanism and reliable guarantee to realize the phased objectives of struggle, is the dependable leading passage of guiding, promoting, and guaranteeing the comprehensive deepening of reform. The CPC is the leading core of the great rejuvenation of the Chinese nation and the fundamental guarantee for comprehensively deepening the reform and advancing the rule by law. Only by comprehensively and strictly governing the party and consistently improving the Party's governing capacity and governing level according to the constitution and the laws can we play our leading and core role in guaranteeing the process of comprehensively building a moderately prosperous society, comprehensively deepening the reform, and comprehensively ruling the country by law.

The Report of the CPC to its 18th National Congress clearly put forward several requirement as follows in order to ensure the building of a well-off society in an all-round way by 2020. The first requirement is to have more political courage and wisdom to deepen the reform of key areas. The second requirement is to address all disadvantages in ideology and institutional mechanisms hindering scientific development. The third requirement is to build a systematic, perfect, scientific, normative, and effectively operated institutional system. The fourth requirement is to make institutions of all aspects more established and mature. The fifth requirement is to build a systematic, perfect, scientific, normative, and effectively operated institutional system. The sixth need is to expedite the advancement of an institutionalized, normalized, and procedural socialist democracy. The seventh requirement is to expand citizens' effective and orderly participation in politics from various areas. The eighth requirement is to bring all works of the state under the rule of law. On November 17, 2012, General-Secretary Xi Jinping stated in an article titled *Firmly Center on Upholding and Developing Socialism with Chinese Characteristics, Study, Propagandize and Implement the Spirit of the 18th National Congress of the CPC* that the report of the CPC to its 18th National Congress depicted the great blueprint of comprehensively building a moderately prosperous society, accelerating the advancement of socialist modernization and seizing a new victory of socialism with Chinese characteristics. The blueprint came as the political declaration and action program of our party to unite and lead Chinese people of all ethnic groups to move forward on the socialist road with Chinese characteristics and to comprehensively build a moderately prosperous society. The blueprint also shows the direction for the works of leaders of the current Central Committee.

Of course, comprehensively building a moderately prosperous society includes the strategic goal of preliminarily building "moderate legal prosperity" for China by 2020. Moderate prosperity is not only an organic part of an all-round well-off society but also an important law-based guarantee for building a well-off society in an all-round way. Moderate prosperity, from a value perspective, pursues freedom and equality, democracy and the rule of law, fairness and justice, happiness and caritas, harmony and order, and full realization of human rights and dignity. From an institutional point of view, moderate prosperity pursues the people's democracy, the supremacy of the constitution and the law, ruling the country by the constitution, governance by law, administration by law, impartial judicature, governing power by law, and trying to build the rule of law in China. From a target perspective, moderate prosperity pursues the realization of comprehensive implementation of the rule by law as the basic strategy, basic establishment of a law-based government, consistent enhancement of judicial credibility, and practical respect and guarantee of human rights and bringing all works of the state under the rule of law. From a practical point of view, the pursuit of moderate prosperity is to abide by the law, enforce the law strictly, prosecute law-breakers and act by law, and try to realize good law and proper governance. At the same time, moderate legal prosperity also provides a sound law-based environment and effective law-based guarantee for building an overall well-off society through the specific institutional arrangements, normative means and educational compulsory function of the rule by law.

Just like the two wheels of a vehicle or the two wings of a bird, comprehensive rule by law and comprehensive deepening of reform supplement act upon each other. In the speech delivered at the Fifth Meeting of the 18th Central Commission for Discipline Inspection, General-Secretary Xi Jinping made clear that the dialectical unity of "break" and "establishment" has been demonstrated by the important deployment of the all-around deepening reform that was made at the 3rd Plenary Session of the 18th Central Committee of the CPC and the strategic deployment on comprehensively advancing the rule by law at the 4th Plenary Session of the 18th Central Committee of the CPC. In the theory of legal system reforms with Chinese characteristics, the focus of the overall deepening in reform is to deepen economic system reform according to *The Decision* of the 3rd Plenary Session of the 18th Central Committee of the CPC. This means that the economic system reform is the emphasis of the all-round deepening of reform, and the core issue is to better handle the relations between government and market, giving market a decisive role and making government better able to perform its functions in resource allocation. The essence of comprehensively ruling the country by law put forward at *The Decision* of the Fourth Session of the Central Committee of the CPC is to advance the political system reform within the framework of the constitution and on the track of the rule of law in an organized, guided, progressive, active, and steady manner. The core issue is to keep to a high degree of unity of the Party and the law and implement the Party's leadership in the whole process and all aspects of the rule by law. Thus it can be seen that the relationship between comprehensively ruling the country by law and comprehensively deepening the reform include the mutually supplementary relations between political system reform and economic system reform and the top design arrangement of doing two jobs at once and attaching equal importance to each. Comprehensively ruling the country by law is the basic mode and path for guiding, promoting, and guaranteeing an all-around deepening of reform. There is a need to use law-based thinking to handle the relations between the rule of law and the reform, keep to the unity of reform decisions and legislative decisions, and give full play to the role of legislation in guidance, promotion, regulation, and guarantee. At the Sixth Meeting of the Leading Group of Central Committee for all-round deepening reform held on October 27, 2014, Xi Jinping noted that there is a need to dovetail legislation and reform policies, make major reforms have lawfully recognized evidence, and make legislation actively adapt to the requirement of reform and development; there is a need to consider legislative issues involved in reforms when studying reform plans and measures and thus promptly propose legislative requirements and suggestions; there is a need to turn those proven practices into laws in a timely way; there is a need to give authorization according to statutory procedures when the practical condition is not mature and pilot programs need to be implemented first; and there is a need to timely revise and annul the laws and regulations that are inadaptable to reform requirements.

All major reforms should have lawfully recognized evidence. When there is a need to revise a law, legislation should come before law revision. When issues can be solved through law interpretation, the law should be interpreted promptly before revision. A law should be resolutely annulled if needed before revision. In so doing, reforms could proceed orderly according to the law. There is a need to carry out reforms within the framework of the current constitution and laws and make the best of the reform space and institutional condition reserved by the constitution and the law to make bold exploration and courageous innovation. The constitution is the fundamental law of the state, the general regulation on administering state affairs and ensuring national security. The constitution has the supreme legal status, authority, and effect, and is fundamental, overall, stable, and effective long-term. When issues cannot be solved through interpreting the constitution and creating, revising, annulling, and interpreting laws for reform experiments that indeed require breaking the current constitution and laws, legislative authorization of reform experiments can be adopted to provide a legal basis for reform experimental works through the authorization and approval of competent organs.

To be strict in Party discipline in an all-round way, the rule by law as the basic strategy for the Party to lead the people to govern the state and the society on the one hand and the rule of law as the basic way for the Party to run the state and deal with politics on the other hand has to be adhered to. To be strict in Party discipline in an all-round way, there is a need to adhere to governing by the constitution and the laws and acting within the framework of the constitution and laws. To be strict in Party discipline in an all-round way, there is a need to insist on the Party's leadership in legislation, guarantee of law enforcement, and support for and leadership in law observation. The Party's leadership should be implemented in the entire process of scientific legislation, strict law enforcement, impartial judicature, and law abidance by all the people and in all aspects of the rule by law, governance by law, administration by law, and the building of a law-based state, government, and society. There is a need to persist in a high degree of unity and consistency of the Party's leadership and the socialist rule of law. The socialist rule of law must keep to the Party's leadership while the Party's leadership must rely on the socialist rule of law. In the practice of keeping to governance by law, the Party needs to properly handle relations between its leadership in legislation and the scientific legislation of legislative bodies, between its guarantee of law enforcement and the strict law enforcement of administrative organs, between its support for judicature and the impartial judicature of judicial organs, and between its leadership in law abidance and the law abidance by all the people. The ruling party not only needs to persevere in administrating by the constitution and the laws and acting by law but also prevent from running the state by the Party and exceeding its duties and meddling in others' affairs. The ruling party should keep to the unity of the rule by law as the basic strategy and the governance by law as the basic way according to the requirements of *The Decision* of the 4th Plenary Session of the 18th Central Committee of the CPC. The Party's direction of the overall situation should be united with the performance of duties and the conduction of works of the people's congresses, governments, the CPPCC, adjudication organs, and procuratorial organs according to the law and constitutions. The Party's leadership in enacting and implementing the constitution and laws should be united with the Party's adherence to acting within the framework of the constitution and the laws. The Party should be adept in turning its propositions into the will of state through legal procedures, making the candidates recommended by Party organizations become leaders of organs of political power through legal procedures, leading the state and society through organs of political power, and safeguarding the authority of the Central Committee and the unity and solidarity of the entire Party and the whole nation through democratic centralism.

The key to being strict in Party discipline is to administer the Party according to laws, regulations, and institutions and to put powers in the cage of laws and institutions. *The Decision* of the 4th Plenary Session of the 18th Central Committee of the CPC proposed the objectives of building the system of socialist rule of law with Chinese characteristics. These objectives are to put in place a perfect legal norm system; a highly efficient implementation system, a strict supervision system and a strong guarantee system for the rule of law, and a perfect inner-Party legal system. This indicates that the inner-Party legal system is not just an important part of the national system of rule of law, and the institutional arrangement, and measures, but also the standard for comprehensively ruling the country by law. Moreover, the inner-Party legal system is the basis and standard for being strict in Party discipline and the criteria and rules that must be followed and applied for the ruling party to run the state and deal with politics from the perspective of the state rule of law.

Based on the strategic layout and thinking of "four comprehensive objectives," there is a need to realize that comprehensively advancing the rule by law is an important part of building a modern socialist country with Chinese characteristics, the fundamental guarantee for comprehensively developing the people's democracy, and the important content of and the main way to realize modernized state governance. There is also a need to realize that comprehensively advancing the rule by law is the internal demand for deepening the reform of the socialist market economic system, the basic channel to realize socialist equity and justice, the root for anticorruption and power management, and the inevitable requirement for accelerating the building of a socialist law-based system and law-based state. Moreover, there is a need to further deepen understanding of the significance of comprehensively advancing the rule by law from the following perspectives.

First, from the perspective of the value and function of the rule by law, comprehensively advancing the rule by law has a bearing on our Party's state governance and rejuvenation, on the people's happiness and good health, and on lasting peace and order of the Party and the country. Beyond that, comprehensively advancing the rule by law represents an essential requirement and important guarantee for keeping to and developing socialism with Chinese characteristics and a certain requirement for realizing the modernization of a state governance system and governance capacity. Therefore our Party underscores the development of the rule of law and identifies the rule by law as the basic strategy for leading the people to govern the state and identifies governance by law as the basic way to run the state and deal with political affairs.

Second, from the perspective of the direction of the rule by law, comprehensively advancing the rule by law is the fundamental requirement for and only way to solve a host of major issues faced in developing the cause of the Party and the state. These issues include emancipating and strengthening social vitality, promoting social equity and justice, regulating and restricting public powers, guaranteeing full realization of human rights, maintaining social harmony and stability, and ensuring the lasting peace and order of the Party and the state. General-Secretary Xi Jinping profoundly pointed out that China is entering a critical juncture of building a well-off society in an all-round way and a crucial stage of the reform. He also noted that the Party is facing an unprecedented arduous task of reform, development, and stability, and unprecedented contradictions, risks, and challenges, so the position and function of the rule by law in the overall plan of the Party and the state is more prominent and important. He also added that the rule of law is an important support for the state governance system and governance capacity. On top of that, comprehensively advancing the rule by law is a fundamental requirement for addressing a series of major issues faced in developing the Party and national undertakings, such as emancipating and enhancing social vitality, promoting social equity and justice, maintaining social harmony and stability, and ensuring the lasting peace and order of the Party and the state. In order to boost continuous and healthy development of Chinese economy and society and keep exploring the vast potential for future development of the socialist cause with Chinese characteristics, there is a need to comprehensively propel the building of a socialist country under the rule of law and provide institutional plans for solving these issues.

Third, from the perspective of the internal relations of the "four comprehensive objectives," comprehensively ruling the country by law is a certain requirement and important guarantee for building a moderately prosperous society, realizing the Chinese dream of the great rejuvenation of the Chinese nation, comprehensively deepening the reform, improving and developing the socialist system with Chinese characteristics, comprehensively being strict in party discipline, and enhancing the Party's governing capacity and level.

Fourth, from the perspective of the new situation and tasks faced by the Party and the state, comprehensively ruling the country by law is conducive to better planning the domestic and international situations as a whole, better maintaining and utilizing the period of important strategic opportunities for the development of China, and better planning social force as a whole. In addition, comprehensively ruling the country by law can also help balance social interests, adjust social relations, regulate social behaviors, and make the Chinese society full of vigor and order in the profound reform. Moreover, comprehensively ruling the country by law can help realize strategic objectives like economic development, clear and bright politics, cultural prosperity, social justice, sound ecology, and peaceful development of China.

7.3 COMPREHENSIVELY RULING THE COUNTRY BY LAW MUST KEEP TO THE INTEGRATION OF THE SOCIALIST LAW-BASED THEORY, LAW-BASED ROAD, AND LAW-BASED SYSTEM

The theory of socialist rule of law with Chinese characteristics is part and parcel of the theoretical system of socialism with Chinese characteristics and the result of Chinese communists' profound summary of the successful experiences and painful lessons in building the socialist rule of law with Chinese characteristics based on the basic principles of Marxist state and laws, the beneficial results learned and absorbed from human law-based civilizations at all times and of the entire world, and modern China's national condition and practice of modernization construction and rule by law. The theory of socialist rule of law with Chinese characteristics is the inheritance, innovation, and great development of Marxist view of law and the latest development of boosting the sinicization of Marxist legal ideology. The theory of socialist rule of law with Chinese characteristics is also the important theoretical guidance, ideological basis, and theoretical support for comprehensively advancing the rule by law and accelerating the building of a socialist country under the rule of law. The core and main idea of the theory of socialist rule of law with Chinese characteristics is to take Marxism–Leninism, Mao Zedong Thought, Deng Xiaoping Theory and the Important Thought of "Three Represents," and Scientific Outlook on Development as the guidance to thoroughly implement the spirit of important speeches of General-Secretary Xi Jinping, and keep to an organic unity of upholding the Party's leadership, ensuring that the people are masters of the country and ruling the country by law. The core and main idea of the theory of socialist rule of law with Chinese characteristics is also to unswervingly take the road of socialist rule of law with Chinese characteristics, resolutely safeguard the authority of the constitution and the laws, the people's interests, social equity and justice, national security and stability in accordance with the law, and provide a powerful law-based guarantee for realizing the "200-year" objective of struggle and the Chinese dream of the great rejuvenation of the Chinese nation.

In the introductions to *The Decision* of the 4th Plenary Session of the 18th Central Committee of the CPC, General-Secretary Xi Jinping made the following points. The key to comprehensively advancing the rule by law is whether we have the right direction or strong political guarantee. Specifically speaking, it is to keep to the Party's leadership and the socialist system with Chinese characteristics and implement the theory of socialist rule of law with Chinese characteristics. The Party's leadership is the most essential feature of socialism with Chinese characteristics and the most fundamental institutional guarantee for comprehensively advancing the socialist rule of law. The socialist system with Chinese characteristics is the fundamental institutional foundation of the system of socialist rule of law with Chinese characteristics and the fundamental institutional guarantee for comprehensively advancing the rule by law. The system of socialist rule of law with Chinese characteristics is the theoretical guidance and academic support of the socialist rule of law system with Chinese characteristics and the guide to action of the comprehensive advancement of the rule by law. These three aspects are actually the core and main idea of the road of socialist rule of law with Chinese characteristics, which have regulated and ensured the institutional property and progressing direction of the system of socialist rule of law with Chinese characteristics.

The theory of socialist rule of law with Chinese characteristics is the scientific theoretical system based on the road of socialist rule of law with Chinese characteristics, the system of socialist of rule of law with Chinese characteristics, and China's practices of comprehensively advancing the rule by law. This scientific theoretical system mainly consists of the following four parts.

First, the thought value theory of the socialist rule of law with Chinese characteristics involves political philosophy, philosophy of law, and related values, core concepts, basic categories, and main contents of the theoretical system of socialism with Chinese system, principally including Marxist theory of state and law, Marxist views of state, party, democracy, law, rule of law, human right, equality, justice and power, Marxist science of law, and Sinicized innovation and development, etc.; and socialist law-based spirit, socialist law-based ideology, socialist law-based concept, socialist law-based value, socialist constitutional and law-based principle, socialist law-based thought, socialist law-based idea, socialist culture of the rule of law, socialist law-based doctrine, etc.

Second, the theory of institutional norms of socialist rule of law with Chinese characteristics involves the basic institution of rule of law, legal norm, system of law, system of rule of law, procedure of rule of law, and structure of rule of law, among other categories and contents, including the theory related to the system of socialist rule of law with Chinese characteristics, the theory related to the socialist law-based government with Chinese characteristics, administration by law and executive law enforcement system, the theory of judicial power, judicial system, judicial procedures, legal supervision system, impartial judicature system, and judicial system reform, and the system and theory of governance by the constitution and the laws and administering the Party by rules, etc.

Third, the theory of practical operation of the socialist rule of law with Chinese characteristics involves the application of law-based theories and principles, law-based behavior, law-based practice, implementation of the constitution and the laws, legal system operation, among other categories and contents, typically including scientific legislation, strict law enforcement, impartial judicature, law abidance by all the people, and all links of rule of law development, etc.

Fourth, the theory of correlation of the socialist rule of law with Chinese characteristics involves the external relations of the existence, operation, and development of the rule of law, involves the mutual effect, influence, and coexistence of the rule of law and some external factors, among other phenomenon and contents, mainly including the relations between the socialist rule of law with Chinese characteristics for one part and the socialism with Chinese characteristics, the road of socialism with Chinese characteristics, the socialist theory with Chinese characteristics, the socialist system with Chinese characteristics, comprehensive deepening of reform, comprehensively being strict in Party discipline, building a well-off society in an all-round way, realizing the Chinese dream of the great rejuvenation of the Chinese nation, etc.

The road of socialist rule of law with Chinese characteristics is the development path of the rule of law identified based on the long-term practice of the Party in leading the people to advance the development of socialist democracy and rule of law since the founding of the New China, especially based on the theoretical studies, practical explorations, and institutional innovation of comprehensively implementing the rule by law as the basic strategy and accelerating the building of the country under the rule of law after the 15th National Congress of the Party. The road of socialist rule of law with Chinese characteristics was also identified through constantly deepening and developing the recognition of the socialism with Chinese characteristics, constantly deepening the recognition of the socialist democratic politics with Chinese characteristics, and constantly deepening the recognition of comprehensively advancing the rule by law and building the socialist country under the rule of law. The road of socialist rule of law with Chinese characteristics is the right path determined by our Party, which acted upon China's national conditions and reality, building an overall well-off society and realizing great rejuvenation of China and the Chinese dream. The road of socialist rule of law with Chinese characteristics is the right path identified after our Party has summarized the practical experiences of building the socialist rule of law in China, learned from the beneficial results of the law-based civilizations of various countries and absorbed by the essence and nutrients of the traditional legal culture of the Chinese nation. The road of socialist rule of law with Chinese characteristics is a historical achievement made by our Party, which has profoundly summarized experiences and lessons in building the socialist rule of law with Chinese characteristics in the past, especially since the convocation of the 3rd Plenary Session of the 11th Central Committee of the CPC. The road of socialist rule of law with Chinese characteristics is the historical achievements made by our Party after the proposal of strengthening of the rule of law and democratic institutionalization and legalization in order to guarantee the people's democracy. The road of socialist rule of law with Chinese characteristics is the historical achievements made by our Party after the identification of the rule by law as the basic strategy for its leadership over the people to run the state and deal with politics and the identification of the governance by law as the basic way for the Party to run the state and deal with politics for a long time. The road of socialist rule of law with Chinese characteristics is the historical achievements made by our Party after active building of the socialist rule of law.

The road of socialist rule of law with Chinese characteristics is the product of the unity of history and reality and the combination of theory and practice. In the four coordinates of historic position, the road of socialist rule of law with Chinese characteristics has its own space-time location and time features.

First, relative to the mode and road of the rule of law of capitalist countries like Britain, France, Germany, and the United States, what we choose is the road of socialist rule of law. In terms of essence and nature, China's rule of law is socialist while the rule of law of these other countries is capitalist. These two roads and modes of the rule of law are totally different in nature and must not be confused. Therefore we should by no means copy or indiscriminately imitate the western capitalist mode of rule of law.

Second, relative to the mode and road of the rule of law of former socialist countries like Soviet Union and Eastern Europe and modern socialist countries like Vietnam and Cuba, what we choose is the road of socialist rule of law with Chinese characteristics. A number of integrated factors have determined that we could only choose the road of socialist rule of law with Chinese characteristics and only learn from but not copy or clone the mode and road of the rule of law of socialist countries like the Soviet Union and Vietnam. These integrated factors include the Chinese nation's historical genes and historical evolution, China's historical and cultural tradition, realistic national conditions, and social conditions.

Third, relative to the discussions and descriptions of Marxist classical writers about an ideal socialist society and its state and laws, we are now and will be in the primary stage of socialism for a long time and China's rule of law is the rule of law and rule by law at the primary stage of socialism. Therefore there are still some inadaptable and incompatible issues in building the rule of law compared with the development requirement of the Party and national undertakings, the masses' expectation, and the advancement of the objective of modernizing state governance system and governance capacity.

Fourth, relative to the mode of the legal culture and legal system of the Chinese law system, we are now walking on the development road of modernized rule of law that adheres to openness, inclusiveness, and disciplinary spirit of innovation. This road represents advanced productivity, advanced production relation, and advanced culture on the basis of Chinese historical inheritance, cultural tradition, and social and economic long-term development, progressive improvement, and endogenous evolution. We are now walking on the development road of modernized rule of law facing the world and the globe and learning from the beneficial results of human law-based civilizations.

The system of socialist rule of law with Chinese characteristics is mainly composed of three aspects. First, it is the theoretical value and spiritual culture of the rule of law, including the value, spirit, ideology, theories, beliefs, culture, thinking about the rule of law, constitutional, and legal authority of socialism with Chinese characteristics. Second, it is the institutional system and operating system of the rule of law, including a perfect system of legal norms, a highly effective law-based implementation system, a strict law-based supervision system, a strong law-based guarantee system, and an impeccable inner-Party system of laws and regulations and system of legal norms. Third, it is the behavioral activity and practical operation of the rule of law, including scientific legislation, strict law enforcement, impartial judicature, law abidance by all the people, governance by law, administration by law, acting by law, seeking legal support for any case, solving problems by law and depending on the law to resolve contradictions, laws that must be strictly observed, law-breakers that must be brought to justice, etc.

The theory of socialist rule of law with Chinese characteristics, the road of socialist rule of law with Chinese characteristics, and the system of socialist rule of law with Chinese characteristics form an organic whole. They have together constituted the theoretical support, path direction, and institutional guarantee for comprehensively advancing the rule by law and accelerating the building of a socialist country under the rule of law. They have together fully demonstrated the confidence in theory, path, and system of the socialist rule of law with Chinese characteristics. Comprehensively advancing the rule by law must consciously adhere to an organic whole of the theory, path, and system of the socialist rule of law with Chinese characteristics and guarantee the advancement of the rule by law along the right direction and path of socialism with Chinese characteristics.

7.4 COMPREHENSIVE RULE BY LAW MUST KEEP TO "AN ORGANIC UNITY OF THE THREE"

"An organic unity of the three" is the essential feature of the socialist democracy with Chinese characteristics and the fundamental principle for comprehensively advancing the rule by law. The Party's leadership is the fundamental guarantee for the people to be masters of the country and the rule by law. The people's role as masters of the country is the essence and core of the socialist democracy. The rule by law is the basic strategy for the Party to lead the people to govern the state. The three are united in the great practice of socialism with Chinese characteristics and in the strategic objective of building a modern and powerful socialist country and realizing the great rejuvenation of the Chinese nation. The three are united in the practice of building the socialist rule of law with Chinese characteristics in China. In order to adhere to "an organic unity of the three", we must ensure the people's role as masters of the country as the basis and set up the target of strengthening the vitality of the Party and the state and motivating the people's enthusiasm, and eventually expand the socialist democracy and develop the socialist political civilization. China is a socialist country under the people's democratic dictatorship and the people are masters of the country. Comprehensively advancing the rule by law and ensuring the people's role as masters of the country are the objectives that should not be shaken. The rule by law is the basic channel to realize the people's role as masters of the country, an effective way to ensure the realization of the people's role as masters of the country, and the basic strategy for the Party to lead the people to run the state and deal with politics. The Party's leadership, the people's role as masters of the country, and the rule by law do not have coordinate relations. The people's role as masters of the country is the objective, and people's interests are above everything else. The Party's leadership and the rule by law are the principal means to ensure that the people are masters of the country.

The Party's leadership is more important than the rule by law. The rule by law is a great exploration led by the Party to guarantee that the people are masters of the country. Therefore comprehensively advancing the rule by law and keeping to the Party's leadership turn out to be the fundament and key. The Party's leadership is the most essential feature of the socialism with Chinese characteristics and the most fundamental guarantee for the socialist rule of law. A basic experience of building the socialist rule of law in China is to implement the Party's leadership in the entire process and all aspects of the rule by law. The constitution of China has established the leading status of the CPC. Keeping to the Party's leadership is the fundamental requirement of the socialist rule of law and the root and lifeline of the Party and the state. Keeping to the Party's leadership has a direct bearing on the people's interests and happiness, and represents the essence of the comprehensive advancement of the rule by law. Our party is the ruling party, persists in governance by law, and plays a major role in leading and guaranteeing the comprehensive advancement of the rule by law. Then, what's the relation between the Party's leadership and the rule of law? Under the political philosophy and constitutional mode of western "tripartite" political system and multiparty system, political parties and the rule of law of western states more often than not have a diversified, misplaced, separated, and different relationship. Western political parties represent different classes, stratums, and interest groups. Western rule of law claims to represent the common will of all the people and the will of the state. Contradictions and conflicts are bound to exist in this kind of political system featuring multiple interest orientation and its claimed neutrality, equality, and justice. In essence, it is inevitably hard to unite its political party with the rule of law. Under the socialist system led exclusively by the CPC, under the economic system based on the public ownership identified and guaranteed by the Chinese constitution and laws, and under the political system that the people are masters of the country, on the political basis that the Party represents the people's common interests and does not have any private interests, the relations between the Party and the people, the Party and the state, and the Party and the law are harmonious, consistent and highly united rather than contradictory.

Comprehensively advancing the rule by law is a great and systematic project for building the rule of law and thus must be carried out under the unified leadership of the Party. Also, there is a need to actively, steadily, orderly, effectively, and comprehensively implement the rule by law by taking an overall plan in all kinds of basic values including freedom and equality, democracy, and the rule of law, fairness and justice, safety and order, and respect and happiness; in all links including legislation, law enforcement, judicature, law abidance, and law protection; in all aspects like ruling the country by law, directing military affairs by law, administering power by law, safeguarding legal rights by law, governing by law, administering by law and acting by law; in all kinds of legal forms like domestic and international laws, central and local laws, substantial and procedural laws, public and private laws, enacting and implementing laws; and in all kinds of relations, such as the relations between the centrality and the locality, between local areas, between government and society, between the state and individuals, between home and abroad, between the rule of law and reform, between stability and development, between fairness and efficiency, and between democracy and centralism.

Keeping to governance by the constitution and the laws is a certain requirement of comprehensively advancing the rule by law and the basic way for our Party's leadership and governance. Ruling the country by law is firstly to rule the country by the constitution, and the key to governing by law is to govern by the constitution. Under the new situation, our Party needs to fulfill its major responsibilities in governing and rejuvenating the country, and must strictly administer the Party according to the Party constitution and run the state and deal with political affairs according to the constitution. If it wants to lead the people to enact and implement the constitution and laws, the Party must act within the framework of the constitution and the laws and truly realize its leadership in legislation, guarantee law enforcement, and take the lead in law abidance. As such, the close connection of the rule of law with the modernization drive of the Party and the state and the deepening of the reform has been raised to an unprecedented strategic position and political height. This demonstrates that our Party has realized its fundamental changes from a revolutionary party to the ruling party in ideology and politics. In addition, this demonstrates that our Party has changed from a revolutionary party mainly relying on movements and administrative means to manage the state and the society to a ruling party mainly relying on constitutional and legal norms and law-based methods to run the state and deal with political affairs in the strategy for running the state and governing style. The Party has become more conscious in keeping to changes in democratic governance, scientific governance, governance by law, and administration by law, more actively advancing the modernization of the state governance system and state governance capacity (the modernization typically refers to legalization, democratization, scientification, and information). Our Party has used the rule by law as the basic strategy and the rule of law as the basic way to further consolidate our Party's governing status, entrench our Party's ruling foundation, and improve our Party's governing authority. Comprehensively advancing governance by law must keep to the Party's leadership in legislation, guarantee of law enforcement, support for judicature, and leadership in law abidance. The Party needs law-based thinking and a law-based mode to advance governance by the constitution and governance by law and to practically realize its leadership in legislation, guarantee in law enforcement, support for judicature, and leadership in law abidance.

Comprehensively ruling the country by law must focus on advancing governance by law, while comprehensively advancing governance by law must enhance the Party's leadership in legislation and further improve the procedures of major legislative decision-making by the Party. All matters involving major adjustment of systems and policies must be reported to the Central Committee for discussion and decision. The Party's Central Committee proposes suggestions on constitutional amendments to the National People's Congress and amends the constitution in accordance with the procedures regulated by the constitution. Major issues to be formulated and amended must be reported to the Party's Central Committee by the Party Group of the National People's Congress. In the process of deepening the political system reform and advancing the building of a law-based government, there is a need to ensure that governments at all levels keep to the Party's leadership and the law-based track to conduct works. There is also a need to innovate the law enforcement system, improve law enforcement procedures, boost comprehensive law enforcement, uphold strict law responsibility, and build an authoritative and highly effective administrative system by law featuring the integration of power and responsibility. There is a need to speed up the building of a law-based government featuring functional science, statutory rights and liabilities, strict and clear law enforcement, openness and fairness, honesty and highly efficiency, and law abidance and integrity. There is a need to strengthen the Party's support for judicial works. Party and governmental offices and leaders should support the courts and procuratorates to independently exercise powers and functions in accordance with the law. There is a need to support in institution judicial organs to independently exercise powers and put in place a record, report, and accountability system for leaders who intervene in judicial activities and meddle in specific cases. No political and governmental organ and leading cadre are allowed to do anything violating statutory responsibilities and obstructing judicial impartiality. No judicial organ is allowed to meet the requirement of political and governmental organs and leading cadres for intervening in judicial activities. Any political and governmental organ or leading cadre intervening in judicial organ's handling of cases shall be given a policy discipline punishment. Criminal sanctions would be given to those who have caused unjust, fake, and false cases according to the law. Party organizations at all levels and communists must take the lead in abiding by the law. Party organizations at all levels and Party leaders must profoundly realize that safeguarding the authority of the constitution and the laws means safeguarding the authority of the common will of the people and the Party. Defending the dignity of the constitution and the laws is to defend the dignity of the common will of the people and the Party. Guaranteeing the implementation of the constitution and the laws is to guarantee the realization of the common will of the people and the Party. Leading cadres at all levels must uphold the law in awe and veneration, bearing in mind that the red line of the law shall be insurmountable and the bottom line untouchable. Leading cadres at all levels must take the lead to act by law and shall not violate the law when exercising powers, shall not put in words to replace the law, or suppress the law by power, or bend the law for personal gain. Party organizations of the people's congresses, governments, judicial organs, and procuratorial organs at all levels must lead and supervise their units to abide by the constitution and the laws, resolutely investigate law-breaking activities and illegal power uses, among other behaviors.

7.5 COMPREHENSIVE RULE BY LAW MUST KEEP TO COORDINATED DEVELOPMENT OF SCIENTIFIC LEGISLATION, STRICT LAW ENFORCEMENT, IMPARTIAL JUDICATURE, AND LAW ABIDANCE BY ALL THE PEOPLE

In the early stage of the reform and opening up, Mr. Deng Xiaoping put forward the well-known "16-character guideline" for building the rule of law in China. The "16-character guideline" can be explained as: there must be laws for the people to follow; laws must be strictly observed and enforced; law-breakers must be brought to justice; and all people are equal before the law. This guideline has guided historical achievements in building the socialist rule of law in China. At present, the system of socialist laws with Chinese characteristics has taken shape; the construction of law-based government is advanced with steady steps; the judicial system keeps improving; and socialist law-based ideas keep improving significantly. Entering the new phase and new starting point of historical development, the report of the Party to its 18th National Congress put forth the "new sixteen-character guideline" for building the rule of law-based on Deng Xiaoping's thought on the rule of law. The "new 16-character guideline" can be explained as "scientific legislation, strict law enforcement, impartial judicature, and law abidance by all the people." In the speech delivered at the 30th anniversary celebrating the promulgation and implementation of the current constitution, General-Secretary Xi Jinping emphasized that we need to take the constitution as the highest legal norm, continue to improve the system of socialist laws with Chinese characteristics guided by the constitution, and include national causes and works in the track of legal system. General-Secretary Xi Jinping also emphasized that we need to implement the principles that there must be laws for the people to follow; laws must be strictly observed and enforced; law-breakers must be brought to justice; and all people are equal before the law. Moreover, he clearly put forward the requirements for implementing the rule by law as the basic strategy, accelerating the building of a socialist country under the rule of law, comprehensively advancing the process of scientific legislation, strict law enforcement, impartial judicature, and law abidance by all the people.

7.5.1 Scientific Legislation as the Premise for Comprehensive Rule by Law

Scientific legislation is the legislative process and legislative result of adhering to scientific spirit, adopting scientific methods, and following scientific laws. General-Secretary Xi Jinping pointed out that moving forward with scientific legislation and democratic legislation is the fundamental channel for improving the quality of legislation. He also said that the core of scientific legislation lies in respecting and demonstrating objective laws while the core of democratic legislation is for the people and relying on the people. He noted that there is a need to improve the scientific legislation and democratic legislation mechanism, innovate the mode of public participation in legislation, and extensively listen to opinions and suggestions of all aspects.

The system of socialist laws with Chinese characteristics guided by the constitution has taken shape in China, and there are laws for the people to follow in all aspects of national and social life in general. These are tremendous achievements in building the rule of law in China. However, in China's legislative works, some laws and regulations still fail to reflect objective laws and the people's will, comprehensively and are not strong in pertinence and operability. In addition, the phenomena of departmentalization, fighting for powers, and buck passing remain salient in legislative works. Some laws after formulation and implementation are hard to apply, execute, and observe, and are not effective. Some individual laws even exist in the name only. General-Secretary Xi Jinping pointed to references emphasizing that China needs to further improve the quality of legislation and further enhance the efficiency of legislation. Some legislation has actually become a game of interests, but sometimes it cannot solve the problem for a long time, and other times it is not workable at all. Some areas utilize laws and regulations to implement regional protectionism, preventing the whole country from forming an open, competitive, and well-organized market order and damaging the unity of national rule of law.

Advancing scientific legislation means to focus on solving these issues in institution and mechanism. Law is the key to governance while good law is the precondition of proper governance. A system of socialist rule of law with Chinese characteristics must keep to the advancement of legislation first, give play to the leading and driving role of legislation, and seize the critical juncture of enhancing the quality of legislation. There is a need to abide by the philosophy of putting people first and making laws for the people, implementing the socialist core values, and making every law conform to the constitutional spirit and reflect the will of the people and have support of the people. There is also a need to implement the principles of impartiality, fairness, and openness in the entire legislation process, improve legislative systems and mechanisms, persist in promoting the making, revising, annulling, and interpreting laws simultaneously, and make laws and regulations more timely, systematic, targeted, and effective.

There is a need to well implement the following reform deployments according to the new requirement of *The Decision*: improve the systems and mechanisms for legislative works dominated by the NPC with legislative powers and make full use of the dominant role of the people's congresses and their standing committees in legislative works; strengthen and improve government legislative system building, perfect administrative laws and regulations and regulation development procedures, and improve the mechanism for the public to participate in government legislation; define the boundary of legislative powers, and effectively prevent departmental benefits and local protectionism from being legalized in system, mechanism and working procedure; enhance legal interpretation, clearly define the meaning of laws and regulations and the applicable legal basis in a timely manner; define the limit and range of local legislative powers and endow legislative powers to cities and local areas consisting of several districts according to the law; reinforce the organization and coordination of the people's congresses in legislative works, modernize the mechanism for legislative drafting, argumentation, coordination, and deliberation and the mechanism for consulting with the people's congress of the lower level, put in place the system for grassroots point of contact for legislation, and boost legislative refinement; improve the mechanism for legislative organs to communicate with the public, conduct legislative consultations, and extensively gather social consensus; perfect the voting procedure for draft laws, and individually vote important articles; and intensify legislation in key areas. There is a need to safeguard citizens' rights, accelerate the improvement of the legal system reflecting fair rights, fair opportunities, and fair regulations, and guarantee that citizens' physical rights, property rights, and basic political rights, among other rights, are not violated. There is a need to safeguard the fulfillment of citizens' all rights, including economic, cultural, and social rights, and bring the guarantee of citizens' rights under the rule of law. On top of that, there is a need to enhance the entire society's consciousness of respecting and safeguarding human rights and improve citizens' rights relief channel and method.

7.5.2 Strict Law Enforcement is Key to Comprehensive Rule by Law

About 80% of existing laws in China are enforced by state administrative organs at all levels. About 80% of all Chinese civil servants are public employees of state administrative organs. As long as the state administrative organs enforce 80% of existing Chinese laws and state administrative organs' public employees account for 80% of all Chinese civil servants the primary mission of building the rule of law in China will be basically accomplished. In this case, adhering to administration by law and strict law enforcement is key to realizing the stated objective of comprehensive rule by law. General-Secretary Xi Jinping pointed out that government is the subject of law enforcement and there is a need to make great effort to solve issues such as failure to observe the law, lax law enforcement, unpunished law breakers, and even suppressing the law by power, trading power for money, and bending the law for personal gain, among others extremely hated by the general public. Currently, the main problem existing in China's administration by law is the poor effect of law enforcement. In China, it is common to see that most laws are difficult to enforce in practice, written laws are disconnected from laws in real life, "hidden rules" are ubiquitous, and legal authority is difficult to be established.

We need to strengthen the implementation of the constitution and the laws, maintain the unity, dignity, and authority of the socialist legal system, and form a law-based environment under which people are not willing to, cannot, and dare not to break the law. We also need to realize the vision of ensuring strict observance and enforcement of laws and prosecution of law-breakers. Administrative organs are an important subject for implementing laws and regulations, so they should take the lead to enforce the law strictly and maintain public interests, people's interests, and social order. Law enforcers must be loyal to the law. Leading agencies and leading cadres at all levels should enhance their ability to use law-based thinking and law-based methods and try to use the rule of law to build consensus to reform, regulate development behaviors, promote conflict resolution, and guarantee social harmony. They also should strengthen the supervision over law enforcement activities, resolutely eliminate illegal interventions in law enforcement activities, and firmly prevent and overcome local protectionism and departmental protectionism. They should firmly punish corruption, and ensure the liability that comes with power, supervise power exercise, and prosecue law-breakers.

7.5.3 Impartial Judicature is the Vital Task of Comprehensive Rule by Law

Impartiality is the lifeline of the rule of law, and impartial judicature plays an important leading role in social justice. Denial of justice plays a destructive role in social justice. Realizing impartial judicature is an important task of comprehensive rule by law. However, China is facing some protruding issues in judicial areas at the moment, such as unjust judicature and lower level of judicial credibility. Other salient issues existing in judicial areas are that some judicial personnel do not have a good work ethic and are dishonest in handling cases, money, relationships, and even take bribes from plaintiff and defendants, etc. The deep-seated reason for unjust judicature lies in the imperfect judicial system, unscientific allocation of judicial powers and power operation mechanism, and unsound judicial guarantee system for human rights.

As General-Secretary Xi Jinping noted, we should try to make the masses feel fairness and justice in every judicial case, and all judicial organs should firmly center on this objective to improve works and focus on solving deep-seated issues influencing juridical justice and constraining judicial capacity; we should keep to the principle of judicature for the people, improve the style of judicial works, practically solve difficult problems faced by the general public in initiating legal proceedings through hospitable service, especially work harder to provide legal assistance to people in straitened circumstances to protect their lawful rights and interests; judicial workers should have a close contact with the masses, regulate judicial behaviors, work harder to realize judicial publicity, respond to the masses' attention and expectation of just and open judicature; and we should ensure that judicial organs and procuratorial organs exercise judicial powers and procuratorial powers independently and impartially. We also should improve the judicial management system and the judicial power operation mechanism, regulate judicial behaviors, strengthen the supervision over judicial activities, and try to make the masses truly feel fairness and justice in every judicial case.

The Decision of the 4th Plenary Session put forth that impartial judicature and judicial credibility should be boosted and improved from the following aspects: further improve the system ensuring independent and impartial exercise of judicial and procuratorial powers according to the law and continuously optimize the allocation of judicial powers. We should perfect the systems and mechanisms for public security organs, procuratorial organs, judicial organs, and judicial administrative organs to perform their own duties and to coordinate and interact in exercising investigation power, procuratorial power, judicial power, and executive power. We should advance strict judicature, keep to taking fact as the basis and taking the law as the criterion to improve the legal system under which fact finding conforms to the objective truth, case result conforms to actuality and fairness, and case-handling process conforms to justice. We should improve the system of people's assessors, guarantee citizens' jury right, and facilitate the openness of adjudication, procuratorial affairs, police affairs, and prison affairs. We should reinforce the guarantee of human rights and judicature, enhance the institutional guarantee for the right to know, the right of statement, the right to defend and debate, the application right, and the right to appeal of parties and other litigant participants involved in the process of proceedings. We should improve the legal system for implementing legal principles like legally prescribed punishment for a specific crime, no punishment for doubtful cases, and illegal evidence exclusion. We should strengthen the prevention of using torture to coerce a statement from a source, practically solve law enforcement difficulties, enact compulsory enforcement law, and regulate judicial procedures, such as seal up, detention, congelation, and disposal of property rights involved. We should also strengthen supervision over judicial activities.

7.5.4 Law Abidance by All the People Underpins the Comprehensive Rule by Law

In today's Chinese society, some social members respect, believe, abide by, and use the law, but they do not have strong consciousness of the rights and protection of the law. Some national staff, especially leading cadres with a weak understanding and scarce capacity of acting by law, deliberately break the law, replace the law with words, suppress the law by power, and bend the law for personal gain. Since the reform and opening up, the Central Government and local governments have made great efforts to conduct publicity and education of law, but fail to form the structure of law abidance by all the people. Furthermore, the authority of the law has often been ignored, and cases like widespread and flagrant violation of the law and violent resistance against the law are common. Law abidance by the people underpins the comprehensive rule by law, so there is a need to focus on solving the above problems.

The authority of law originates from the inner support and true belief of the people. People's rights and interests should be guaranteed by law, while the authority of law should be safeguarded by the people. We must promote the socialist law-based spirit, build the socialist culture of the rule of law, strengthen the enthusiasm and proactivity of the entire society to strictly enforce the rule of law, and form a social atmosphere of feeling pride for law observance and shame of violation of laws. In so doing, all people would become loyal advocators, conscious observers, and resolute defenders of the socialist rule of law. Any organization or individual must act within the framework of the constitution and the laws; any citizen, social organization, and state organ must take the constitution and the laws as the standard of behavior, exercise rights or powers, and perform obligations or duties in accordance with the constitution and the laws. We must carry out in-depth publicity and education of law, promote the socialist law-based spirit in the entire society, and guide all the people to abide by the law. We must depend on the law to solve issues and form a good atmosphere of feeling pride for law abidance. We should keep to the combination of legal education and law-based practice, extensively carry out governance activities by law, and improve the level of social management under the rule of law. Leading cadres of all levels should take the lead in acting by law and abiding by the law. Organizations and departments at all levels should take acting by law and law abidance as the paramount condition for evaluating and recognizing cadres. Apart from the effective institutional designs and arrangements of the publicity and education on traditional rule of law to keep pace with the time, *The Decision* also put forward the following reform and construction tasks from the perspective of the rule of law as a systematic project. We should advance multilevel and multifield governance by law, keep to systematic governance, governance by law, comprehensive governance, source governance, and improve the level of social governance under the rule of law. We should make use of the active role of citizen conventions, village regulations and agreements, industry rules, and group charters, among other social regulations in social governance, and make use of the active role of mass organizations and social organizations in building a law-based society. We should build a perfect legal service system, improve the legal aid system, modernize the judicial aid system, and perfect the unified judicial identification management system. We should also improve the mechanism for safeguarding legal rights and resolving conflicts according to the law, construct the institutional systems that play a significant role in safeguarding the people's rights and interests, and establish and improve the mechanism for early warning of social conflict, the interest expression mechanism, the consultation and communication mechanism, and the relief and assistance mechanism. We should smooth the legal channel for coordination of the masses' interests and guarantee of rights and interests, include petition in the track of the rule of law, and improve the mechanism for preventing and defusing social disputes. We should also advance comprehensive governance of social security, improve the leadership responsibility system, and so on and so forth.

From the perspective of citizens' active law abidance, deepening the publicity and education of the rule of law and promoting the law-based spirit require the citizens not only to manage themselves and passively abide by the law by negative acts, but also to benefit all the people in the world and "have confidence in legislation, coordinate in law enforcement, rely on judicature, and conscientiously abide by the law and try to uphold the law" in an active and factitive manner as masters of the state. Having confidence in legislation means adhering to democratic legislation, enabling the general public to take part in legislation directly or indirectly, and guaranteeing that China's legislation is the concentrated reflection of fairness and justice and the people's will and interests. As such, the people should be sure of the fact that respecting the law, abiding by the rule of law, and maintaining judicial authority are to respect their own will, maintaining their own interests and safeguarding their own happiness. Coordinating in law enforcement means to actively support state administrative organs to administer by law, coordinate administrative law enforcement organs to seriously perform duties, engage in law enforcement activities including public security, social order, industry and commercial administration, transportation safety, tax law enforcement, food safety, production safety, and financial order and environmental resource protection on the basis of having confidence in the law and the rule of law. In the relationship between law enforcer and the object of law enforcement, administrative organizations for law enforcement and citizens are neither cat and mouse, police and bandit, enemy to each other, nor master and servant, official and citizen, grandfather and grandson. Instead, they are fish and water, service provider and service enjoyer, manager and managed subject. So long as administrative organs for law enforcement and their law enforcers correctly realize their relations, identify their roles, and are strict and impartial in law enforcement rather than choosing fishing, brutal, barbarous, rent-seeking, restrictive, selective, moving, weak, hysteretic law enforcement, the broad masses would definitely support and coordinate the impartial law enforcement of administrative organs. Relying on judicature requires the entire society to believe in the rule of law and requires the broad masses to have confidence in law. Relying on judicature also requires the entire community to rely on the judicial system and judicial mechanism to solve problems. In a law-based society, judicature is the last line of defense for resolving contradictions, settling conflicts, and realizing social equity and justice, and the most authoritative and effective institutional arrangement for citizens to safeguard their rights, "seek explanations," settle disputes, and seek relief. Ideas and wrong practices that are not based on the rule of law should be thoroughly changed when seeking solutions for conflicts and disputes, including petition, mass disturbance, making rumors, and resort to social connections, relationship, nepotism, and explosion. Trying to uphold the law requires citizens to consciously respect and abide by the law, have courage in resorting to the law to fight against illegal activities and criminals, and against unlawful acts damaging national interests, social order and others' rights, and against state organs and their civil servants' behaviors of power abuse, malpractice and corruption.

7.6 COMPREHENSIVE RULE BY LAW MUST KEEP TO AN INTEGRATED DEVELOPMENT OF LAW-BASED COUNTRY, LAW-BASED GOVERNMENT, AND LAW-BASED SOCIETY[5] AND A COMMON ADVANCEMENT OF THE RULE BY LAW, GOVERNANCE BY LAW AND ADMINISTRATION BY LAW

General-Secretary Xi Jinping has noted, on many occasions, "an integrated development of the three" and "a common advancement of the three," as a key issue of the comprehensive rule by law in this new historical period. On February 23, 2013, Xi Jinping pointed out in his speech delivered at the fourth collective study of the Political Bureau of the CPC Central Committee that we need to comprehensively implement the spirit of the 18th National Congress of the CPC. He also said that we need to take Deng Xiaoping Theory, the Important Thought of "Three Represents," and Scientific Outlook on Development as the guidance to comprehensively advance scientific legislation, strict law enforcement, impartial

[5] Concerning "law-based society," the Chinese jurisprudential circle does not have a universally recognized and unified definition but has certain consensus and recognition of the concept. Scholars believe that law-based society should have a broad sense and narrow sense alike because the word "society" has a broad sense and narrow sense (*society in the narrow sense refers to the range of human activity and settlement, such as habitat, village, township, city, etc.; society in broad sense refers to a country, a large area or a cultural circle, such as the British society, the Eastern society, the western world*). The content of "law-based society" in the broad sense covers law-based forms like "law-based country," and "law-based government"; law-based society" in a narrow sense is a concept different from "law-based country" and "law-based government," and the form of the rule of law with independent value requirement and expression form. Most scholars agree on the concept of "law-based society" in a narrow sense. Some scholars note that law-based society is a concept relative to the society under the rule of man, civilized social form of humanity, and social form established on the basis of special law-based cultural values and exists under the system of the constitution and the laws, and a harmonious, orderly and stable social form in which state power and social relations operate according to clear-cut law-based order. A law-based society should pursue and reflect the following principles: the supremacy of the constitution and the laws, social democratic rule of law, respect and guarantee of human rights, equality of everyone before the law, supervision and retraction of public powers, fairness, justice and order, unity, integrity, and harmony. Scholars also believe that, under the thinking of building the rule of law in China, law-based country, law-based government, and law-based society are an organic whole, but they are different from, connect to, and supplement each other. In this system, the role of a law-based country and law-based government play an irreplaceable role in the formation and the development of a law-based society while a law-based society is an important foundation of law-based country and law-based government. The three are equally important and must develop in an integrated manner.

judicature, and law abidance. He noted that we need to keep to common advancement of the rule by law, governance by law and administration by law, and integrated development of law-based country, law-based government, and law-based society, and keep opening up new prospects of the rule by law. In the speech delivered at the 60th anniversary celebrating the founding of the National People's Congress on September 5, 2014, Xi Jinping pointed out again that we need to keep to a common advancement of the rule by law, governance by law and administration by law, integrated development of the law-based country, law-based government, and law-based society, and continuous improvement of the rule of law across the entire society.

In the introductions to *The Decision* of the 4th Plenary Session, General-Secretary Xi Jinping noted that "The 18th Central Committee of the CPC proposed that the rule of law is the basic way of running the state and dealing with political affairs and there is a need to accelerate the building of the socialist country under the rule of law and comprehensively advance the rule by law. Moreover, by 2020, the rule by law as the basic strategy would be implemented across the board, a law-based government would be established, judicial credibility would keep improving, and human rights would be practically respected and guaranteed. The 3rd Plenary Session of the 18th Central Committee further pointed out that building the rule of law in China must keep to a common advancement of the rule by law, governance by law and administration by law and an integrated development of law-based country, law-based government and law-based society. Comprehensively implementing these deployments and requirements has a bearing on accelerating the building of a socialist country under the rule of law, implementing the top design of comprehensive deepening of reform, and a long-term development of the socialist cause with Chinese characteristics. It is thus clear that "an integrated development of the three" and "a common advancement of the three" are the certain requirement of continuous deepening and expansion of the comprehensive rule by law on the one hand and the important manifestation of the thought of "comprehensively advancing the rule by law is a systematic project" on the other hand. "An integrated development of the three" and "a common advancement of the three" require strengthening the top design, systematic design, strategic design, and overall arrangement of the development of the rule of law, but not taking stopgap measures. "An integrated development of the three" and "a common advancement of the three" require that the rule by law must proceed under the concentrated and united leadership of the Central Committee of the CPC, but not that each does things or acts in his own way. Advancing state governance by the constitution aims at building a constitutional order. Advancing governance by law aims at building a law-based Party. Advancing administration by law aims at building a law-based government. Advancing judicial reform aims at realizing judicial impartiality. Advancing law abidance by all the people aims at building a law-based society. Advancing direction of army by law aims at building a law-based army. Advancing governance by law aims at building law-based provinces and cities.

Under the strategic deployment of comprehensively advancing the rule by law and accelerating the building of a socialist country under the rule of law, law-based country, law-based government, and law-based society are an organic whole, but they are different from each other and connect and supplement each other. The three are united in the great practice of building the rule of law in China and together constitute the main part of the system of the socialist rule of law with Chinese characteristics. In the strategic layout of building the rule of law in China, our goal is to build a socialist country under the rule of law by comprehensively advancing the rule by law; comprehensively advancing administration by law aims at speeding up the building of a law-based government; a law-based society would be formed while a law-based country and law-based government are established.

A law-based country is a long-term target of building the rule of law in China, and there is a need to comprehensively advance the process of scientific legislation, strict law enforcement, impartial judicature, and law abidance by all the people. Law-based government is the key to building the rule of law in China, and the core is to regulate and restrict government powers and enhance the capacity to apply law-based thinking and law-based methods to defuse social conflicts. The core is also to make the market play a defining role in resource allocation, and realize the separation of administrative functions from that of enterprises, separation of public service units from government, division between government, and capital and separation of government functions from commune management. A law-based society is an important part of building the rule of law in China, and the core is to carry forward the socialist core values and promote strength, prosperity, democracy, civilization, harmony, freedom, equality, justice, rule of law, patriotism, devotion to work, integrity, and friendship. The core is also to form a law-based thinking, law-based ideology, and culture of the rule of law in which all social members consciously believe in, revere, observe, apply, and safeguard the law. Integrated development of law-based country, law-based government, and law-based society constitutes a driving structure of one body with two wings. They are mutually complementary and promoted, and together constitute a very important part of building the rule of law in China.

General-Secretary Xi Jinping pointed out that we need to adhere to common advancement of the rule by law, governance by law, and administration by law and integrated development of law-based country, law-based government, and law-based society, and continuously open up new prospects of the rule by law. Building the rule of law in China should keep to the constitutional idea that all powers of the state belong to the people, and most extensively mobilize and organize the people to exercise state powers through the people's congresses at all levels according to the provisions of the constitution and the law, as well as manage national, social, economic, and cultural affairs through various channels and forms. Building the rule of law in China should also keep to common construction, common possession, and common development. Based on the principle of democratic centralism, on the system of state political power, and on the activity principle identified according to the constitution, the people's congresses exercise state powers, practice rational division of labor and mutual coordination among decision-making power, executive power, and supervision power, guarantee state organs to exercise powers and functions and perform duties and responsibilities according to statutory limits of authority and procedures, and guarantee state organs to unitedly and effectively organize various undertakings. According to the system and principle identified by the constitution, we need to handle properly the relations between the central government and local governments, correctly deal with national relations, and appropriately handle interest relationships in all aspects. We also need to mobilize all positive factors, and consolidate and develop a political situation featuring national unity, vibrancy, security, and harmony. In building the rule of law in China, the government should set an example and practically advance administration by law. People's governments of all levels and their working staff should loyally perform duties and responsibilities bestowed by the constitution and the law, protect the lawful rights and interests of the people, legal persons and other organizations, and improve administrative and management efficiency. People's governments of all levels and their working staff should lower management costs, innovate administrative approaches, and strengthen administrative transparency. People's governments of all levels and their working staff should boost a coordinated development of socialist material civilization, political civilization, and spiritual civilization, and build a moderately prosperous society in an all-round way.

In summary, China is experiencing a major strategic adjustment in the rule of law, which is a transformation forming the socialist system of law with Chinese characteristics into a system of the rule of law with Chinese characteristics, from centering on legislation to focusing on implementing the constitution and the law, from a great country under the law to a strong country under the rule of law, and from economic GDP to law-based GDP. At this new and unprecedented historical starting point, China must make an overall plan to comprehensively building a well-off society, comprehensively deepen the reform, and comprehensively and strictly run the Party in order to comprehensively advance the rule by law and accelerate the building of the system of the socialist rule of law. China must also open up new prospects for building the socialist rule of law with Chinese characteristics in the great practice of the overall strategic plan's "four comprehensive objectives."

REFERENCES

Arblaster A: Democracy (Rongfei S, et al., translator), Changchun, 2005, Jilin People's Publishing House.

Bangzuo W: Social ecological analysis of Chinese political system, Shanghai, 2000, Shanghai People's Publishing House.

Barber B: Strong democracy (Bin P, Runzhou W, translators), Changchun, 2006, Jilin People's Publishing House.

Berman HJ: Law and revolution: the formation of the western legal tradition (Weifang H, et al., translator), Beijing, 1992, Encyclopedia of China Publishing House.

Brandt W, Kreisky B, Palme O: Future of social democracy (Donghong D, translator), Chongqing, 1990, Chongqing Publishing House.

Breton A, et al: Understanding democracy: economic and political perspectives (Dan M, et al., translators), Shanghai, 2000, Xuelin Publishing House.

Buchanan JM: Liberty, markets, and state (Xinqiao P, Fumin M, translators), Shanghai, 1989, Shanghai Joint Publishing Company.

Buyun L: The road towards rule of law in China, Beijing, 2013, China Social Sciences Publishing House.

Cicero MT: The republic and the laws (Huansheng W, translator), Beijing, 1997, China University of Political Science and Law.

Coicaud J-M: Legitimacy and politics (Xinping T, Yuanfei W, et al., translators), Beijing, 2002, Central Compilation & Translation Press.

Dahl R: Dilemmas of pluralist democracy (Zhengming Y, translator), Beijing, 1989, Qiushi Press.

Dahl R: On democracy (Baiguang L, et al., translator), Beijing, 1999, The Commerical Press.

Dezhi T: Between democracy and the rule of law, Beijing, 2006, People's Publishing House.

Dingguo W, et al: On democracy and legal system by Xie Juezai, Beijing, 1996, Law Press China.

Dingjian C: China's journey toward the rule of law: legal reform, 1978–2008, Beijing, 2008, Social Sciences Academic Press.

Dingjian C: Democracy is a kind of modern life, Beijing, 2010, Social Sciences Academic Press.

Dye T, Zeigler H: The irony of democracy (Zhanping S, et al., translators), Beijing, 1991, World Affairs Press.

Gaomin N, et al: Theoretical discussions on separation of party and government, Beijing, 1988, Chunqiu Publishing House.

Guanglei Z: The governmental process of contemporary China, Tianjin, 1997, Tianjin People's Publishing House.

Habermas J: Reconstruction of historical materialism (Guanyi G, translator), Beijing, 2000, Social Sciences Academic Press.

Hager BM: The rule of law: a lexicon for policy makers (Mansfield Center for Pacific Affairs, translator), Beijing, 2005, China University of Political Science and Law Press.

Hainian L: Ruling the country by law is the summary of historical experiences, Beijing, 2013, China Social Sciences Publishing House.

Heftel C: An ex-congressman's proposal to clean up congress (Fuwu H, et al., translators), Beijing, 2002, Foreign Languages Press.

Held D: Models of democracy (Jirong Y, et al., translators), Beijing, 1998, Central Compilation & Translation Press.

Held D: Democracy and the global order. From the modern state to cosmopolitan governance (Wei H, et al., translators), Shanghai, 2003, Shanghai Century Publishing Group.
Hengshan Z, et al: Governance by law: studies on the governance of the communist party of China, Beijing, 2012, Law Press China.
Huning W: Democratic politics, Hong Kong, 1993, Joint Publishing (Hong Kong) Company Limited.
Jianbian Y: Democracy is a good thing, Beijing, 2006, Social Sciences Academic Press.
Jingben R, Xinjun G: Comparative studies of political parties, Beijing, 2002, Central Compilation and Translation Press.
Kluckhohn C, et al: Culture and individual (Jia G, et al., translators), Hangzhou, 1986, Zhejiang People's Publishing House.
Lindblom CE: Politics and market (Yizhou W, translator), Shanghai, 1996, Shanghai Joint Publishing Company.
Lummis D: Radical democracy (Yuanqi L, translator), Beijing, 2002, China Renmin University Press.
Malinowski B: A scientific theory of culture (Xiaotong F, et al., translator), Beijing, 1987, China Folk Literature and Art Publishing House.
Marks S: The riddle of all constitutions: international law, democracy, and the critique of ideology (Zhiyan F, translator), Shanghai, 2005, Shanghai Century Publishing Group.
Mill J: Representative government (Xuan W, translator), Beijing, 1982, The Commercial Press.
Montesquieu CL: The spirit of law (Yanshen Z, translator), Beijing, 1961, The Commercial Press.
Mu Q: An introduction to culturology, 1981, (Taipei) Taiwan Zhongzheng Publishing House.
Peilin C: Parliamentary politics, Hong Kong, 1993, Joint Publishing (Hong Kong) Company Limited.
Ping J: The hundred years' of democratic constitutional movement in China, Lanzhou, 1998, Gansu People's Publishing House.
Puqu W: Basis of political science, Beijing, 1995, Peking University Press.
Roskin M, et al: Political science (edition 6) (Zhen L, Feng W, et al., translators), Beijing, 2001, Huaxia Publishing House.
Sartori G: The theory of democracy revisited (Keli F, et al., translator), Beijing, 1993, Orient Press.
Schumpeter J: Capitalism, socialism and democracy (Liangjian W, translator), Beijing, 1979, The Commercial Press.
Shangli L: Study on contemporary China's political form, Tianjin, 2000, Tianjin People's Publishing House.
Shaowen H: Rule by law and the party's leadership, Hangzhou, 1998, Zhejiang People's Publishing House.
Shklar JN: American citizenship: the quest for inclusion (Mangui L, translator), Shanghai, 2006, Shanghai Century Publishing Group.
Sunstein CR: Designing democracy: what constitutions do (Chaowu J, et al., translator), Beijing, 2006, Law Press China.
Thesing J, Jung W: Democracy, Chinese edition, Beijing, 2005, Law Press China.
Thucydides History of the peloponnesian war (Defeng X, translator), Beijing, 1978, The Commercial Press.
Tieying L: On democracy, Beijing, 2001, People's Publishing House.
Tocqueville A: Democracy in America (Guoliang D, translator), Beijing, 1988, The Commerical Press.
Tongzu Q: Chinese law and Chinese society, Beijing, 2003, Zhonghua Book Company.

Tylor E: Primitive culture (Shusheng L, translator), Shanghai, 1992, Shanghai Literature and Art Publishing House.
von Hayek F: Law, legislation and liberty (Zhenglai D et al., translator), Beijing, 2000, Encyclopedia of China Publishing House.
von Hayek FA: The Road to Serfdom (Yi W, et al., translators), Beijing, 1997, China Social Sciences Publishing House.
Warren ME: Democracy and trust (Hui W, translator), Beijing, 2004, Huaxia Publishing House.
Wei H: The process of government, Hangzhou, 1998, Zhejiang People's Publishing House.
Wei P: Essays in Rule of Law and the "Myth of Democracy", Hong Kong, 2003, Hong Kong Press for Social Sciences LTD.
Wiarda HJ: Comparative democracy and democratization (Yuan R, translator), Beijing, 2004, Peking University Press.
Wieslander B: The parliamentary ombudsman in Sweden (Jie C, translator), Beijing, 2001, Tsinghua University Press.
Young HT: China party government and the market (Chinese version), Beijing, 2002, Economic Daily Press.
Zongling S: Modern western law philosophy, Beijing, 1983, Law Press China.

INDEX

Note: Page numbers followed by "*f*", "*t*" and "*n*" refer to figures, tables and footnotes, respectively.

T

U

Edwards Brothers Inc.
Ann Arbor MI. USA
October 3, 2017